Privatization, Public Policy and Public Corporations in Canada

Privatization, Public Policy and Public Corporations in Canada

edited by

Allan Tupper
and
G. Bruce Doern

The Institute for Research on Public Policy/
L'Institut de recherches politiques

Legal Deposit Fourth Quarter
Bibliothèque nationale du Québec

Canadian Cataloguing in Publication Data

Main entry under title:

Privatization, public policy and public
corporations in Canada

Prefatory material in English and French.
ISBN 0-88645-082-9

1. Corporations, Government -- Canada -- Case
studies. 2. Privatization -- Canada. I.
Tupper, Allan, 1950-. II. Doern, G. Bruce,
1942-. III. Institute for Research on
Public Policy.

HD4008.P74 1988   354.7109'2   C89-098511-1

The camera-ready copy for this publication was created
on a Xerox 6085 Desktop Publishing System.

The Institute for Research on Public Policy/
L'Institut de recherches politiques
P.O. Box 3670 South
Halifax, Nova Scotia B3J 3K6

Contents

Foreword

This book examines the role of public enterprise in Canadian public policy in the context of international and domestic pressures to privatize. In its narrowest sense, privatization encompasses the whole or partial sale of state-owned companies but more broadly and importantly it embraces actions to reduce the role of government and enhance market forces in an effort to produce a more competitive economy. In this larger sense, privatization includes deregulation, trade liberalization and the contracting out of government services.

The 1984 election of the Progressive Conservative government of Brian Mulroney brought to power the first federal government in the post-war era committed to reducing the state-owned sector. As it assumed power, it joined several Conservative provincial governments also interested in restraining the state. Accordingly, the authors make the performance of the Mulroney Government concerning public corporations and privatization a major focus of this book. The book also examines privatization and public enterprise at the provincial level, albeit more selectively.

On one level, the purpose is to explore the significance of these recent developments for understanding the shifting boundaries between the state and markets. On another level, the purpose is to provide readers with practical knowledge and a sense of the origins, goals, evolution and performance of selected public corporations. This "micro level" knowledge is as crucial as the "macro level" developments for several reasons, but especially as it relates to privatization. First, existing Crown companies are bureaucratic entities with lives of their own and with goals that are partially internally driven. Second, they exist in industrial sectors whose political and economic dynamics vary considerably. Third, whether they are retaining or selling public corporations, governments quickly learn that they are not dealing with unadorned entities, Crown jewels, as it were. Individual enterprises, as the authors point out, are much more like onions, surrounded by layers of other governing instruments and relationships, including regulations, tax provisions, subsidies and "understandings".

Tupper and Doern conclude that the Conservatives in Canada have proceeded cautiously because they are more pragmatic than, for example, the modern British Conservative party and because they govern a country in which public opinion is not hostile to public enterprise. They have sought to lessen the role of government, but the evidence on whether or not they have succeeded must be examined carefully. With respect to state enterprise there is evidence of actual expansion when measured by data on assets but considerable contraction when measured by data on equity infusions, debt financing and employment in some key firms. More significant change has probably been achieved through deregulation than through the sale of government owned firms.

There are, however, limits to passing judgements at this general level. Sooner or later one must deal with evidence at the sectoral level. The present study surveys the dynamics of the several sectors in which particular Crown corporations function. In this context the temptation to see all such dynamics as the mere interplay of self interest among regional and industrial interests is resisted. A closer look reveals the important role of analysis and information, of salutary crises, and of changing technologies and economic forces in shaping the environment of the firms examined.

A similar set of views at different levels accompanies the authors' conclusions about the accountability of state enterprise. They have no difficulty concluding that the accountability regime has improved over the past decade. This, they hope, will induce a greater sense of confidence in the performance of state-owned firms in Canada. It is clear, however, that it will not end disputes about particular enterprises as Canadians continue to experiment with the shifting boundaries between states and markets.

This book is a completely revised and expanded version of a collection of essays on public corporations in Canada first published in 1981. Its publication reflects the Institute's continuing concern with the changing role of public enterprise in the governance and economic life of Canada. The overview and individual studies contained in this book deal with some of the most crucial public policy issues of our time. These are themes and questions which the Institute will continue to pursue in future research and forthcoming publications.

Rod Dobell
President

November 1988

Avant-propos

Cet ouvrage examine le rôle de l'entreprise publique en matière de politique générale canadienne et dans le contexte des pressions exercées, à l'intérieur du pays et internationalement, en faveur de la privatisation. Dans son sens le plus strict, on entend par privatisation la vente entière ou partielle d'entreprises possédées par l'État, mais en un sens plus général et plus important, la privatisation comprend les mesures qui tendent à réduire le rôle du gouvernement et à encourager le libre jeu des forces du marché, afin de rendre l'économie plus concurrentielle. Dans ce dernier sens, la privatisation inclut la déréglementation, la libéralisation du commerce et le recours au secteur privé pour assurer les services gouvernementaux.

Avec l'élection du gouvernement progressiste conservateur de Brian Mulroney, en 1984, le Canada se dotait, pour la première fois depuis la guerre, d'un gouvernement fédéral décidé à réduire le secteur étatisé. En prenant le pouvoir, il s'alliait à plusieurs gouvernements provinciaux conservateurs déjà engagés dans cette voie. Aussi les auteurs consacrent-ils la majeure partie de leurs efforts à l'analyse du comportement du gouvernement Mulroney à l'égard des corporations publiques et de la privatisation. Ils examinent également la question de la privatisation et de l'entreprise publique au niveau provincial, mais d'une manière plus sélective.

D'un certain point de vue, l'intention est de saisir le pourquoi de ces récents changements, afin de mieux comprendre la signification des frontières mouvantes qui séparent l'État des marchés économiques. Par ailleurs, il s'agit de donner aux lecteurs des renseignements pratiques et une idée plus claire sur les origines, les buts, l'évolution et les résultats de certainos sociótés contrôlées par le gouvernement. Pour plusieurs raisons, et spécialement parce qu'il a des rapports avec la privatisation, ce savoir à un "micro-niveau" est aussi important que l'évolution constatée à un "macro-niveau". D'abord, les sociétés de la Couronne existantes sont des entités bureaucratiques douées d'une vie propre ainsi que d'objectifs en partie fixés par elles-mêmes. Ensuite, elles relèvent de secteurs industriels dont les activités politiques et économiques varient considérablement. Enfin, soit qu'ils les gardent ou soit qu'ils les vendent, les gouvernements se rendent vite compte que les corporations publiques ne sont pas de simples entités sans personnalité: ce sont en vérité des joyaux de la Couronne. Les auteurs font remarquer que les entreprises individuelles ressemblent davantage à des oignons, protégées qu'elles sont par plusieurs couches d'autres moyens d'administration et d'autres types de relations, tels que les réglementations, les mesures fiscales, les subventions et les "accords tacites".

Dans leurs conclusions, Tupper et Doern reconnaissent que les Conservateurs canadiens ont procédé avec prudence, sans doute parce qu'ils sont plus pragmatiques que, par exemple, les membres du parti conservateur actuel de Grande-Bretagne, et également parce qu'ils sont à la tête d'un pays qui n'est pas hostile à l'entreprise publique. Les Conservateurs canadiens ont cherché à diminuer le rôle de l'État, mais la question de savoir s'ils ont ou non réussi dans leur tentative doit être examinée avec soin. En ce qui concerne l'entreprise étatisée, on constate, dans certaines entreprises de premier ordre, une expansion réelle si l'on se rapporte aux actifs, et une régression considérable si l'on se réfère aux nouveaux investissements, au financement des dettes et à l'emploi. Les changements significatifs sont probablement dus beaucoup plus à la déréglementation qu'à la vente de ses entreprises par l'État.

À ce niveau général, la faculté de juger a toutefois ses limites. Tôt ou tard il faut tenir compte des faits au niveau sectoriel; aussi la présente étude passe-t-elle en revue les activités des différents secteurs auxquels appartiennent des sociétés de la Couronne données. Dans ce contexte, les auteurs résistent à la tentation de ne voir dans de telles activités que le simple jeu des intérêts régionaux et industriels respectifs. Un examen plus approfondi révèle le rôle important de l'analyse et de l'information, ainsi que celui des crises bénéfiques, des changements technologiques et des forces économiques, dans la constitution de l'environnement des firmes étudiées.

Les auteurs utilisent, à différents niveaux, un ensemble de critères similaires qui leur permet d'aboutir à leurs conclusions sur la responsabilité de l'entreprise étatisée. Ils reconnaissent que le régime de responsabilité publique s'est amélioré au cours de la dernière décennie. Ce fait, espèrent-ils, devrait inciter le public à avoir davantage confiance dans les possibilités de réussite des entreprises étatisées au Canada. Il est toutefois évident qu'aussi longtemps que régnera l'incertitude dans la délimitation des frontières séparant les gouvernements des marchés économiques, il ne sera pas possible de mettre un terme aux discussions qui portent sur certaines entreprises particulières.

Cet ouvrage est la version augmentée et entièrement revue d'une série d'études sur les corporations publiques au Canada publiée pour la première fois en 1981. Cette nouvelle édition témoigne de l'importance que l'Institut continue à accorder au rôle en pleine évolution de l'entreprise publique dans le gouvernement et la vie économique du Canada. La vue d'ensemble et les études particulières que ce livre renferme présentent des problèmes de politique générale qui sont parmi les plus importants de notre temps. Ce sont des thèmes et des questions que l'Institut continuera d'explorer dans ses recherches futures et dans ses publications à venir.

Rod Dobell
Président

Novembre 1988

Preface

In 1981, the Institute for Research on Public Policy published *Public Corporations and Public Policy in Canada* edited by Allan Tupper and G. Bruce Doern. The success of that volume led us to conclude that a series of detailed case studies of particular public corporations was an effective way to study modern Canadian public enterprise. But by 1988 so much had changed in the world of Canadian public enterprise that the Institute decided to commission the present volume. As in the 1981 collection, our case studies stress contemporary trends and address specific firms within the context of a common set of questions. Accordingly, this volume comprises an editors' introduction, eight case studies and an overview of recent developments in three provinces. This collection should not be seen, however, as a mere updating of our 1981 work. For one thing, six of the corporations studied (Via Rail, the Alberta Energy Company, Hydro-Quebec, Teleglobe Canada, the Farm Credit Corporation and the Federal Business Development Bank) are new to this volume. Moreover, those corporations that are re-examined (Canadian National Railways, Air Canada, Petro-Canada and the Potash Corporation of Saskatchewan) have been subject to a thorough updating *and* reinterpretation in light of major changes over the last decade.

We believe that the case study approach forces readers to probe and understand Canadian state enterprise within a series of complex, distinct and diverse industries rather than exclusively at the level of rhetoric. The cases also show how difficult it is to sustain sweeping generalizations or "iron laws" about the behaviour, development and future prospects of Canadian public enterprise. A confluence of ideology, unpredictable economic circumstances and international developments will shape the public enterprise sector in the future.

In forging the volume, we were also interested in employing, where desirable and possible, the emerging insights of economics and management science as these relate to the study of public enterprise. Readers are warned that no "party line" governed the approach of the editors or the authors to the study of public enterprise. As a result, various methodologies and approaches are employed, different issues are sometimes emphasized and a range of conclusions emerge.

In preparing the volume, we were deeply concerned with the dynamics, probable consequences and underlying politics of privatization. After all, a sharp political focus on privatization is a key feature in the environment of most Canadian public firms in the 1980s. But we tried to ensure that a genuine concern with privatization did not become a trendy obsession. Our cases reveal that the pace of privatization has often been slow, that circumstances within particular industries may render it unfeasible and that Crown corporations will remain as important policy instruments at both levels of government. Vexing questions about their control and accountability, their relations with the private sector, the extent of their regulation and their performance will confront Canadian governments for the foreseeable future.

Many debts are accumulated in the preparation of a volume such as this. John Langford, in his work with the Institute for Research on Public Policy and as a contributing author, enthusiastically supported the project from its conception. All our authors cheerfully met the deadlines and demands of frequently fussy editors. Leah Modin of the Department of Political Science, University of Alberta skilfully word-processed the introduction as its component parts were shuffled between Edmonton and Ottawa. Douglas Kerr, a doctoral candidate in political science at the University of Alberta, provided invaluable assistance in the final phases of the volume's production. Finally, on behalf of the authors, we would like to thank the Institute for Research on Public Policy for its unfaltering support for this undertaking.

Allan Tupper and G. Bruce Doern
November 1988

The Authors

Johanne Bergeron is a member of the Department of Political Science, University of Ottawa.

John F. Devlin is a doctoral candidate, Department of Political Science, Carleton University.

G. Bruce Doern is a member of the School of Public Administration, Carleton University.

Philippe Faucher is a member of the Department of Political Science, University of Montreal.

Ken Huffman is a Research Associate at the Institute for Research on Public Policy, Ottawa.

John Langford is Director, School of Public Administration, University of Victoria.

Jeanne Kirk Laux is a member of the Department of Political Science, University of Ottawa.

Maureen Appel Molot is a member of the Department of Political Science and Associate Director, Norman Paterson School of International Affairs, Carleton University.

Larry Pratt is a member of the Department of Political Science, University of Alberta.

Richard Schultz is a member of the Department of Political Science and Director, Centre for the Study of Regulated Industries, McGill University.

Garth Stevenson is a member of the Department of Politics, Brock University.

Allan Tupper is Chairman, Department of Political Science, University of Alberta.

Chapter I

Canadian Public Enterprise and Privatization

Allan Tupper and G. Bruce Doern

The central purpose of this book is to examine the role of public enterprise in Canadian public policy in the context of international and domestic pressures to privatize in the 1980s. In its narrowest sense privatization encompasses the whole or partial sale of state-owned companies but more broadly and importantly it also embraces actions to reduce the role of government and enhance market forces to produce a more competitive economy. In this larger sense, privatization includes deregulation, trade liberalization, and the increased contracting out of government services.

The 1984 election of the Progressive Conservative government of Brian Mulroney brought to power the first federal government in the post-war era committed to reducing the state-owned sector. As it assumed power, it joined a virtual sea of Conservative provincial governments also interested in restraining the state. Accordingly, the performance of the Mulroney government concerning public corporations and privatization is a major focus of this book. We also examine privatization and public enterprise at the provincial level, albeit more selectively.

At the macro level, our purpose is to explore the significance of these recent developments for understanding the shifting boundaries between the state and markets. Is the role of government declining or is it being reformulated? Does the new configuration make sense given the challenges Canada faces? Are there any clear principles that suggest when state ownership or markets are the preferred choice or are we left only with the resultant outcome of a clash of rival interests? Has the political and managerial accountability of government enterprises improved after an unprecedented period of scrutiny? These and other related questions are central to this book.

Our second purpose is to provide readers with practical knowledge and a sense of the origins, goals, evolution and performance of selected public corporations. This "micro level" knowledge is as crucial as the macro level developments for several reasons, but especially as it relates to privatization. First, existing Crown companies are bureaucratic entities with lives of their own and with goals that are partially internally driven. Second, they exist in industrial sectors whose political and economic dynamics vary considerably. Third, whether they are retaining or selling public corporations, governments quickly learn that they are not dealing with unadorned entities, Crown jewels, as it were. Individual enterprises are much more like onions surrounded by layers of other governing instruments and relationships, including regulations, tax provisions, subsidies and "understandings".

Some of the companies examined (Petro-Canada, Air Canada and Canadian National Railways) were examined in our earlier book on this subject and are analyzed again.[1] The change in focus, however, is quite stark and is itself an indicator of how greatly the paradigm of debate has changed since 1980. At time of writing none of the "Big Three" federal crowns has been privatized. But the intention to partially privatize Air Canada has been announced and the pressures on the other two are real. Other companies are new to this book and cover sectors not previously examined. These include the combined banking, agriculture, and small business sector through a comparative analysis of the Farm Credit Corporation and the Federal Business Development Bank. The telecommunications sector is also represented by an analysis of Teleglobe Canada, a firm that has already been sold by the Mulroney government. A chapter plumbs the political economy of privatization in Ontario, Quebec and Saskatchewan.

Inevitably in a book such as this, there is unevenness in the sectors covered. For example, the resource sector is covered by chapters on Petro-Canada, the Alberta Energy Company, the Potash Corporation of Saskatchewan and Hydro-Quebec. The cultural sector, on the other hand, is not addressed except in our general review of the Mulroney government's record.

Each chapter addresses a number of basic issues about each company. These include its origins and goals, its evolution and performance as an organization and policy vehicle, its response to the privatization and restraint pressures of the 1980s and its likely future prospects. In the case of the firm already privatized, the chapter examines the dynamics of the sale and comments on the actual or likely post-privatization conduct.

In this chapter, we present some basic information about public enterprise in Canada as well as our own assessment of the evidence accumulated by the individual authors. The chapter comprises five sections. The first section briefly surveys developments and pressures in the international political economy including the particular impact of the British privatization ethos on Canadian Conservatives. This is followed by a discussion of key characteristics of public enterprise in Canada at both the macro and micro or sectoral levels. The third section explores key issues and trends in the study of public enterprise through an examination of the contributions of political science, economics and management theory. We examine whether a mature political economy of state enterprise is emerging. The fourth section explores the performance of specific enterprises especially since the mid 1970s when the restraint era can, roughly speaking, be said to begin. Finally, we draw together from the chapters and from other recent analyses, an assessment of state enterprises as managerial and accountable entities both as individual companies and as stables of enterprises that, even with privatization, governments must continue to manage and monitor.

Comparative Developments and the International Political Economy

Without doubt the main impetus for the changing views on the role of state enterprise has come from the international environment. In one sense, the pressures of the international political economy began with the first oil crisis in 1973 and escalated with the stagflation and meagre economic growth of the mid and late 1970s.[2] With the onset of what many regard as a policy induced recession in 1981-82, the worst since the 1930s, governments faced unprecedented pressures. Underlying these changes were still other even deeper determinants. One was the emergence of several newly industrialized states capable of competing in such sectors as automobiles, textiles and electronic goods. A second was the robotization of mass production industries. A third was the revolution in the nature of capital and financial markets that, through computerization, allows capital to move at lightning speed across national boundaries.

All of these changes were only gradually and imperfectly recognized by western and third world governments, which, not surprisingly, exhibited vastly different capacities to respond to these changes.[3] Since political debate requires rhetorical and ideological packaging to capture more complex underlying phenomena, it was also the case that western political systems varied in the ways in which political ideas were expressed.

The clearest critique emerged from political conservatives, often referred to as neo-conservatives or simply as the new right, but more accurately as neo-liberals.[4] Strongly criticising the role of government as being not only excessive but also the fundamental cause of the economic and social malaise, conservatives pushed aggressively for liberalization under several banners, including freer trade, deregulation, tax reduction, expenditure restraint and privatization. These issues and terms came to dominate political debate.

The rise and nature of conservatism varied widely among western countries. It was most ardently expressed in the United States and the United Kingdom under the Reagan and Thatcher governments respectively. In other western countries, the massaging process took longer and penetrated less deeply. The mode of debate also varied, with some seeing the debate focus on industrial policy, thus casting the net quite widely, while in other states the debate stressed fiscal matters, notably a concern over deficits. The literature and debate of the period also noted key differences between small and large western countries, between trade dependent and less trade dependent countries, and between countries which had different institutions for policy-making and interest representation.[5]

The key point in the above account is that there is no straightforward causal journey among these major events, their specific mode of political expression and particular acts of privatization.[6] The movement toward the privatization of some state enterprises in Canada has clearly been influenced by a general pattern of change but often in subtle ways, and, as the case studies of individual enterprises show, not always in the same direction.

With respect to privatization, defined as the whole or partial sale of state enterprise, the most direct influence on Canada was the Thatcher government's program. But the nature of this influence must be carefully understood both as it unfolded in Britain and as it seeped into Canadian political debate and action.

The North American image of the Thatcher privatization program is often too readily summed up as an aggressively planned set of actions decisively and purposely taken. In fact, the process was far less clear cut.[7] Its progression is best seen in relation to each of Thatcher's terms in office which were closely watched and analyzed by Canadian political and bureaucratic officials.

Thatcher's 1979 election manifesto made only modest promises about privatization. Indeed, British Conservatives were initially concerned that privatization might be unpopular. In practical terms, since no one had done it before on any scale, there was a great deal of "learning by doing". The early privatizations in the 1979-83 period focused on a small number of profitable firms including British Aerospace and the National Freight Corporation. Revenue raising goals from sales were not the key priority. Instead the focus was managerial and financial. The intention was to discipline some companies by subjecting them to market forces. In the 1980-82 period, Thatcher and key ministers had attempted to solve Britain's fiscal problems by cutting back on social programs. Expenditure reduction goals, however, were not met in this manner due to the resistance of other ministers and to the general unpopularity of such cutbacks. A very divided Cabinet then looked to other areas of the public purse on which they were more united. As a result, as David Heald points out, "privatization was a unifying policy because of their near-unanimous hostility to the concept and practice of industrial nationalization"[8]. Even then, a more confident and ambitious approach to privatization only began in 1982-83 when, following the Falkland's war, the re-election of Thatcher seemed assured.

Only in the second Thatcher term did large scale privatization occur. The focus was the monopoly public utilities such as British Telecom, British Gas and British Airways. At this stage, revenue raising goals rather than competitiveness became extremely important as mass public share offerings were involved. This goal became entwined with a more generic political appeal by the Thatcher regime that it was establishing a new share-owning capitalist society. The privatizations were becoming politically popular to an extent that not even the most ardent Thatcherite could have imagined. Somewhat lost in this second phase was any apparent concern for whether these actions were producing the true economic goals of privatization, namely liberalization and enhanced competition. Also given less attention was the fact that the Thatcher government had to erect a new array of regulatory agencies to police the new private monopolies. By 1987, however, the Thatcher program had certainly produced results in relation to other goals. It had halved the size of Britain's nationalized sector and raised $44 billion for the Treasury.

The third Thatcher term set out to "finish the job" by selling off further shares in enterprises but also extending privatization more deeply into the social service and education spheres. The October 1987 stock market crash created severe problems for the sale of further shares in British Petroleum and took some political bloom off the privatization rose. There can be no doubt, however, that in the 1980s as a whole, the Thatcher privatization program had had a profound impact on Britain and on the world.

By the mid 1980s, France and Japan announced large privatization programs and were in the process of carrying them out.[9]

Under combined American and British influence, the World Bank made privatization and market oriented policies a major condition of its lending and development activities.

The links between the British program and the privatization initiatives of the Mulroney and Clark Conservative governments are rhetorically direct but practically very subtle. The initial 1979 work by Sinclair Stevens in the Clark government was inspired by visits to some of the then small band of Thatcher advocates. But the early visits also showed that not even the British, in the first two or three Thatcher years, seemed to know how to privatize. By late 1984, the Mulroney Conservatives were again enamoured of the British example. But in the pre-British Telecom sale period, much of the British experience, while music to some Tory ears, was not practically useful in the Canadian context. This was because most of the "candidate companies" for sale in Canada — essentially the initial Sinclair Stevens checklist of 1979 that included Canadair, deHavilland, Teleglobe Canada and Eldorado Nuclear — were either money losers or not easily amenable to a mass public share offer. The federal government clearly learned some tips of the trade from the British proponents but basically had to go through their own phase of "learning by doing".

General Characteristics of
Canadian Public Enterprise

Given the international impetus traced above, the comparative size of the Canadian state owned sector assumes greater importance as a reference point. While comparative data is not highly developed, there is general agreement that Canada falls in the middle of the pack with a level of government ownership greater than the United States and Japan but much less, for example, than that of Austria, Britain and France.[10] The politically most important aspects of these comparisons deal with the United Kingdom and the United States.

Concerning the British comparison, the most relevant bench-mark is that the British state sector, as the Thatcher era began, was about twice that of Canada's in relation to the two economies. The Thatcher goal, with the advantage of hindsight, can be seen as one of trying to reduce the British state owned sector to a level that Canada's was *already* at as the 1980s began. The American comparison is more subtle and complex. Historically, it has allowed Canadians to see themselves as having a very large state owned sector. In comparison with the United States, this perception is accurate but in relation to most of the rest of the western world it is not. But many conservatives in Canada saw only the United States comparison and viewed Canada's situation adversely and even as evidence of rampant socialism, a view that would be almost laughable in a Western European context. On the U.S. side of the political equation, the larger use of state enterprises in Canada assumed greater practical importance in the 1980s. American business interests threatened by foreign competition increasingly began to argue in trade countervail cases that the activities, sometimes the mere existence, of these firms was an unfair trade subsidy.

While such international comparisons became commonplace in the 1980s, one must employ other data to gauge the size and nature of the Canadian public enterprise sector. Recent studies have highlighted the following facts and trends:

- In the mid 1980s there were 259 wholly government owned or effectively controlled enterprises, which in turn owned 268 subsidiaries.[11] (see Table 1)

- The 259 parent firms accounted for 26 percent of the net fixed assets of all Canadian corporations but less than 5 per cent of total employment in the economy. They account for over 35 per cent of total government employment but only about 16 per cent of total public sector employment (which includes the education and hospital sectors).[12]

- The provincial government sector is larger than the federal sector in terms of assets, particularly because of the large size of hydro electric utilities.[13]

- The creation of public enterprises accelerated in the 1960s and 1970s, especially at the provincial level.

- In terms of assets and employment, the growth kept pace with that of the total corporate sector.

- Federal government payments to its own enterprises to cover losses and equity infusions quadrupled from about $1 billion in 1976-77 to $4.6 billion in 1987-88.[14]

- Federal enterprise employment as a percentage of total public sector employment declined from 9.5 per cent in 1965 to 6.6 per cent in 1982 while provincial enterprise employment increased from 5.2 per cent to 7.6 per cent.[15]

- Mixed enterprises in which governments owned significant share holdings of private firms increased in the latter half of the 1970s and early 1980s. Though difficult to measure directly, much of this growth was accounted for by public investment funds such as the Caisse de Dépôt et placement in Quebec and the Alberta Heritage Savings Trust Fund.[16]

Table 1

Number of Government-Owned Enterprises (GEs) and Government-Controlled Enterprises (GCEs), 1985[1]

	Parent		Subsidiary[3]		Total	
	Wholly owned	Effectively controlled[2]	Wholly owned	Effectively controlled[2]	Parent	Subsidiary[3]
Federal[4]	43	13	46	35	56	81
Provincial						
Newfoundland	10	2	2	4	12	6
Prince Edward Island	10	2	1	6	12	7
Nova Scotia	14	4	6	2	18	8
New Brunswick	11	1	4	1	12	5
Quebec	43	-	49	30	43	79
Ontario	32	-	24	1	32	25
Manitoba	22	-	7	-	22	7
Saskatchewan[5]	7	-	17	-	7	17
Alberta	15	1	4	11	16	15
British Columbia	23	-	17	1	23	18
Yukon/NWT	4	-	-	-	4	-
Jointly owned[6]	2	-	-	-	2	-
Subtotal	193	10	131	56	203	187
Grand total	236	23	177	91	259	268

1   As of December 31, 1985.

2   "Effective control" requires ownership of a substantial proportion of shares (usually 30 per cent or more), which exceeds the holdings of all other shareholders, singly or in combination.

3   The numbers pertain only to the subsidiaries directly held by publicly owned or controlled corporations.

4   The Canada Development Investment Corporation does not conform to the definition of "government enterprise" used here, as it is not "commercial." Its subsidiaries are commercial and, as such, are included. Similarly, 125459 Canada Ltd., which is 63 per cent owned by the federal government and is the parent company of Fishery Products International, is not included, while FPI itself is.

5   Wholly owned subsidiaries include 16 enterprises held by the Crown Management Board. The CMB performs no commercial function and is excluded.

6   The Atlantic Lottery Corporation is jointly held by the four Atlantic provinces; the Western Canada Lottery Foundation is jointly held by the three Prairie provinces.

Source: Annual Reports, Public Accounts, and Statistics Canada's Corporate Ownership Mapping System (1985 database).

Source: Canada. Economic Council of Canada, *Minding the Public's Business* (Ottawa: Minister of Supply and Services, Canada, 1986), p. 7.

- Canadian public opinion data on general impressions of Crown Corporations did not reveal any strong antipathy to their overall role.[17] Anywhere from 37 to 67 per cent of respondents viewed them "somewhat favourably", with the higher levels of support (all above 50 percent) in the Eastern provinces and Saskatchewan and the lowest in British Columbia and Alberta.

These data and trends constitute the background of the political economy of Canadian public enterprise in the 1980s. They produce a menu of facts, selectively employed by supporters and critics of public enterprise. In varying ways public enterprise could be generally seen to be either too big or just about right, and out of control or well constrained and even declining, depending on the indices used and the level of government to which one was referring.

To these macro data we need to add a micro or sectoral portrait. For it is the combined macro and micro elements of the picture that allow us to analyze the Canadian privatization debate. At the sectoral level, the following points are vital:

- As Chart 1 shows, the proportion of state-owned assets to total assets for each sector of the economy varies widely. The highest by far is electric power with over 90 per cent with transportation and communications at about 50 percent and 25 percent, respectively, followed by mines (resources), finance, and trade with much smaller percentages. Employment data broadly parallels these patterns.[18]

- In the 1970s and early 1980s the mines (resource sector), including oil and gas had the fastest rate of growth in assets as a proportion of total assets, followed by the finance sector. At the federal level the finance sector in the 1970s was the fastest growing leading to growing concerns by the Auditor General and financial authorities about the overall liabilities of the Government of Canada.[19]

- In the same period, the transportation sector declined in its proportion of state-ownership and the communications sector increased. This reflected both the underlying changes in technology and changes in modes of nation building. It also arguably reflected what many believed was a serious underinvestment by government in the transportation sector.[20]

Chart 1

Assets of GEs and GCEs as a Proportion of Total Assets for Each Sector, Canada, 1959 and 1983[1]

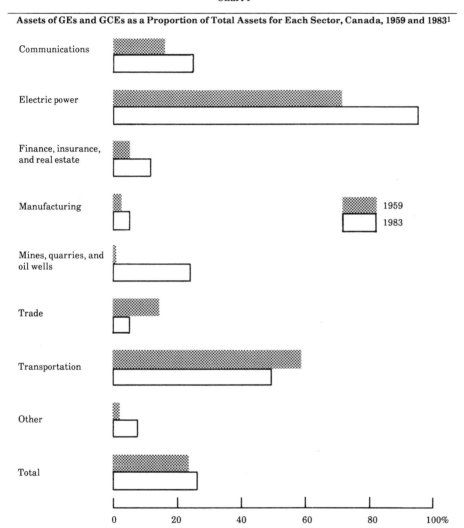

Communications

Electric power

Finance, insurance, and real estate

Manufacturing

1959
1983

Mines, quarries, and oil wells

Trade

Transportation

Other

Total

0   20   40   60   80   100%

[1] "Assets" include net fixed assets and the inventories of parent companies and of directly held, unconsolidated subsidiaries.

Source: Total sectoral assets from Statistics Canada, *Corporation Financial Statistics*, Cat. 61-207, and Department of National Revenue, Taxation Division, *Taxation Statistics, 1962*; govermnment-enterprise assets from Annual Reports, Public Accounts, and Statistics Canada data (derived from *Federal Government Enterprise Finance*, Cat. 61-203, and *Provincial Government Enterprise Finances*, Cat. 61-204).

Source: Economic Council, *Minding the Public's Business*, p. 12.

Taken together, these data reveal some of the inherent contradictions and changes in the debate about Canadian state enterprise. First, there was concern about growth and proliferation (e.g., the spurt of subsidiaries being established). But for most of the 1970s when the Crown corporation debate heightened the federal government was not in fact the main growth culprit even though it received the brunt of the political criticism. Second, the growth of the public sector's presence in the resource sector politicized Crown Corporations out of proportion to the size of this sector's growth because it struck jurisdictional nerves on resource ownership and influenced the oil and gas industry which ardently views itself as a "free enterprise" sector.[21] Third, public opinion was not overly hostile about the size of the state owned sector but there was growing criticism of the overall role of government,[22] a climate easily played upon with respect to particular Crown Corporations either because regional criticism could occur (Alberta objections to Petro-Canada or Quebec MPs' anger at separatists in CBC's Radio Canada) or financial mismanagement could be shown (e.g., Atomic Energy of Canada Ltd. or Canadair). A fourth factor was fiscal concerns that ranged from a "ballooning" federal deficit which brought renewed attention to the quadrupling of federal payments to cover the losses of its Crowns, to sectoral issues such as the growing set of liabilities of the federal banking or financial crowns. These debates were often played out among fiscal professionals in less public political arenas.

Such developments set the context for our analysis. But the subtleties of the debate and the nature of political action can only be understood by a parallel examination of the way the study of public enterprise has proceeded. In short, we need to know more precisely what intellectual currents and ideas preceded, accompanied, and followed the shift in paradigms towards the emergence of privatization.

Studying Public Enterprise

Since the late 1970s, major changes have occurred in the political environments of Canadian public enterprise. The aggressive, and much discussed, "province-building" strategies of the provincial governments have been replaced by more conservative provincial economic policies characterized by a concern with fiscal restraint and in most cases a lesser economic role for government. Restraint is particularly noteworthy in the western provinces whose economic strategies have been dashed by severe downturns in commodity markets. Moreover, Quebec nationalism is often said to be waning as that province's political agenda reflects a growing concern with conventional economic issues at the expense of more traditional concerns about the preservation of a distinctive community. More broadly yet, in contrast to a decade ago, contemporary politics reveal an obvious concern about the extent of state intervention and a related concern with questioning in a general sense government involvement in the Canadian economy.

As the political and ideological landscape shifts, so too have the focus and interests of students of public corporations. Until recently, political scientists exhibited the greatest interest in Crown corporations. Their particular focus was on the problem of integrating semi-independent commercial state firms with the conventional practices of democratic politics and accountable government. But in the 1980s new perspectives emerged and the hegemony of political science has been challenged by the insights of modern economics and management theory. A related Canadian development is the expanded role for businessmen in the debate about state intervention. Indeed, some of the more controversial recent literature is written by members of the business community who actively and energetically espouse their visions of the proper balance between intervention and market forces in shaping the Canadian economy.[23] Our purpose in this section is to review and to assess old and new perspectives to see whether there has emerged through this broadening of scholarly interest a richer grasp of the role, nature, and effectiveness of Canadian Crown corporations, in short, a political economy of state enterprise.

To be sure, considerable diversity of opinion exists among scholars and other observers about the role of Crown corporations and about broader trends in economic policy. This having been said, most recent literature is critical of Crown corporations as institutions, partial to market forces as a solution to contemporary economic woes and supportive of privatization. Whether scholarly contributions shape or reflect the broader constellation of political and economic power is an open question. But it can be safely said at time of writing that, both intellectually and politically, supporters of Crown corporations are on the defensive. Indeed, noteworthy by its absence in the literature of the 1980s is any sustained, supportive account, comparable to Herschel Hardin's *A Nation Unaware*, of the contribution of Crown corporations to Canadian development.[24]

Recent Contributions of Political Science

Political science remains concerned with the control and accountability of state firms. But it has not stood still in the face of political and economic change. It has broadened its focus theoretically and empirically and ventured into new areas.

Our 1981 volume, *Public Corporations and Public Policy in Canada,* was an early effort by political scientists to expand the discipline's agenda for the study of public enterprise.[25] While somewhat concerned with the framework of political control and accountability, our focus was the role of Crown corporations in the policy process. Through case studies, we related Crown corporations to the regulatory process, the dynamics of federal-provincial relations and the changing domestic and international political economy. A particular concern was the *behaviour* of Crown corporations particularly as it related to the resolution of tensions between commercial and policy goals.

State Capitalism: Public Enterprise in Canada by Jeanne Kirk Laux and Maureen Appel Molot illustrates the range and sophistication of political science's concerns in the late 1980s.[26] The volume stresses the role of profit-seeking state firms in competitive industries. Its empirical focus is wide ranging and examines federal and provincial firms, wholly-owned and "mixed ownership" corporations and Crown corporations in the resource and manufacturing sectors. And while noting the formal framework of control over Crown corporations, Molot and Laux are primarily interested in how a range of political, economic, financial and managerial concerns determines the behaviour of public corporations and how the expansion of Canadian public enterprise shapes and is shaped by the "mixed economy". Their investigation, in common with a good deal of the contemporary literature, relies on the contributions of economists and management theorists as well as those of political scientists.

Another area of progress is in the examination of "bailouts" where the state intervenes, sometimes through public ownership, to maintain a firm that seems not to be viable on conventional economic grounds. While all democratic governments engage in such undertakings and while Canadian governments exhibit no particular propensity to undertake them, the "bailout" phenomenon is the subject of intense partisan and expert debate. As Michael J. Trebilcock argues, such debate is probably inevitable insofar as "bailouts" focus attention on the tradeoffs between short term political goals and broader concerns about structural economic change.[27] One viewpoint laments such interventions as dangerous challenges to the market economy and as clear evidence of the folly of allowing "social" considerations to dominate policy-making. A relatively large literature now exists on the topic.[28] It probes, through case studies and general analysis, the circumstances under which "bailouts" occur, their frequency, the means of intervention employed by the state, and in a broad sense the costs, benefits and consequences of such interventions.

The modern democratic state employs a complex arsenal of instruments of economic intervention. But despite such diversity, scholars have generally focused on the wholly owned Crown corporation to the detriment of other important means of intervention. One such form of intervention, the "mixed enterprise", is now the object of considerable scholarly attention. While watertight definitions are elusive, a mixed enterprise is a firm owned jointly by government and private investors. The precise nature of the mix varies substantially.

Our knowledge of the dynamics of mixed firms has grown substantially in the last decade. For example, E. Craig Elford and W.T. Stanbury undertook an exhaustive survey of the size of the Canadian mixed enterprise sector.[29] Moreover, general accounts of the economic performance of Canadian government firms have recently been extended to embrace the mixed enterprise form. And some scholars have tried to develop ambitious, deductive models that seek to explain the behaviour of mixed firms in a capitalist economy.[30] Such contributions are noteworthy, but the most fruitful work on Canadian mixed firms is found in the writings of Stephen Brooks, a political scientist.[31] Brooks explores, through case studies, the internal dynamics of mixed enterprises paying particular attention to instances of conflict between the state's pursuit of policy purposes and private shareholders' concern with profit. Brooks' general conclusion is that the mixed enterprise is a rather limited policy instrument and one prone to severe tensions between the conflicting imperatives of profit and policy purposes. Tensions between the partners often lead to situations where either the government abandons its desire to pursue policy goals through the mixed enterprise or where private shareholders withdraw from the firm altogether. Brooks' careful work undercuts the benign image of mixed firms that portrays them as at the cutting edge of intervention and as instruments for harnessing the virtues of public and private ownership within a single firm.

The expansion of our understanding of mixed enterprise has practical significance. As several of our authors note, a Canadian concept of privatization holds that Crown corporations should be converted into mixed enterprises through the sale of equity to individual or institutional Canadian investors with the state retaining a significant ownership stake. The emergence of a school of thought critical of mixed enterprise suggests the need for considerable caution when prescribing such a solution. Mixed enterprises may sometimes be flexible instruments of intervention and management but, as noted above, they are likely to be prone to serious internal conflict.

In the 1980s, political scientists have extended our knowledge about the interplay between federalism and the creation and operation of government firms. In this vein, a concern is that governments might employ, with possibly contradictory results, public ownership as a weapon in their struggles for superiority *vis-à-vis* other governments in the federation. Put differently, the drives of governments in a competitive federation might lead to an expansion of public ownership *independent* of considerations of the broader economic consequences and possibly unrelated to deficiencies in market performance. But in a careful survey of the issues, K. Huffman, J. Langford, and W.A.W. Neilson argue that such concerns are exaggerated. They acknowledge, however, that there exists the potential for significant intergovernmental conflict over the scope and purposes of public ownership.[32] Canadian attention focused on these issues in 1983 when the federal government unexpectedly announced that it planned to limit, through Bill S-31, provincial government ownership of interprovincial firms to ten per cent.[33] Allegedly designed to prevent provincially inspired "balkanization" of the Canadian economy, the proposal met fierce opposition from the province of Quebec which correctly saw it as threatening the investment strategies of its pension fund, the Caisse de Dépôt et Placement. Although the bill was ultimately withdrawn, the debate over S-31 highlighted the potential conflict between provincial entrepreneurship and the integrity of the national economy. Moreover, it heightened scholarly and political interest in the activities of large provincially-controlled pools of capital such as Quebec's Caisse de Dépôt and the Alberta Heritage Savings Trust Fund. A modest, but useful, literature has emerged about such financial institutions.[34] It has probed the degree to which policy considerations, rather than conventional investment criteria, have shaped the investment strategies of these public bodies. A related concern, particularly about the Caisse, is the extent of state involvement in the management of firms where an equity stake has been acquired. The broad conclusion is that such provincial intermediaries are highly selective and subtle in their interventions with the Caisse having had a greater impact, but in a very small number of firm specific interventions.

One important area that political scientists are now exploring is popular and elite attitudes toward public enterprise in general and particular firms. As we have already noted, research by Richard Johnston reveals, if not powerfully supportive public attitudes toward public firms, then certainly general support and an absence of an overarching public hostility toward Crown corporations. Moreover, recent research by Donald Blake provides insights into the views of Liberal and Progressive Conservative party activists about Crown corporations.[35] Interestingly, a substantial majority of activists in each party accept a role for Crown corporations, although the Liberal majority is larger than the Conservative. Indeed, only in the case of Air Canada and particularly Petro-Canada do Conservative activists, unlike Liberals, demand complete privatization. A majority of activists in both parties see the need for at least partial state ownership of such controversial firms as the Canadian Broadcasting Corporation, Via Rail and Atomic Energy of Canada. Blake's data thus reveal perceptible, if not substantial, differences of opinion between Liberals and Conservatives about Crown firms and privatization. But he also notes how such inter-party comparisons ought not to blind readers to the existence of significant *intraparty* controversies about the economic role of governments and Crown corporations. In particular, the contemporary Liberal party seems divided about the role of government ownership.

Such findings have theoretical and practical implications. They suggest the spectrum of opinion in which either an extension of public ownership or privatization is likely to occur and give clues to the disposition of the two parties toward particular firms. More broadly, they point to substantial elite and mass support for Crown corporations, although it remains unclear why individuals, groups or parties support or oppose particular Crown firms. Many economists and proponents of privatization will find such data intriguing as they have often argued that a major obstacle to privatization lies in the continuing support of Canadians for government ownership. Whether, as they further imply, such support merely reflects a lingering nostalgia about the nation-building roles of Crown corporations remains to be seen.

Noteworthy advances have also been made in our understanding of the creation of Crown corporations. For example, Marsha Chandler has studied the effects of partisanship on the establishment of public firms by Canadian provincial governments.[36] Her broad conclusion is that parties of the "left" (NDP/CCF and PQ) are more likely to establish Crown corporations than their "nonleft" rivals. Perhaps more significantly, parties of the left employ public ownership for different reasons than their opponents. "Nonleft" governments are prone to establish "facilitative" state firms whose purpose is to foster conditions conducive to the profitable expansion of the private sector. Public ownership of this sort is conservative in impact and can be seen as a substitute for other less direct forms of state assistance to industry like grants and loans. Governments of the left, on the other hand, are willing to establish "redistributive" Crown corporations, those oriented to altering the balance of political and economic power. In a related vein, Jorge Niosi maintains that the use of public ownership by Canadian governments, particularly those of the nonleft, is a function of three perennial features of Canada's political economy — a complex class structure characterized by the development of powerful regional elites, most recently in Quebec and Alberta, uneven regional economic development and Canada's broader subordination to the economic, political and military dominance of the United States.[37] The interplay between these forces has frequently propelled Canadian governments into public ownership. Niosi's work links the expansion of state entrepreneurship to patterns of economic development notably the "regionalized" nature of Canada's economic structure, the influence of federalism, and the country's class structure with particular reference to the existence of divisions within business.

The Advent of the Economists

Our understanding of Canadian public enterprise has recently been enhanced by the contributions of Canadian economists. Indeed, what is most surprising about the impact of economists is neither its quality nor its ideological bent but rather its lateness. For a perennial concern about public enterprise in Canada and abroad is its efficiency compared to private enterprise either generally or in the same industry.

In examining public firms, most Canadian economists have struggled with the political environment. They have generally acknowledged Canada's greater historical commitment to public ownership as compared with the United States, recognized that privatization has political and economic dimensions, and perhaps most importantly, grappled with the public enterprise as a unique and complex organizational form that embraces commercial and political dimensions in a manner different from either a private firm or a government department. For example, in his survey of the efficiency of government, mixed and private firms, D.G. McFetridge notes that the very notion of efficiency must be carefully spelled out when dealing with government enterprises.[38] For McFetridge, efficiency has at least three dimensions – commercial efficiency, efficiency in the delivery of political services and market efficiency defined as an absence of monopolistic behaviour. Such notions of efficiency extend the debate beyond its often simplistic dimensions by recognizing that government firms must be evaluated as political *and* economic undertakings. For example, while the commercial efficiency of government firms might sometimes be inferior to that of the private sector, their institutional characteristics might make them superior to private firms in the delivery of services to citizens. This having been said, it must also be noted that very little headway has been made by economists or others in evaluating the performance of social and political undertakings by Crown corporations. As Sandford F. Borins and Barry E.C. Boothman note pessimistically in their comprehensive review of the economic and managerial literature on Crown corporations: "One of the frustrations of this review is that in no case could we find research which attempts to measure systematically the costs of achieving policy objectives, and rarely have researchers taken such costs into account when making assessments of performance."[39]

A controversial contribution of modern economics is "property rights" theory.[40] This approach, while diverse, is centrally concerned with the impact of various ownership structures, notably the capital market, on the performance of firms and the behaviour of managers. Operating under the assumption that managers maximize their own utility rather than that of owners or their organization, property rights theorists see the modern joint stock company as the organizational framework best capable of controlling managerial behaviour and determining good corporate performance. Several characteristics of capital markets are said to limit management's self-serving tendencies and to ensure owner control. For one thing, capital markets are objective measures of investors' assessment of managerial performance. Through the sale or acquisition of shares, investors signal their sense of corporate performance. Similarly, capital markets perform the important role of reducing "monitoring costs" for individual investors. As Borins and Boothman put it: "The capital market, by evaluating the price of a firm's shares, provides an objective standard for comparing the managerial performance of different firms. The market capitalizes expectations about the future performance of a company, which provides the owners with an indication of how outsiders with an incentive to be informed evaluate the firm's management."[41]

A Crown corporation faces a radically different ownership structure and incentive system, one which property rights theorists see as decidedly inferior and one that determines the allegedly inferior performance of state firms. In the absence of an equity market, citizens, as shareholders in state firms, have no easy way of gaining information about corporate performance or signalling their concerns to management. Moreover, the cost of monitoring, supervision and control of Crown corporations, which must be undertaken through political processes, is said to be higher than the cost of monitoring firms through capital markets. Citizens are thus likely to be passive observers of state firms. Building from these perspectives, property rights adherents advance a number of claims about management behaviour in government firms, all of which imply inferior performance. As outlined by Thomas J. Courchene, these include the notions that public managers will minimize profit so as to maximize political support, engage in cross-subsidization where possible and routinely employ "too low" discount rates and thereby expand capacity too quickly.[42] Seen in this light, it is not surprising that property rights theory has influenced and provided intellectual guidance to advocates of privatization.

Property rights theory is hotly contested on empirical and theoretical grounds.[43] For one thing, many skeptics, notably J.K. Galbraith and others following in the intellectual tradition of Berle and Means, reject property rights' underlying premise that capital markets discipline management. And the empirical literature on the topic is clearly inconclusive given different methodologies and assumptions about how to define and measure output, and how to treat conditioning factors such as regulatory regimes and other kinds of state subsidies when making head-to-head comparisons. More importantly for our purposes, property rights theorists are criticized for providing a superficial account of public firms that fails to capture their key institutional features and to take into account administrative features that might serve as efficiency-inducing substitutes for equity markets. More broadly yet, various scholars reject the notion that politicians have neither the interest nor the capacity to demand efficient performance from Crown corporations. Critics ask why politicians should tolerate managerial efficiency and point to a number of institutional characteristics of Crown corporations, including budgetary competition for resources and the framework of controls, that can induce efficiency. In a stimulating treatment of this issue, Sandford Borins probed the administration and organization of Canadian Crown corporations during the second World War.[44] Among other things, he observed how the federal government, operating in an admittedly unique economic and political environment, developed a framework of organizational, financial and personnel incentives that contributed to the management efficiency of a stable of Crown firms. Such findings do not disprove the broad assertions of the property rights school, but they certainly suggest that property rights approach overstates the problem of controlling and monitoring public enterprise managers in the absence of equity markets.

The "Managerial" Perspective

Scholars, managers and politicians have long recognized the role of dominant personalities in shaping the strategies and behaviour of Crown corporations. Such figures as Adam Beck at Ontario Hydro, Wilbert Hopper at Petro-Canada and Donald Gordon at the CNR are recognized for exerting powerful influences over their enterprises for extended periods. Our understanding of such personal influences has recently been extended by a literature that probes the factors that shape the economic, financial and political strategies of public enterprises. No consensus has yet emerged on the key forces, but one observer notes several salient determinants of enterprise strategy including the corporation's financial autonomy/dependence on the state, the nature of corporate goals, the nature and extent of its competition and the firm's precise relationship with the state.[45]

The managerial approach, like the other perspectives, is quite diverse. But its adherents see the modern public corporation as a unique institution that responds to the often conflicting imperatives of political commands and market signals. In so responding, however, senior managers enjoy autonomy in selecting their strategies. Moreover, while acknowledging the importance of the formal framework of control, managerial theorists ultimately see the state enterprise in a *bargaining* relationship with its various controllers and rivals. The actual authority relationship often differs markedly from the formal one as determined by statute, convention and organization chart. In the ensuing bargaining, actors employ a range of strategies and tactics as determined by their resources. But as Jean-Pierre Anastassopoulos argues the process is at heart a political one. As he puts it: "The time has now come to consider the fact that top managers and ministers are human beings possessing a personality, ideas and commitment of their own, and a power or influence which they use to support their personal interests and objectives. When they are decision-makers, these men and women make up their mind according to their own vision of the best choice, through their personal convictions, through the information they have as well as through the opinions of the persons who surround them."[46]

The work of Anastassopoulos and R. Kent Weaver are illustrative of recent trends in the "managerial" approach. Anastassopoulos argues that the state enterprise engages its masters and competitors at three different levels. The first and most important is the "socio-economic" plane where the corporation's broad strategy may conflict with the state's basic policy goals and where conflict may be intense. A second focus of interaction is the "organizational" level where the state firm deals with other agencies in the public sector. Finally, the drama is played out at the "political" level where managers, politicians and other actors employ "power games" in pursuit of their vision of the public interest. Each level of interaction differs from the other in the range of interests involved, the intensity of conflict, and the instruments of conflict resolution. Weaver's stimulating work probes the behaviour of state railroad firms as part of a broader study of industrial strategy in Canada and the United States.[47] Proceeding from the assumption that the goals of public enterprise managers will differ from those of politicians, Weaver argues that public enterprises normally follow one of three distinct strategies — security, autonomy or public service. The security strategy sees managers pursuing the enterprise's long-term survival by securing its budget and minimizing threats to managerial tenure. On the other hand, the autonomy strategy maximizes managerial freedom by reducing dependence on the state and by pursuing profit maximization. Finally, the public service strategy sees relatively altruistic managers pursuing their version of the public interest by downplaying profitability and stressing the provision of socially desirable services. In a broad sense, Weaver argues that managers have some discretion in their choice of strategy although such discretion is circumscribed by the firm's financial dependence on the state and by formal state controls over the firm. Other relevant determinants are the nature of national political institutions and the goods and services provided.

A Political Economy of Public Enterprise?

Our review of recent developments in the literature reveals a refreshing expansion of ideas, frameworks and methodologies. The perspectives of different disciplines, notably economics, adds new dimensions and welcome controversy to our deliberations. But has this expansion of interest led to a new synthesis, a genuine political economy of state enterprise in the face of growing specialization within and between disciplines? Answers to such a question are necessarily subjective and will ultimately depend on one's sense of the purposes of scholarly inquiry and one's ideas about the roles of governments and markets. For example, a scholar concerned with the class basis of politics is likely to see property rights theory as very conservative and based upon deeply deficient assumptions about the nature of political life.

While different disciplines have undoubtedly expanded others' horizons, there remain major, possibly irreducible, gaps between them. For example, political scientists and economists pay significantly different amounts of attention to the "social" and "political" obligations of state firms. For political scientists such noncommercial undertakings constitute the essence of state firms, but while acknowledged, they do not fit readily into economists' assessments of overall performance and are often ignored. More broadly, the economist's concerns are the firm's efficiency and the economy's overall health, while the political scientist, employing admittedly "looser" and more diverse frameworks with varying degrees of success, struggles with the broader constellation of political forces with a focus on the social groups and forces that influence state firms. Similarly, without trying to exaggerate differences or to attribute rigid ideological positions to disciplines, most economists are trained to see government "intervention", not merely state firms, as obstacles to the efficient allocation of resources. Their resultant policy prescription is generally to reduce the incidence and impact of such interventions thereby setting the stage for relatively unhindered markets to shape economic life. Economists' efforts to recognize political variables are laudatory, but ultimately their training, their assumptions and premises, and their orientation toward the state lead them to conservative conclusions about government enterprise. A noteworthy example of these tendencies is the Economic Council's recent study, *Minding the Public's Business*.[48] Critics of this document, including several dissenting members of the Council, note its deep concern with the principles of neo-classical economics and its penchant to recommend privatization without a full political and economic assessment of particular state firms. For their part political scientists may arguably have a conceptual bias that favors state action. They may be inclined not to ask questions about how Crown companies operate in relation to structural changes in the sector(s) in which they compete.

Such different disciplinary perspectives are further complicated by the existence of substantially different methodologies and levels of quantification. Few political scientists, for example, are capable of undertaking the complex analyses necessary to determine the allocative efficiency of Crown corporations. At best, scholars from different disciplines will continue to borrow fruitfully from one another. And sometimes, as witnessed by the growing skepticism of experts about mixed enterprise as a policy "solution", scholars proceeding from different premises and intellectual traditions will arrive at broadly similar prescriptions. But such intellectual confluence is more accidental than contrived and the deep specializations of disciplines continue to impede the emergence of any kind of single minded political economy of state enterprise.

The Performance of Public Enterprise

What lessons do our cases generate about the performance of government enterprise? Have they achieved their goals? Have they operated "efficiently" and have they been able to reconcile the imperatives of commercial efficiency with their social and political obligations? Before answering such questions, we will review the burgeoning literature about the commercial efficiency of Canadian Crown corporations and thereby set our cases in a somewhat broader context.

Several valuable recent surveys demonstrate the diversity of the literature on the commercial efficiency of state enterprise.[49] Authors have employed different methodologies, utilized competing definitions of efficiency, and probed different firms and industries at different periods of economic and political development. Efficiency can refer to financial efficiency where the focus is on the cost structure of comparable public and private firms. A broader view of efficiency refers to dynamic or allocative efficiency and hence the capacity of the firm to innovate and compete in a more fundamental sense. In addition, these investigations have proceeded from different economic and political assumptions. Such diversity prompted Borins and Boothman to conclude: "Each type of efficiency measure entails significant problems of calculation or has serious limitations in explanatory power. Profitability is the least satisfactory form of measurement because it encompasses any and all determinants of efficiency, and simply may not be in accord with the designated social role of a public enterprise. Few empirical studies have approached the essence of an "ideal" measure, and many have produced results which are methodologically suspect . . . ." [50]

Such complexity notwithstanding, one generalization is that Canada's "mature" Crown corporations, generally those operating in the railroad, air transport, telecommunications, and electrical generation industries, are as cost efficient as their private counterparts. This finding is noteworthy insofar as these are the largest firms which consume substantial resources and which influence economic life in a variety of ways. They are also among the most frequently discussed candidates for privatization even though economists warn that privatization is unlikely to improve efficiency significantly, unless there are accompanying efforts to deregulate. A related argument is that newer government firms operating in turbulent competitive environments such as in the high technology sector might perform in a decidedly inferior way to private firms in terms of allocative efficiency.[51] Another variation on the theme is provided by Richard Pryke, an observer of the British nationalized industries, who maintains that public firms perform notably more poorly in times of economic distress.[52] Such a hypothesis has not yet been explicitly probed by Canadian scholars.

A second generalization is that commercial efficiency is a function of a firm's environment rather than its ownership *per se*. In this vein, economists argue that the pattern of regulation and deregulation, the nature of competition, and the structure of incentives facing managers are more important determinants of performance than ownership. One noteworthy exception to this line of reasoning might be the experience of mixed ownership firms which observers have concluded have not performed well and whose inferior performance seems attributable to the firm's ownership structure. According to D.G. McFetridge: "With respect to mixed enterprise, the conclusion here is that it is more likely to constitute the worst than the best of all possible worlds. It does not combine the benefits of transferable ownership with efficient provision of political services, as some have suggested."[53]   Such findings, when read in context with some of the critical work of political scientists, raise further questions about the wisdom of "partial" privatization of Crown corporations.

While the data may be limited, tentative, and sometimes contradictory, observers have not been reluctant to interpret it as they see fit. For example, Thomas J. Courchene sees the data as conclusive insofar as the results of various studies do *not* demonstrate any inherent or decisive superiority of public enterprise performance.[54] For him, the data buttress the case for privatization.   Similarly, having concluded their exhaustive survey of the literature, Borins and Boothman feel obliged to distance themselves from even a hint that they might favour an expansion of public ownership even though their research acknowledges that Canadian public enterprise is not inherently deficient.[55]   And in a slightly different vein, three members of the Economic Council of Canada in a public dissent to the conclusions of a major Council study on state enterprise, argue that the Council often recommended privatization of particular firms even though no assessment was undertaken of the costs and benefits of particular projects and services.[56]   In assessing the performance of Crown corporations and when making policy recommendations, observers are able to interpret data creatively so as to foreordain particular policy conclusions.

Garth Stevenson's account of Canadian National's evolution highlights many of the problems encountered in the evaluation of a Crown corporation's performance. He demonstrates how CN must respond to complex political and economic pressures. The railroad continues to operate many miles of unprofitable track while also facing pressures to maintain its workforce. It must also respond to "deregulation" within Canada and the United States, to shifting patterns of trade and investment within Canada and to the imperatives of technological change. The Mulroney government's hostility to CN's efforts to diversify into new areas further complicates its environment and capacity to respond to change. In such a complex setting, the precise impact of political and economic forces on commercial performance is almost impossible to isolate. As a result, arguments about CN's effectiveness remain rooted in political attitudes about the role of state enterprise and the place of profit therein. And to a greater degree than the performance of most Crown corporations, CN's undertakings remain a source of partisan controversy between the Liberals and Progressive Conservatives.

John Langford and Ken Huffman's assessment of Air Canada points in the same direction. They note that no consensus has emerged about the national airline's commercial performance, although on balance the airline seems competently managed.

Moreover, they observe a continued blurring of political and commercial forces within the airline.   Such blurring has been lessened, however, with the passage in 1978 of a revised Air Canada Act which stresses profitability as a corporate goal and as a criterion for performance evaluation.

Philippe Faucher and Johanne Bergeron's analysis of Hydro-Quebec reveals the centrality of that firm to debates about Quebec's economic development and industrial strategy options.   Particularly insightful is their assessment of Hydro's procurement policy as an instrument of provincial policy.   Among other things, they note how Hydro-Quebec, without noticeable provincial government pressure, developed a preferential purchasing policy that advantaged local producers.   Their conclusion is that Hydro's massive economic power has been intermittently used to develop Quebec's industrial capacity, but that the effects have not been as great as claimed by Hydro and that no "grand plan" has ever been agreed to between the firm and successive Quebec governments.   Their analysis points to the need for careful evaluations of the purchasing activities of large Crown corporations with a view to determining their political rationales, their economic costs and benefits and their extent.

Bruce Doern and John Devlin's account of the Farm Credit Corporation and the Federal Business Development Bank reveals several of the contradictions manifest by the behaviour of Canadian Crown corporations.   These admittedly small firms, situated on the fringes of Canada's financial sector, raise complex policy questions and political controversies.   When public financial intermediaries pursue a cautious, "break even" strategy they are accused of orthodox behaviour and reviled by their clienteles for not behaving differently from private lenders.   On the other hand, aggressive strategies by government financial intermediaries are resisted by private financial institutions who portray such initiatives as intrusions.   As a result, government lenders face unique constraints and expectations.   Under these circumstances, assessments of their performance are complex and ultimately shaped by a series of political premises about the role of financial intermediaries.

Richard Schultz's analysis of Teleglobe Canada reveals the case of a Crown Corporation which, prior to its recent privatization, was very profitable.   His study shows that, contrary to much mythology, public firms can be run profitably over the long term.   He notes, however, that Teleglobe's superior performance is a function of its *de facto* monopoly, its freedom from regulation, its happy location in a rapidly expanding international industry, and its capacity to retain profits for further expansion.   Throughout its history as a Crown corporation, Teleglobe was free from political control, although its long-term autonomy raised contradictions that surfaced during the firm's privatization.

The cases of the Alberta Energy Company (AEC), Petro-Canada and the Potash Corporation of Saskatchewan (PCS) attest to the problems of assessing the performance of Crown-owned resource firms. For example, Maureen Molot and Jeanne Laux argue that PCS's performance was adversely affected by the dramatic international downturn in potash prices and demand in the 1980s. Facing intense competition and slumping demand, PCS was forced to pursue a survival strategy which made difficult the pursuit of such provincial government objectives as economic diversification. Harsh economic realities reinforced other powerful pressures toward orthodox commercial behaviour at the PCS. Their analysis also reveals how PCS's precarious position caused dilemmas for the "free-enterprise" Progressive Conservative government of Grant Devine. Although philosophically committed to privatization, the Conservatives adopted an interventionist and protective strategy for PCS in the face of turmoil in international markets.

This brief and necessarily selective review of some of our case studies reveals the complexity of performance evaluation within the context of particular industries, differing competitive environments, and fluctuating economic and political circumstances. Indeed, analysis of detailed case studies reveals the difficulty of developing generalizations about the performance of state firms. Moreover, our contributors have tried to assess the *overall* political and economic performance of Crown corporations. Their efforts ultimately result in fuller and richer, although necessarily more subjective, evaluations given the well known problems of separating the political, social and economic functions of state firms.

Performance and Privatization

To gauge the extent of privatization, the instrument mix in implementing such choices, and the effects of such decisions requires analysis at several levels. The performance of the Mulroney Government can be assessed by looking at: its policy statements; aggregate data in the 1984-88 period; the major sales of Crown corporations; and a range of other decisions affecting the firms examined in this book.

The Mulroney Conservatives have more seriously scrutinized the federal stable of Crown enterprises than any previous federal government. Their first statements on Crown corporations, however, did not even use the term privatization. The rhetorical themes were cast in the language of economic renewal through markets, overall expenditure restraint, and the better management of Crown corporations. Government ownership was to be reduced but the approach was incremental and the rhetoric was restrained. The Mulroney Conservatives were determined to reassure Canadians that they were not "Thatcherite" Tories.

Not until the May 1985 Budget Speech, following several months of confusion (especially over Air Canada's future) was an explicit privatization policy announced.[57] It stated that a Crown Corporation should be sold unless it could be shown to be fulfilling a policy purpose. It also set out basic principles for privatization (see Table 2) including: close consultation with management, unions and the provinces: the nature of market competition in the sector; a commitment not to sell at distress prices; the possible need to divest large corporations in stages; and foreign ownership considerations.

Table 2
Conservative Principles for Privatization

1. The government will be sensitive to the concerns of management and employees of corporations that may be considered candidates for sale. While recognizing that negotiations must be conducted confidentially, every effort will be made to keep these groups informed of significant developments and to ensure that their legitimate interests are not jeopardized.

2. The type of market competition and the impact on consumers that is likely to develop after a sale will be an important consideration for each divestiture.

3. Provincial governments will be consulted to ensure that provincial and federal privatization programs do not conflict.

4. Crown corporations will not be sold at distress prices merely to transfer them quickly to the private sector. A large deficit and normal fiscal prudence dictate that the privatization program should proceed at a measured pace with careful consideration of all the issues, not the least of which is the receipt of a fair and reasonable price for each asset.

5. The divestiture of large corporations may need to be accomplished in stages, in which case there will be periods of mixed, private and public ownership. In these situations the government will consider the nature of its participation and provide assurances to private sector investors that it will be guided in exercising its ownership rights by the same commercial objectives that guide corporations' private sector shareholders.

6. In recognition of the diverse nature of the various corporate holdings, issues such as the method of sale, eligible purchases, foreign and domestic ownership restrictions, purchaser commitments and government obligations and commitments will be examined on a case-by-case basis, rather than being subject to a general approach.

Source: G. Bruce Doern and J. Atherton, "The Tories and the Crowns: Privatizing and Restraining in a Political Minefield," in *How Ottawa Spends 1987-88*, ed. by Michael J. Prince (Toronto: Methuen, 1987), p. 169.

Aggregate data on the Mulroney years confirm the careful Tory approach, although a tilt to privatization in some of the indicators is clear.[58] Crown corporation assets have in fact grown, primarily due to the expansion of Petro-Canada and Air Canada. Employment has remained steady. On the other hand, infusions of equity capital have been slashed and clear evidence exists of Tory insistence that Crown corporations obtain more of their financing from private markets.

The three major sales of public enterprises involved de Havilland, Canadair and Teleglobe. Early in 1988, it was announced that Eldorado Nuclear would first be merged with the provincially owned Saskatchewan Mining Development Corporation and then gradually privatized. These four federal firms were those initially targeted for sale in 1979 by the Clark Conservatives. In each case, and in the four as a whole, a privatization "learning curve" is evident. Unlike the well-known British mass share offers, each of these sales was individually negotiated. And except for Teleglobe, each firm was in financial difficulty.

Because these firms were picked for privatization well before an explicit Tory policy on privatization was enunciated, they do not conform to the overall dictum that in the absence of a policy role Crown firms should be privatized. Indeed, in both their Crown owned status and in their privatized state they have *de facto* policy obligations. At the very least, there are strong governmental expectations that they will perform in certain ways. This does not mean that there is no difference when ownership changes from public to private. But it does mean that one must look closely at the actual conditions of sales and at other policy changes that accompany the various deals. One must also appreciate that the decisions themselves are the product of an interplay among at least four factors: the sectoral dynamics of the industry in which the Crown corporation is located; the regional issues and perceptions it raises; the place of particular decisions to sell on the government's overall priority list at any given time; and the demands for other changes being made by relevant federal departments and by prospective buyer(s).

An analysis of the de Havilland and Canadair sales by Doern and Atherton shows that while the sales of two chronic money losers earned the Tories considerable political credit for the overall handling of the issues,[59] the politics and economics were difficult and the complex nature of the bargains struck made it difficult to assess their future effects. De Havilland was sold to the giant American firm, Boeing, while Canadair was sold to Quebec based and Canadian owned Bombardier. While Table 3 shows some key features of the two deals, including a set of continuing obligations and control elements, even it understates the complexity of the dynamics of the deal. This is because underlying the deals were concurrent changes leading to the

Table 3
A Comparative Look at the de Havilland
and Canadair Privatizations

Category	de Havilland Sale	Canadair Sale
Date sold	November, 1985	August, 1986
Purchasing company	Boeing Commercial Corporation	Bombardier
Privatization process	Negotiated sale	Negotiated sale
Purchase price	$90 million + $65 million + $28.5 million (royalties) (nominal value)	$120 million + $11.5 million (airport) + $3 million (dividend) + 1 CF-18 + $173 million (royalties) (nominal value)
Government objectives	1. To maintain a competitive export-oriented aerospace industry. 2. To advance aerospace technology 3. To maintain employment. 4. To give appropriate recognition to regional-development priorities.	1. To maintain a competitive export-oriented aerospace industry in Quebec and Ontario. 2. To advance aerospace technology. 3. To maintain employment.
Control elements	1. Tax limitation on the use of $400 million in deferred taxes. 2. World product mandate. 3. First right of refusal on sale of property adjacent to airport. 4. Lease of airport. 5. Reduction of $65 million at 1:5 for funds spent on new purchases.	1. Retention of $150 million in non-voting retractable or redeemable shares. 2. World product mandate. 3. Retention of rights of technology. 4. First right of refusal on sale of airport.
Issues	Foreign ownership Rights to technology Purchase price Privatization process Product liability insurance	Capability of Bombardier CF-18 contract

Source: G.B. Doern and J. Atherton, "The Tories and the Crowns," p. 175.

deregulation of the airline industry and hence enhanced prospects for the sale of smaller commuter aircraft. While space does not allow any detailed account of these sales, it is evident policy issues were critical and the privatized firms carry with them obligations that only the disingenuous observer could label as purely commercial. At the same time, a significant change of ownership has occurred and new management exists in firms where there clearly had been a serious malaise.

A similar range of dynamics are evident in Schultz's account of Teleglobe Canada. In this case, Teleglobe's *de facto* monopoly over overseas telecommunications, the fact that Teleglobe was not regulated by the CRTC, and complex international issues converged in a climate of rapid technological change. Since many complex policy issues had not been settled prior to the call for bids by prospective purchasers, confusion reigned and the privatization unfolded in a policy vacuum. One of the reasons for the confusion was that the Teleglobe sale, unlike the de Havilland and Canadair sales (which had been handled by one department) involved the new Privatization Secretariat and the Department of Communications in greater conflict over both substantive issues and timing. Moreover, the Minister of Finance was anxiously awaiting the several hundred million dollars from the sale which would allow him to show that he was sticking to his fiscal plan of deficit reduction. Schultz criticizes Teleglobe's privatization for being obsessed with sale price, for being devoid of broader public debate and input, and for being hastily undertaken before complex telecommunications policy questions had been resolved. He wonders whether the result will ultimately be the replacement of a public monopoly by a private one. Once again, we note how the detailed analysis of particular firms reveals an interplay of political, bureaucratic and economic forces that are seldom embraced in the broader political and rhetorical debates about privatization.

Beyond these sales one must look to an even more subtle set of choices made by the government itself or by particular Crown corporations in anticipation of, or in the context of, the new "pro-market" ethos. Air Canada and Petro-Canada, as chapters 3 and 4 show, grew in the 1984 to 1988 period. For the former this was a direct result of the need to prepare for "deregulation" and a new competitive environment. For the latter it was the unexpected availability of the downstream assets of Gulf Canada, parts of which Petro-Canada was allowed to buy by the Progressive Conservative government. In both cases, it is possible to argue that the government was "fattening up" the two companies for later privatizations or partial share offers. But the government's, especially Prime Minister Mulroney's, political antennae are extremely sensitive about both companies. Public opinion still favours their continuation as public entities.[60] Larger share offerings also had to be sensitive to the state of the stock market, especially following the October 1987 crash. And as the free trade debate reached its peak in 1988 and an election looms, the Mulroney Government seems reluctant to sell both of its flagship Crown companies.

Other companies examined in this book also provide evidence of the impact of Conservative policies. Chapter 2 shows that Canadian National's environment changed by a sequence of events, beginning with American deregulation which adversely affected its north-south market shares, continuing with Canadian deregulation under the Tories, and then with severe cutbacks in staff and the sale of some of its subsidiaries in the 1984-1988 period. Stevenson shows the complexity of the arguments about CN's privatization. The firm's management has supported privatization for some time as a means of increasing its freedom from government control and improving the railroad's financial performance. However, CN's uncertain profitability remains the prime obstacle to its immediate privatization. And the prospects for privatization are ironically complicated by the Mulroney government's insistence on forcing CN to sell its non-rail assets. Finally, important decisions remain about the form of CN's privatization. Should the federal government retain an ownership stake? And if so, how large a share? What policy directive powers should Ottawa retain? Should non-residents, other railroads especially CP and institutional investors be allowed to acquire shares?

The analysis of the FBDB and the FCC, two banking Crowns, shows the impact of diverse privatization pressures and the differences in the political constituencies of the two agencies. Changes in the Bank Act in the late 1960s, changes then called "bank reform" but which today would be called deregulation, subjected the two banks to much more competition and resulted in some loss of their market share. In the Mulroney period, the main evidence of privatization is the requirement that the banks obtain their financing from private markets, and in the reductions in staff and the closing of local branches, especially in the case of the FBDB. The FCC has more successfully resisted such pressures in part because, in the 1984-1988 period, the agriculture sector was in greater economic difficulty than the small business sector. It is a sector, moreover, that continues to be supportive of government intervention.

Finally, any survey of the Mulroney privatization record must mention Tory policy for such Crown enterprises as the post office and the CBC. In part because of strong pressure from the Tory caucus, the Cabinet has certainly been prepared to do battle on issues related to privatization. Thus the 1987 postal strike was partly an issue over franchising or contracting out and over the end of door-to-door delivery in new urban sub-divisions. The CBC was targeted for special treatment because of the strong caucus view that it was too "centralist," too "eastern biased" and anti-Conservative. Accordingly it suffered significant budget cuts, and was strongly challenged when an all-news network was awarded to the CBC and not to a private firm.

In general, the Mulroney record on privatization is one of slow and deliberate movement but with an approach that is very conscious of the pitfalls and of the underlying fact that Canadian public opinion is not overly critical of the current level and form of public enterprise.

While the Mulroney government's agenda and actions have focused attention on Ottawa, privatization is also an important issue in several provinces. Maureen Molot's study of the recent experience of Ontario, Saskatchewan and Quebec, provinces with different economic and political traditions, reveals the variety of the provincial experiences and the gap between the rhetoric and practice of privatization. She argues that even the contemporary scene is ambivalent as governments simultaneously *expand* certain public enterprises while trying to reduce the scope of their undertakings in other areas. Moreover, the politics of privatization are difficult. In Quebec, for example, privatization is controversial as sales have yielded lesser revenues than anticipated, as job losses have been higher than predicted and as problems of regional economic development have emerged. In Saskatchewan, the Progressive Conservative government of Grant Devine discovered that an ideological commitment to privatization is difficult to implement. The province's Crown corporations are politically popular and the collapse of commodity prices left Saskatchewan vulnerable to economic decline. Under these circumstances, the provincial government finds its economic options limited by harsh economic realities. Crown corporations remain an integral part of the government's response to the economic downturn. Saskatchewan has undertaken, however, to encourage citizen participation in provincial economic life through the device of public share offerings in several provincial Crown corporations. Such undertakings convert Crown corporations into mixed firms and could well transform their behaviour by institutionalizing an internal drive for profits. And in an interesting speculation, Maureen Molot and Jeanne Laux suggest that the assets of the Potash Corporation of Saskatchewan might be sold to the giant American firm, International Minerals and Chemical Corporation (IMC). In this vein, they note that PCS is not a good candidate for a public share issue. It is a large firm operating in a very volatile market, a fact already well known to conservative Saskatchewan investors. Molot and Laux also point to the close ties that have emerged between PCS and IMC under the Conservative government. A determined push by the party's right wing might lead to PCS's sale to the American firm. Such a sale would be controversial given successive Saskatchewan governments' commitment to increasing provincial control over resource development. A debate will also emerge about the impact of any such sale on corporate concentration and competition in the potash industry.

Crown Corporations: The Accountability Dilemma

Privatization is itself a response to the notion that existing accountability regimes cannot adequately control Crown corporations. But the larger accountability issue nonetheless remains. Indeed this was the issue that dominated political debate about public enterprise in Canada from the mid-1970s until 1984. An array of studies by the Auditor General, the Lambert Royal Commission on Financial Management, the Privy Council Office and by provincial governments dealt with a classic set of issues and questions.[61] At the centre of these was the perennial puzzle of how to structure decision-making processes to ensure political accountability and responsiveness while also allowing for commercial independence. Accountability relationships involve at least three dimensions, the "reporting" aspect (accountability to whom?), the performance aspect (accountability for what?) and the sanctions and rewards aspect, part of which involves the need to ask the question "accountability over what time frame?"

Accordingly, the tension between Crown corporations as politically accountable bodies and as commercial entities involves a series of issues including: the adequacy of financial data on the enterprise's performance and on the government's performance where social and policy goals are intertwined in that performance; the even greater difficulty, especially for firms in "entrepreneurial industries," of devising measures of allocative efficiency or "foregone gains" when the firm fails to take advantage of opportunities;[62] inadequate guidance and monitoring by boards of directors; and weaknesses in the Parliamentary and Cabinet scrutiny of public firms as a whole or as a stable of enterprises, along several dimensions (the formation of new firms and subsidiaries, as an aggregate pool of investment funds, and in terms of borrowing requirements).

After several failed attempts in the late 1970s and early 1980s, some progress in reforming accountability regimes became evident in the 1980s. Figure 1 shows the variety of regimes in existence in the provinces and at the federal level. The centre-piece of federal reform came with the passage in 1984 of the Part XII provisions of the *Financial Administration Act*. The key provisions were: the uniform requirement for annual approval of capital budgets, rolling multi-year corporate plans and borrowing requirements; the requirement for comprehensive audits by the Auditor General; the ability of the government to issue directives which must be tabled in Parliament; the statutory requirement that the directors of Crown corporations must always consider the "best interests of the corporation"; and improved reporting requirements for accountability to Parliament, including the automatic referral of annual reports to standing committees of the House of Commons. The lead agency for the new accountability regime is the Crown Corporations Directorate which reports jointly to the President of the Treasury Board and the Minister of Finance.

Few doubt that the formal apparatus of accountability is superior to that of the pre-1984 period. It must be recognized, however, that the system described thus far assumes the normal existence of these enterprises. In the Mulroney era, however, a second closely related system also exists. It is centred in the Ministry of State for Privatization and Regulatory Affairs, whose purpose is to challenge the continued existence of many of these firms. The secretariat for the ministry is the staff agency for the Cabinet Committee on Privatization, Regulatory Affairs and Operations. Thus the machinery is linked to Conservative efforts to deregulate and to pursue regulatory reform.[63] A related aspect of the accountability system under the Tories is that Crown Corporations are now subject to the provisions of the *Competition Act*. Prior to 1985 they were exempt from such a control.

Ideally, the privatization process develops through several stages of review and decision. Following an initial determination that a particular company should be considered for privatization, a working group is formed. It then determines the policy role of the company (if any) and other contingencies involved and develops a plan. It reports to the cabinet committee which decides on the extent and form of privatization. This decision is normally ratified by the Cabinet Committee on Priorities and Planning which gives the order to proceed. Later a more specific divestiture decision requires approval by cabinet.

For a number of reasons, the dynamics are more complicated than the formal process. First, the journey to the point of divestiture may require a host of actions including restraint, selling off subsidiaries, recapitalization or even outright expansion. Second, there have been differences over which agency ought to be the lead agency and also conflict among departments about what policy obligations now exist or ought to exist in the post-privatization period. Some of these were due to lags in developing the machinery. For example, the de Havilland and Canadair sales were handled by the

Figure 1: Government-Enterprise Control: An Overview of Seven Jurisdictions

	British Columbia	Saskatchewan	Manitoba	Ontario	Quebec	Nova Scotia	Canada
Control specified in Crown corporation legislation		*Crown Corporation Act*					*Federal Administration Act – Part XII*
Control resides with: – designated minister – central agency	X Ministry of Finance	X Crown Management Board	X Department of Crown Investments	X Management Board Ministry of Treasury and Economics	X Ministry of Finance Treasury Board	X Management Board Ministry of Finance	X Treasury Board
Capital budget – approval required	**[1]	X	X	X	A few[2]	X[2]	X
– tabled in legislature							X Summary tabled
Operating budget – general approval required	**[1]						
– approval required for revenue-dependent corporations			A few[4]	X	A few[2]	X[2]	
Borrowings: approval required, direct borrowing[5]	X	X	X	X	X	X[3]	X
Corporate plan: – approval required	X	X	At developmental stage	X	X	**[3]	X
– tabled in legislature				X[6]	X Only for Hydro-Québec[7]		X
Chief executive officer: remuneration set by of directors	X (According to Treasury Board directives)	Reviewed by CMB	Proposed by board	X (According to Management Board guidelines)		Sometimes	

	British Columbia	Saskatchewan	Manitoba	Ontario	Quebec	Nova Scotia	Canada
Board of directors:							
- may include minister	X	X	Only one GE			X	X
- may include public servants	X	X	X	X	X	X	X
Audit							
- private-sector auditor	Sometimes	Most	A minority[8]	Sometimes[9]	Sometimes	Sometimes	Corporations in Part II of Schedule C
- comprehensive audit required							X
Main legislative Committees	Public Accounts Committee	- Crown Corporations Committee - Public Accounts Committee	- Committee on Economic Development - Public Utilities & Natural Resources Committee - Agricultural Committee	- Public Accounts Committee - Procedural Affairs Committee - Select Committee on Ontario Hydro	- Standing Committees	- Public Accounts Committee - Industry Committee	- Public Committee - Standing Committees

X   Yes.
1   Approval might be considered to be implicit in the presence of the minister or the board of directors.
2   A few self-financing corporations, Lotto-Québec and Société des alcools du Québec, must submit both their capital and operating budgets for approval.
3   Capital and operating budgets are examined by Management Board as part of the overall planning and budgetary process within the province. While there is no general requirement for the submission of corporate plans, the planning strategy of enterprises such as Sydney Steel and Nova Scotia Power Corporation are subject to regular and thorough review.
4   The budgets of the Manitoba Agricultural Credit Corporation and the Manitoba Crop Insurance Corporation are examined in the context of the government's review of the budget of the Department of Agriculture.
5   Approval may involve initial authorization, which will permit the corporation to borrow directly within certain limits. Corporations in Saskatchewan, Manitoba, Quebec, and Nova Scotia need not seek approval when they go to the capital market, so long as the borrowing is within approved limits and they do not require an explicit government guarantee.
6   This is now being made a general requirement for all commercially oriented agencies in Ontario. While the corporate plan is not tabled, the Memorandum of Understanding is.
7   Hydro-Québec's capital budget is generally examined when the legislature reviews the corporation's request for rate increases.
8   Corporations that are privately audited are, moreover, subject to an "overview audit" by the Provincial Auditor.
9   Corporations receiving more than 50 per cent of their required revenue from, or generating significant revenues for, the consolidated revenue fund are expected to be audited by the Provincial Auditor.

Source: Economic Council of Canada, *Minding the Public's Business*, pp.110-111.

Department of Regional Industrial Expansion and by the Canada Development Investment Corporation, the holding company that owned the shares of the companies initially targeted for sale in 1979. But others, as the Teleglobe case shows, involved significant policy conflict within the government. Third, there are the inevitable twists and turns of decisions on particular companies caused by the government's changing priorities as well as those of particular departments.

The accountability process in the Mulroney era is also driven by the anticipatory and reinforcing behaviour of the Crown corporations themselves. The senior management of companies such as Air Canada and Eldorado Nuclear actively pressured for privatization. Other companies such as CNR were prepared to practice the new gospel of restraint, partly because they knew the strength of the Tory commitment and partly because market conditions required it. Our cases reveal the extent of managerial involvement in privatization. They caution us not to see privatization only as an ideologically driven exercise.

Thus, in the latter half of the 1980s the accountability regime in Ottawa is dual in nature. One part assumes business as usual for Crown corporations but with a more rigorous scrutiny of corporate plans and capital budgets. The second is driven by the Tories careful but unmistakeable privatization process. Together they add up to a period of unprecedented political and managerial attention being given to state enterprise.

Conclusion

The latter half of the 1980s has witnessed a profound shift in the debate about public enterprise in Canada. The privatization ethos took root abroad but has begun to be implemented by the Mulroney Conservatives and by several provincial governments. If the Mulroney government wins a second majority government, the privatization program is likely to be carried out with greater confidence since the early learning curve will have been completed. If not, the pace of privatization will be arrested or stop altogether.

The Conservatives have proceeded cautiously first because they are not Thatcherites at the ideological level and secondly because they govern a country in which public opinion is not hostile to public enterprise. They have sought to lessen the role of government but the evidence on whether they have succeeded must be sifted through carefully. With respect to state enterprise there is evidence of actual expansion when measured by data on assets but considerable contraction when measured by data on equity infusions, debt financing and employment in some key firms. More significant change has probably been achieved through deregulation than through the sale of government owned firms. We must reserve judgement as to whether this is a net reduction overall in the role of the state since other actions in policy areas and instruments not examined here may involve expanded activities for government.

Do the privatization initiatives make sense given the challenges Canada faces? The answers depend on a series of normative political and economic questions and critieria. In the context of democratic politics, the policies can be said to be "correct", if for no other reason than that the Conservatives sought and obtained an electoral mandate to restrain and reduce the role of government. In an economic sense, the policy is plausible to the extent that it helps induce a sense of change and responsiveness in a world economy that demands constant adaptation. At this level, however, one must again differentiate the act of selling Crown corporations from other probably more significant actions such as deregulation. Such arguments will, and should be, strongly disputed by those who hold different ideological views about the relative roles of governments and markets.

There are, however, immediate limits to even attempting to make judgements at this macro level. Sooner or later one must deal with evidence at the micro level or sectoral level. Our case studies indicate the varied dynamics of instrument choice in the specific political economies in which Crown corporations or privatized firms function. There may be an irresistable temptation to see all such choices as just the resultant clash of self interest among regional and industrial interests. A closer look, however, reveals the important role of analysis and information, of salutary crises and of how changing technologies lead to new mixes of policy, institutional and market based responses.

A similar macro-micro set of views must accompany any conclusions about the accountability of state enterprise. We have no difficulty concluding that the overall regime has improved over the past decade. Hopefully, this will induce a greater sense of confidence in the performance of state owned firms. It is clear, however, that it will not end disputes about particular enterprises as Canadians continue to experiment with and adapt to the shifting boundaries between states and markets.

Notes

1. See *Public Corporations and Public Policy in Canada,* ed. by Allan Tupper and G. Bruce Doern (Montreal: Institute for Research on Public Policy, 1981).

2. See John Zysman, *Governments, Markets and Growth* (Ithaca: Cornell University Press, 1983).

3. See Michael Trebilcock, *The Political Economy of Economic Adjustment* (Toronto: University of Toronto Press, 1986).

4. See Desmond S. King, *The New Right: Politics, Markets and Citizenship* (London: Macmillan, 1987).

5. See Zysman, *op. cit.* and Peter J. Katzenstein, *Small States in World Markets* (Ithaca: Cornell University Press, 1985).

6. See Jeanne Kirk Laux and Maureen Appel Molot, *State Capitalism: Public Enterprise in Canada* (Ithaca: Cornell University Press, 1988).

7. See Cento Veljanovski, *Selling the State: Privatisation in Britain* (London: Weidenfeld and Nicolson, 1987) and David Heald, "The United Kingdom: The End of Nationalization, and Afterwards?" Paper presented to Conference on *Privatisation in Western Europe,* Nuffield College, Oxford University, November 1987.

8. Heald, "The United Kingdom," p. 13.

9. See "Privatising Fling," *The Economist,* (19 April 1986) pp. 15-19, and "Privatisation: Everybody's Doing it Differently," *The Economist,* (21 December 1985) pp. 71-79.

10. See Canada, Economic Council of Canada, *Minding the Public's Business* (Ottawa: Minister of Supply and Services Canada, 1986), p. 1.

11. *Ibid.,* p. 7.

12. *Ibid.,* p. 7. See also Sharon Sutherland, "Federal Bureaucracy: The Pinch Test," in *How Ottawa Spends 1987-88,* ed. by Michael J. Prince (Toronto: Methuen, 1987), p. 87.

13. Economic Council of Canada, *Minding the Public's Business*, p. 7.

14. Sutherland, "Federal Bureaucracy: The Pinch Test," Table 2.1, p. 86.

15. *Ibid.*, Table 2.2, p. 87.

16. See, E.C. Elford and W.T. Stanbury, "Empirical Evidence on Mixed Enterprises in Canada," in *Papers on Privatization*, ed. by W.T. Stanbury and Thomas E. Kierans (Montreal: Institute for Research on Public Policy, 1985), pp. 275-302.

17. See Richard Johnston, *Public Opinion and Public Policy in Canada* (Toronto: University of Toronto Press, 1985), pp. 181-184.

18. Economic Council of Canada, *Minding the Public's Business*, pp. 8-11.

19. See Tupper and Doern, *Public Corporations and Public Policy in Canada*, pp. 5-6 and Economic Council of Canada, *Intervention and Efficiency* (Ottawa: Minister of Supply and Services Canada, 1982).

20. See Canada, Royal Commission on the Economic Union and Development Prospects for Canada, *Report*, Volume Two, pp. 252-256.

21. See Robert D. Cairns, "Exhaustible Resources and Public Firms in Canada," *Government Enterprise: Roles and Rationale* (Ottawa: Economic Council of Canada, 1985), pp. 379-423, and J.D. House, *The Last of the Free Enterprisers: The Oilmen of Calgary* (Toronto: Macmillan of Canada, 1979).

22. Johnston, *Public Opinion and Public Policy in Canada*, pp. 189 and 214.

23. See for example the articles by Tom Kierans, Maurice Strong and Paul E. Martin in *Re-mixing the Economy*, ed. by Tom Kierans (Montreal: Institute for Research on Public Policy, 1986), pp. 2-3, 4-10, and 54-57 respectively.

24. Herschel Hardin, *A Nation Unaware: The Canadian Economic Culture* (Vancouver: J.J. Douglas, 1974).

25. *Public Corporations and Public Policy in Canada,* ed. by Allan Tupper and G. Bruce Doern (Montreal: Institute for Research on Public Policy, 1981).

26. Jeanne Kirk Laux and Maureen Appel Molot, *State Capitalism: Public Enterprise in Canada* (Ithaca: Cornell University Press, 1988).

27. Michael J. Trebilcock, "The Political Economy of Business Bailouts in Canada," in *Domestic Policies and the International Economic Environment,* ed. by John Whalley with Roderick Hill (Toronto: University of Toronto Press in co-operation with the Royal Commission on the Economic Union and Development Prospects for Canada, 1985), pp. 199-213.

28. See, for example, Sandford F. Borins with Lee Brown, *Investments in Failure: Five Government Corporations that Cost the Canadian Taxpayer Billions* (Toronto: Methuen, 1986) and Michael Trebilcock *et al., The Political Economy of Business Bailouts* (Toronto: Ontario Economic Council, 1985).

29. Elford and Stanbury, "Empirical Evidence on Mixed Enterprise in Canada."

30. See for example Catherine C. Eckel and Aidan R. Vining, "Elements of a Theory of Mixed Enterprise," *Scottish Journal of Political Economy,* 32 (February 1985), pp. 82-94.

31. See, for example, Stephen Brooks, "The Mixed Ownership Corporation as an Instrument of Public Policy," *Comparative Politics* 19 (January 1987), pp. 173-191 and *Who's in Charge? The Mixed Ownership Corporation in Canada* (Montreal: Institute for Research on Public Policy, 1987).

32. K.J. Huffman, J.W. Langford, and W.A.W. Neilson, "Public Enterprise and Federalism in Canada," in *Intergovernmental Relations,* ed. by R. Simeon (Toronto: University of Toronto Press and the Royal Commission on the Economic Union and Development Prospects for Canada, 1985), pp. 131-178.

33. For details see Allan Tupper, "Bill S-31 and the Federalism of State Capitalism," Discussion Paper 18 (Kingston, Ont.: Institute of Intergovernmental Relations, 1983).

34. See for example Stephen Brooks and A. Brian Tanguay, "Quebec's Caisse de dépôt et placement: a tool of nationalism," *Canadian Public Administration*, 28 (Spring 1985), pp. 99-119 and Stephen Brooks "The State as Financier: A Comparison of the Caisse de dépôt et placement du Quebec and the Alberta Heritage Savings Trust Fund," *Canadian Public Policy*, 13 (September 1987), pp. 318-329.

35. Donald Blake, "Division and Cohesion: The Major Parties," in *Party Democracy in Canada,* ed. by George Perlin (Scarborough, Ontario: Prentice-Hall Canada Inc., 1987), pp. 32-53.

36. Marsha Chandler, "State Enterprise and Partisanship in Provincial Politics," *Canadian Journal of Political Science*, 15 (1982), pp. 711-740.

37. J. Niosi, *Canadian Capitalism* (Toronto: James Lorimer and Company, 1981), pp. 69-117.

38. D.G. McFetridge, "Commercial and Political Efficiency: A Comparison of Government, Mixed, and Private Enterprises," in *Canadian Industrial Policy in Action*, ed. by D.G. McFetridge (Toronto: University of Toronto Press and the Royal Commission on the Economic Union and Development Prospects for Canada, 1985), pp. 195-231.

39. Sandford F. Borins and Barry E.C. Boothman, "Crown Corporations and Economic Efficiency," in *Canadian Industrial Policy in Action*, ed. by D.G. McFetridge (Toronto: University of Toronto Press and the Royal Commission on the Economic Union and Development Prospects for Canada, 1985), pp. 122-23.

40. The following section relies heavily on *ibid.,* and McFetridge, "Commercial and Political Efficiency."

41. Borins and Boothman, "Crown Corporations and Economic Efficiency," p. 84.

42. Thomas J. Courchene, "Privatization: Palliative or Panacea," in *Papers on Privatization*, ed. by Tom Kierans and W.T. Stanbury (Montreal: Institute for Research on Public Policy, 1985), pp. 16-17.

43. For further details see Borins and Boothman, "Crown Corporations and Economic Efficiency," pp. 86-88.

44. Sandford F. Borins, "World War II Crown Corporations: Their Functions and their Fate," in *Crown Corporations in Canada: The Calculus of Instrument Choice*, ed. by J. Robert S. Prichard (Toronto: Butterworth and Co. and the Ontario Economic Council, 1983), pp. 447-75.

45. Yair Aharoni, "Managerial Discretion," in *State-Owned Enterprise in the Western Economies*, ed. by Raymond Vernon and Yair Aharoni (London: Croom Helm, 1981), pp. 189-191.

46. Jean-Pierre Anastassopoulos, "State-owned Enterprises: Between Autonomy and Dependency," *Journal of Public Policy*, 5 (October 1985), pp. 521-539.

47. R. Kent Weaver, *The Politics of Industrial Change* (Washington, D.C.: The Brookings Institution, 1985), especially chapter 6.

48. Canada, Economic Council of Canada, *Minding the Public's Business* (Ottawa: Minister of Supply and Services Canada, 1986).

49. See in particular Borins and Boothman, "Crown Corporations and Economic Efficiency," and McFetridge, "Commercial and Political Efficiency."

50. Borins and Boothman, "Crown Corporations and Economic Efficiency," p. 104.

51. See for example McFetridge, "Commercial and Political Efficiency."

52. Richard Pryke, *The Nationalised Industries: Policies and Performance Since 1968* (Oxford, U.K.: Martin Robertson, 1981).

53. McFetridge, "Commercial and Political Efficiency," p. 226.

54. Thomas J. Courchene, "Privatization: Palliative or Panacea."

55. Borins and Boothman, "Crown Corporations and Economic Efficiency."

56. Economic Council of Canada, *Minding the Public's Business*, pp. 147-49.

57. Department of Finance, *Budget Papers* (Ottawa: Minister of Finance, 23 May 1985), pp. 26-28.

58. See G. Bruce Doern and John Atherton, "The Tories and the Crowns: Privatizing and Restraining in a Political Minefield," in *How Ottawa Spends 1987-88*, ed. by Michael J. Prince (Toronto: Methuen, 1987) pp. 172-174.

59. *Ibid.*, pp. 150-163.

60. See the Globe-Environics Poll, *Globe and Mail*, (5 March 1988), p. D2. For both companies the data indicate at least 50 percent oppose selling and 31-33 percent support it. There are some regional variations but they are not very significant.

61. See Canada, Auditor General, *Report of the Auditor General of Canada to the House of Commons* (Ottawa: Supply and Services Canada, 1976); Canada, Royal Commission on Financial Management and Accountability, *Final Report* (Ottawa: Supply and Services Canada, 1979); and Saskatchewan, Crown Investments Review Commission, *Report* (Regina: Queen's Printer, 1982).

62. For a discussion see Economic Council of Canada, *Minding the Public's Business*, Chapter 8.

63. See Ken Stein, "Privatization: A Canadian Perspective," in *Privatization: Tactics and Techniques* (Vancouver: Fraser Institute, 1988).

Chapter II

Canadian National Railways and Via Rail

Garth Stevenson

Canadian National Railways is the largest and oldest Crown corporation in Canada, at least at the federal level, and one of the largest state enterprises in the world. Although in terms of assets it ranks behind the electric power utilities of Quebec and Ontario, it exceeds both of them in revenues. In terms of either criterion, it ranks among the top ten industrial corporations in Canada. No other public institution, apart from the Post Office, is as ubiquitous a presence in so many Canadian communities. In earlier years, it pioneered both radio broadcasting and commercial aviation, and can claim to have spawned two other Crown corporations of almost equal prominence: the Canadian Broadcasting Corporation and Air Canada.

Apart from its vast size, CN's peculiar character has made it more conspicuous than other Crown corporations, although possibly to a diminishing extent. It is a trite observation that railways have played a greater role in Canadian history, politics, and economic development than in those of any other country. Described in the novels of Hugh MacLennan, painted by the Group of Seven, and commemorated in song by Gordon Lightfoot, they remain deeply embedded in the national consciousness. In more concrete ways, CN has affected large numbers of Canadians. Until recently, it was Canada's largest employer and it remains one of the largest, although improved productivity has allowed railway employment to decline in

45

recent years even when traffic has been increasing. Traditionally, many of its services, such as passenger trains, telegraphs, express parcel delivery, and hotels, were of a retail character, consumed directly by large numbers of individuals who were easily made aware of their deficiencies, but at the same time highly sensitive to any threat of their removal. While less true than in the past, this is still true enough to involve CN in more than its share of political controversies.

Evolution and Environment

Ownership of railways by the Canadian state began at Confederation, when the new federal state acquired an assortment of railway lines in New Brunswick and Nova Scotia, as well as the obligation to build the Intercolonial Railway between those provinces and central Canada. Subsequently, Laurier's government began construction of the National Transcontinental Railway from Moncton to Winnipeg, which was completed by 1915. Two years later Borden's government established CN to operate these lines as well as the Canadian Northern, Grand Trunk Pacific and Grand Trunk railways, all of which had been, or were about to be, nationalized.[1] Subsequently CN took over the Hudson Bay Railway, built to appease discontented prairie farmers during the 1920s, and the Newfoundland Railway, which the federal government acquired under the Terms of Union between Newfoundland and Canada.

CN in its present form thus cannot be attributed to any single decision or to any single motive. It arose from a number of decisions taken by different governments, both Liberal and Conservative, for different reasons, over a period of more than eighty years. Public ownership was never viewed as an end in itself but as a means to many ends: fulfilling political and constitutional obligations, protecting Canada's credit rating, which would have suffered from the bankruptcy of either the Canadian Northern or the Grand Trunk, and providing railway service to areas, such as northern Manitoba and northwestern Quebec, that had been neglected by private enterprise. An additional motive for the establishment and retention of CN was to avoid a monopoly by the privately-owned Canadian Pacific, particularly in the West where such a monopoly had existed, and been resented, prior to the completion of the Canadian Northern. Paradoxically, state enterprise in this instance was viewed as a means to ensure "competition", the virtues of which are more frequently cited as an argument against state enterprise than as an argument in its favour.

From its inception, CN found itself in the peculiar, and at the time probably unique, situation of a state enterprise sharing the market with a private corporation of approximately equal size that had itself depended heavily on state assistance in its formative years and resented the emergence of a state-owned rival. To nationalize the mighty Canadian Pacific, whose annual revenues at that time were comparable to those of the federal state itself, was unthinkable in a country still heavily dependent on British portfolio investment. To place the other transcontinentals under CP's control or to allow their abandonment was equally unthinkable, particularly in the West. Thus the odd situation that emerged resulted from the balance of political forces that then existed.

In the competition between the two systems, the Crown corporation, at least initially, suffered serious handicaps. CP was a well-integrated and highly profitable system with a national and international reputation second to none. CN was a collection of railways not designed to operate as a single system. Much of the trackage was redundant, while other portions, such as the National Transcontinental, were incapable of generating enough traffic to pay their expenses. Interest charges on the inherited debts of its predecessors were a heavy burden. There were few precedents for a state enterprise of such vast size, and many Canadians, particularly in the two central provinces, regarded the whole idea with suspicion. CP, whose president in those days was automatically considered the unofficial head of the business community, missed few opportunities to keep the suspicion alive. Until the Second World War, the competition between the two railway companies had an almost ideological character, as though neither company fully accepted the legitimacy of its rival's existence.

With the collapse of the Union government in 1921, party politics became, and has remained, a part of the environment within which CN operated. Although some Canadians have persuaded themselves that the Conservative Party embodies an element of "collectivism" that makes it more supportive of state enterprise than the "individualist" Liberal Party, railway history provides no evidence to support this assumption. In fact the reverse would be closer to the truth.

Railways in Canada have always been associated with politics. Prior to the formation of the Union Government, the CP was Conservative, the Grand Trunk was Liberal, while the Canadian Northern tried to keep a foot in both camps and eventually had the sympathy of neither. The Intercolonial tended to be subject to the political influence of the incumbent party. After 1921, since the Liberals were usually in office, they became the defenders of the Crown corporation, while the Conservatives returned to their normal alliance with CP. The polarization of attitudes showed most clearly in 1932 when the Bennett government forced the resignation of the CN's president, Sir Henry Thornton. Throughout the interwar period, complaints about the burden of maintaining a nationalized railway system were a common theme of Conservative oratory, as suggested by the following exchange between a Conservative and a Liberal member of the eighteenth Parliament:

> Mr. Speaker, what good thing can be said for this white elephant?
> Well, it has a grand trunk![2]

Mackenzie King often denounced CP in his diary, and on one occasion wrote that it was controlled by "Downing Street."[3] According to Dalton Camp, the CN hotel in Halifax was identified with the Liberal Party and avoided by conscientious Conservatives.[4] These traditional attitudes and alignments have survived and were particularly evident during parliamentary debates on the alteration of CN's capital structure in 1978. The Mulroney government's insistence that CN dispose of its profitable non-rail activities was in sharp contrast to the views of previous governments, and suggested that Tory "hostility" to CN was by no means extinct in the 1980s.

Although the fact was only dimly realized at the time, CN was established just as the period of rapid railway development and expansion was coming to an end. Throughout its history, therefore, it has had to deal with the problems of a relatively slow-growing industry facing increasingly vigorous competition from other modes of transport. At the same time, socio-economic change was transforming the country that the railways built into one to which they have had some difficulty in adapting.

Air transport eroded much of the market for long-distance railway passenger service after 1945, but it had little impact on the freight business that has always been the major part of railway operations in Canada. Pipelines appeared at about the same time but tended to create their own traffic rather than diverting that which already existed. Highway transport by car, truck, and bus, which was already becoming important in the 1920s, proved to be by far the most important competitor of the railway. It took over much of the passenger traffic at an early stage, and by the 1950s was a serious competitor for much of the freight traffic as well. Its effect on CN can be seen in Table 1, which shows the decline of passenger traffic and the relatively slow growth of freight traffic, at least up to 1960. After 1960, however, the growth in freight traffic was much more encouraging.

In the long term, the growth of competitive modes did not so much curtail the size as it altered the character of the railway operation. The new modes, especially the motor vehicle, proved much better suited to what might be called the retail side of transportation:

small shipments, short distances, and most passenger traffic. The railway, on the other hand, is better suited to high-volume, long-distance, capital-intensive rather than labour-intensive shipment of bulk freight. To take advantage of this fact required not only technological changes in railway operations, but even more importantly, changes in the political attitudes and constraints that have surrounded Canadian railways since the middle of the nineteenth century. Regulated freight rates based on the assumption of railway monopoly, and obligations to provide services for which other modes were better suited, made it difficult for railways, including CN, to adapt to their new circumstances. By 1960, CN's freight traffic had shown no net increase over a decade in which the Canadian economy had grown substantially.

In the 1960s, CN's fortunes began to improve. Dieselization was not completed until 1960, despite a very early start under Thornton's presidency, but its impact on productivity was soon apparent. Centralized traffic control, automated classification yards, specialized rolling-stock, unit trains, continuous welded rail and concrete ties, containers for some kinds of freight, and increased integration between rail and highway services were other innovations adopted on a large scale. The National Transportation Act of 1967, following the recommendations of the Macpherson Royal Commission on Transportation, gave the railways greater freedom to set rates and withdraw from unprofitable services. The effect of these changes can be seen in the tables. While the number of CN employees declined sharply in the 1960s and did not increase in the 1970s, freight traffic and rail operating revenues increased rapidly in both decades. Even the passenger business revived to some extent, although much of the "new" passenger traffic was diverted from CP as the latter abandoned most of its services between 1959 and 1966.

Changes parallel to those on the railway also affected the communications industry, which ranks second in importance among CN's activities. Competitive modes, in this case mainly the long-distance telephone, eroded much of the market for the traditional birthday and anniversary telegraph business. However, the communication of information by a variety of sophisticated means has become indispensable to most businesses. Communications is a major participant in this kind of activity and an important contributor to CN's overall profits.

Thus both the transportation and communications sectors of CN have been transformed from labour-intensive and largely retail operations directly serving large numbers of individuals to capital-intensive, large-scale operations providing service mainly to large

Table 1
Canadian National Physical Data

	Canadian Track Miles Operated	Employees	Freight Ton-Miles (Billions)	Passenger- Miles (Millions)
1925	21,936	98,382	18.0	1380
1930	23,650	101,046	16.9	1214
1935	23,652	75,053	13.5	770
1940	23,603	82,831	21.5	1125
1945	23,498	105,624	34.6	3338
1950	24,188	112,874	32.0	1408
1955	24,235	116,853	35.7	1464
1960	24,945	101,799	34.0	1208
1965	24,613	91,378	46.1	1782
1970	25,214	80,528	56.0	1738
1975	24,959	82,856	69.3	1330
1980	22,224	74,014	88.0	-
1981	22,719	73,287	87.9	-
1982	22,617	67,113	77.8	-
1983	22,475	63,496	86.7	-
1984	22,440	66,234	97.4	-
1985	22,050	61,124	91.6	-
1986	21,792	56,715	94.2	-

Source: Annual Reports and (for track miles from 1980) Statistics Canada Publication 52.003. Data from 1981 onwards include the Northern Alberta Railways.

Table 2
Canadian National Financial Data
(Millions of Dollars)

	Gross Operating Revenues	Operating Income	Interest Payments	Net Income
1925	249.4	33.1	42.9	-9.8
1930	251.0	22.2	67.9	-35.7
1935	173.2	14.2	61.6	-47.4
1940	247.5	45.0	62.0	-17.0
1945	439.7	73.8	49.0	24.8
1950	562.6	44.1	47.4	-3.3
1955	693.9	43.7	33.0	10.7
1960	723.4	- 6.5	61.0	-67.5
1965	914.7	28.5	61.9	-33.4
1970	1167.7	45.8	75.5	-29.7
1975	2025.3	-68.1	110.6	-178.7
1980	3705.6	303.6	110.9	192.7
1981	4334.5	358.9	170.8	193.2
1982	4227.3	97.1	240.4	-223.0
1983	4659.3	465.4	268.4	212.3
1984	4987.5	552.9	349.1	242.0
1985	5017.8	440.0	336.2	117.6
1986	4881.8	281.0	382.3	-86.3

Source: Annual Reports

corporations. This change is still by no means complete, and has been frequently resisted by employees, consumers, and the politicians who represent them, but it has none the less occurred. In the long term, it will make CN less politically conspicuous and controversial than it has traditionally been. At the same time, it may expose it to new pressures and constraints while eroding much of the traditional political support that has counterbalanced the hostility of its competitors.

Apart from changes in the character of transportation itself, larger changes in the Canadian economy and society have required adaptation, not always with complete success, by Canadian National. Railways in Canada were traditionally associated with British portfolio investment, east-west trade, and a strong central government; they have survived into the era of American direct investment, north-south trade, and rampant provincialism. CN adapted fairly well to continental integration because of the extensive American subsidiaries that it inherited from the Grand Trunk, itself a product of an earlier period of continentalism. The Canada-United States Autopact made the Grand Trunk Western main line through Michigan of particular importance. Provincialism on the other hand has been associated with highway building and the rapid growth of truck and bus competition, regulated and encouraged by the provincial governments. Provincial governments have also increasingly sought to influence federal transport policy, usually in ways not welcomed by CN.

Both regional and sectoral shifts in the balance of forces within the Canadian economy have had important consequences for CN. Because of its heavy investment in fixed physical plant, and in specialized rolling stock, railroading adapts slowly and with difficulty to both kinds of changes. For historical reasons CN, in contrast to CP, has a disproportionate share of its trackage in the Atlantic provinces, where economic growth has been slow. Another problem of excess capacity, shared by both transcontinental railways, is the dense network of grain-related prairie branch lines constructed in the heyday of the wheat economy, between 1900 and 1930. In both East and West, however, any suggestion that redundant facilities and services be removed threatens powerful vested interests, stirring up a hornets' nest of political protest that has been highly successful in preventing adaptation to new circumstances.

Adapting to growth is more pleasant than adapting to stagnation, but can create problems of its own. In the 1970s the growth of the Canadian economy was again concentrated in the West, and the growth was largely based on commodities for which rail transportation is particularly suited, such as coal, potash, sulphur and lumber. CN had always been a more eastern-oriented railway than

CP, but by the end of the decade 70 per cent of its freight traffic was in the West. The capacity of the Winnipeg-Vancouver main line was strained to the limit, particularly west of Edmonton where the topography increased the capital cost of track improvements. CN nonetheless decided to double-track its line between Edmonton and the Yellowhead Pass, an ironic decision since two parallel lines on this route had actually existed for a brief period prior to nationalization. The main lines west of the pass, to Vancouver and Prince Rupert, were also improved at considerable cost. These expenditures were probably justified, but they increased CN's burden of debt and by the time they were completed the more euphoric predictions regarding the growth of the Western economy had been overtaken by events.

As shown by tables 1 and 2, CN's freight traffic grew rapidly in the 1970s and its financial performance towards the end of the decade gave cause for satisfaction. Between 1976 and 1981 its operating profits exceeded its interest charges for six years in succession, a feat that had never been achieved before. The optimistic mood at CN headquarters dissolved abruptly in 1982, when traffic declined sharply because of the recession and net income was negative for the first time in seven years. Traffic recovered in the following year, but financial performance has been somewhat uneven since that time, partly because the upgrading of the railway in response to the resource boom of the 1970s has increased debts and thus increased the burden of interest charges.

The operating results for 1985 had disturbing implications for the railway. For the first time in CN's history, freight traffic declined in a year in which the gross national product increased in real terms. The centre of economic growth had shifted away from the West, where the railways still dominate the movement of freight and where CN has concentrated its capital investment in recent years, towards southern Ontario. More significantly, the Canadian economy seemed to be shifting away from resources and agriculture, which generate most of the railways' traffic, towards manufacturing, which moves most of its output by truck, and service industries, which generate no freight traffic at all.[5] If this is a long-term trend, as seems likely, the future of railway freight transportation could be rather bleak.

As Table 1 shows, CN has responded to these adverse circumstances with massive reductions in employment. Between 1979 and 1986 the number of employees declined by 20,000, or more than 25 per cent. While some of these employees were transferred to Via Rail, which took over responsibility for the passenger service, the vast majority represented positions that simply ceased to exist.

An additional source of concern for CN management was the revival of railroads in the United States. In 1980 the United States Congress passed the Staggers Act, which deregulated railway freight rates, facilitated the abandonment of unprofitable trackage, and allowed U.S. railroads to sign confidential contracts with individual freight shippers, rather than charging the same rate to all. Between 1967 and 1980 CN had enjoyed a freer regulatory environment than its American counterparts, but the shoe was now on the other foot. U.S. railroads, most of which had fallen behind CN in productivity after 1967, were able to make significant gains as a result of the Staggers Act. By 1986 CN estimated that the ten most productive U.S. railroads exceeded CN on the average by 40 per cent in terms of the volume of freight traffic per employee.[6] The railways of North America comprise in many respects a single network, so that these facts were of more than academic interest. At least a quarter of CN's traffic consists of the movement of freight between Canada and the United States, mainly in a southbound direction.[7] For much of this traffic (e.g. the movement of lumber between British Columbia and the eastern United States) CN competes directly against its American counterparts. The greater productivity of the latter and their freedom from many constraints imposed on Canadian National, particularly the obligation to publish its rates, made it difficult to retain much of this traffic.

In 1983 CN and CP jointly claimed that they had lost $100 million worth of traffic to American competitors since the passage of the Staggers Act. The Minister of Transport, Lloyd Axworthy, asked the Canadian Transport Commission to investigate the situation. The CTC reported the following year that the rail regulatory regimes of the two countries were no longer in harmony, and it recommended that Canadian railways be allowed to make confidential contracts with shippers for their transborder traffic. It recommended further study before any decision to extend the same principle to traffic within Canada.[8] Axworthy's successor, Don Mazankowski, promptly directed the CTC to undertake a more broad-ranging inquiry. Although CN and CP seemed less convinced about the virtues of deregulation on the domestic scene, the CTC recommended that confidential contracts should be allowed for domestic traffic also. Thinking possibly of the free trade agreement that had already been recommended by the Macdonald Royal Commission, the CTC argued that this was necessary not to protect Canadian railways, but to enable Canadian shippers to meet American competition on equal terms.[9] The recommendation was incorporated in Mazankowski's white paper on deregulation, *Freedom to Move*, which appeared two months after the CTC report.[10] *Freedom to Move* in turn led to the new National Transportation Act of 1987, whose consequences for CN are considered in a subsequent section of this chapter.

One of the few happy developments of the early 1980s, from CN's point of view, was the passage by Parliament of the Western Grain

Transportation Act in 1983. Prior to this, the railways received no direct compensation for their obligation to carry grain out of the prairie provinces at a freight rate set in 1897, the so-called Crow's Nest rate. Although it derived its popular label from the fact that it was originally the *quid pro quo* for a federal subsidy to extend CP over the mountain pass of the same name, the rate was entrenched in the Railway Act in 1925 and thus made binding on CN, which had not even existed at the time of the original agreement.[11] By the 1970s the rate had become so uneconomic that the two railways refused to invest either in purchasing freight cars to carry the grain or in the routine maintenance of grain-related branch lines. The Canadian Wheat Board and the provincial governments assumed the former task and Transport Canada agreed to subsidize the latter, but the railways were still suffering heavy losses. Although regarded as sacred by western grain producers, the statutory rate was resented by western livestock processors, since it lowered the price of grain in central Canada and thus benefited their competitors. With the support of the railways and of academic economists, they argued that the rate should be raised to a normal level and compensation paid to the grain producers for their increased costs. The government appeared at first to favour this solution, but eventually adopted a compromise: the rate would increase only gradually, and compensation for the continuing shortfall of railway revenues would be paid to the railways each year. This was not CN's first preference, but at least its losses on grain traffic would be compensated. In 1986 CN was paid $360,636,707 under the terms of the Western Grain Transportation Act, while a slightly smaller amount went to CP.[12]

A subject that absorbs a large part of management's attention is that of relations between CN and its employees. In contrast to some newer industries, railroading is characterized by a large number of specialized craft unions, and efforts to create a single all-encompassing organization have not been successful. Fourteen different unions represent CN's railway employees and this total does not include the organizations representing employees in non-rail activities such as communications and hotels. The diversity of organizations contributes to complex work rules which, in the judgement of management, are serious obstacles to improvements in productivity. The rapid decline in the numbers of employees, and efforts by management to impose further reductions, have caused the climate of labour-management relations to deteriorate in the 1980s, and 1987 saw the first nation-wide railway strike in fourteen years. The strike was ended, as usual, by Act of Parliament, but the solution imposed by the state conceded much less to the employees than had been conceded on earlier occasions. It also imposed unusually harsh penalties on any employees who might defy Parliament's order.

This strike was largely the result of demands by CN and CP management that job security be eliminated so that the number of employees could be reduced in the event of declines in traffic. Increased competition from the United States, and from trucking, as well as the imminent deregulation of their own industry, convinced the managements of both major railways that this was essential. Another important issue was the desire of management to eliminate the traditional conductor's vans or cabooses at the end of freight trains, based on the argument that the job of the rear end crew could now be performed by an electronic device. The unions argued that removing the caboose would increase the risk of accidents (which are already remarkably numerous on Canadian railways) but were obviously concerned as well about the implications for employment. In one of its last decisions, at the end of 1987, the CTC ruled that cabooses could be eliminated, subject to certain conditions. Labour-management relations in CN are likely to remain difficult for the fore-seeable future.

As a Crown corporation CN faces political and social pressures in regard to its employment policies and practices from which CP is largely exempt. In the 1960s the low proportion of senior manage-ment positions held by francophones became a controversial issue, and in the 1980s there are demands to hire more women, at all levels, in a traditionally male-dominated industry. (In 1986, 36 per cent of the employees hired were women, although women still comprised less than 10 per cent of all employees at the end of the year.)[13] In addition, CN is often criticized when it eliminates jobs in regions of high unemployment, particularly in Atlantic Canada where the govern-ment railways have been a major employer since Confederation, and where CP has only a minimal presence. A major controversy of this kind erupted in 1986, when CN announced its intention to close its Moncton workshops and to concentrate all maintenance of rolling stock at Winnipeg and Montreal. The uproar subsided to some extent, although by no means completely, when Canadian General Electric agreed to buy the workshops and to hire some of the employees.

Relations with the State

The structural relationship between a state enterprise and the state may suggest the assumptions and goals that guided the founding of the enterprise. At the same time, it affects the ability of the state and of other interests in society to orient the enterprise's own behaviour to their purposes. Except for one brief intermission, the structural relationship between CN and the state has been essentially unchanged since 1922. For this reason, and because it was the prototype for later Crown corporations, the original relationship is of interest.

In defining the structure of CN and its relationship to the state, the precedent provided by the Intercolonial was deliberately rejected. The Intercolonial had become famous, in some circles notorious, for the role that party politics and patronage played in its operations. The Drayton-Acworth Royal Commission, on whose advice CN was established, recommended a type of structural relationship that would place the government railways beyond the reach of "politics," enabling them to operate as nearly as possible like a private enterprise. This advice was congenial to the Union government, which represented a rejection of what was viewed as the pettiness of traditional party politics and an emphasis on defining supposedly more elevated national goals.[14] In broader terms, the "decline of politics" in this period (as in the United Kingdom at an earlier period) can be seen as part of the modernization of the capitalist state in response to demands coming largely from the business community.

Sir Robert Borden believed that the Intercolonial had suffered from political pressure, but that the nationalized railways, if insulated from direct government control, could function as effectively as a private corporation. A specific precedent that appealed to him was the Suez Canal Company, which operated like a private corporation although the British government was the only shareholder.[15] As an interim measure, all railways owned by the government were placed by order-in-council under management of the Canadian Northern in November 1918. Since the government had forced the resignation of the Canadian Northern's two promoters, Mackenzie and Mann, this left power in the hands of their general manager, D. B. Hanna, who shared to an exaggerated degree Borden's distaste for political interference in railway operations. In preparation for the acquisition of the Grand Trunk, legislation was adopted the following year to replace these interim arrangements with a permanent structure, which still exists today. This continued to follow the model of a private corporation as closely as possible.

Formally, CN exists entirely at the pleasure of Parliament, which could repeal the Canadian National Railways Act. In fact, there has been only one instance when this power was pushed close to its limit. Following the resignation of Thornton in 1932 Parliament adopted an act that replaced the CN board of directors with three trustees, replaced the office of president with that of "chief operating officer," and directed the corporation to co-operate as closely as possible with CP.[16] Although the statute explicitly denied that its goal was to amalgamate the two systems (a solution repeatedly proposed by CP), some observers were sceptical. Most of these provisions were replaced by the incoming Liberal government in 1936, although the provisions for co-operation between the two railways remained on the statute book for somewhat longer.

In normal circumstances management enjoys a large degree of autonomy but the Canadian National Railways Act does assign certain powers of control and supervision to Parliament, the cabinet, and the Minister of Transport. CN's relationship with the state, like that of other Crown corporations, is also governed by the Financial Administration Act (FAA). The Crown corporations bill adopted by Parliament in June 1984, while the Liberal party was still in office, made a number of changes to the Canadian National Railways Act as well as to the FAA, and has thus altered the formal relationship between CN and its only shareholder.[17] As described elsewhere in this volume, the 1984 legislation was a response to allegations that Crown corporations were insufficiently accountable to their political masters.

Among other changes, the 1984 amendments formalized a situation that already existed *de facto* by incorporating in the FAA a provision that the cabinet can issue binding directives to any Crown corporation. Such directives must now be tabled in Parliament, a requirement that did not exist in the past. Complying with a directive may involve financial costs, and CN management has long taken the view that the government should provide financial compensation if it imposes any costly obligations on the corporation. An earlier draft of a Crown corporations bill, produced by the short-lived Clark government in 1979, would have made such compensation obligatory. However, the bill which Parliament adopted in 1984 does not.

Also since 1984, CN is required to submit a corporate plan each year to the Minister of Transport, and such plans require cabinet approval. Prior to 1984 cabinet also had to approve the annual capital budgets of Crown corporations, but this power is now exercised by the Treasury Board. CN, along with a few other Crown corporations of a commercial character, continues to be exempted from the necessity of submitting its operating budget, as distinct from its capital budget, to the political authorities. On the other hand, the legislative changes of 1984 now require it to seek cabinet approval before creating any subsidiary or acquiring shares in any other enterprise. These provisions might seriously restrict its freedom to diversify or to extend its railway network in the United States. The cabinet also retains its traditional powers under the Canadian National Railways Act to determine the location of the head office and to approve construction of new branch lines up to twenty miles in length. Construction of longer lines requires the approval of Parliament, under a provision of the Railway Act that applies to all railways under federal jurisdiction.

The cabinet also appoints, and can remove from office, both the chairman and the president of CN. Prior to 1984 the president was nominated by the board of directors, although subject to approval by the cabinet. Directors were previously appointed and removed by the cabinet, but the 1984 legislation transferred this responsibility to the Minister of Transport, subject to cabinet approval.

The board of directors is theoretically the main link between the state in its capacity as the only shareholder and the management of CN. There are twelve directors (as compared to seven prior to 1958) who are appointed for a renewable term of three years. Since 1984, the Canadian National Railways Act provides that no more than half of the board shall retire or be removed in any calendar year, a provision that provides some continuity and possibly some protection against political interference. At the end of 1986 one director had been on the board since 1974, but none of the others had served more than five years.

There are no formal qualifications required of appointees to the board, apart from Canadian citizenship, but in practice most have been business or professional persons close to the governing political party. Regional balance is an important consideration, and at the end of 1986 eight of the ten provinces were represented on the board. As recently as 1983 there were no women, but at present there are three. The first black person ever to sit on the board was appointed in 1985. As suggested by the preceding remarks, the board has an important representational and symbolic function, as well as being a source of political patronage. Unlike CP's board, it does not serve as a link between the railway and other large corporations in the private sector. Few if any CN directors could be considered part of the corporate elite.

Although major capital expenditures and major executive appointments are approved by the directors, they do not seem in practice to challenge the autonomy of management to any significant extent. Most directors do not have any professional background or experience in transportation. There is no evidence that the cabinet uses the directors either as a channel of communication with management or as a means of influencing its decisions. In the private sector, it is common for a director to act on behalf of a major shareholder in the enterprise, but although CN has only one "shareholder," which appoints all the directors, this pattern does not seem to prevail.

The position of chairman of the board dates only from 1974, and only since 1984 has the designation of one board member as chairman been obligatory. The first chairman, who served for eight years, was General Jacques Dextraze, who had previously been chief of staff of the Canadian Armed Forces. In 1982 he was succeeded by Jack Horner, a former cabinet minister who had lost his seat in the 1979 election. Two years later Horner was replaced by Edmonton alderman Elizabeth Hewes, a political ally of the then Minister of Transport,

Lloyd Axworthy. Hewes was dismissed by the Progressive Conservative government in 1985, and subsequently elected to the Alberta legislature as a Liberal. In her place, the president of CN, J.M. Leclair, was promoted to the chairmanship while retaining the title of Chief Executive Officer. On Leclair's resignation at the end of 1986, the chairmanship was assumed by Brian Gallery, a prominent Progressive Conservative fundraiser from Montreal and a friend of the Prime Minister, who had been appointed to the board six months previously.

Except between April 1985 and December 1986, the president of CN has always been the chief executive officer. Early presidents were not immune to political pressure. D. B. Hanna was appointed by the Borden government and resigned after a disagreement with Mackenzie King. His successor, Sir Henry Thornton, was forced out of office by R. B. Bennett, a move which some have attributed to Bennett's partiality towards the Canadian Pacific.[18] There appears to have been some uncertainty as to whether the Diefenbaker government would renew the appointment of Donald Gordon, but in the end it did so.[19] In recent years changes of government have had no apparent effect on the presidency, but the fact that the president's term of office is only three years may make him sensitive to the political environment. The selection of Robert Bandeen in 1974, after careful consideration of at least one other candidate, was apparently a signal to CN that it should adopt a more profit-oriented strategy, with less emphasis on social obligations, a message which it certainly took to heart during Bandeen's eight years as chief executive officer. Bandeen's two successors, J. Maurice Leclair and Ronald Lawless, have also been promoted from within the corporation. They differed in background, however, since Leclair was a medical doctor and former deputy minister while Lawless has spent most of his working life with the railway.

While the political executive thus has many direct ways of exercising influence over CN, Parliament has very few, a fact that will not surprise knowledgeable students of Canadian government. CN must submit an annual report to Parliament, which is considered by the Standing Committee on Transport in the House of Commons and by the Standing Committee on Transport and Communications in the Senate. The cabinet must table in Parliament any directives given to CN, as well as a summary of the annual capital budget once that has been approved. Questions related to CN may be addressed to the Minister of Transport in the House of Commons, and some sort of answer is usually provided. However, the declining influence of railways on the average voter, and the fact that passenger service is now provided by a separate Crown corporation, have made such questions far less frequent than they were twenty or thirty years ago.

Apart from occasional amendments to the relevant statutes, the main opportunity for parliamentary input is the consideration of the annual report by the House of Commons standing committee on transport. The chief executive officer and other senior personnel appear before the committee to make opening statements, and a fairly comprehensive discussion follows. Parliament gains some information from these proceedings, but management arguably gains more: the opportunity to publicize its views on issues of public policy and, on occasion, to disagree publicly with the government of the day.

An issue that perhaps illustrates the ambiguity and occasional conflict in CN's relationship with its political masters is that of purchasing policy. As a Crown corporation CN has always been under some pressure to "buy Canadian" and it has normally taken this obligation for granted, at least up to a point. When the transcontinental passenger trains of both major railways were re-equipped in the early 1950s CP purchased state-of-the-art stainless steel rolling stock from the Budd Company of Philadelphia, then the world's leading producer of luxurious passenger trains. CN settled for old-fashioned and less attractive equipment that was built in C. D. Howe's bailiwick of Thunder Bay, and its share of the market did not recover from this decision until the 1970s, when it began to offer lower fares than its competitor.

A more recent illustration of the same problem concerns the more mundane subject of steel rails, which suffer severe wear from heavy freight trains and must be replaced at frequent intervals. CP purchases its supply from Algoma Steel, a company in which it has a financial interest. CN also buys some from Algoma, particularly for the western half of its network, but the bulk of its supply comes from the Sysco steel mill in Cape Breton. Because of its geographical remoteness from the automobile industry and other major users of steel, that heavily subsidized enterprise is almost totally dependent on CN to maintain a semblance of usefulness. In 1982 CN responded to a decline in its traffic by cancelling an order for rails from Sysco, a decision that provoked considerable criticism in Nova Scotia. Early in the following year it agreed to purchase in 1983 the rails that it would normally have needed a year later, in return for a promise by the federal and Nova Scotia governments that each would pay a third of the additional inventory costs and interest charges that resulted from this decision. The remaining third of the additional costs was paid by CN itself.

CN's official position on Sysco is that it wants the mill to remain in existence so that there will continue to be some competition in the steel rail industry, but there have been allegations that Algoma's products are of better quality. It may be noted that CN (and Via Rail) continued to buy some diesel locomotives from the Bombardier plant in Montreal for some years after CP opted to rely completely on the General Motors Diesel plant in London, Ontario. General Motors diesels have enjoyed overwhelming predominance on other North American railways for thirty years, and it is reasonable to assume that maintenance costs would be lower with a standardized fleet.

Although a government directive of 1974 instructed CN to be profitable, dependence on the government still interferes with the pursuit of that objective to some extent. Disagreements with the government of the day allegedly contributed to the resignations of two chief executive officers, Robert Bandeen in 1982 and J. Maurice Leclair in 1986.[20] It is thus not surprising that CN management generally supports the idea of privatization, a subject that is considered in more detail below. An additional reason for supporting the idea is a revival of concern in recent years over the ratio of CN's debts to its equity.

As mentioned above, a very significant change in CN's capital structure was made by Act of Parliament in 1978. This was actually the third such measure, with others having been adopted in 1937 and 1952. All three were introduced by Liberal governments, welcomed by CN itself, and opposed by the Conservative Party and CP. An understanding of the capital structure, and of the controversies to which it has given rise, is essential in order to understand the relations between Crown corporation, private enterprise, and the state.

"Rail debts are at the heart of the present rail problem" was the judgement of Lesslie R. Thomson, who published a massive analysis of Canadian railways and their problems during the Great Depression.[21] As Thomson pointed out, the nationalization of the railways that became part of the CN prevented them from shedding their debts through bankruptcy, which was and remains the usual therapy prescribed for ailing North American railways. Because of this "negligence," as he called it, Canadian National entered the Depression with a debt-to-equity ratio of approximately four to one. Even in prosperous years, its operating profits, although respectable, could not cover the burden of its interest payments.

This situation was the principle source of the handicap that CN suffered in its competition with CP. The inability to earn enough to cover the interest charges damaged the morale of both management and employees and contributed to the widespread belief that state enterprise was inherently inefficient, while the constant need to seek funds from Parliament kept the Crown corporation at the centre of political controversy. CP and its political allies argued that CN was a burden on the backs of all taxpayers, that CP, as the largest taxpayer, put money into the public treasury while CN took it out, and that it

Table 3
Canadian National Capital Structure
(Millions of Dollars)

	Long-Term Debt	Government Equity	Debt-Equity Ratio
1925	931.3	265.6	78:22
1930	1168.6	265.6	81:19
1935	1154.8	265.6	81:19
1940	1199.9	669.5	64:36
1945	573.2	777.3	42:58
1950	659.0	776.4	46:54
1955	896.0	1591.9	36:64
1960	1680.3	1721.1	49:51
1965	1368.1	1843.2	43:57
1970	1044.0	1984.4	34:66
1975	2066.1	2224.6	48:52
1980	1591.0	2944.9	35:65
1981	1784.2	3059.6	37:63
1982	2274.8	2840.9	44:56
1983	2357.8	3112.6	43:57
1984	2692.4	3324.3	45:55
1985	3172.2	3418.5	48:52
1986	3358.3	3004.6	53:47

Source: Annual Reports

was unfair to expect CP as a taxpayer to contribute funds that were
turned over to its competitor, enabling the latter to compete more
effectively. CN did not have to earn money to finance its capital
expenditures, but could always get money from Parliament, giving it
an unfair advantage. If all the railways were placed under CP
management, the deficits would disappear and the taxpayers would be
relieved of their burden.[22] These arguments were widely believed, at
least in Quebec and southern Ontario, but their plausibility depended
on CN retaining the burden of debt that kept it in a position of
dependence on Parliament. Thus CP and its allies had a vested
interest in the existing capital structure of the CN, and resisted any
moves to change it to the latter's advantage.

The Canadian National Railways Capital Revision Act of 1937
was the first effort to deal with this situation. It cancelled most of the
stock of the Canadian Northern and certain debts to the Crown that
CN had inherited from the Grand Trunk. Over a billion dollars of
additional debts to the Crown were transferred to a new entity known
as the Canadian National Railways Securities Trust. This measure
caused CP to undertake in the city of London what John W. Dafoe
termed "an organized campaign to damage the credit of Canada . . . , in
the hope that the government can thus be intimidated to yielding to
Sir Edward Beatty's demands."[24] Nonetheless, it went only a short
distance towards resolving the problem. More than a billion dollars
worth of debts to private bondholders remained.

By 1952, the CP and British finance capital had lost most of their
power to intimidate the Canadian government. By the Capital
Revision Act of that year, one half of CN's remaining debts to the
Crown were transformed into preferred stock paying a nominal
dividend of 4 per cent. Interest payments on some additional debts to
the Crown were suspended for ten years. The government was
required until 1960 to purchase more preferred stock to an amount
equal to 3 per cent of CN's gross revenues in each year, a practice
actually continued well into the 1970s although there was no
statutory obligation to do so.[25]

This measure was supposed to eliminate the pre-nationalization
debts once and for all and to give CN a debt-to-equity ratio comparable
to CP. Unfortunately it overestimated the assets by some $800
million through failing to take accumulated depreciation into
account.[26] Over the next quarter-century, CN borrowed heavily to
finance massive expenditures on new equipment, so that by the 1970s
its debt-to-equity ratio was again unsatisfactory, despite continuing
purchase of preferred shares by the government.[27]

The third Capital Revision Act cancelled $808 million of CN's
debts to the Crown, as well as all the preferred stock purchased by the
government since 1952, and increased the book value of the no-par-

value ordinary stock, also held by the government, by an amount equal to the value of the cancelled obligations. It also provided that 20 per cent of CN profits would henceforth be paid to the Crown as a dividend, with the remainder reinvested in the company.[28]

This legislation was supported by the Liberals and New Democrats and opposed by the Progressive Conservatives, indicating the durability of partisan railway alliances now more than half a century old. Progressive Conservative spokesmen expressed anxiety that the legislation would adversely affect the interests of CP, and also of the trucking industry. Both the Canadian Trucking Association and CP argued that CN's debts were the result of its capital expenditures since 1952. Both expressed concern that if the debts were removed, CN would undertake more capital expenditure with borrowed funds than it could afford, on the assumption that it would again be relieved of its debts by Parliament at some future date. Both had an obvious interest in minimizing capital expenditure by their state-owned competitor. If a state enterprise spends too little on improving its physical capital, it is derided for backwardness and inefficiency, but if it spends too much, it is criticized for extravagance.

CN has invested heavily in improvements since 1978. Its management now proudly claims that their railway is more modern and more productive than its privately-owned competitor, a claim that is probably justified. On the other hand, as Table 3 shows, CN's debt-equity ratio has again begun to deteriorate, just as its opponents predicted in 1978. The solution this time is more likely to be sought through privatization than through another increase in the equity held by the state.

Goals and Structures

In a recent book on railway policy in North America, Kent Weaver has classified public enterprises according to which of three strategies they pursue: security, autonomy, or public service.[29] The first refers to an enterprise which is mainly concerned with ensuring its own survival by maximizing its political support. Capital is allocated so as to minimize discontent on the part of customers, employees, persons otherwise dependent on the enterprise, and their political representatives, since the latter may have the power to determine whether the enterprise remains in existence. The second type, the autonomy strategy, refers to an enterprise whose major concern is to maximize its own freedom from constraints imposed by the state. The means to this end is the pursuit of profitability, since a healthy balance sheet will end financial dependence on the state and thus limit the state's ability to impose conditions in return for its support. Finally, the public service strategy is based on a more idealistic urge to contribute to the welfare of society, rather than pursuing the welfare of the enterprise as an end in itself. While the first two strategies have diametrically opposite implications with regard to the retention or otherwise of unprofitable services and facilities, the implications of the third strategy in this regard are more complex and ambiguous. The allocation of capital will be based on the larger social objectives, whatever they are, with neither making friends nor making profits as the primary consideration.

Although Weaver does not say so, there could be a logical sequence of these three strategies. A newly established state enterprise, whose political mandate is fresh in the minds of its managers, might be expected to pursue a strategy of public service without much concern for either its balance sheet or the dangers of antagonizing sections of the public. This could lead to serious controversy, threatening the very survival of the enterprise and causing it to retreat to what Weaver calls a security strategy. This would achieve its goal of self-preservation but at the cost of making the enterprise increasingly cumbersome, unprofitable, and dependent on the state. Eventually management and the state, for different reasons, would agree on the desirability of an autonomy strategy based upon the pursuit of profitability. This would relieve the state of a financial burden while relieving the enterprise of its dependence on the state. Eventually this arms-length relationship might lead to a divorce by mutual consent, or in other words the privatization of the enterprise.

This appears to be exactly what has happened in the case of CN, although the final phase has not yet reached its culmination. The public service strategy corresponds with the presidency of Sir Henry Thornton, from 1922 until 1932. The security strategy was pursued from Thornton's fall until 1974, when Robert Bandeen was appointed as president with specific instructions to make CN into a profitable enterprise. The autonomy strategy has been pursued ever since, although the government has not always been entirely consistent in its support of that strategy. Privatization began to be considered, by both government and management, as early as 1976, and seems likely to take place in the 1990s.

While the choice of an autonomy strategy in recent years is understandable, its appropriateness is by no means universally accepted. An examination of the proceedings of the House of Commons Standing Committee on Transport indicates that significant support persists in Parliament for the view that CN should not pursue profitability, and should not be judged by the same criteria as a private enterprise like CP. The goal of profitability may be rejected for one or both of two contrasting reasons.

One basis for this view is what might be described as free enterprise fundamentalism: the belief that it is simply immoral for the state to occupy, even partially, a profitable field of activity that could be left to private entrepreneurs. As long as CN appeared to be inherently unprofitable, it was not very vulnerable to criticism of this kind, at least with respect to its railway operation. The improved financial results of recent years, however, have produced demands for complete or partial "privatization" as well as excessive criticisms of CN's activities that are both conspicuous and profitable, such as the CN Tower on Toronto's waterfront. During debate on the Capital Revision Act of 1978, Senator Duff Roblin openly expressed the view that diversification into profitable fields of activity was legitimate for CP but not for CN:

> As [a] free enterpriser, I feel that the Canadian National Railways should avoid the temptation to try to model itself on that other company, and become a conglomerate.[30]

During committee hearings on the same legislation, Don Mazankowski, subsequently Minister of Transport in the Clark and Mulroney governments, asked President Bandeen whether "the public" would accept the idea of a Crown corporation making a profit.[31] Although Mazankowski's own views, and his motives in asking the question, are not clear from the record, the question is a real one and has yet to be conclusively answered.

Perhaps paradoxically, the admirers of state enterprise, and of CN in particular, frequently join with its detractors in demanding that it renounce the goal of making a profit. For example, NDP transport critic Les Benjamin, during the same committee hearings referred to above, challenged President Bandeen's view that CN should be compensated directly for its unprofitable services, suggesting instead that it should use the profits from its profitable services to subsidize them. He admitted that this would prevent CN from showing an overall profit, but saw no reason why it should do so.[32]

Even from the viewpoint of corporate self-interest, it could be argued that CN still requires the political support it has received over the years from Liberals, the moderate left, and residents of the Canadian hinterlands. That support has traditionally been based on the view that CN not only competed with, but was in some way different from, CP. It may be eroded if CN's single-minded pursuit of commercial profitability makes the two corporations appear indistinguishable.

From a broader perspective, the question may legitimately be asked whether in a country of vast distances, physical barriers, and fragile unity, whose regions are more easily linked with adjacent portions of the United States than with one another, a transport policy based on normal commercial criteria is at all appropriate. If it is not, then the main rationale for a Crown corporation involved in several fields of transportation and communication would seem to be that it is, at least potentially, a tool by which objectives of a more "political" character can be implemented by the state. If the Crown corporation resists the idea of being used in this way, or is otherwise unsuitable to the task, is there any justification for its existence?

CN's pursuit of an autonomy strategy in recent years has led to important changes in its internal structure and in the range of activities which it pursues. The former has been transformed from one based primarily on geography to one based primarily on function. The latter has moved from concentration on the railway to increasing diversification and then back towards an increasingly single-minded preoccupation with the railway.

Historically the basis of railway organization in North America was geographical. The basic unit was the subdivision, a segment of track corresponding to the distance a steam locomotive could travel without replenishing its supply of fuel and water. Subdivisions were grouped into divisions and divisions into larger units, if the overall size of the railway made this desirable. Managerial control was nonetheless highly centralized.

CN traditionally followed this pattern except that the divisions were known as "areas". In the early 1960s there were eighteen of them, not counting the Grand Trunk Western which was organized as a separate railway with headquarters in Detroit, apparently to avoid offence to patriotic Americans. At about that time the eighteen areas were grouped into five regions with headquarters in Moncton, Montreal, Toronto, Winnipeg and Edmonton, each headed by a vice-president. Some decentralization of managerial authority to this level took place. Eventually in the 1970s the "areas" were deemed to be superfluous and were abolished. Communications (originally known as telegraphs) and hotels were outside of this organizational structure, but functions such as express, trucking, passenger service and coastal steamships were treated as parts of the main enterprise.

In 1976 a fundamental change took place. The geographical organization of the railway was preserved, but the railway, now known as CN Rail, became merely one of several self-contained "profit centres" reporting to corporate headquarters. Besides setting overall policy, headquarters was responsible for providing certain services to the "profit centres", including public relations, industrial relations, legal and medical services, and CN's private police force.

Beside CN Rail, the "profit centres" included CN Passenger Services, Trucking and Express, Hotels and Tower, Grand Trunk

Corporation, Telecommunications, CN Marine, CN Investment Division and Canac Consultants Limited. Trucking and Express were associated, although not completely integrated, because almost all express shipments by this time were carried by truck rather than on passenger trains. Hotels and Tower owed its odd name to the CN Tower in Toronto, which might more logically have been included with Telecommunications. Grand Trunk took over subsidiaries in Vermont and Minnesota, as well as the Grand Trunk Western, but the line to Portland, Maine, also known locally as Grand Trunk, continued to be treated as part of the Canadian railway. CN Marine took over the coastal shipping and ferryboats in Atlantic Canada, CN Investment Division was responsible for miscellaneous activities such as oil and natural gas, while Canac provided consulting services to railways overseas. Subsequent additions to the list included Terratransport, organized in 1979 to take over the bus service and narrow gauge railway in Newfoundland, and CN Real Estate. "Profit centre" was a singularly inappropriate term for many of these enterprises, but this fact was actually a major reason for the whole exercise. Separating them in this way made it possible to identify the ones that were actually or potentially profitable and to seek relief from the burden of those that were not, either through subsidy, contract, privatization, or transfer of responsibility from CN to some other agency of the state. CN argued that if it was expected to be profitable, it could not logically be expected to cover the costs of services that were maintained for political or social reasons. Subsidies would be welcome, but CN's preference was for contracts that would provide incentives for efficiency and productivity. A precedent for this type of arrangement existed as early as 1966, when CN signed a contract with the Government of Ontario to operate commuter trains on the latter's behalf in the Toronto area. This operation known as GO Transit, was completely distinct from CN's own passenger services, and the rolling stock belonged to the province.

CN Passenger Services was intended to have a short life, since railway passenger service was considered hopelessly unprofitable by 1976. Under the terms of the National Transportation Act of 1967 the government subsidized 80 per cent of the losses of passenger services which the Canadian Transport Commission had deemed to be required by the public convenience and necessity, but CN now demanded either complete reimbursement for its losses on unprofitable services or the right to terminate them. In 1977 the government responded by forming Via Rail Canada (described in the last section of this chapter) and most passenger services were taken over by the new enterprise within two years. CN's losses on Montreal commuter service were ended by a contract with the Montreal Urban Community in 1982. Two minor passenger services (Toronto-North

Bay and Edmonton-Waterways) were still the responsibility of CN Rail in 1987, but the unremunerated 20 per cent of their losses was a relatively minor burden. CN claims that its contract with Via Rail does not completely cover the real costs of servicing that operation, but Via Rail itself claims that the costing formula used to calculate the amount of payment is too generous to CN and CP.

Express and trucking proved to be major headaches for CN. The express business was highly labour-intensive and inefficient but politically popular because for the many Canadians who used it it was a more convenient and cheaper alternative to the post office. In the hope of reducing its losses it was combined in 1983 with CN's other trucking operations under the name of CN Route. Although trucking, in contrast to express, had previously earned modest profits, the combined operation never did so, even though considerable rationalization took place. In 1985, when the losses of CN Route soared to a record level of $42.6 million, CN decided to withdraw from the trucking business. CN Route was sold to the private sector the following year.

The hotels were less damaging to the balance sheet, but their profits were small or non-existent, and the disappearance of CN's passenger trains, with which they had been closely associated, seemed to undermine the rationale for their existence. Several were disposed of individually to local businessmen or, in one case, to the government of Ontario. The idea of withdrawing completely from the hotel business was first considered in the late 1970s, but at that time was rejected by the directors. Between 1982 and 1985 CN tried to interest Air Canada in sharing ownership of the hotels. Discussions were held but Air Canada showed little enthusiasm. CN then tried to sell the hotels to CP, which also declined. In 1987 CN announced publicly that it would like to dispose of the remaining hotels, and would consider any reasonable offer. Subsequently the Minister of Transport confirmed rumours to the effect that the CN Tower would also be privatized. In January 1988 the CN Hotels were sold to CP, which had apparently reconsidered its earlier reservations. The CN Tower was not included in the deal.

The Newfoundland railway is a politically sensitive problem in which the provincial government has become involved. The railway was originally built by private enterprise but was later taken over by the Newfoundland government. Like the railways in many British colonies, it was built to a narrow gauge of 1067 millimetres, instead of the 1435 millimetres used in both Europe and North America. By the terms of union with Canada, it became the responsibility of the federal government, which entrusted it to CN. CN made some effort to modernize the line, but traffic was light and losses were heavy. Buses were substituted for passenger trains in 1968, but the buses were also unprofitable. In 1978 the Sullivan Royal Commission recommended abandoning the railway.[33]

Since the federal government refused to run the political risks that would result from abandoning the railway, and since Newfoundland declined CN's offer to return it to provincial ownership, the formation of Terratransport was the best available solution. Management continued to hope that at some future date CN might be relieved of the obligation to operate the Newfoundland railway, either through abandonment or through the transformation of Terratransport into a Crown corporation completely separate from CN. In the early 1980s the Newfoundland railway was rationalized by an almost complete substitution of containers for ordinary rolling stock. However, operating revenues of Terratransport in 1985 covered less than 40 per cent of operating expenses.[34] The Mulroney government's task force on possible ways to reduce federal expenditures repeated the recommendation that the railway be abandoned, and Transport Minister Don Mazankowski tried to secure the acquiesence of the Newfoundland government by promising major expenditures on other modes of transport. His successor John Crosbie, a Newfoundlander, bowed to public pressure and promised to retain the railway at least until 1990. Although CN has repeatedly urged that it be compensated for what it calls an "imposed public duty", federal governments for over a decade have ignored this request. It appears that regional cross-subsidization is a major unstated objective of federal railway policy.

Although CN gained neither compensation for, nor relief from, its obligations to provide rail and bus service in Newfoundland, both approaches were tried in the case of CN Marine, the "profit centre" which operated steamship and ferry services in Atlantic Canada. This operation has always been heavily subsidized by the government, but in 1979 the subsidy was replaced by a contract, under which CN agreed each year to provide a specified package of services in return for a fixed payment. Any gains in productivity or any success in attracting additional business would thus result in "profits" for CN, rather than simply reducing the amount of the subsidy. These arrangements worked well, from CN's point of view, for several years. In 1979 the "profit" of CN Marine, or in other words the excess of the contract payment over the operating loss, was $7.8 million, and by 1984 it had risen to $21.9 million.[35] The Mulroney government, however, decided to separate CN Marine from CN, without consulting the latter. In 1985 CN Marine became a new Crown corporation under the name of Marine Atlantic, and was allowed to begin its new life with no debts on its balance sheet.

The Mulroney government's obvious preference for divesting CN of its non-rail operations, made explicit in a public statement by the

Minister of Transport late in 1987, forced the corporation to reconsider the emphasis on diversification that characterized its corporate strategy from 1974 until 1984. Diversification had been viewed as a means of protecting the balance sheet against the effects of cyclical fluctuations in railway revenues, with real estate and natural resources as the main areas of interest. In 1979 CN's miscellaneous activities were grouped into a new profit centre known at first as CN Holdings and after 1981 as CN Enterprises. In the early phase of the Trudeau government's National Energy Program, CN considered becoming a major participant in the Canadianization of the petroleum industry, but the collapse of energy prices and the growing political resistance to the NEP brought these ambitions to an end. CN Enterprises was abolished in 1985.

By far the most important of the non-rail activities, and the one that CN was most determined to retain, was CN Telecommunications, which changed its name to CN Communications in 1981. Although less than one tenth as large as the railway in terms of operating revenues and expenses, CN Communications has always contributed a disproportionately large share of the overall profits, even in years when the railway results were better than usual. An additional reason for wishing to retain this profit centre is the increasing importance of sophisticated communications for railway operations. Nonetheless, the Mulroney government instructed CN in 1987 to sell its two profitable telephone companies, Northwest Tel and Terranova Telecommunications. This would still leave CN in possession of the largest part of CN Communications, namely its share of CN-CP Telecommunications. Under the terms of the agreement between the two railways that set up this partnership in the 1950s, CP would have the right of first refusal if CN disposed of its share, and the privately owned railway would undoubtedly avail itself of the opportunity to become the sole owner.[36] CN would thus have to purchase communications services from its major competitor, unless it could make some arrangement with Telecom Canada, the consortium dominated by Bell Canada.

An even more important profit centre in terms of interdependence with CN Rail is the Grand Trunk Corporation, which includes most of CN's railway operations in the United States. Until 1980 these consisted entirely of lines owned by the Grand Trunk or, in one case, the Canadian Northern before nationalization. The rationale for acquiring them, namely to increase the parent company's share of transborder traffic, has gained additional importance because of the Staggers Act, the subsequent deregulation of Canadian railroading, and the prospect of bilateral free trade. In 1980 Grand Trunk acquired the Detroit, Toledo and Ironton Railroad, giving it access to the important rail gateway of Cincinnati. Soon afterwards it tried to gain access to both Minneapolis and Kansas City by offering to purchase the remains of the bankrupt Chicago, Milwaukee, St. Paul and Pacific Railroad. However, a higher bid was submitted by the Soo Line, a majority of whose shares are owned by CP. In 1985 the Interstate Commerce Commission authorized the absorption of the Milwaukee by the Soo Line. Meanwhile, in 1983, CN considered disposing of its weakest American subsidiary, the Central Vermont, but eventually decided to retain it. Since most U.S. railroads are now controlled by one of seven giant systems, additional major changes in the shape of the Grand Trunk network are unlikely.

The shape of CN Rail's Canadian network has also undergone significant changes in the 1980s. More than two thousand miles of track have been abandoned since 1979 including two sections, totalling 246 miles, of the former National Transcontinental main line between Moncton and Winnipeg. The Northern Alberta Railways were added to the network in 1980, after CN bought the 50 per cent share formerly held by CP. In 1985 CN and CP jointly acquired from Conrail the Canada Southern Railway, which connects Detroit with Buffalo and Niagara Falls by way of southern Ontario.[37] This line, which had never before been under Canadian ownership, controls three of the four rail connections between southern Ontario and the United States. (The fourth, at Sarnia-Port Huron, was already controlled by CN.) The Canada Southern also provides better access to Windsor and Fort Erie than CN 's own lines, and will in effect replace them.

In the long term, the most significant impact on the future of CN Rail may be that of the free trade agreement between Canada and the United States. Railways are less closely linked with economic nationalism today than they were in 1911, when CP Chairman Sir William Van Horne waged a public campaign against Reciprocity. Exports to the United States, such as lumber, newsprint, potash and motor vehicles, already account for a large share of railway freight traffic. The acquisition of the Canada Southern, and the recent expansion of both the Soo Line and the Grand Trunk, suggest that CN and CP had already come to terms with continentalism, and their public support for Canada-United States free trade is thus not surprising. On the other hand, long-term shifts in trade patterns resulting from the agreement might reduce freight traffic in both directions between central Canada and the western provinces, and between central Canada and the Maritimes. This bridge traffic must pay the high fixed costs of CN's extensive trackage in northern Ontario and New Brunswick, the legacy of the second and third transcontinental railways that were built to compete against CP. The effects of the free trade agreement may thus increase CN's incentive to reduce its trackage, a subject discussed below.

Apart from continental free trade, the most significant developments to the end of the twentieth century are likely to be deregulation and, possibly, privatization. The first, which presents both opportunities and dangers, became a fact in 1987 with the adoption by Parliament of a new National Transportation Act. The second has not yet taken place but would seem to be a logical culmination both of CN's recent corporate strategy and of the Mulroney government's policies. Its feasibility in turn will be largely governed by the success with which CN Rail is able to respond to deregulation. An examination of these two issues will conclude the consideration of CN's problems and prospects in this chapter.

A New Regulatory Framework

As noted in an earlier section of this chapter, the revision of the regulatory framework for Canadian railways that took effect at the beginning of 1988 was very largely the consequence of similar action taken eight years earlier in the United States. Since the Staggers Act had brought about a dramatic improvement in the fortunes of U.S. railroads, apparently without adverse consequences for other sectors of the economy, it naturally attracted favourable attention in Canada. The railways themselves wanted to eliminate regulatory constraints that interfered with their own efforts to improve productivity and compete more effectively against their American counterparts, particularly for transborder traffic. On the other hand, policy-makers in Ottawa were more concerned with the interests of freight shippers, and with their ability to meet American competition, than with the problems of the railways. The political reasons for this were not difficult to fathom. Freight shippers numbered in the thousands, and were an important constituency for the business-oriented Progressive Conservative party. The major railways numbered only two, and one of them was a Crown corporation at a time when sympathy for state enterprise was distinctly unfashionable. To paraphrase one of John Diefenbaker's aphorisms, there were more votes to be won on Main Street than in Central Station. Thus the legislation that finally found its way onto the statute books was viewed by CN with very mixed feelings.

Although popularly described as "deregulation", what took place is more accurately described as the imposition of a new and different regulatory framework on Canadian railways. Freight rates, apart from those on prairie grain, had virtually been deregulated twenty years earlier, in contrast to the United States where they were tightly regulated until the adoption of the Staggers Act. The principal change that the Canadian legislation of 1987 (Bill C-18) made in this regard was that it followed the example of the Staggers Act by allowing confidential contracts between railways and shippers. This was of course in the mutual interest of both railways and shippers, and was welcomed by CN and CP. Some less important changes were made that were also beneficial or at least acceptable to the railways. These included relaxation of the requirements regarding the filing of freight rates, procedures for the mediation of rate disputes, and a provision that railways and shippers could negotiate special agreements to limit the carrier's liability for loss, delay or damage. The railways even accepted a provision that ended their traditional (and since 1967 explicit) power to set rates in collaboration with one another, regardless of the Combines Investigation Act. These changes brought the Canadian regulatory framework into harmony with that of the United States. Since both major Canadian railways control trackage on both sides of the border, and since the post-Staggers regulatory regime in the United States has proved beneficial to their U.S. counterparts, this could only be to their advantage.

Section 156 of the new National Transportation Act, which was added to Bill C-18 while it was in the House of Commons, may also benefit Canadian railways. This section provides that if a foreign government (discreetly not specified by name) discriminates against Canadian railways, the government of Canada may seek the elimination of the discriminatory law or practice by consulting with the foreign government concerned. If this does not have the desired effect, the Canadian government may take whatever action it deems appropriate, presumably including retaliation against the railways of the unnamed foreign country.

A number of other provisions in the new act are clearly designed to protect shippers against the railways, and are viewed as potentially damaging by CN. For example Section 134 provides that where the origin or destination of any freight traffic is accessible by only one railway, that railway shall at the shipper's request agree to a competitive line rate to or from the nearest point served by another railway. In other words a shipper at St. Catharines, which is served only by CN, could have the option of shipping freight fifteen miles to Welland on CN, and then from Welland to Vancouver on CP. If CN does not agree to a competitive line rate as defined above, Sections 136 and 137 allow the shipper to appeal to the National Transportation Agency (which replaces the old CTC) and the agency can impose a rate on the railway.

Section 148 provides that the National Transportation Agency may give any railway company permission to:

(a)   take possession of, or occupy any lands belonging to any other railway company

(b)   use the whole or any portion of the right-of-way, tracks, terminals, stations or station grounds of any other railway company, and

(c)   exercise full rights and powers to run and operate its trains over and on any portion of the railway of any other railway company . . . .

This provision violates a principle that has been sacrosanct throughout the history of railroading, namely that each railway company has the exclusive right to use its own lines and can control access to them by others.   One of CN's vice-presidents told the House of Commons Standing Committee on Transport that it would "effectively convert private property to public use."[38]   In a speech a year earlier, another CN vice-president called it "confiscation — without adequate compensation — of investments made by individual railways."[39]

Section 152 of the new act deals with interswitching, or the handling of one railway's freight cars and trains by another railway. It extends from four miles to thirty kilometres, and in some cases more, the distance from the other railway's lines within which this service is obligatory, and allows the National Transportation Agency to set the terms and conditions including compensation, if any, regarding the performance of the service.

All of these provisions are designed to protect shippers from any exercise of monopoly power by a railway, even though more than a quarter of a century has passed since the McPherson Royal Commission argued that the railways no longer possessed such power, except in rare circumstances.   Since Canada and the United States are the only countries in the world with more than one railway competing for the same traffic, and since the Staggers Act contains no provisions analogous to those described above, the Mulroney government's concern in this regard is unprecedented, and probably unwarranted.

For various reasons CN feels particularly threatened by these provisions, well-intentioned though they may be.   CN National serves many more locations than CP, and has about 50 per cent more trackage in Canada than its competitor.   It thus stands to lose much more by making its on-line traffic accessible to its competitor than it will gain in return.   CN has also invested more heavily in recent years than CP in improving its infrastructure, yet it will now be expected to share the benefits of these investments with its competitors. Furthermore, while the Act provides for at least formal equality of privileges as between CN and CP, it opens the trackage and traffic of those two railways to other competitors who are not required to offer anything in return.   The two provincial railways, British Columbia Railway and Ontario Northland, will benefit from Sections 134, 148, and 152 but, since they are not federally regulated, they cannot be required to offer reciprocal privileges to CN and CP. Even more significantly, American railroads that operate a few miles of track in Canada can use Sections 134, 148, and 152 to take traffic from CN and CP but since the Staggers Act does not have any comparable provisions, the Canadian railways cannot retaliate against the extensive networks operated by those same railways in the United States.[40]

A further set of provisions in the new Act are on balance slightly favourable to CN's interests, but are faulted on the grounds that they do not go far enough in freeing the railways from regulatory constraints. The provisions in question are those dealing with the abandonment of branch lines and other trackage. The constraints imposed on the railways in this regard have always been, and remain, formidable. Most of the grain gathering network on the prairies (minus some lines which the Hall Royal Commission judged in 1977 to be useless, and which were abandoned soon afterwards) has been entrenched by order-in-council until the year 2000. About 15 per cent of CN Rail's Canadian trackage falls into this category.[41] Abandonment of trackage elsewhere has proved to be difficult, although not always impossible, for the railways. Although CN has abandoned considerable trackage in recent years, it would like to abandon much more. In 1987 it estimated that one third of its Canadian trackage carried 90 per cent of its freight traffic, another third carried about 9 per cent, and the remaining third carried practically no traffic at all. Although some of the traffic originating on the less-used lines, or destined there, also travels over the heavily used main lines, most of it could be carried by truck to a main line point and then transferred to the railway, or carried by rail along the main line and then delivered by truck. If CN Rail abandoned two-thirds of its track it would probably retain about 80 per cent of its traffic.[42]

The new Act gives the National Transportation Agency powers to regulate or prevent the abandonment of trackage that are not very different from the powers previously exercised by the CTC. It does allow the railways one loophole that was not envisioned by the drafters of the old act, namely the transfer of unwanted trackage, provided the Agency approves, to short line carriers that may be able to operate it more cheaply by paying sub-standard wages. This practice has become widespread in the United States since the Staggers Act and the first Canadian instance occurred in 1986, when CN transferred the Stettler subdivision in Alberta to a local entrepreneur styling himself the Central Western Railway. There will probably be many more such transfers in Canada over the next few years.

Two sections added while the bill was in the House of Commons were intended to make abandonment of lines more difficult for the railways. Section 159 says that no railway company may abandon more than four per cent of its route mileage in any of the first five years that the act is in operation. Section 168 says that abandonment of a line will be deferred for a year if Via Rail is using it for passenger service or planning to do so. It also says that Via Rail may apply to take over a line that a railway wishes to abandon. It is possible that a number of CN lines will be transferred to Via Rail over the next few years, particularly in Quebec and Ontario, but lines used by Via Rail comprise only a very small fraction of the surplus trackage that CN would like to abandon.

On balance the new National Transportation Act is thus more of a drawback than an advantage from CN's point of view, particularly since it simultaneously takes steps to deregulate the trucking industry. CN will be exposed to more competition from American railroads, from trucks, and even from CP. The abandonment of surplus trackage is not really made any easier, and the problem of actual or potential social obligations (such as Terratransport) is completely ignored. The estimated loss of revenue over a five year period as a result of the Act is in the neighbourhood of one billion dollars.

The Prospects for Privatization

Privatization of CN has been under consideration, at least intermittently, for more than a decade. Several ministers of Transport, beginning with Otto Lang in the late 1970s, have considered the idea, and CN itself has conducted two internal studies of its feasibility, in 1981 and 1984. Although privatization seems likely to take place before the end of the century, certain difficulties have so far prevented it from moving to the top of the government's agenda.

From the viewpoint of CN's management, privatization would have certain advantages and no real disadvantages. By definition, it would bring to an end the government's ability to issue directives and otherwise influence corporate policy. It would also presumably involve, either before privatization or very soon afterwards, the removal of uncompensated social obligations like the operation of the Newfoundland railway and bus service. The most important reason why management favours privatization, however, is that it would facilitate access to capital without causing further deterioration in the debt-equity ratio. CN's annual capital requirements are in the neighbourhood of $500 million, and its profits have never come close to this figure. As noted above and in Table 3, the debt-equity ratio was temporarily improved by the recapitalization of 1978 but has deteriorated again since that time. As early as 1982 Dr. Leclair warned that a further recapitalization might soon be required and that the next recapitalization, in contrast to that of 1978, might require an actual transfer of cash from the government to the company, rather than simply a cancellation of debt. At the same time he warned that CN's credit rating might suffer if no action was taken.[43] This prediction was proved correct in 1986 when Standard and Poor's reduced CN's credit rating from AAA to AA.

Privatization would also have advantages for any federal government, quite apart from ideological and political considerations that are possibly unique to the Progressive Conservative party. CP and the trucking industry would no longer be able to argue, as they still do from time to time, that their competitor derives an unfair advantage from its relationship with the government. The government would no longer be held responsible in Parliament and by the electorate for the social consequences of CN's efforts to improve its productivity. Above all, the government would be able to avoid the unpalatable choice between providing the capital that CN will need and allowing CN's facilities to deteriorate. These advantages might well be considered to outweigh any benefits that the government may still derive from being able to use the Crown corporation as an instrument of public policy.

The main difficulty standing in the way of privatization is also in some ways the strongest argument in its favour: CN's uncertain financial performance and prospects. As Dr. Leclair said in September 1986, "The real issue from our point of view is not who owns us but whether anyone would want to."[44] CN failed to earn a profit in 1982 and again in 1986, while its profits in other years have been modest in relation to its assets and gross revenues. Its ability to earn profits under the regime of the new National Transportation Act remains to be demonstrated. Although its main line operations are at least as productive as those of CP, it carries a much heavier burden of uneconomic trackage, including the Newfoundland Railway, the Hudson Bay Railway, and the lines in Prince Edward Island. Without significant changes, investors might well hesitate to purchase equity in the corporation. In October 1986, not long before he resigned as chairman, Dr. Leclair said that it would have been easy to privatize CN two years earlier (i.e. in 1984) but that it would be difficult in 1986, and probably not feasible for another three years.[45]

The levelling off of railway freight traffic, the operating loss suffered by CN Rail in 1986, and the uncertainties regarding "deregulation" all undoubtedly contributed to this gloomy assessment. An additional factor, however, and one that may have contributed to Leclair's resignation, is the Mulroney government's policy of forcing CN to dispose of its non-rail activities, whether profitable or not. As noted above, by no means all of the non-rail activities have been consistently profitable. However, they have always been profitable when considered as a group, and have performed more consistently than the railway. Speaking to a conference on deregulation and privatization shortly after the Mulroney government took office, a senior official of CN warned against what management sometimes refers to as "cherry-picking", namely the piecemeal sale of the non-rail assets:

> I believe that CN is not simply a railway but an entrepreneurial institution; its institutional strength extends well beyond its railroading capabilities . . . . If CN remains a Crown corporation, it would substantially weaken its capabilities - financial and otherwise - to split apart and sell off its non-rail enterprises. Moreover, that would weaken its saleability. Once CN is privatized, it should be left to market forces and to the best judgement of its management to determine what its conglomerate nature will be. [46]

This advice, whose validity is confirmed by the successful example of CP, has not been heeded by the Mulroney government. In their zeal to privatize the non-rail assets they have made more difficult, and perhaps indefinitely postponed, the privatization of CN itself.

In the event that the present government or a future one decides to privatize CN, and that CN's financial performance and prospects allow this, a number of decisions will have to be made. The most fundamental is whether privatization should be total or partial, in other words whether the state should retain some of the equity. If privatization is to be partial, then the proportions of state and private ownership will have to be determined. Whether privatization is partial or total, Terratransport will presumably have to be separated from CN and retained in the public sector. The government will also have to determine what limitations should be placed on the ownership of the shares. It would be highly undesirable for significant ownership to be acquired by non-Canadians, or for any ownership to be acquired by railway companies in the United States, or by CP. It might also be desirable to restrict the holdings of individual shareholders to a low percentage. Any such restrictions could only be enforced if they were embodied in an Act of Parliament.

Almost seventy years have passed since Canada decided to nationalize about half of its railway system, while leaving the largest and most successful private enterprise intact. That uniquely

Canadian compromise may have left only two possible outcomes in the long run: either CN would be defeated, politically or commercially, by CP, or else it would compete with it successfully but in doing so come to resemble it. It was the second outcome that occurred. Whether privatization follows or not, Canada has clearly accepted the American model of commercial competition between railways rather than the usual model of a state monopoly that subsidizes other sectors of the economy. In both Canada and the United States, however, passenger service is an exception to this rule, as will now be discussed.

Via Rail

An important consequence of CN's shift towards a profit-oriented autonomy strategy in 1974 was its decision to dispose of its passenger service. Although CP had become disillusioned with passenger service about a decade earlier, CN had continued to improve and promote its passenger service through the 1960s. The contrast between the policies of the two companies was particularly noticeable in the Quebec to Windsor corridor, where CP virtually withdrew from the passenger business while CN increased the speed and frequency of its services, reduced fares, and even bought new equipment, including the ill-fated Turbotrains. Even in the long-distance transcontinental market CN increased its market share to about 60 per cent by offering lower fares than CP and by purchasing second-hand rolling stock in the United States to supplement its unpopular Canadian-built equipment. Thus by 1974 CN was carrying almost five times as much passenger traffic as its competitor.[47] Although both companies received subsidies for their passenger services, the subsidies were limited by law to 80 per cent of their losses, as estimated by the CTC. According to the railways, their actual losses were somewhat higher than the CTC estimates.

In 1974, the same year that they directed CN to be profitable, the Liberals promised improved railway passenger service in their successful campaign for re-election. With both railways dragging their feet, and with conclusive evidence that passenger service was inherently unprofitable, this pledge could only be carried out at the expense of the taxpayer. The railways would not perform the task in return for partial subsidies, a point which CN emphasized in the spring of 1975 by adding sixteen hours to the schedule of its transcontinental service.

Seeking a solution, the government turned for inspiration to the United States, where an Act of Congress in 1970 had established Amtrak to take over the passenger service of twenty different railroads. Under the U.S. legislation, railroads were allowed to abandon passenger services if they agreed to join Amtrak, which acquired the passenger rolling stock and operated trains over the tracks of its members. Amtrak did not, at least formally, become a state enterprise until 1978, by which time it had (in 1976) become the owner of the "Northeast Corridor" trackage between Washington, New York and Boston.[48]

Via Rail Canada, the Canadian counterpart of Amtrak, was created in February 1977 by the simple expedient of adding a symbolic one dollar to the estimates of Transport Canada. The ostensible purpose of this expenditure was "to deem Via Rail Canada a railway company incorporated pursuant to Section 11 of the Railway Act." Via Rail would not own any tracks (and still does not) but would take over the passenger services from both CN and CP. Initially it was a subsidiary of CN and drew most of its managerial personnel from that source, including its first Chief Executive Officer, Frank Roberts. The government intended to make Via Rail a separate Crown corporation as soon as possible, and actually did so, by order-in-council, in 1978. In October of 1978 Via Rail took over the transcontinental services (Montreal and Toronto to Vancouver) from both major railways, and in April 1979 it took over their remaining passenger services, apart from commuter trains in the Montreal area.

In contrast to Amtrak, Via Rail has changed little in terms of organization and structure since it was established. It has a chairman, a chief executive officer and a board of directors appointed by the cabinet. Until 1982, and again from January 1986 until June 1987, the chairman and the chief executive officer were the same person. For operational purposes Via Rail is divided into four regions (Atlantic, Quebec, Ontario and West) each headed by a vice-president. This structure is obviously borrowed from CN, except that CN divides the West into two regions. Via Rail also has seven other vice-presidents, with various functional responsibilities, located at the head office in Montreal. It has had four chief executive officers in its brief history. Roberts was succeeded in 1982 by Pierre Franche, the former head of the National Harbours Board, and Franche was succeeded at the end of 1985 by Lawrence Hanigan, who had previously headed the urban transit authority in Montreal. Hanigan had been an unsuccessful Progressive Conservative candidate in the 1984 election and was thus widely viewed as a patronage appointment, even though his previous experience certainly made him well-qualified for the position. In 1987 Hanigan was succeeded by Denis de Belleval who had previously headed Ports Canada (the new name for the National Harbours Board). De Belleval is also an experienced politician, having been Quebec's Minister of Transport from 1979 to 1981.

Table 4
Via Rail Financial Data
(Millions of Dollars)

	Operating Expenses	Revenues	Government Payments
1980	462.5	135.8	330.2
1981	554.8	160.8	399.8
1982	583.7	156.1	434.1
1983	615.5	167.5	451.2
1984	565.7	170.7	397.8
1985	716.0	197.0	523.6
1986	682.1	202.1	461.9

Source: Statistics Canada Pub. 52-003

Via Rail's board of directors, like that of CN, consists of patronage appointees who are not expected to devote their full time to their duties. Until January 1985 the board also included two public servants, one from Transport Canada and one from the Department of Labour. At that time the new Progressive Conservative government dismissed the entire board, including the chairman, and replaced it temporarily with a three-member task force headed by Dr. Hugh Horner, the former Deputy Premier of Alberta. After the task force submitted its report in May the government appointed Hanigan as chairman and eleven other directors. Hanigan became chief executive officer, as well as chairman, when Franche resigned at the end of the year.

Because of its extreme financial dependence on the state (see Table 4) Via Rail enjoys far less autonomy, in form and in fact, than CN. Via Rail is listed in Part I of Schedule C of the Financial Administration Act and thus must submit its operating budgets, as well as its capital budgets, in advance to the Minister of Transport for approval by the Treasury Board. The government's capital advances to Via Rail are in addition to the operating subsidies shown in Table 4, and have averaged around $100 million per annum. New rolling stock for the corridor routes and facilities for equipment maintenance have accounted for the largest shares of this expenditure. Since its capital expenditures can at best be considered as means to reduce losses, rather than to make profits, Via Rail's capital budgets are scrutinized far more carefully by the Treasury Board than are those of CN. In May 1987, for example, the Mulroney government rejected the major recommendation of Hugh Horner's task force by deciding not to authorize purchase of new bi-level passenger cars for the trans-continental service. Instead, it told Via Rail to refurbish the existing equipment, which was already more than thirty years old.

Although Kent Weaver argues that Via Rail attempted to pursue a "public service" strategy under Frank Roberts, any tendencies in this direction were ended in July 1981. By order-in-council, adopted while Parliament was not in session and overruling numerous decisions of the CTC, the government abolished about one fifth of Via Rail's services, effective November 1981.[50] Among the services eliminated were the Montreal-Sudbury and Winnipeg-Edmonton-Vancouver sections of the transcontinental service, as well as the service between Montreal, Saint John and Halifax. Passengers bound from Montreal and Ottawa to Western Canada were forced to go by way of Toronto. As shown in Table 5, the seemingly random nature of the cutbacks had the consequence that traffic fell more sharply than the volume of service provided. Some of the most popular trains were eliminated while a number of lightly patronized services were retained. To make matters worse, local trains were added on portions of the discontinued long-distance routes and attracted no patronage whatsoever. Neither Via Rail's management nor the CTC were even consulted about these changes, which were the work of Transport Canada and of its minister, Jean-Luc Pepin.

Pepin's successor, Lloyd Axworthy, restored service from Winnipeg (which he represented in Parliament) to Edmonton, and the other discontinued long-distance services were restored by the Mulroney government in 1985. Nonetheless, the damage was done. As Table 5 shows, Via Rail's traffic has never again attained the level of 1981, and its morale suffered even more severely. The Pepin cutbacks were the equivalent for Via Rail of what the forced resignation of Sir Henry Thornton in 1932 was for CN. Since 1981 Via Rail has pursued a survival strategy, endeavouring to stay alive in the face of powerful opposition from the Treasury Board and Transport Canada. The latter department, whose main business is managing airports, makes little secret of its wish that railway passenger service would disappear. Another powerful opponent is the intercity bus industry, which claims that Via Rail's fares are too low and drive away its traffic. Voyageur Colonial, Via Rail's main competitor east

Table 5
Via Rail Traffic Data

	Train-KM Operated (Millions)	Revenue Passenger-KM (Millions)	Revenue Passenger-KM per Train KM	Revenue Passengers (Thousands)
1980	24.5	2720	111.0	6836
1981	23.7	2689	113.5	7489
1982	19.9	2114	106.2	6522
1983	19.6	2046	104.4	5865
1984	19.7	2067	104.9	6056
1985	20.8	2199	105.7	6335
1986	21.0	2060	98.1	5735

Source: Statistics Canada Pub. 52-003

of Toronto, had close ties with the former Liberal government. Via Rail has friends in both houses of Parliament, but this asset is of limited value in Canada's executive-dominated system of government. By contrast, congressional support has allowed Amtrak to flourish, despite the Reagan administration's repeated efforts to abolish it.[51]

Two significant problems for Via Rail have been its dependence on the railways and the absence of a statutory basis for its existence. Via Rail's management and its allies in Parliament have repeatedly called attention to both problems almost since it was established, but governments have been slow to respond. Although Via Rail, like Amtrak, owned its rolling stock from the outset, it was otherwise dependent on CN and CP for tracks, stations, operating personnel, and for equipment maintenance. Payment to the railways for the operation of trains over their lines is governed by a formula known as costing order C-6313, devised by the CTC, before Via Rail was established, as a guide to estimating railway losses from passenger service. Via Rail has persistently claimed that this formula overestimates the real costs to the railways, while CN and CP have claimed the opposite. In 1983 the government authorized construction by Via Rail of its own facilities for the maintenance of rolling stock,

and in 1984 CN agreed in principle to transfer to the Via payroll all
employees involved in passenger service. Details remained to be
worked out, but by the end of 1986 all employees involved in
passenger service, except locomotive crews, were working directly for
Via Rail and negotiations to transfer the locomotive crews were in
progress. In 1986, for the first time in its history, payments to CN and
CP accounted for less than half of Via Rail's expenses. Costing order
C-6313, however, is still in effect. A number of stations have been
transferred to Via Rail but many, including those at Montreal and
Toronto, still belong to the railways.

Although Amtrak carries about half of its passengers on
trackage which it actually owns, thus reducing its dependence on the
railways, Via Rail is unlikely to find itself in a comparable situation.
Some trackage no longer required for railway freight may be
transferred to Via Rail, particularly in the Ottawa area and in
Southwestern Ontario, but Via Rail's most important route
(Montreal-Toronto) also carries a high volume of freight traffic for CN.
Soon after his resignation Pierre Franche proposed a completely new
Montreal-Ottawa-Toronto line dedicated exclusively to passenger
service, but the very high capital cost of such a project and the level of
the federal deficit make this an unlikely prospect in the near future.[52]

Via Rail has repeatedly urged that it be given a statutory basis,
partly to protect itself against arbitrary government action like that
of July 1981. The same suggestion was repeated by a special
committee of the Senate in June 1984. Bill C-97, described as an act
respecting railway passenger transportation, was introduced by the
government and given first reading in February 1986, but was never
adopted. It would have established Via Rail as a Crown corporation
with no share capital and with the power to borrow money, subject to
the approval of the Minister of Finance. It would have listed all of Via
Rail's services and restricted the cabinet's power to eliminate them
without the approval of Parliament. It would also have given Via Rail
access to data on the costs incurred by CN and CP as a result of its
operations, and would have legislated the principle that passenger
trains be given scheduling priority over freight. These two provisions
responded to two of Via Rail's major complaints against the railways.

Bill C-97 would also have established cost recovery targets for
different categories of passenger service. The "corridor" services
between Quebec City and Windsor, where Via Rail carries 70 per cent
of its passengers, would have been expected eventually to break even.
Services connecting central Canada with the Atlantic and Pacific
coasts would have been expected to cover 60 per cent of their costs and
all other services, except for a few in remote areas with no highways,
would have been expected to cover 40 per cent. If these targets were
not met, the bill provided that the cabinet could discontinue services

or, in the case of the transcontinental services, reduce them to a frequency of three times per week in each direction.

These targets were far in excess of Via Rail's actual performance. In 1984 the corridor services had an overall cost recovery of 35 per cent, the eastern and western transcontinental services 25 per cent, and the remaining services ranged from 25 per cent down to an incredible 1 per cent. The best figure for an individual service was 43 per cent for Ottawa-Toronto. The overall figure for Via Rail as a whole was 26 per cent.[53] By contrast, Amtrak recovered 50 per cent of its costs in the same year. Converted into Canadian dollars, Amtrak's revenues were six times as high as those of Via Rail while its expenses were only three times as high.[54]

Bill C-97 would have made discontinuance of "corridor" and "regional" services that failed to meet the cost recovery targets obligatory after four years unless a "province or other body" agreed to support them financially. Since the targets were unrealistic, this was in effect a proposal to unload the costs of railway passenger service onto the provinces, even though it has been recognized as a federal responsibility since Confederation. Admittedly Amtrak trains that run entirely within one state are usually subsidized by the state concerned, but this seems less appropriate in Canada, where the provinces are fewer and larger and where the national capital is located within one of the provinces. About half of Via Rail's passengers begin and end their journeys within a single province.

Given its financial performance, Via Rail can obviously not be privatized. Its abolition has frequently been urged by various "experts" but Canadians appear to want passenger trains, and no industrialized country has actually tried to do without them.[55] To do Via Rail justice, its cost recovery is better than that of Marine Atlantic (the former CN Marine). On the other hand, its traffic is not growing and it remains a heavy drain on the public treasury. Eliminating all except the corridor services would cut the deficit by two-thirds but would be politically unacceptable in the Maritimes and the West. Eliminating the "regional" and "remote" services would make Via Rail more comparable to Amtrak, which runs all of its trains between major cities, but would reduce the deficit by less than one third. Amtrak experience suggests that new equipment for the transcontinental service would reduce operating costs and perhaps increase traffic by making the service more reliable. Such equipment could be purchased most cheaply in the United States, but as the Department of National Defence has discovered, regional pork-barrelling tends to become the first priority when Canadian governments make large capital expenditures. The facts of Canadian geography and politics seem to rule out easy solutions to Via Rail's problems.

Notes

1.   John A. Eagle, "Sir Robert Borden, Union Government and Railway Nationalization," *Journal of Canadian Studies* 10 (November 1975), pp. 59 66.

2.   Quoted in Tommy Douglas, "What Politics Needs Most — More Laughter," *Maclean's* (28 March 1959).

3.   *The Mackenzie King Record,* Volume 1, 1939-44, ed. by J.W. Pickersgill (Toronto: University of Toronto Press, 1960), p. 647.

4.   Dalton Camp, *Gentlemen, Players, and Politicians* (Toronto: McClelland and Stewart, 1970), p. 113.

5.   Canadian National, *1986 Annual Report,* p. 7.

6.   Canada, House of Commons, Standing Committee on Transport, *Minutes of Proceedings,* 10 June 1982, pp. 56.72 to 56.73.

7.   *Ibid,* p. 56.54.

8.   Canadian Transport Commission: *Inquiry into effects in Canada of U.S. rail regulation* (Ottawa, December 1984).

9.   Canadian Transport Commission: *Inquiry into effects in Canada of U.S. rail deregulation; implications for Canadian domestic and import/export rail traffic* (Ottawa, June 1985).

10.   *Freedom to Move: A Framework for Transportation Reform* (Ottawa: Supply and Services Canada, 1985).

11.   David Harvey, *Christmas Turkey or Prairie Vulture* (Montreal, Institute for Research on Public Policy, 1980) discusses the economics of the Crow's Nest rate.

12.   Canadian Transport Commission, *1986 Annual Report,* p. 99.

13.   Canadian National, *1986 Annual Report,* p. 17.

14.   John English, *The Decline of Politics* (Toronto: University of Toronto Press, 1977).

15.   *Robert Laird Borden: His Memoirs,* ed. by Henry Borden (Toronto: Macmillan, 1938) p. 653.

16. *Canadian National-Canadian Pacific Act*, S.C., 1932-33, chapter 33.

17. *An Act to Amend the Financial Administration Act in Relation to Crown Corporations*, S.C., 1984, ch. 31.

18. D'arcy Marsh, *The Tragedy of Henry Thornton* (Toronto: Macmillan, 1935).

19. Joseph Schull, *The Great Scot: A Biography of Donald Gordon* (Montreal: McGill-Queen's University Press, 1979), pp. 209-17.

20. Bandeen's unexpected resignation in February 1982 was attributed by some observers to the political fallout from his controversial decision to purchase shares in the Cast shipping group. This episode is described in Jeanne Kirk Laux and Maureen Appel Molot, *State Capitalism: Public Enterprise in Canada* (Ithaca, Cornell University Press, 1988), pp. 85-88. The resignation of Leclair, who had served most of his career as a public servant under Liberal governments, came at a time when CN was under pressure from the Mulroney government to dispose of its profitable non-rail assets.

21. Lesslie R. Thomson, *The Canadian Railway Problem* (Toronto: Macmillan, 1938) p. 890.

22. These arguments are sympathetically discussed in John Murray Gibbon, *Steel of Empire* (Toronto: McClelland and Stewart, 1935), and D.H. Miller-Barstow, *Beatty of the C.P.R.* (Toronto: McClelland and Stewart, 1951).

23. *Canadian National Railways Capital Revision Act*, 1937, S.C. 1937, Chapter 22.

24. Quoted in Robert Bothwell and William Kilbourne, *C.D. Howe: A Biography* (Toronto: McClelland and Stewart, 1979), p. 99.

25. *Canadian National Railways Capital Revision Act*, 1952, S.C. 1952, Chapter 36.

26. Canada, House of Commons, Standing Committee on Transport and Communications, *Minutes of Proceedings*, 3 April 1978, pp. 26-27.

27. Canada, Senate, *Debates*, 24 May 1978, p. 821.

28. *Canadian National Railways Capital Revision Act,* S.C. 1977-78, Chapter 34.

29. R. Kent Weaver, *The Politics of Industrial Change* (Washington: Brookings Institution, 1985), pp. 148-170.

30. Canada, Senate, *Debates,* 17 May 1978, p. 791.

31. Canada, House of Commons, Standing Committee on Transport and Communications, *Minutes of Proceedings,* 4 April 1978, pp. 18-19.

32. *Ibid,* pp. 61-65.

33. Canadian National, *Initial Submission to the Commission of Inquiry into Newfoundland Transportation* (September 1977, mimeo).

34. Canadian National, *1985 Annual Report,* p. 27.

35. Canadian National, *1979 Annual Report,* p. 22, and *1984 Annual Report,* p. 33.

36. Canada, House of Commons, Standing Committee on Transport, *Minutes of Proceedings,* of June 1985, p. 15.22.

37. On Conrail, see Weaver, *op. cit.,* pp. 97-113 and 209-224. The Canada Southern was owned by the New York Central System, which was merged into the Penn Central in 1968. Conrail was formed as a state enterprise after the bankruptcy of the Penn Central. It was privatized in 1987.

38. Canada, House of Commons, Standing Committee on Transport, *Minutes of Proceedings,* 2 March 1987, p. 12.14.

39. Remarks by P.L. Schwartz to the Canadian Institute of Traffic and Transportation, Toronto, June 23, 1986 (mimeo) p. 2.

40. Canada, House of Commons, Standing Committee on Transport, *Minutes of Proceedings,* 2 March 1987, p. 12-15.

41. Canadian Transport Commission, *1986 Annual Report,* pp. 79-80.

42. Canada, House of Commons, Standing Committee on Transport, *Minutes of Proceedings,* 2 March 1987, p. 12.18.

43. Canada, House of Commons, Standing Committee on Transport, *Minutes of Proceedings*, 10 June 1982, p. 68.8.

44. "A journey begun," remarks by J. Maurice Leclair to the Canadian Daily Newspaper Publishers association, Vancouver, 18 September 1986 (mimeo), p. 12.

45. "Trop endetté, le CN ne peut etre privatisé avant trois ans," *La Presse*, (20 Octobre 1986).

46. E. Maroti, "CN: A Case Study," compiled from remarks to the I.R.P.P. conference, "Weaving a new industrial policy: concentration, deregulation and privatization," Toronto, 22-23 February 1985 (mimeo), pp. 6-7.

47. Canadian Transport Commission data, unpublished.

48. For a comparison of Amtrak and Via Rail see Weaver, *op. cit.*, pp. 227-267.

49. P.C. 1978-952, 23 March 1978.

50. P.C. 1981-2171, 6 August 1981. The cutbacks were announced on 27 July 1981.

51. For a fuller discussion see Garth Stevenson, "Bureaucratic Politics versus National Integration: The Case of Railway Passenger Service" in *The Integration Question*, ed. by Jon H. Pammett and Brian Tomlin (Don Mills: Addison-Wesley, 1984) pp. 182-204.

52. "Former Via boss backs electric train system," *The Globe and Mail*, (13 March 1986).

53. Canadian Transport Commission data reproduced in *Economic Growth: Transportation: A Study Team Report to the Task Force on Program Review* (Ottawa: Supply and Services Canada, 1986) pp. 228-229. The data do not correspond precisely with the Statistics Canada data reproduced in Tables 4 and 5.

54. This calculation is based on data from Weaver, *op. cit.*, p. 231.

55. The case for abolition is presented by J. Lukasiewicz, "Public Policy and Technology: Passenger Rail in Canada as an Issue in Modernization," *Canadian Public Policy*, 5 (1979), pp. 518-532.

Chapter III

Air Canada

John Langford and Ken Huffman

Introduction

Air Canada – until 1965, Trans-Canada Airlines (TCA) – was created by an Act of Parliament in April 1937, began limited operations later that year, and became Canada's national carrier in 1939.[1] In half a century it has evolved from an operation based on two planes connecting five Canadian cities to a leading international carrier with a fleet of 110 jets serving 36 North American cities and 27 cities in Europe, Asia and the Caribbean. Another 72 communities in Canada are connected to the Air Canada system through "alliance partner" subsidiaries.[2]

While the government's precise rationale in establishing the airline as a public corporation in 1937 remains to a degree inscrutable, and the goals of the corporation are curiously ambivalent, there is little doubt that the direct management and indirect regulatory intrusions by the federal government have been the most significant factors in the operation of the corporation since its inception. A measure of the intimacy of the relationship between the corporation and its political mentors is the fact that C.D. Howe, who was the principal architect of the airline in the 1937 Cabinet which brought down the bill, remained as its designated minister and undisputed "super-chairman" in an unbroken series of Liberal governments lasting for 20 years. The role of the government – particularly in the exercise of direct management power – suggests that there have been significant differences between Air Canada and Canadian Airlines International as operating entities.*

While there is some evidence that Air Canada has been slower than other airlines to adjust to changing market conditions, there is little evidence that the public airline has performed less adequately in the long term. Having weathered an unstable management and organizational environment in the 1980s, Air Canada faces new challenges. In addition to adjusting to deregulation and digesting a number of new regional "partners", the airline faces uncertainty about its ownership status. And beyond the issue of privatization rest crucial decisions especially about the financing of costly new aircraft in the 1990s.

The Origins of Air Canada

The origins of Air Canada and the role played by the federal government in its inception, qualify as ancient history by contrast with most of the other public corporations examined in this volume, and many of the details are readily accessible in the works of Ashley, Corbett, Bothwell and Kilbourn, and others.[3] Unfortunately, a review of this rather complex tale reveals a confusing picture of the rationale lying behind the federal government's creation of one of its most important public corporations. Corbett picturesquely comments that:

> Canada seems to have established a publicly-owned monopoly of scheduled inter-urban air services in a fit of absence of mind, as Britain is said to have acquired her Empire.[4]

That the federal government intended to play a major role in the development of civil aviation in Canada is beyond dispute. Its wide authority in this area was endorsed by the Supreme Court and the Judicial Committee of the Privy Council and by the early 1930s "the government's organization for forming and carrying out civil air policy grew smoothly and continuously in advance of the development of airline services."[5] Beyond the formation of a Department of Transport in 1936, these efforts involved the support of route survey and airmail flights, the development and administration of safety regulations and the planning and construction of a national network

---

* "Canadian" is the product of the 1987 takeover of CP Air, the other trunk carrier, by Pacific Western Airlines (PWA), formerly a regional carrier. In this paper the airline name used will be that which is appropriate for the year being discussed, i.e., TCA until 1965, then Air Canada, and CP Air until 1987, then Canadian.

of airports and navigational aids.[6] The government's efforts in the civil aviation area were always in advance of private sector initiatives which for economic reasons arising from fundamental geographic considerations and, later, the depression, were extremely limited in Canada by contrast with other developed countries.[7]

As a result of this retarded private initiative there was by 1936 strong pressure for the creation of a national intercity air service for passengers and mail. In part, the pressure came from the expansionary tendencies of private American airlines. The anticipated development of north-south links between various American and Canadian cities raised the spectre of Canada's east-west trunk line needs being met by the new services across the northern United States joining the termini of the north-south linkages with Canada. The Post Office Department, anxious to have access to a vehicle which would allow it to cash in on the lucrative air mail business, was frustrated by the lack of a national air service. Bothwell and Kilbourn add – in somewhat creamy prose – that:

> In the depths of the Depression, the airways offered hope of dramatic future growth and a way out of despair. They also offered a potential new east-west link for a trans-continental nation, reinforcing that of the railways, and counterbalancing the north-south pull of the highways which first became an economic force in the 1920s.[8]

As Tupper and others have argued, the environmental combination of retarded private initiative and the threat of foreign domination traditionally called for some form of nation-building or "community development" activity by the federal government.[9] Further, as Baldwin and Trebilcock and Prichard have pointed out, key elements of a classic economic rationale for choosing to produce this national airline service publicly (rather than regulate and/or subsidize its private provision) were also present in the environment facing the government in 1936-37.[10] In terms of industrial structure, there were no private firms ready to make the leap to national carrier status. Moreover, the expectation that the Post Office would be the biggest purchaser of the new airline's services lent force to the argument in favour of folding the airline into the public sector. The Post Office would get the best rates possible in the long run and, internal to government, could be used to subsidize the airline in the short run. In any case, the government had already created or was in the midst of creating the infrastructure required to support a national air service, making the marginal cost of the final step less significant. The desirability of the alternative instrument of regulation was limited not only by functional considerations such as the complexity of achieving effective cross-subsidization of routes through a multi-plicity of private firms in the future, but also by the simple fact that there was no requirement in 1937 to arbitrate between existing producers and consumers of national air service. Finally, a monopoly public corporation provided more scope for exacting the political benefits potentially available through cross-subsidization of routes by reducing the need for the distribution of profits to forestall takeovers.

Unfortunately, while objectively the case for the creation of a public corporation seems almost overwhelming it is not easy to find persuasive evidence that the major political actors within the government saw the environment, even implicitly, in quite these terms. Certainly, there was widespread consensus within the Cabinet on the nature of the threat from U.S. airlines, the needs of the Post Office, and the fragmentation of private air services in Canada. Facing these pressures, it is not surprising that the government acted to bring into existence some form of national airline. Ideologically, however, Howe and his colleagues were far from Canadian apostles of the Morrisonian vision of government ownership of the "ramparts of the economy" and there was, as a consequence, no philosophical attachment to the instrument of public ownership. Much more disturbing, in terms of the clarification of the rationale question, is the sense that the major actors involved in the decisions to create both the National Harbours Board and TCA seemed blissfully unaware of the political differences between a public and a private corporation and, therefore, did not in any literal sense rationally choose the public over the private corporate instrument.

It is most significant that Howe, the major actor within the Cabinet on the TCA decision, did not seem to differentiate clearly between a public and private corporation. Focussing on the common qualities which they both shared—"management by experts" and a board made up of businessmen—Howe appeared simply to ignore the implications for the public corporation of having the government as a direct or indirect shareholder and (often) key creditor and powerful individuals like himself as designated ministers. Bothwell and Kilbourn note that Howe's vision of a Crown corporation was of a "publicly owned enterprise . . . to be managed as efficiently, absolutely and aggressively as if he himself were the private entrepreneur at the head of it, and no nonsense about politicians meddling with the management."[11] The result is a curious paradox which defies analysis in terms of the widely mooted rationales noted earlier. Howe, the Liberal, argued for free enterprise, referred to TCA as a "private corporation", and effected the creation of a public corporation; while Bennett, the leader of the opposition Conservative party, opposed both the bill creating TCA and Howe's talk of a private corporation arguing instead for the creation of a government-owned monopoly. In the event, Trans-Canada Airlines seemed to be a more accurate reflection of Bennett's vision rather than Howe's.[12]

The fluidity or ambiguity of the approach taken by Howe and the government is reflected in the development of the legislation. The Cabinet's first Trans-Canada Airlines proposal was for the formation of what would now be labelled a shared or mixed ownership venture whereby the CNR (acting for the government), the CPR and Canadian Airways of Winnipeg (in which each railway owned a 10 per cent share), would create a national airline. The government was prepared to sweeten this proposal by covering the operating losses of the new company; however, it also wanted to limit the return on capital invested to 5 per cent per annum and insisted on representation on the board as a *quid pro quo* for meeting operating losses and providing airports and navigational aids.[13] The noteworthy feature of this proposal is the government's preference for the combination of the indirect shared ownership through the CNR and subsidization instruments (in the context, of course, of continued regulation and the provision of infrastructure) over either outright public or private ownership. The antipathy towards the latter alternative seems to have been based largely on C.D. Howe's distrust of James Richardson, the founder and president of Canadian Airways, and his unease concerning the pressure of other private financial interests who wanted all or part of the new national franchise.[14] Unhappy with the experience of the competition between the two railways, Howe and his senior Cabinet colleagues seemed determined not to allow the possibility that the national air service could be divided up amongst competing private interests.

If this initial proposal was designed with the implicit intention of discouraging the participation of CPR and Canadian Airways and leaving the government free to create a wholly public monopoly, then it succeeded. Sir Edward Beatty of the CPR refused the shared ownership/subsidization formula, which the government had embodied in draft legislation in early 1937, on the grounds that the CNR and the government were indivisible and that he could not ask his shareholders to invest in a corporation the board of which would be dominated by CNR and Department of Transport representatives.[15] The bill, which was finally presented to the House in March 1937, would have allowed private interests ("interested in aviation" and approved by the Minister) to purchase up to 49.8 per cent of the 50,000 shares in TCA (worth $5,000,000 at par) from the CNR. The railway was to hold all of the shares for the government until such time as the latter chose to acquire them or some were sold to private interests.[16] However, had the shares been sold to private interests, the three CNR and the three government appointees on the Board would still have continued to outweigh the three private directors under the revised

proposal so that participation remained anathema to the CPR and, in
the event, no shares were ever sold to private interests.[17] However
inadvertently, the Liberal Government under C.D. Howe's strong
influence created a thoroughly public airline. With the inception of
TCA, the state took the leading role in the provision of national and
international air service in Canada.

The Goals of the Corporation

The 1937 legislation sets down the mandate of TCA in the following
manner:

> to establish, operate and maintain air lines or regular
> services of aircraft of all kinds, to carry on the business of
> transporting mails, passengers and goods by air, and to
> enter into contracts for the transport of mails, passengers
> and goods by any means, and either by the Corporation's
> own aircraft and conveyances or by means of the aircraft
> and conveyances of others, and to enter into contracts with
> any person or company for the interchange of traffic ... ;
> and to carry on its business throughout Canada and outside
> of Canada.[18]

It is obvious — and, therefore, hardly noteworthy — that a fundamental
goal implicit in this statement of purposes is that TCA run a safe and
efficient national and international airline. Beyond this, however,
and also implicit in this statement of purposes and other contemporary expressions of the government's intentions is a goal package
significantly different from the widely mooted commercial objectives
of a comparable private airline. The first element of this package is
the role of TCA as an instrument of national policy. While the airline
was not given a total monopoly of air services in Canada (northern
bush flying and local feeder services were to be left for private
enterprise) it was provided with an effective monopoly of all intercity
routes; moreover, it was anticipated that TCA would be given a
complete monopoly (*vis-à-vis* other Canadian airlines) of all
international air services. But with the absence of any regional air
policy this monopoly meant to Howe and the Cabinet that the airline
could and would be asked to provide services on "such other arteries as
are designated by the government as being of national importance."[19]
It was also accepted as part of this goal package that TCA would not
be a profitable venture. In fact, the more specific references to routes,
tariffs and the transportation of air mail in the Act make it clear that
even with cross-subsidization and the establishment of fares and
freight rates competitive with other similar services in North America

operating deficits were anticipated. Howe summed it up most optimistically:

> The set-up is such that the company will be protected against loss, but its profits will be very strictly limited. In other words, it is organized to perform a certain national service, and it is expected that the service will be performed at or near cost.[20]

Despite the firm's insistence that it operated as a "normal" private airline, Air Canada's goals remained virtually unchanged for nearly forty years. But change began in the 1970s in the wake of the 1967 *National Transportation Act* and was reflected in ministerial pronouncements, corporate "mission" statements and, most importantly, the wording of the *Air Canada Act* of 1978.[21] The legislation recognized that, while remaining an instrument of national policy (like other wholly-owned public corporations), Air Canada should act as such an instrument by responding to market pressures. The primary purpose of the corporation, according to the legislation, is to establish and operate the *business* of an air carrier.[22] The encouragement of regional airlines in the 1960s, the termination of the air mail contract arrangement between the government and the airline, and the recognition of CP Air and Wardair and other charter operators as competitors signalled the breakdown of the traditional relationship between the "instrument of policy" goal and the route monopoly. These trends accelerated in the 1980s as the effects of U.S. deregulation dribbled over the border and new entrants and alliances emerged to take advantage of an anticipated "open skies" policy.

Accenting the tendency to view Air Canada as a business, the Act widened the statement of capacities and activities for the company to include the power to diversify the operation into the tour and accommodation fields to allow it to keep pace with other airlines. Linked to these developments is the legislation's change in philosophy concerning profits. Profits are no longer abhorred. In fact, the Act, on the face of it, positively exhorts the corporation's board, "in discharging its responsibilities" to "have due regard to sound business principles, and in particular the contemplation of profit."[23]

The 1978 legislation reinforced the sense that the original goals of TCA to be an efficient, safe and non-profit monopoly instrument of national policy were being supplanted — or at least paralleled — by the notion that Air Canada should be an efficient and safe profit-making airline competing on a more or less equal footing with other carriers. And over the past decade, particularly with the ascendancy of the Mulroney Conservative government, the balance between the policy instrument and profit goals has tilted toward the latter. That is not to

say that the policy goal is totally moribund.   Decisions such as the
1985 transfer of overseas flights from Gander to St. John's, Nfld., the
debate about the qualifications of board members and the airline's
response to serious drops in demand during the 1982-83 recession
keep the policy instrument issue alive.

Another perspective on the question of mandate casts doubt on
the usefulness of thinking about the goals of either private- or public-
sector purely in the above institutional manner (i.e., the former
traditionally maximizes profits while the latter traditionally pursues
wider social goals). Baldwin, following the arguments of the public
choice school, suggests that, in behavioral terms, a public firm like Air
Canada has "an objective similar to other organizations, whether they
be public or private – that of self-perpetuation". Developing a model
of rational political behavior for Air Canada based on the goal of self-
perpetuation, Baldwin argues that public ownership of Air Canada
militates against the pursuit of the goal of profit maximization
regardless of the airline's monopoly status in earlier days or the ebb
and flow of legislated mandates. At its simplest level, the thesis is
that to survive the public airline adopts policies which adversely
affect profit levels but maximize its "political" support among users,
employees and its single shareholder, the government. A number of
examples are available which illustrate the pursuit of political
support. First, (as a later section will explain), Air Canada, until the
1980s, avoided route competition by cross-subsidizing losing or
"social" routes. Second, in the 1950s the airline regularly juggled
depreciation expenses to regulate net income. Former president
Gordon McGregor describes how write-offs were increased in boom
years to reduce profit levels, thus reducing pressures for lower fares or
new competitors. In lean years the bottom line was boosted by cutting
depreciation rates or extending the lives of assets.[24] Third, in the
1970s when the federal government was actively promoting
bilingualism in the delivery of public services, Air Canada was very
cooperative in training employees and facilitating the use of French
on the job.[25] Finally, recently Air Canada was noticeably less
aggressive than competitors in instituting staff cuts in response to
falling demand. One explanation for this behaviour could be a lesser
concern with profit levels than with the political fallout from layoffs of
hundreds of employees.[26] While this essay does not specifically
pursue the validity of Baldwin's claim, it is important to note that this
model does force us to look at Air Canada's behavior outside the
confines of traditional hypotheses concerning the contrasting goals of
private and government firms.

The Evolution of a Public Airline: 1937-1988

On the surface there may appear to be little that is exceptional in the development of TCA/Air Canada over the fifty-one years since its inception.[27] Establishing its corporate headquarters in Montreal and its operational centre in Winnipeg, TCA began its modest operation with the takeover of the Vancouver-Seattle route from Canadian Airways on September 1, 1937 and the launching of training flights on other legs of what would become the transcontinental route. By April 1939 this route was opened between Vancouver and Montreal and was completed through to Halifax two years later. The war slowed down but did not entirely stifle the development of TCA. Using modified Lancaster bombers, a trans-Atlantic service began carrying mail in 1943. By the end of the war some five hundred flights had been made.

The most noteworthy aspect of the early post-war evolution of TCA was the movement to a new generation of aircraft. From Lockheed 10A's and 14's and converted Lancasters, the fleet evolved to DC-3's and the pressurized North Star, a Canadian hybrid of the DC-4 and DC-6. The latter allowed the airline to expand its long range route coverage to the South, to include Bermuda, the Bahamas, Jamaica, Trinidad and Tampa. The introduction of Super Constellations in the 1950s allowed for a similar expansion in the North Atlantic sector to encompass Paris, Zurich and Brussels by 1958 and further southern network growth to include Mexico City and Antigua. The quality of passenger service on domestic routes was also significantly upgraded in the 1950s with the adoption of the turbo-prop Viscount which became the backbone of the domestic fleet. On the cargo side, TCA began serving a wider market by the mid-1950s through the use of three Bristol freighters and the conversion of three North Stars.

The early 1960s mark a distinctive point in TCA's evolution. The introduction of the first commercial jet, the DC-8, to the fleet dramatically altered the quality of service on domestic and international long-range routes. With the addition of the turbine-powered Vickers Vanguard to service shorter routes, the airline's piston-engine era ended. The arrival of the short-range DC-9 jet in 1966 heralded the transition to an all-jet fleet—a process that was complete by 1974. Notwithstanding the transformation of its fleet, Air Canada's route expansion was less dramatic during this decade. A bilateral agreement with the U.S. opened up new destinations to the south (such as Miami and Los Angeles) beyond the traditional transborder cities to which Canadian airlines had been restricted. In addition, Moscow and Copenhagen were added to the existing European network.

The major operational phenomenon during this period, beyond the new generation of aircraft, was the enormous growth in traffic. As one Air Canada publication put it: "Whereas it took 18 years for TCA to carry its first 10 million passengers, traffic volume in the early 1960s rose at an unprecedented rate. In 1964, the airline carried 4.1 million passengers; in 1966 5.2 million and in 1968 6.4 million."[28] Air Canada — as its name officially became in 1965 — had become a major international carrier. In 1968 its 16,656 employees generated revenues of $388 million and record profits of $8.1 million from a fleet of 107 aircraft including 27 DC-8's, 30 DC-9's, 17 Vickers Vanguards and 33 Vickers Viscounts.

Since 1968 Air Canada's operations have been characterized by the following features: severe and continuing cost pressures with a focus in the 1970s on fuel costs and in the 1980s on labour costs; huge capital outlays for new equipment and innovative methods of financing fleet expansion; a slower pace of route expansion (and some contractions); rapid increase followed by stagnation in growth of traffic volumes; increasing diversification away from the straight-forward operations of an airline; growing importance of cargo, including courier services to compete with Canada Post; increased competition as traditional monopoly routes were opened; and the prospects of a somewhat problematic change in its capital structure, ownership and relationship with the government.

The introduction of a new generation of wide-bodied jets, route diversification and growth in traffic are closely linked. Air Canada took delivery of its first Boeing 747 in 1971 and its first Lockheed L-1011 in 1973. These "jumbo" jets led to some disturbing short-run overcapacity problems, but over the longer term provided the airline with the seats required for a significant increase in revenue passengers over the 1970s. These aircraft, along with the shorter range fleet workhorses the Boeing 727 and the DC-9, dominated fleet development in the decade. In the 1980s fuel economy continued to play a key role in fleet planning. The cost of new aircraft led many airlines to retrofit existing aircraft with new engines. Air Canada pared its fleet over the decade, getting rid of the fuel guzzling DC-8's (retaining eight for exclusively cargo services) and replacing some of the earlier DC-9's with new "stretch" models. The only entirely new aircraft received during the decade was the Boeing 767, whose design reflects the 1970s focus on fuel efficiency and the market shift to large capacity aircraft. In the early 1980s the Air Canada fleet peaked at 127 aircraft and has gradually declined so that in 1987 there were 110 aircraft, plus four L-1011's on lease to other airlines.

In the 1980s the airline was forced to respond to weak market demand on some international routes and cut back or eliminate service. Service to a number of "prestige" European and U.S. cities was terminated (e.g., Moscow, Copenhagen and Dallas). Meanwhile, more flexible bilateral agreements allowed Air Canada to provide new services to select (i.e. profitable) markets. Flights to New York City were expanded to allow a choice of airport destinations among Kennedy, La Guardia and Newark. Rules were relaxed to allow a range of discount possibilities on scheduled services into British and continental airports. Potentially the largest plum obtained in the 1980s was the right to begin service to south Asia through Bombay and Singapore. Particularly important for the viability of this route was attaining the so- called "fifth freedom" right to pick up passengers in London for carriage to Asia on its four weekly flights.[29] Not only does this open up a new and increasingly important passenger market for Air Canada, but it is a key link in the long term goal of achieving a world-wide cargo service. As deregulation in Canada increases competition and reduces market dominance, the airline must look to other markets or services to prosper.

Table 1 shows how the 1980s have been characterized by stagnant passenger growth as new competitors emerged in markets and the economy slowly recovered from the effects of the worst recession in fifty years. In 1987 Air Canada carried 11.0 million passengers, more than 1.8 million fewer than in 1979. On a positive note, cargo and contract revenues more than doubled to $773 million in the same eight year period. While passenger revenue remains dominant, other revenues have expanded their share of total revenues from 15 per cent in the late 1970s to 25 per cent in 1987. The airline managed to report a profit of $45.7 million in 1987 in spite of a labour disruption late in the year, which cost the airline up to $70 million dollars off its bottom line, and rapidly escalating costs of labour and expenses related to the provision of passenger services.[30] In its fifty-one years of existence TCA/Air Canada has a record of thirty-four profits and seventeen losses.

In the 1970s horizontal integration and diversification became marks of Air Canada's operations. An early sign of these developments was the airline's participation in the establishment of Air Jamaica in 1969. In 1972 Air Canada broadened its operational base with the establishment of Air Transit to run an experimental STOL aircraft commuter service between Montreal and Ottawa for the federal Ministry of Transport. Since the abortive efforts to form a joint airline with Canadian Pacific in the 1930s, the inefficiencies inherent in a small and dispersed Canadian market made possible mergers a recurring theme in air transport policy. In 1974 a proposal to purchase a one-third interest in charter rival Wardair was terminated by mutual consent. The next opportunity to expand domestically came with the 1977 purchase of Nordair, a decision which was apparently influenced by the intervention of the federal transport minister, Otto Lang. The government wanted to rationalize

Table 1
Air Canada: Operating Statistics and Financial Data

Year	Revenue (1) Passenger Miles (000's)	Revenue Ton Miles (000's)	Total Revenue ($000's)	Total Assets ($000's)	Net Profit ($000's)
1938			591	3,411	(818)
1943			9,380	8,270	147
1948	350,112	41,112	31,728	36,024	(2,933)
1953	759,320	89,150	62,237	45,480	256
1958	1 625,689	185,516	120,555	119,066	547
1963	2 701,899	331,114	199,390	269,342	527
1968	5 616,011	732,456	387,628	508,391	8,184
1969	5 740,299	788,528	404,652	594,912	1,548
1970	6 427,811	946,241	478,259	707,900	(1,072)
1971	6 426,830	957,283	508,341	800,020	1,662
1972	7 901,378	1 141,059	583,262	834,251	8,648
1973	9 600,971	1 349,491	698,050	917,800	6,123
1974	10 268,087	1 390,515	848,582	1 157,000	(9,255)
1975	10 110,077	1 396,154	957,180	1 289,400	(12,473)
1976	10 705,040	1 458,307	1 057,484	1 132,100	(10,455)
1977	11 297,000	1 508,000	1 187,655	1 227,000	20,006
1978	12 017,000	1 609,000	1 322,587	1 310,900	47,485
1979	14 414,000	1 860,000	1 595,172	1 505,800	55,369
1980	15 176,000	1 911,000	1 981,000	1 688,300	57,042
1981	14 351,000	1 848,000	2 258,200	1 866,900	43,400
1982	13 590,000	1 757,000	2 305,900	2 037,000	(35,600)
1983	12 728,000	1 710,000	2 313,600	2 186,000	3,100
1984	13 905,000	1 891,000	2 499,400	2 494,900	28,100
1985	14 130,000	1 947,000	2 722,500	2 544,500	(14,800)
1986	14 425,000	2 023,000	2 885,200	2 922,900	40,400
1987	14 358,000	2 021,000	3 131,100	3 084,800	45,700

Notes (1) Scheduled services only.

the air transport system in eastern Canada and Lang ultimately wished to see a grouping of Quebecair, Nordair and, perhaps, Eastern Provincial Airlines (EPA). Unfortunately, the main bid for Nordair was from Great Lakes Airlines in southwestern Ontario, which retained the enthusiatic support of the Ontario government to expand into a full-fledged regional carrier. In order to avoid the potential loss of identity for Nordair in a Great Lakes takeover (and the political fallout in Quebec), as well as to preserve the possibility of future regional airline integration, Lang asked Air Canada to act as intermediary to bring Quebecair and Nordair together. The plan was for Air Canada to buy both of the regional airlines, merge them, and sell the stronger, larger airline. The Air Canada purchase of Nordair was the first controversial act in a convoluted seven year regulatory and political battle which touched old wounds of French-English relations and the rivalry between Ontario and Quebec.[31] At the time Transair, a northwestern Ontario, Manitoba and Saskatchewan regional carrier, had recently been taken over by Pacific Western Airlines (PWA), which in turn was controlled by the Alberta government. This meant three of the five regional carriers were government owned (and a fourth, EPA, had its bonds guaranteed by a province). As soon as the deal was completed, the federal government began seeking a suitable private-sector purchaser for Nordair on the grounds that ownership of a regional airline by a trunk carrier violated evolving regional air policy.[32] Air Canada only found an acceptable buyer for Nordair in 1984 when Innocan Incorporated, partly owned by the Canada Development Corporation and Air Canada's pension fund, bid for Nordair. It is ironic that Innocan's first takeover choice, Eastern Provincial Airlines, had been taken over by the other major trunk carrier, CP Air, earlier in 1984 thereby signaling the death of the government's regional air policy.

With the 1984 announcement of the "New Canadian Air Policy", the doors were flung open for the greatest binge of takeover activity in Canadian transport history. Unlike the experience in the U.S., where deregulation produced an initial wave of fierce competition and expansion, followed by a series of acquisitions of airlines near corporate death, in Canada the airlines opted to forego open competition in favour of gaining market share through takeovers of smaller airlines which could feed into the trunk system. Over the past four years, most major regional carriers have been taken over by Air Canada or CP Air/Canadian. Air Canada has acquired ownership interests in Air BC (100 per cent), Air Ontario (75 per cent), Austin Airways (75 per cent) (now joined with Air Ontario), Air Nova (49 per cent) and NWT Air (100 per cent). In addition, the airline recently moved to fill a gap in its regional service by creating a new airline, Air Alliance, to serve Montreal, Quebec City, Bagotville and Ottawa.

These arrangements allow Air Canada to connect with dozens of communities where the demand would not justify jet service. However, in the takeover wars Air Canada has lost the major battles for the carriers which would protect its market share — particularly the largest and most efficient of the regionals like Nordair and EPA.

After the major reorganization of the early 1970s Air Canada's operations were broadened further by other forms of diversification. In cooperation with CNR, it established a management and technical consulting firm, CANAC, which sold its services to other companies and governments.[33] The airline also leased access to its advanced computerized reservation system, ReserVec II, to a number of Canadian and international airlines. More significant was the change in approach to the delivery of service which accompanied an increasing emphasis on marketing within Air Canada. One aspect of this operational change was the effort of the airline to sell a wider variety of tourist services (eg. hotel accommodation, car rentals, etc.) to the airline seat purchaser. This involved the establishment of a subsidiary corporation, Venturex Ltd., (later transformed into a tour wholesaling subsidiary, Touram Inc.), and the operation of hotels in the Caribbean through Allied Innkeeper Ltd. In a preview of deregulation in the 1980s even the seats were sold differently, with the potential customer being offered "Rapidair" rather than mere air travel between Toronto and Ottawa or Montreal, "Nighthawk" flights to the south, and "charter class fares" to compete with the burgeoning air charter operations.

As noted, the new *Air Canada Act* expanded the airline's capacity for diversification through vertical integration. MATAC Cargo Ltd., GPA Group Ltd., Innotech Aviation Industries, Aerospace Realties (1986) Ltd., Global Travel Computer Holdings Ltd. and three newly acquired courier services (Express Messenger Systems, Northern Express Messenger Systems and Gelco Express) are companies in which Air Canada has taken an ownership position over the past decade. Most services are very profitable areas of corporate activity and allow the company to enhance its core airline business. For example, GPA Group leases aircraft and develops a market for used aircraft, thus Air Canada can reduce its debt by selling and leasing back an aircraft *and* receive a share of the GPA profit on the transaction.[34]

Diverisification in services has expanded in response to deregulation and advances in computer applications which allow precise forecasts of demand on specific flights months in advance. To balance out seasonal fluctuations in passenger load and to cover the fixed costs of excess capacity, Air Canada has had "seat sales" over the past three years where prices have been discounted up to 75 per cent off regular economy fare. These sales have become so institutionalized that more than 60 per cent of Air Canada passengers now travel at a discount.[35]

Factors in the Airline's Development and Performance

Many of the features of Air Canada's development since 1937 are unexceptional in that they form a generally common pattern shared by many major world airlines – public or private. External factors such as the development and availability of new technologies for aircraft and ancillary equipment, the boom in distant holiday travel demand, and the cost of fuel supplies have affected the operations of most airlines in a roughly similar manner – although obviously in some cases other variables intervene to mitigate or accent the impact of a specific factor. On the whole, TCA/Air Canada's choices of available new aircraft technology have been in line with the needs and timing requirements of the airline, despite the vagaries of a fragmented route structure (a complex mixture of long and short domestic and international routes with varying passenger load density characteristics).[36]

Until 1980, traffic generally grew exponentially as the airline took advantage of the worldwide boom in air travel.[37] As passenger growth stagnated in the 1980s the airline has had to become more innovative (even if borrowing heavily from ideas pioneered in the U.S.). Marketing techniques such as seat sales to fill empty seats with passengers who would (hopefully) have not travelled otherwise, "connaisseur", "executive class" and other specialty services to attract the regular business traveller, and "Aeroplan", the frequent flyer program introduced in 1985 which seeks to generate loyalty and repeat business, have all been utilized to hold off the competition induced by deregulation and slower domestic traffic growth.

From 1974 to 1980 increases in the cost of aviation fuel were the most significant factor in the escalation of operating costs.[38] This was the case despite the fact that federal oil pricing tended to soften the impact of such price increases on Canadian airlines. In the 1980s the situation was reversed and Canadian carriers were forced to pay more than their international competitors as Canadian prices failed to reflect the drop in world oil prices until energy deregulation took hold in 1986.

If such factors have been to a degree common to most airlines, others are specific to TCA/Air Canada. One is the internal management and leadership of the airline. The other is the pervasive role of government as shareholder, air transport policy-maker and regulator.

Air Canada From the Inside

While it is extremely difficult on the basis of the available data to explore the salience of the internal management factor in any detail, the bare outlines of the story suggest that this variable may be of considerable significance and worthy of more detailed attention.[39] It is widely agreed that there have been three management phases in the history of TCA/Air Canada.[40] The first, an "operational" phase, extended from 1937 to 1968 and featured a senior management cadre largely drawn--at least in the latter half of the period—from the operational ranks of the airline. This period was dominated by the presidency of Gordon McGregor who ran the airline from 1948 to 1968. The management organization was highly centralized and stream-lined, with McGregor acting as both chief executive and chief operating officer and with at most four vice-presidents reporting to him. Not unexpectedly during this phase, the emphasis was on operations—providing a no-frills passenger and freight service. As a result, the airline engaged in little diversification and tended to downplay many of the more trendy aspects of modern management such as strategic planning and marketing. For the early part of the period, CNR provided a wide variety of management services (accounting, advertising, legal, purchasing, etc.) to the airline.[41] In their study of the first forty years of management strategies at Air Canada, Mintzberg, Brunet and Walters note that during its first decade TCA was a "truncated organization" with all major decisions made by government or CNR officials.[42]

The second management phase ran from approximately 1968 to 1976.[43] This period was dominated by the massive reorganization which followed a management study by McKinsey and Company and was a distinct departure from the first period in a number of ways. First, the senior management responsibilities were split between a chairman who functioned as chief executive officer and a president with the role of chief operating officer. After 1973, the office of president was reduced to staff and advisory responsibilities. Second, both of the new appointees to these positions in 1968 came from outside of Air Canada; Yves Pratt, the chairman from private law practice and John Baldwin, the president from 14 years as deputy minister of transport at the federal level. Third, there was a massive decentralization of management with—by 1976—as many as 22 vice-presidents reporting to the two senior officers. Finally, there was a strong movement within management away from operations towards a marketing and strategic planning approach.

The impact of these changes on operations was mixed. On the plus side, the new marketing perspective made management more receptive to both the diversification of service beyond merely flying planes, and somewhat more aggressive and innovative approaches to the selling of these and the more traditional services offered by the airline. These traits and the increasing orientation of the new management towards "commercial viability" and "profit-making" were essential complements to the gradual changes in public policy on competition which were confronting the airline during the 1970s. But by the end of this second era, it became clear that the new management style was imposing significant costs. For example, morale was badly shaken by heavy-handed efforts to change approaches and internal organization. More than a decade after the reorganization, Mintzberg et al. found that "opinions remained very divided on this restructuring" with many believing that senior management lost control of the process to McKinsey and Company. In the event, most insiders felt that, "while the operations of the airline kept functioning throughout these years in their (by now) highly structured way, the senior management levels did not really settle down again until 1976" when Claude Taylor, a twenty-seven year veteran of the airline, became CEO.[44] The wider distribution of management power also had a negative impact on vertical and horizontal communications and financial and corporate control within the airline. The authority of the multitude of new vice-presidents and the two senior officers was never clarified as executive responsibilities shifted away from the presidency to the chairman. The turmoil of the period was characterized by the running joke of managers telling their secretaries when leaving for lunch: "If my boss calls while I'm out, for God's sake get his name."[45] The darker side of the organizational problems is revealed in the convoluted tale of mismanagement and loss of control centring around the freewheeling activities of the Marketing branch which are catalogued in the Estey report.[46]

A third management phase began with the appointment of Claude Taylor as president and chief operating and executive officer. The nature of the appointment betrays the retreat from the excesses of the second phase and suggests an attempt to restore the centralized management system of the first era. The president became the recognized management authority within the corporation and the chairman returned largely to more traditional oversight and liaison roles. Only under these conditions could the government contemplate the patronage appointment in early 1979 of an ex-Cabinet minister, Bryce Mackasey, to the chair. In January 1979 the board reallocated the respective duties of the chairman and the president with the incoming chairman, Mackasey, losing responsibilities for subsidiaries and legal matters to the president.[47] Predictably, Mackasey's tenure was short when the government changed in the spring of 1979. Instability at the apex of the board continued with two interim chairmen and a 1981 appointee, Rene Amyot, who resigned in 1983 several months after RCMP investigations of wrongdoing in the establishment of new corporate headquarters.   Finally in 1984, Claude Taylor was appointed chairman and for the first time since the 1960s the board and management had stable leadership.

In the late 1970s Taylor intended to follow the lead of American Airlines, moving to an organization structure focussing on product groups and thinning the ranks of senior managers reporting to him. Reorganizations in 1980, 1983 and 1986 (the latter carried out by Taylor's successor as CEO, Pierre Jeanniot) have largely accomplished the first goal.   In 1986, the concept of business units, each with its own bottom line responsibility and accountability, was extended from the initial experiment with cargo and enRoute Card units to the backbone of the airline — two units to cover passenger operations (Passenger Canada and Passenger International).[48]   This is not to suggest that the transition was continuous; for example, a group enterprises division established in 1980 when Air Canada believed that it had to be "more than an airline", was sacrificed during the 1983 struggle for survival.[49]   The goal of thinning senior management has been more elusive.   While management ranks have been sharply reduced, the number of vice-presidents is unchanged since the 1970s. The severe market collapse of 1982-1983 led first to a voluntary reduction program which cut management by 1/6 or 650 people.   In 1985, layoffs and attrition took another 400 management positions while the number of vice-presidents has stayed around 25.[50]

Taylor's, and now Jeanniot's eras as president are marked by a need to contain costs.   In the 1970s fuel costs were the major concern and the airline was a leader in finding ways to reduce consumption. Labour costs have been a major concern in the 1980s but Air Canada has been unwilling or reluctant to act as vigorously as its private sector competition.   For example, Wardair won a long and bitter strike with its flight attendants in 1985 and thereby established a "two-tier" wage structure with lower rates for new employees.   Similarly, CP Air undertook massive cuts in the wake of its disastrous 1983 operating results, while Air Canada relied on a voluntary program, at least initially.   It is unclear whether Air Canada's reluctance to retrench was based on anticipated political fallout (and subsequent government intervention), by remnants of the paternalism of employee relations during the McGregor era, by the strong "people" orientation of the airline under Taylor's stewardship or simply by calculations about the direction of the economy and labour market needs. However, there is little doubt that memories of poor morale from the time of the McKinsey reorganization left their mark on the willingness of managers to turn the organization on its head again.

Another key aspect of internal corporate management is the role and effectiveness of the board of directors.   Here, again, one can do little more than suggest possible relationships between the viability of

TCA/Air Canada's board over time and the evolution of the airline's operations. It is hardly an exaggeration to note that for the first twenty years of TCA's existence, the board played almost no role in the leadership or management of the corporation.

It is widely agreed that C.D. Howe both "made" the boards and dictated the policies which they should adopt.[51] At a CNR board meeting in April, 1937, Howe oversaw the placement of six of his men from the CNR and the Department of Transport on the new TCA board. His immediate impact on personnel matters did not stop here, however. Howe also manoeuvred the appointment of an American, Philip Johnson, to the key post of vice-president of operations. As the president, S.J. Hungerford, was also the president of CNR, this made Howe's protege the effective chief operating officer of the airline.[52] The board did not play a significant role as a buffer between the airline and the government and, in common with most boards in the period, did little to review or audit in any meaningful manner the activities of management. Even without the overpowering influence of C.D. Howe this situation prevailed almost to the present day. The Estey report makes it clear that the board's role was poorly articulated in the 1970s and that the board was poorly informed of key activities by management and took little initiative on its own to inquire into the affairs of the corporation.[53] The committee system remained primitive and ineffective, and appointments to the board (like all federal Crown corporations) continued to be made largely on a patronage basis. The 1978 act increased the size of the board, improved the method of recruitment and spelled out a wider role and set of responsibilities for the board of directors.[54] But the patronage approach to appointments continued to hamper the board in providing the buffer, liaison and leadership roles which the literature on public sector corporations increasingly argues should be key features of the corporate model. For example, the entire board was asked to resign in 1985 following the 1984 change of government. The new Tory appointees included a former premier, a former MP and one individual who suggested that her qualifications included a driver's licence.[55]

The government as shareholder and regulator

The tradition of government involvement in the affairs of the corporation extends well beyond patronage appointments. Without doubt, the major external factor affecting the evolution of the airline has been the actions of its present sole shareholder, the federal government. The government's influence on TCA/Air Canada has been and continues to be both direct and indirect. In a direct sense, from the outset, the government—for many years in the person of C.D. Howe—has been a major force in key managerial decisions which in the private sector would generally be the responsibility of the senior management and the board of a corporation. Over the years other players including Transport Canada officials, the Cabinet, the Department of Finance, the Treasury Board Secretariat, and, latterly, the Ministry of State for Privatization and Regulatory Affairs have made their mark on the operation of the airline. Over the years government involvement in Air Canada has evolved from near total control to more modest control following the passage of the 1978 Act to recent moves through deregulation and impending privatization toward effective autonomy.

In an indirect sense, the government has also been a major force in the development of the corporation through its power to create air transport policy and exert ultimate authority over the federal agencies which have exercised the regulatory powers with respect to Canadian airlines since 1937. These include the Board of Railway Commissioners until 1938, the Board of Transport Commissioners to 1944, the Air Transport Board up to 1967, the Air Transport Committee of the Canadian Transport Commission (CTC) until 1987, followed by the neophyte National Transportation Agency. This regulatory power has been exercised most significantly to affect the level of competition faced by TCA/AC. Competition on both domestic and international routes has been almost exclusively dependent on government policy, its ultimate control over entry and exit through licensing and its power to negotiate bilateral agreements with other governments.

In the early years the most significant vehicles for shareholder intrusion were the formal powers available to the government under the *TCA Act* to dictate the route structure and schedule of the airline, aspects of the quality of service offered, and the rates to be charged for travel, freight and the transporting of air mail. These powers were written into the original legislation in the cabinet's power to authorize the minister of transport and the postmaster general to enter into contracts (the Trans-Canada Contract and the Trans-Canada Mail Contract respectively) with the airline to cover these key features of the corporation's operation.[56] Both contracts provided that the government should be responsible for meeting the operating deficits of the airline, thus putting the government in an influential role as subsidizer and effectively diminishing the airline's incentive at the outset to operate on a cost-recovery or profitable basis.

The enormous powers of direction, management and financing accorded the government under these contract arrangements did not remain static over the ensuing decades. In 1938, the scope of the Trans-Canada Contract was extended to include destinations outside of Canada. This provision permitted the government to become the negotiator, on behalf of the airline management, of the key features of

the company's international operations, particularly – in the early
period – on the potentially lucrative North Atlantic routes.[57] The
contract arrangements were further altered in 1945 to allow cabinet
the power to amend the Trans-Canada Contract whenever it saw fit
and to include whatever "terms" it chose.[58] This latter "deal you can't
refuse" amendment power was also extended to the air mail contract.
In addition, the latter contract arrangements were amended in 1945
to alter the basis upon which the Post Office's payments were
calculated in its favour, and revise the process by which the air mail
contract was negotiated to give the cabinet more power to deal with
disputes between the airline and the Post Office.[59] In 1953, the
cabinet relinquished its right under the Trans-Canada Contract to
deal specifically with TCA's schedules (despite the retention of the
override power to dictate "terms" in the broadest sense). It also
relieved itself, under the same set of amendments to the *TCA Act*, of
the responsibility of meeting the operating deficit of the airline.[60]
This left the government in the powerful position of being able to
dictate to a significant degree the nature of the airline's operations
without being forced to assume financial responsibility for consequent
losses. In 1961, the government declared that in the future, route
structure decisions for TCA would be handled in common with the
applications of other airlines by the Air Transport Board and that
TCA would give up the privilege of exclusive access to the mainline
route set down in the contract.[61] After 1967, the Air Transport
Committee of the CTC gained control of the regulation of passenger
fares thereby removing their consideration from the Trans-Canada
Contract. It is important, however, to keep the latter two changes in
the direct relationship between the government and TCA/Air Canada
in perspective. Despite the apparent diminution of the government's
power in favour of the regulatory agency, the government still
retained a firm hold on route structure and fare decisions through its
effective domination of the regulatory process. While formally the
province of the CTC from 1967 until deregulation in 1988, routes and
fares were subject to policy guidance by the minister of transport and
decisions could be appealed to the federal cabinet.[62]

The enormous management and subsidization roles implicit in
the contracts are not the final measure of the government's formal
powers with respect to TCA/AC. In the 1937 legislation, the
government also accorded itself – through the minister of transport – the powers to name the corporation's auditors and decide when
the airline should begin paying for ancillary services (e.g. landing
fees) rendered by the government.[63] In the 1945 amendments, the
government gained the right to approve the acquisition or creation of
subsidiaries by the airline and subject them to route and airmail
contracts.[64] Finally, under the *Financial Administration Act* of 1951,

the government took on the important power of approval of the capital budgets of "proprietary" corporations such as TCA/Air Canada.[65]

A review of the history of the airline clearly suggests that the government's formal and informal super-management powers *vis-à-vis* the airline have had a measurable impact on the evolution of its operations between 1937 and 1988. Route structure, fares and service quality are major areas in which the government's influence has been felt. On the international level, the government's powers to negotiate bilateral agreements with other governments and dictate which Canadian airline will fly the routes obtained has been, and remains, a key factor in the development of TCA/Air Canada's international network. Filtered through the government's regulatory role, the impact of this power on TCA/Air Canada has been substantial. Not only has the public airline received the lion's share of international and trans-border routes, but it has also been forced by the government to fly some losing prestige routes (e.g. Montreal-Moscow). Domestically, under the demands of the Trans-Canada Contract and the more subtle interplay of pressure between the government and the airline's management, the airline has taken on and serviced (often charging fares well below cost) a number of "social routes" in the name of the "national interest" which purely commercial considerations would never have let it develop. These include regional and feeder routes in British Columbia, the Prairies and Foothills, the Great Lakes, Northern Ontario, Eastern Quebec and the Maritimes. The effect of political pressure can best be illustrated by examples such as the airline's decision to extend service to Trois Rivières during the period when the Minister of Transport was an MP from that area.[66] The fact that the airline took the initiative, often without documented direct prodding by the government during the 1950s particularly, to extend its "social route" network does not diminish the case to be made for the pervasiveness of the government's influence on the public airline's operations. In these instances, Baldwin contends the airline is moving to placate its indirect sole shareholder by engaging in cross-subsidization to the extent that anticipated profits from profitable routes will cover both losses from servicing a social route and the level of retained earnings viewed by the airline to be necessary to cover anticipated capital expenditures.[67]

In effect, then, the government's power *vis-à-vis* the airline not only had a direct impact on route structure, fares and quality of service, but also may be an important explanatory variable with respect to the level of profit reported by the airline. In the context of his more general thesis that TCA/Air Canada has adjusted its behaviour to assure its own survival, Baldwin argues that there is ample evidence that the airline has generally pursued a policy of cross-subsidization at the expense of profits despite its strong rhetorical attachment to the profit-making goal. Up to 1945, and to a lesser degree until 1950, the government "signalled" TCA (through legislation and the insistence that retained earnings be used to cover deficits) that it would cover its operating deficits but that it did not like them. After 1950, the airline was given the message that the government would not automatically cover deficits. In the earlier period, there was little incentive for the airline to earn a profit of any kind. In the latter period, the only incentives for earning a profit were to amass funds for the periods of heavy capital expenditures and to engage in cross-subsidization to maximize political support.

The subsidization of money-losing social routes is no longer the key feature of Air Canada's operation that it was up until the 1970s. Gradually the government stopped pressuring the airline to take on new routes and Air Canada was eventually allowed to drop services as competitors emerged and restrictions on the routes of CP Air and others were lifted. Air Canada (with the cooperation of the Canadian Transport Commission and the government) moved to a fully compensatory fare structure which recognized the significant fixed costs (e.g., selling tickets, and handling passengers and aircraft) associated with low-mileage routes.[68] By 1981 the airline argued that it was no longer cross-subsidizing any domestic passenger services.

Aircraft and infrastructure choice are other areas where the government's formal and informal powers of management and direction have exerted direct impacts on the operations of TCA/Air Canada. Corbett argues that aircraft choice is a key variable in the "fortunes" of the airlines which he studied:

> No other managerial decision seems to matter so much. The right aircraft introduced at the right time brings commercial success: a mistake or bad luck in the choice of aircraft leads to trouble. Some of the airlines we have studied have a consistent record of successful choices, while others have a mixture of good and bad. And it also happens that the airlines whose choices have been successful are those whose managements have enjoyed long terms of service and have either been left free of government interference or have put a determined resistance against it.[69]

At the CNR board meeting in April 1937, Howe announced that "his department had placed tentative orders for three existing Lockheed planes and four of the newest Lockheed 14H 'twin-engine monoplanes' just being developed"; CNR was to take over the orders until the TCA board "could in turn be assigned the aircraft."[70] Effectively, then, the government dictated the initial fleet development of TCA, choosing amongst a variety of available piston aircraft before the management of the corporation was in place. Baldwin notes that, in the event, this choice of aircraft was not inappropriate in view of the passenger load factors which emerged in the early years of operations and the superior speed for Lockheed series aircraft.[71] Corbett contends that TCA made two questionable fleet decisions — the choice of the Canadair "North Star" in 1946 and the decision to hang on to them after 1950 — and both decisions were made by C.D. Howe as the designated minister and not by TCA's management.[72] The initial choice "was dictated by a government faced with a newly developed wartime aircraft industry and the problem of its postwar conversion."[73] The government has on other occasions (the choice of the DC-9 over the Caravelle in 1966) "discussed" aircraft choice with the corporation's management and even effectively delayed a choice (the decision to order the Boeing 767 instead of the A-310 Airbus in 1979). In the case of the intervention on the decision to purchase the Boeing 767 the government of the day certainly took a very liberal interpretation of the act's allowance for "directions of a general nature."[74] In April 1988 there were suggestions that an announcement on ordering the Airbus A-320 to replace the Boeing 727 was delayed during a provincial election campaign in Manitoba to avoid political fallout from news of the potential loss of maintenance jobs.[75] But the views of management on aircraft choice have in the end prevailed.

The government apparently exercised its power to direct the airline's activities again in 1979, this time in the choice of aircraft for particular services. Air Canada was held back from the introduction of wide-bodied aircraft on the Prairies until its competitor, Transair, was in a position to introduce a similar service.[76]

Another publicized intrusion by the government into the airline's infrastructure decision-making, which also involved the Winnipeg maintenance facility, was directed at the corporation's operations and quality of service in western Canada. In 1963, the government was insistent that TCA/Air Canada continue to maintain its Winnipeg maintenance operation instead of consolidating it in Montreal as management desired.[77] It was estimated in 1963 that the continued operation of two facilities would cost the airline an additional $19.8 million over seven years.[78] The eventual sale of the Winnipeg operation in 1969 did not end the story. As a result of a promise during the 1974 election campaign, the Liberal government forced Air Canada to re-establish a maintenance base in Winnipeg employing eight hundred workers. Interestingly a local Liberal candidate in the election, James Richardson, retained his seat by eight hundred votes! Like Phoenix, the maintenance base issue emerged again during the build-up to the introduction of legislation permitting the partial privatization of Air Canada. In the one month period between the announcement of the intention to privatize and the tabling of Bill C-129 in Parliament on 19 May 1988, the government was persuaded to insert a legal guarantee that maintenance facilities would be preserved in Winnipeg.[79]

The final area in which the government has had a direct managerial impact on operations is human resource policy and customer service. On the instructions of the government, the firm has moved to provide services to its domestic customers in both official languages. This legitimate extension of the government's bilingualism policy has caused personnel disruptions and increased operating costs due to language training and translation of training manuals. It provides an interesting illustration of the extent to which the government is prepared to think of Air Canada as an instrument of national policies removed from the immediate ambit of air transport. Pursuing this theme in a 1973 statement on air policy, the minister of transport noted that "the government expects Air Canada to perform a special role as a model corporation in such fields as decentralization, bilingualism, and labour and technological change".[80] By 1979, Air Canada offered basic training and management development courses in both official languages, and, in its Annual Report notes that less than 1 per cent of surveyed customers had been unable to receive service in the language of their choice.[81]

The 1978 *Air Canada Act* altered the government's powers with respect to the airline without diminishing its capacity to play a major role in the corporation's affairs.[82] The government relinquished the right to dictate route and air mail contracts to the airline but gained the "front-end" power to issue policy directives to the airline that could transform its objectives in an instant and could force the airline to perform a non-commercial task with no guarantee of adequate compensation.[83] The airline gained the right to borrow in private markets, subject to the approval of the government.[84] Under this act and the 1984 legislation amending the *Financial Administration Act* (which affects all Crown corporations),[85] central agencies of government gain significant powers and influence over a number of corporate decision-making areas. For example, there is extensive contact with central agencies as the corporation develops its budget and corporate plan and these documents must be approved by the Treasury Board and the cabinet respectively. Each individual borrowing exercise requires the approval of the minister of finance and the cabinet must approve the acquisition or sale of any subsidiaries. Some observers argue that some of these areas should legitimately be left to internal management control.[86]

The 1978 act altered the capital structure of the airline, effecting the transformation of the debt/equity ratio to approximately 60/40 (from 97/3) through the cancellation of the large debt to CNR and the federal government's purchase of $329 million worth of Air Canada shares. In the process, Air Canada ceased to be a subsidiary of CNR and became directly and wholly owned by the federal government.[87]

In the 1980s, even though the federal government stopped receiving its annual dividend in 1983, Air Canada's debt/equity ratio once again deteriorated to approximately 75/25 in 1985 as new debt was taken on to carry out fleet replacement. In 1986 the company was able to reduce sharply the ratio to less than 60/40 through the sale and leaseback of a number of aircraft and other assets, the issue of perpetual bonds which are not counted in long term debt, and additions to retained earnings from strong operating results. However, the airline continued to face serious financial problems. In the 1990s when the short-haul workhorses of the fleet, the 727's and DC-9's, need replacing the airline will face a crunch. These aircraft make up more than two-thirds of the fleet and thus, without an infusion of new equity, the estimated $2.4 billion cost of replacement will have a very negative impact on interest costs. To put this sum in perspective, it is equal to more than 80 per cent of the value of all of Air Canada's assets in 1986. The "selling" of this need for a capital infusion had a significant effect on the decision to begin privatization.

The final stage in the devolution of management control from the government to the airline began with the April 1988 announcement that the federal government intends to privatize Air Canada. In making the announcement the deputy prime minister emphasized the change in the environment:

> Rather than competing for a static, regulated market, Canada's airlines are now expanding the market by providing better service across Canada through innovation and efficiency. They are striving to meet the needs of the travelling public rather than the needs of the regulatory agency.
> All airlines including Air Canada, continue to serve important public purposes, but complete Crown ownership is not necessary to carry this out.
> . . . . Indeed, blind devotion to state enterprises would be the only possible reason for not proceeding at this time.[88]

Privatization, as the buzzword of choice for bureaucrats and consultants in the 1980s, has come to mean a number of things and takes a variety of forms but essentially it refers to moving activity from the public sector to the private sector. Narrowly, privatization means disposing of the assets of government corporations, usually through the sale or giveaway of shares representing some or all of the equity in corporations. However, privatization cannot be isolated from the use of other instruments of government policy. For example, deregulation (which is often more important than privatization in determining economic performance), downsizing government (by reducing safety nets or eliminating universality of programs), and contracting out or "hiving off" public services to non-profit organizations and private firms all produce results which can approximate the effect of disposing of assets. The lack of precision in the scope and meaning of the term has led to a great deal of confusion about what privatization means.

Rationales for privatization of public enterprises can be grouped into four broad categories:

— ideology (e.g., removing, as a matter of faith, the "big government" threat to the mixed economy, making room for private sector activity, and creating the environment for public participation in "people's capitalism");

— economic efficiency and competitiveness (e.g., incompatible with deregulation, remove the unfair advantages in cheap capital, and legal and tax immunity, promote efficient use of resources, and encourage unsubsidized competition);

— financial (e.g., realize a "profit", reduce government deficits through reducing demands for cash injections and subsidies, and remove the threat of future capital demands on the federal treasury); and

— symbolic (e.g., placate vocal interest groups by getting rid of the obscure or the unpopular as evidence of government activity, signal to remaining public corporations that they should toe the line, and, by extension, encourage government managers to be efficient and effective).[89]

In trying to come to grips with rationales for privatization, one is driven to the conclusion that no one answer suffices in any particular case. Discussion of privatization began in the late 1970s in Canada. While the Liberals had been talking about privatization, and had set up a holding company, the Canada Development Investment Corporation, to manage and dispose of some assets, their efforts were *ad hoc*. The Conservatives, on the other hand, came to power with a mission to make government smaller and part of that mission involved dismantling many public enterprises. The initial Conservative efforts were based primarily on ideology with elements of battles for turf within the new administration; however the more recent privatizations have been justified by or at least couched in the language of efficiency, economic rationality and financial imperatives. When the Conservatives took office in 1984 the secretary of the Treasury Board had the mandate for coordination of privatization; however, the minister of regional industrial expansion pre-empted the former's efforts by announcing that four Crown corporations were for sale. The confusion persisted even after the process was consolidated in the Office of Privatization and Regulatory Affairs in late 1086.

Part of the confusion surrounding the federal Conservative government's approach to privatization is attributable to a lack of understanding of privatization and a broader failure to articulate a rationale for privatization. Not until 1987 was there a clear (public) statement of privatization objectives.[90] Undoubtedly much of the delay in announcing the Air Canada privatization resulted from the confusion surrounding the bidding process for Teleglobe Canada early in 1987.[91] In both cases uncertainty in the regulatory environment was inescapably linked to privatization.

In the particular case of Air Canada, the notion of privatization has been around as long as the airline. It will be recalled that the enabling legislation in 1937 provided for the sale of up to 49.8 per cent of TCA to private entities "interested in aviation". But since the late 1970s there has been a series of calls for the privatization of Air Canada. Serious discussion and preliminary plans emerged with the election of the Mulroney government in September 1984, although that spring the previous Liberal minister of transport had asked the House of Commons Standing Committee on Transport to consider whether Air Canada should be broken up or privatized and hired Wood Gundy to do an evaluation of the firm. A variety of interests spoke out in favour of privatization including senior management of the airline, Conservative and Liberal politicians, and competitors. In addition, there was active involvement of a group representing 5,000 Air Canada employees in promoting the idea of privatization and taking an ownership position.

Just as momentum was building towards a privatization strategy for the airline the prime minister had a meeting with Louis Laberge, head of the 300,000 member Quebec Federation of Labour, who expressed concerns about job security for employees in the event of a sale. Mulroney left the meeting and blurted out that "Canada needs a national airline and it's going to have one."[92] The prime minister's statement effectively thwarted privatization in the short term; however, in early 1986 speculation again arose that Air Canada might be partly sold and, fueled by statements by cabinet ministers, such speculation mounted through the year. In early 1987 a Gallup poll showed that Canadians were evenly split (42 per cent for and 42 per cent against) on whether Air Canada should be privatized.[93] After a strenuous lobbying effort by Air Canada and exhortation by a number of Canadian newspapers, it was finally reported in August

1987 that Mr. Mulroney had vetoed the sale because of uncertainty about the reaction of the public.[94] Perhaps the prime minister felt that his credibility would be further damaged in light of a public perception of an unequivocal 1985 statement. In any event, the stock market crash in October 1987 knocked more than 30 per cent off the value of other airline stocks and, combined with the problems surrounding the British Petroleum stock offering at the same time, nailed shut any "window" of opportunity which lingered.[95]

The privatization issue would not die; it was a decision in search of a rationale. Where arguments about the incompatability of Crown ownership and deregulation, the demands of efficiency and competitiveness, the airline's need for equity infusion, and the absence of continuing public policy reasons for ownership failed to produce an announcement, other factors came together in 1988.[96] A cabinet shuffle lifted the profile of the ministry of state with the new minister, Don Mazankowski, sitting on the key Priorities and Planning Committee of cabinet which controls the government's agenda. Mazankowski, in an earlier position as minister of transport, had played the central role in initiating the 1984 studies of privatizing Air Canada. Air Canada had increased the pressure for an equity infusion in its 1988 capital budget, as its competitors made large aircraft orders and sought to strengthen their balance sheets by selling assets and paying down debt.

One of the problems with privatizing a national institution like Air Canada once its original mandate has been completed or disappeared, is the corporation's symbolic role, for the creation of TCA was linked with dreams of nation building in the face of U.S. competition. Symbolism remains important—the Economic Council suggested that it may be the "most significant benefit of public owner-ship . . . the satisfaction that Canadians derive from the existence of a national carrier".[97] With the creation of a national trunk service the initial goal for the airline was achieved and TCA's goal shifted to acting as an instrument of federal air policy. However, with deregulation and the evolution of competitive "open skies", much of the policy instrument rationale for a public airline has disappeared.

A further complication of privatization often quickly discovered by governments is that corporations as policy instruments become connected with other policies and programs.[98] In the case of Air Canada, bilingualism is a good example. Apparently one of the serious concerns expressed by Quebec Conservatives was the implications of privatization on the promotion and use of French within the airline. These concerns are reflected in the new legislation which entrenches the application of the *Official Languages Act* to the airline.[99]

Proponents of privatization point to the possibility of direct subsidies for "social" air services which are still in the public interest.

However, as Baldwin points out, the U.S. and U.K. experiences with subsidization were problematic. Subsidies were often mistargeted, inefficient, and difficult to monitor and control.[100] In Canada, the 1978 *Air Canada Act* allows for payments for performing non-compensatory services, but these provisions have not been used.[101] However, this has not stopped representatives of the government from making suggestions that public enterprises might carry out uneconomic activities which are often distant from the corporate mandate. For example, in 1987 the federal sport minister suggested that Air Canada (and other public enterprises) might undertake advertising and promotional efforts to overcome some of the financial problems of the Canadian Football League.

While the 1988 legislation allows for the transfer of all shares to the public, the initial offering will sell off 45 per cent of the government's share. The government will receive *nothing* for the shares sold. All of the proceeds go to the airline; however, the government avoids having to fund new equity for Air Canada, thereby realizing an imputed saving to the treasury. This will be accomplished by issuing new shares. Instead of owning 100 per cent of the current equity of $600 million, presuming the share issue raises $300 million, the government will own 55 per cent of the new equity of $900 million. Thus, the value of the federal shareholding is likely to be diluted by about $100 million following the issue. While holding the majority of shares, the government plans to give up its majority voice by instructing the chairman of Air Canada to vote the 55 per cent government shareholding in accordance with the views of the majority of the publicly-held shares, i.e., the majority government interest will masquerade as a minority.

The minority form of the privatization seems to have been dictated by a number of factors: consistency with the Canadian gradualist approach to deregulation; protecting the integrity of the prime minister by not contradicting his January 1985 statement; polls which showed favourable responses to share issues but negative public views on the "sale" of the airline;[102] and the limited capacity of Canadian capital markets to handle large share issues in the aftermath of the October 1987 crash.[103] The minority share issue also has the support of Air Canada management which has been promoting the idea of minority interests since 1984, citing the examples of such national airlines as Japan Air Lines, Swissair, Lufthansa and KLM. Air Canada president, Pierre Jeanniot described continuing government involvement as the "best of both worlds – a right of regard for the state in its national airline, and access to private capital".[104]

The consensus of the literature is less favourably disposed toward mixed enterprises. Many view them as the worst of all possible worlds. Baldwin argues that mixed enterprises depend on "government forswearing any non-profit objectives... [which] would eliminate most of the reasons for ownership other than the symbolic."[105] The Economic Council's 1986 report on public enterprises concluded that "problems in establishing adequate control mechanisms... lead us to reject the mixed enterprise as a long-term alternative to complete public ownership of Air Canada."[106] Auditor General Kenneth Dye also weighed in with a study of 13 mixed enterprises and cautioned: "This potential move [from Crown corporation to mixed enterprise status] of entities in which large sums of money are invested, from a strong accountability framework into — or through — a less cetain accountability status is a matter of uneasiness".[107] Stephen Brooks studied "mixed ownership corporations" and found the organizational form ambiguous with significant constraints to governments imposing their goals on management.[108] The fact that governments have tried to impose their will on mixed enterprises may lead investors to be leery of investing, in spite of public statements of intent. However, given the limited success in intervention described by Brooks and the recent disavowals of intention to intervene in the privatization announcement, it seems likely that the vehicle of the mixed enterprise is a politically and financially convenient way station on the road to a private airline.

In relinquishing its direct management control over Air Canada, the government is establishing a number of conditions to sustain important public policy goals and, not incidentally, to dilute potential criticism. Bill C-129 limits shareholder ownership of the publicly available shares to a maximum of 10 per cent control with a further cumulative foreign ownership ceiling of 25 per cent of the non-government shares. The legislation also includes operational constraints such as requirements to adhere to the *Official Languages Act,* to preserve the maintenance bases and to maintain corporate headquarters in Montreal.[109] Other constraints mentioned in the April announcements and press releases included: adherence to the *Employment Equity Act,* continuation of employee relations policies and continued provision of bilingual services. From Air Canada's perspective most of these restrictions simply continue existing arrangements and represent good business sense (corporate headquarters and bilingual services) or replicate conditions imposed on all federally regulated companies (employment equity). The conditions on maintenance facilities and labour policies may prove more problematic in efficiency terms. However, management does gain considerable flexibility by severing the direct control ties to government. One of the advantages of any privatization is that it forces the government to make social goals explicit and thus more readily subject to review and compensation – backed by the often noisy voices of shareholders.

For now there are more questions than answers in assessing the direction of the Air Canada privatization. For the airline the benefits are quite clear. Management gains the flexibility to manage its debt:equity ratio and decision making becomes less politicized – managers gain internal "freedom to move." The plan for a wide share distribution, the passive role for federal involvement and the 10 per cent restriction on individual ownership suggest that the share purchase arrangements for employees and management may produce *de facto* control for blocks of Air Canada employee shareholders.

For the government the benefits are less appparent (or the risks are more visible). Air Canada is the "Big Test" of the privatization exercise. Lessons have undoubtedly been absorbed from the early errors but the scale of this effort and the initial public share-offering introduce great uncertainty.[110] The pricing of the shares is likely to be contentious. The government will want to make the shares attractive to investors, both small shareholders and the institutions which will market the shares. At the same time there will be pressure from the airline (which receives the benefits of the issue) to maximize the return and, by implication, taxpayers have an interest in getting the best return for their investment, or in this case, minimizing the dilution of the government share. The evidence from Britain suggests that wide share ownership has been achieved at great cost and the long term impact on share ownership is seen as minimal. The huge offerings and the significant discounts both contributed to the cost.[111] The fact that the funds from Air Canada privatization will be used to fund fleet renewal and the initial offering of a minority interest both suggest that the Canadian government will be more moderate in its approach.

By adopting an arm's-length relationship, except for the specified areas of management constraint, the government is trying to find the balance between intrusion and abandonment of interest. There will be other tightropes to walk: will Air Canada continue to receive preferential treatment in international route bilaterals? How will the government interest be managed? How will the board be appointed and, given the statements of intent on voting the government interest, how independent will the board members be? Will the controls in the *Financial Administration Act* continue to function? Will the airline begin to pay dividends (discontinued in the 1983 recession) again and, if dividends are paid, will the government claim its share? We will return to the issue of privatization in the final section of this paper.

While the government's role as "super manager" has had a significant impact on the operation and performance of Air Canada, it is widely acknowledged that the government acting as "regulator" of competition has been even more important. In the context of the government's exposure to deficit and capital funding, it is hardly surprising that for the first 20 years of TCA's existence, it was extremely protective of the airline. Until 1949, in fact, TCA enjoyed a monopoly on all national and transcontinental routes. As the prime minister put it in 1943: "TCA is the sole Canadian agency which may operate international services. Within Canada, TCA will continue to operate all transcontinental systems, and such other service as may be designated by the government. Competition between air services over the same route will not be permitted. . . ."[112] The decade after 1949 saw an erosion of the public airline's control of international routes, with CP Air gaining access to the Pacific, Mexico, Peru, Holland, Argentina, Portugal and Spain – all destinations which were not serviced by TCA or which the public airline was prepared to trade.

Throughout this period TCA was still protected from direct competition from CP Air and other carriers on its international and transcontinental routes. It was this latter monopoly which collapsed after the election of the Conservative government in 1957. Enthusiastically espousing competition, the new government tentatively put it into practice, after a sobering consultant's report, by granting CP Air one flight per day each way between Vancouver, Winnipeg, Toronto and Montreal.[113] TCA/Air Canada was also confronted after 1961 with direct domestic competition from the growing but economically troubled regional carriers. In a reversal of regional air policy, the Conservative government opened the way for five of the regional airlines to step up from their north-south feeder service role to offer parallel service of the two trunk carriers on mainline route segments. This departure from traditional anti-competition doctrine was perpetuated and extended by the new Liberal government's statement of regional air policy in 1966, the further extension of CP Air's transcontinental service after 1967, and a slightly more equitable redistribution of international routes between the two trunk carriers after 1973. To keep this trend in perspective, it is important to note that these changes still left Air Canada in a dominant position. The redistribution of international and transborder routes in 1965-66 and 1973-74 maintained the principal of complementarity rather than competition on international routes and continued to reserve most key routes for Air Canada. While CP Air was allowed to increase its penetration of the transcontinental route it was still cut off from eastern Canada (beyond Montreal) and was limited to 25 per cent of total transcontinental capacity. It was to take twenty-five years from CP Air's entry to central Canada before the airline achieved its goal of transcontinental service in 1984. Harris concluded in 1978 that:

Government policy would appear to have shifted through the years from a monopoly position for Air Canada in mainline and international aviation to the preservation of its pre-eminent role so that it can act as a chosen instrument to fulfil Canada's public interest in air transportation while providing CP Air with the opportunity to achieve considerable development as an alternative source of public benefit. In doing this the cross-subsidization system of Air Canada has been protected.[114]

This partial reversal of competition policy sent shock waves through TCA/Air Canada's operations after 1957. For some time there was talk of amalgamation with CP Air as being the only means available of reversing the loss of monopoly position. But it came to nothing.[115]   Baldwin argues that the major effect of the initial introduction of competition on the trans-continental routes was to lower profits on one of TCA/Air Canada's "cream" runs. This development, complicated by the capital investments resulting from the introduction of jet technology in the early 1960s, led to three deficit years (1960-62), the consequent development by the airline of a new fare structure featuring increases in the price of services on social-routes – designed to restore equilibrium to the cross-subsidization system – and efforts to drop some social routes entirely.[116]   The extension of CP Air's transcontinental service in the late 1960s led to another round of fare increases, this time focussed more on the transcontinental route itself. The above extension combined with further increases in selective competition on domestic mainline routes caused by the revision of regional air policy in the mid-1960s led perversely to significant fare increases in 1971 for the transcontinental sector and an excess of "quality of service" competition leading to higher operating costs.[117]

Even as it was removing route restrictions on CP Air in the late 1970s, the government continued to intervene in the regulatory process demonstrating the continuing impact of government policy on Air Canada. In January 1978, the cabinet overturned a CTC decision which advocated an extremely limited experiment with domestic Advanced Booking Charters (ABC's) and insisted that a far more extensive and liberal test of ABC's be conducted in the domestic market.[118]   Air Canada had argued that its limited (and vastly oversubscribed) charter class fare program was an adequate response to consumer demand. The cabinet decision opened the door for the first time to regional airlines and (after a delay) charter operators to compete on a reasonably equal footing on interregional routes with the two trunk carriers.[119]   It also forced Air Canada and CP Air to respond to this challenge with a much wider variety of lower fare schemes.

Perhaps less enlightened – but nonetheless predictable – responses to the prospect of increased competition and the threat of passenger diversion are discount pricing to drive out the competition and moves to integrate the competition itself through defensive mergers. Air Canada's purchase of Nordair in 1978 is a classic example of the latter strategy. The CTC approved the acquisition in spite of vociferous opposition by a wide variety of parties who argued that the takeover violated the government's policy of supporting the development of regional carriers, contributed to a curtailment of competition because of Air Canada's control of Nordair's charter business, and was unnecessary as an alternate private purchaser was available.[120] By its behavior, Air Canada seemed less interested in integrating Nordair than in ensuring that the regional carriers stayed weak. For example, even while it was negotiating for the airline, Air Canada actively opposed Nordair's application to take over Transair routes in northern Ontario arguing that the routes weren't really regional. Stevenson notes that the strategy of limiting the damage that regionals could cause through their route ambitions was shared with CP Air; however Air Canada was also trying to curtail CP Air's ambitions. The public airline "saw this as part of a two-front war, having lost its privileged status in relation to CP Air . . . . Probably for this reason, it was somewhat more militant than CP Air in opposing the demands of the regional carriers."[121] The CTC seemed only too willing to condone Air Canada's strategy.

The change in attitude of both government and competitors between Air Canada's 1977 purchase and CP Air's 1985 acquisition of Nordair is remarkable. Stevenson suggests that CP Air's success showed just how weak and politically unpopular Air Canada had become as "shown by the fact it was not allowed to retain control of Nordair, but could not prevent Nordair from eventually falling into the hands of its major competitor. Unlike private enterprises, Crown corporations cannot hope to win many victories without public support."[122] The decision implicit in the 1978 Cabinet decision to let Air Canada be "pre-eminent" but not allow it to swallow up the domestic competition had far-reaching effects in the 1980s. Air Canada was held back, at least psychologically, as the deregulation-induced takeover battles began and CP Air was allowed to pick off two of the regional plums (Nordair and Eastern Provincial Airways) before Air Canada entered the arena.

The 1978 Nordair decision implied that Air Canada would no longer enjoy the same priority status in route allocations which it had in the past. Specifically the government served notice to the CTC that it had no objection to CP Air becoming a competitor of Air Canada in the Atlantic Provinces.[123] However, after the CTC awarded the prime Toronto-Halifax route to CP Air in 1980, the federal government intervened and after a pitched political battle, the cabinet reversed the decision and gave EPA the lucrative Toronto route.[124] However, CP Air did get the Montreal-Halifax route and, combined with the March 1979 relaxation of capacity restrictions on CP Air's trans continental routes, Air Canada and CP Air were now set to go head-to-head across the country. This signalled the first step toward total deregulation.

Decisions like the approval of Air Canada's interest in Nordair and the awarding of licences to regional carriers over the objections of Air Canada and CP Air illustrate the evolving role of the Air Transport Committee.[125] The controversies surrounding many of these hearings illustrated gaps in policy and changing competitive circumstances. By the early 1980s the regulatory regime was under great pressure and Air Canada, as the dominant player in the air industry, had the most to lose. The restriction on CP Air's share of the transcontinental market was lifted in 1979, the regional air carrier policy collapsed with the PWA takeover of Transair and the subsequent 1980-81 licencing of the two regional carriers from the peripheries of the country, PWA and EPA, to serve Toronto; and, in the U.S., deregulation was spreading the gospel of cheap air fares and a wider choice of airlines. Deregulation in the United States proved to hold more than symbolic importance for Air Canada and CP Air — the Canadian airlines found that they were losing passengers across the border to American carriers offering cheaper fares to more distant U.S. and European points.

As government and the air industry in Canada moved toward deregulation in the early 1980s there were a few obstacles and reversals in the path. In August 1981 the minister of transport released domestic air carrier policy proposals which slowed the liberalization trend of the previous few years. The proposals included rigid roles for CP Air and Air Canada as the sole national carriers and the maintenance of the regional carrier policy. Sharp reductions in travel demand in 1982 led to cutthroat competition as seat sales proliferated. By June Air Canada was flying almost one-half of its domestic capacity at a discount (compared to 8-9 per cent in 1978). Both CP Air and Air Canada reported substantial quarterly losses.[126] In August the Air Transport Committee responded to restrict discounts of more than 25 per cent to return trips with minimum stay and two-week advance booking requirements. The action was justified by the perceived threat to "the maintenance of adequate air service." Reschenthaler and Stanbury saw the use of selective evidence to attribute airline problems to deregulation in isolation from other factors, such as the recession, as evidence that the regulatory process was serving to protect the airlines rather than customers.[127]

In May 1984 the minister of transport, Lloyd Axworthy, announced a "New Canadian Air Policy" which proposed significant reductions in regulation of fares, routes and entry. Public hearings produced a division of opinion between "controlled competition", with limited flexibility on pricing but controls on entry (favoured by CP Air and Air Canada, the Air Transport Board and officials from Transport Canada), and deregulation (supported by the minister, consumer groups, and most academic and research analysts).[128] Finally, the new Conservative transport minister, Don Mazankowski, released a white paper ("Freedom to Move") in July 1985 which set out a number of principles aimed at less regulation, greater flexibility and reliance on competition and market forces, while allowing for direct government support for services in the public interest or for those severely dislocated by the new regime.[129] Implementing legislation was introduced in July 1986 and November 1986 and the new *National Transportation Act* came into effect January 1, 1988. The extent of government power under the pre-1988 regulatory regime underlines the change with the new National Transportation Agency. Only northern and remote air routes will be regulated for competition; the focus on other domestic routes will be limited to safety and insurance. If an applicant is "fit, willing and able" it may serve the route. Services may also be dropped easily — only 120 days notice is required to terminate a service. Similarly, approval of fares virtually disappears on domestic routes with the sole caveat that increases in regular fares on "monopoly routes" may be appealed.[130]

In the evolution from no competition in the 1930s to full competition in the 1980s, Air Canada has made some major adjustments. Since restrictions were lifted in the 1970s Air Canada's share of domestic passenger traffic has dropped from almost 70 per cent to a little more than 50 per cent. But as the next section reveals, the airline has managed the transition reasonably well, assisted by the moderate pace of change in Canada.

Outputs and Outcomes: Air Canada's Performance

There is probably no other industry in which corporations are compared on an international basis with such relish as the air industry. A wide variety of statistics are collected on the operations of most airlines and it is therefore possible to compare readily their relative size and economic, technical and safety performance. However, TCA/Air Canada was incorporated to achieve rather vague social or political goals related to nation building and community development — albeit efficiently and safely and at the least cost to the public purse. Therefore economic and technical efficiency, the balance sheet and safety are only part of the performance story. One must also consider the more difficult measurement of effective performance, the degree to which the corporation has achieved the wider goal package for which there are far fewer acceptable measures. Moreover, one is faced with the conundrum that the achievement of social or political goals may be at the expense of the attainment of high levels of economic and technical (but, hopefully, not safety) performance. The existing state of the performance evaluation art gives us few suggestions as to how these two issues can be disentangled. Certainly TCA/Air Canada has never been exposed to any orderly analysis of its effectiveness in relation to the widest statement of its goals. With the contemporary uncertainty concerning the definition of its goals and the pressure to revert to performance measures acceptable to the economic marketplace, it is unlikely that the airline will be subjected to such a broad based assessment in the near future.

By any objective standard of performance, Air Canada has grown over half a century of operations to become an important participant in the international and domestic air transport scene. Until 1980, the normal measures of magnitude (route miles, assets, total revenues, revenue ton miles, revenue passenger miles, and revenue passengers carried) all followed the same general upward slope of growth. Since 1980 a number of factors have combined to slow or reverse the earlier growth trends for a number of measures. The major negative factors have been deregulation, the lingering effects of the 1982-83 recession and competition on Air Canada's traditional bread-and-butter passenger routes which led to excess capacity and price cutting. On the issue of competition it is interesting to note that Air Canada's average fare per mile in 1983 was lower than the four largest, deregulated U.S. carriers: United, American, Delta and Eastern.[131] However, in spite of attractive fares, the number of passengers carried by Air Canada has been stagnant for three years and is at the same level as 1978. From a position in 1980 where it was three times as big as its closest domestic rival, CP Air, Air Canada is now less than one and a half times bigger than Canadian. On the international stage Air Canada ranks in the top fifteen airlines measured by revenue passenger kilometres, freight tonne kilometres, operating revenue and operating profit in 1986.[132]

In the area of economic performance, a number of studies have compared Air Canada's operating efficiency with that of other domestic and international airlines. In 1978, an analysis showed that Air Canada was above the median of a profile of the North American airline industry on such measures as load factor, revenue passenger miles per employee and revenue ton miles per employee.[133] A study by Jordan covering the years 1975-1978 analyzed the operations of seventeen Canadian and U.S. airlines and found that the Canadian airlines compared favourably with the U.S. federally regulated carriers and that the differences in efficiency measures between CP Air and Air Canada were not significant.[134] More recent studies by the federal Treasury Board show that by a number of measures, Air Canada's relative position declined between 1976 and 1985. Much of the deterioration in position is attributable to high growth rates of expenses, particularly in the 1981-85 period. Analysis of annual reports reveals that the most important cost factor has been the growth of "other" expenses, a category that includes costs of sales such as commissions, passenger meals and ground services which climb at a relatively fixed rate independent of the price at which seats are sold. Labour costs have stabilized after a jump resulting from the costs of early retirement and retrenchment as the airline responded to the recession. However, the Treasury Board attributes the high cost structure to low rates of labour productivity and excess capacity. Air Canada ranked last out of nineteen carriers in terms of output (revenue ton miles) per employee between 1981 and 1985.[135]

Another Treasury Board study notes that if Air Canada's productivity gains between 1979 and 1985 (again measured by revenue ton miles per employee) had matched those of CP Air, "it would have required 3600 fewer employees in 1985, thereby reducing costs by about $150 million.[136] As discussed earlier, there may be reasons other than "social" goals for retaining employees during a downturn. Aside from the incredible political furor which 3600 layoffs would cause, it may be advisable to retain skilled employees if the downturn is seen to be temporary. In fact, Air Canada did reduce its labour force in 1983 by 1700 employees (after hitting "bottom" in 1982 with a record loss of $35.6 million and operating revenues not covering operating expenses for the first time), through voluntary measures such as early retirement and work-sharing. However, as the Treasury Board report notes, over the past twenty years there has been a pattern of slow corporate response to traffic downturns. The 1983 staff cuts occurred in the third year of traffic decline.[137]

The other major cost factor identified, excess capacity, is unlikely to improve in the short run as the three national carriers fight for market share in the deregulated environment. Other studies suggest that public corporations have a propensity to overinvest in capacity due to the implicit subsidization of their costs of capital. A study for the Economic Council of Canada found that CP Air's "total factor productivity" was 23.5 per cent higher than Air Canada's in the 1964-81 period. However, when levels of capital stock were controlled for, the differences disappeared. A recent example is the loan which Air Canada obtained from a Swiss bank reportedly at a rate unmatched by any other Canadian airline.[138] Undoubtedly, Air Canada's size gives it some leverage, however, a more pivotal factor is the perception that the government is the ultimate financial backstop for the company. This view is reinforced by the history of equity injections and debt rollovers and cancellations which the federal government has provided to Air Canada and other public corporations. Even though Air Canada has had very limited recourse to the public purse (in line with C.D. Howe's dictum: 'You keep out of the taxpayer's pocket, and I'll keep out of your hair'), the airline is the "beneficiary" of the perception that governments will bail out their creations.

In the greyer area of social or political goals, the data on TCA/Air Canada's performance as an instrument of national policy are even more intuitive. When Ashley attempted to summarize the performance of TCA in 1963, he concluded that "the original intentions of the government on the formation of the corporation have been only partially fulfilled." In his view, while TCA had developed transcontinental services that "compare very favorably in efficiency and rates with those provided in other countries", he noted that the airline had not become entirely self-sufficient as intended.[139] Baldwin, twelve years later, had a somewhat more generous – if equally intuitive – view of the airline's performance in relation to its role as an instrument of nation-building and community development, although he puts a somewhat different interpretation on the nature of the goal being served. He downplayed the loss years suffered by TCA/Air Canada, focusing instead on the "degree of support" manifested for the airline as a result of its policy of providing a relatively high level of service to social routes at acceptable fare levels through the device of internal cross-subsidization. The rough measure of the success of the airline is the political support which it received from areas such as the Maritimes, northern Quebec, and the Prairies (and at a later date, from the business communities in the Ottawa-Montreal-Toronto triangle) which were beneficiaries of the wider public policy aspects of TCA/Air Canada's operation.[140] Of course, Baldwin is arguing more explicitly that the airline did not pursue the political goal because it was a fundamental aspect of its original mandate, but because the political support which the servicing of this goal engendered was essential to the survival of the airline – free from take-over and competition. Writing about the period until 1971, before some of the most significant erosion of Air Canada's monopoly and cross-subsidization positions, Baldwin viewed the public airline as having been to a large degree successful in achieving this continuing and elusive goal of survival.

The airline's efforts to maintain reasonable levels of service across a fragmented international and domestic route structure largely forced on it by the government created significant operational problems related to efficient fleet utilization, and resulted in excess capacity on short-haul routes, low load factors and consequently higher costs and higher fixed-to-total cost ratios than the industry average.[141] However, since the late 1970s Air Canada has rationalized its fleet, given up many short-haul runs, first to regional carriers and now to "alliance partners" and stopped subsidizing other short-haul routes.[142] In fact, Canadian now serves significantly more Canadian communities than Air Canada.

Measurement of performance after the passage of the *Air Canada Act* in 1978 is complicated by the continuing duality of goals. The conflict between commercial objectives and national policy goals evolved over the past decade until Air Canada's mandate clearly centred on the orientation to profit. Following deregulation and in the environment of privatization, organizational "success" is measured on the bottom line.

In the current context it is worthwhile to examine the potential gains in efficiency from transforming the airline into a privately owned corporation. A study by Gillen, Oum and Tretheway notes that public and private sector companies respond to changes in the competitive environment in very similar ways which leads the authors to conclude that ownership is less important than regulation in determining the efficiency of the public sector firm. The study predicts that U.S. style deregulation could cut labour costs by 20 per cent compared to anticipated rates under regulation and that efficiency would improve by up to 8.6 per cent across the industry. The efficiency gains for Air Canada from privatization would have been between 6.7 and 12 per cent in 1981.[143]

Conclusions and Issues for the 1990s

Air Canada's position as an instrument of public policy and the predominant Canadian air carrier has been altered significantly in the 1980s. The competitive environment has been invigorated by the deregulation of rate and route structures. On the other hand, mergers have concentrated the air industry in Canada, following trends in the U.S. and other parts of the world. As market potential in North America diminishes, airlines are looking outward. The industry is becoming globalized as airlines make marketing agreements or undertake mergers to carve up the world. In North America the anticipated ratification of the Free Trade Agreement between the United States and Canada is expected to give a boost to transborder travel and, in consequence, raises calls for a redistribution of routes among Canadian carriers. Finally, for Air Canada privatization promises new challenges as the airline achieves financial independence and tries to maintain its market lead.

While Air Canada maintains a 56 per cent hold on the domestic market, Canadian has increased its share to 39 per cent and Wardair with new services and aircraft is poised to take a major run at Air Canada.[144] Both Canadian and Wardair have strenghtened their balance sheets with share issues and asset sales in 1987. Canadian managed to lower its debt to equity ratio from 5.4:1 at the takeover in early 1987 to 2.3:1 in late 1987 and projects a ratio of 0.43:1 for 1988.[145] Wardair has its debt to equity down to 1.4:1, although it will rise to 3:1 in the next two years as the airline buys eight aircraft for $300 million in order to expand its services to seven Canadian cities west of Montreal.[146] One might suggest that Air Canada might have done more to reduce its debt in anticipation of the challenges ahead. For example, at a time when other transportation companies are shedding non-business assets (e.g., CN has sold its hotels and other subsidiaries while Allegis Corp. has sold its hotel and car rental subsidiaries), and Air Canada is beseeching government for freedom or equity, it seems incongruous that the airline is making question-able investments in courier companies.[147]

With all three major carriers making major aircraft purchases and the Canadian economy more than five and one-half years into expansion, there is a real risk that a situation like the one experienced in 1982 could develop, characterized by excess capacity and predatory price cutting. The increasing concentration in the domestic market through takeovers and agreements has produced a 96 per cent market share for Air Canada and Canadian. Wardair's efforts to crack the duopoly by going after the high yield business customer with 15 per cent discounts, plus the looming capacity problems could be very positive for travellers and very problematic for carriers, particularly Air Canada. Air Canada and Canadian also must deal with the unrecorded liability represented by their frequent flyer plans. Air Canada's Aeroplan has 325,000 members many of whom will be eligible for free flights in 1989-90. While Aeroplan protects Air Canada during the deregulation "shakeout" by providing a real barrier to new entrants and passengers only take otherwise vacant seats, it represents costs in customer service and, as the program moves towards its termination in 1990, there may be some ill-will generated if bookings become tight.

The large number of mergers induced by deregulation may be analagous to airline behavior under regulation. Research has consistently shown that there are no scale economies in airlines.[148] This suggests that the motive may be to limit the opposition. Under regulation we observed how Air Canada and CP Air tried to keep the regionals weak. In the new environment an airline weakens (or eliminates) the opposition by co-opting it. Mergers are going on in other areas too. The former PWA and Air Canada had several links including route cooperation, joint frequent flyer program and shared use of Air Canada's Reservec computer reservation system. In June 1987 Air Canada and Canadian formed a joint venture, Gemini Group, to provide reservation services to travel agents and airlines. Given the overwhelming market share controlled by Gemini and the international problem of bias in the operating programs of computer reservation systems generally, concerns have been expressed that this arrangement may serve to limit new entrants in the Canadian market. At the same time that the federal competition tribunal is examining Gemini, European airlines are consolidating their reservations into two large systems.[149]

The "globalization" of airlines may have implications for Canadian carriers. Now that the U.S. industry is consolidating around several strong airlines, (of the top 20 U.S. airlines, ranked by revenue passenger kilometers, in 1978, *not one* is untouched by mergers in 1987),[150] U.S. airlines are looking for expansion overseas. British Airways and United Airlines recently announced a cooperative agreement to represent each other in areas where they are dominant. In Europe, the head of SAS (Scandinavian Airlines) predicts that there will be just five European "mega-carriers" by 1995.[151] In this context Canada stands somewhat alone. While Canadian and Air Canada have made cooperative marketing agreements (e.g., Air Canada has agreements with Austrian Airlines, Air New Zealand and others), most countries have only one international airline. Given the dependence on bilateral treaties on routes, the presence of two (or three) airlines trying to share routes leads inevitably to problems.[152] Over the years Air Canada management has made a number of suggestions that CP Air merge with them on international services; the most recent occasion was a request to PWA at the time it took over CP Air in 1987. If the globalization process continues, the logic of dividing the world between the two Canadian airlines may become more problematic. Canadian may be more willing to participate in such a joint venture now that it is nearing the same scale of operation as Air Canada, and would be less likely to feel itself the junior partner.

There are also problems looming on the North American front with respect to bilateral air agreements. The agreement dates from 1973 and the combination of three regional airlines plus CP Air which form Canadian have only three minor and three major transborder routes. With growing traffic and the impending privatization of Air Canada, there will be increasing pressure on the federal government to reallocate the existing routes or convince the U.S. to renegotiate the treaty.[153]

The gradual approach to deregulation in Canada seems to have avoided some of the excesses of the U.S. experience. While mergers have occurred in Canada at an equally rapid rate, Canadian travellers and airline employees have been spared the experience of airlines going into voluntary bankruptcy in order to escape from labour and other contracts. This does not mean that labour relations will be tame in Canada, particularly as Air Canada is privatized. Management and administrative employees will be an early target for product improvement because of the higher than average salary bill for this group relative to other Canadian airlines.[154] The involvement of employees in the share issue may help to make any necessary downsizing easier; however, there will be real possibilities of bitter disputes if wage cuts are called for (as happened at Quebecair in the summer of 1987 and PWA when it was privatized by the Alberta Government in 1983).[155]

The mixed enterprise is a necessary and realistic first step toward full privatization which distributes the risk in an uncertain market, allows Air Canada to get its capital infusion of equity and, above all politically, allows the prime minister to be let off the hook on his 1985 statement. As the airline enters a new era there is probably more uncertainty in the environment than at any time since the mid-1970s. Privatization and deregulation offer both challenges and threats. How the government proceeds on the first and how the airline responds to the second will determine the long-term future of Canada's (for now) public airline.

Notes

1. *The Trans Canada Airlines Act*, S.C. 1937, c. 43. The name of the airline was changed by legislative amendment in 1965, see *Air Canada Act*, R.S.C. 1970, c. A-11

2. Air Canada, *Annual Report*, 1986.

3. See C.A. Ashley, *The First Twenty-Five Years: A Study of Trans-Canada Airlines* (Toronto: Macmillan, 1963), ch. 1; D.C. Corbett, *Politics and the Airlines* (Toronto: University of Toronto Press, 1965), ch. 1-3; R. Bothwell and W. Kilbourn, *C.D. Howe* (Toronto: McClelland and Stewart, 1979), ch. 8, Philip Smith, *It Seems Like Only Yesterday* (Montreal, McClelland and Stewart, 1986).

4. Corbett, *op. cit.*, p. 106.

5. *Ibid.*, p. 33.

6. *Ibid.*, pp. 35-6; see also J. Langford, *Transport in Transition* (Montreal: McGill-Queen's University Press, 1976), ch. 2.

7. Important exceptions were the many bush pilot operations in Canada involved in transportation, surveying and forest fire prevention. While pushing ahead of the government's provision of infrastructure, these frontier operations did not represent the nuclei of private inter-city services in the period prior to the establishment of TCA, see Ashley, *op. cit.*, ch. 1.

8. Bothwell and Kilbourn, *C.D. Howe*, p. 105.

9. See A. Tupper, The Nation's Business: Canadian Concepts of Public Enterprise (unpublished Ph. D. thesis, Queen's University, 1977).

10. See John R. Baldwin, *The Regulatory Agency and the Public Corporation* (Cambridge, Mass.: Ballinger, 1975), Ch. 5, and M.J. Trebilcock and J.R.S. Prichard, "Crown Corporations: The Calculus of Instrument Choice," in *Crown Corporations in Canada*, ed. by J.R.S. Prichard, (Toronto: Butterworth and Co. (Canada) Ltd., 1983), pp. 1-98.

11. Bothwell and Kilbourn, *C.D. Howe*, p. 89, and pp. 97-8.

12. See Canada, House of Commons, *Debates*, 22 March 1937, pp. 2041 ff; and 31 March 1937, pp. 2370 ff. This paradox is explored more fully in Corbett, *Politics and the Airlines*, pp. 106-114.

13. See Ashley, *The First Twenty-five Years*, p. 4, and Bothwell and Kilbourn, *C.D. Howe*, pp. 108-9.

14. *Ibid.*, pp. 106-7.

15. In the draft bill the railways would each have four representatives on the board and the Department of Transport one.

16. *TCA Act*, s. 9. The reference to potential purchasers "interested in aviation" makes it clear that the government was not interested in the prospect of a more contemporary form of "privatization" (e.g. CDC, BCRIC or the current proposal for Air Canada) whereby shares are sold or given to members of the general public.

17. In 1953, the Act was amended to allow the CNR to appoint five directors and the government four.

18. *TCA Act*, s. 14.

19.   Canada, House of Commons, *Debates*, 22 March 1937, p. 2042.

20.   *Ibid*, pp. 2042-3.

21.   Air Canada Act, 1977, S.C. 1977 78, c. 5. See also Canada, House
      of Commons, Standing Committee on Transport and Communi-
      cations, *Proceedings*, 2 December 1975, p. 17 and 15 June 1977,
      p. 7.

22.   *Air Canada Act*, s. 6.

23.   *Ibid.*, s. 7(2).

24.   Gordon R. McGregor, *The Adolescence of an Airline* (Montreal:
      Air Canada, 1980), pp. 189-191.

25.   For a discussion of the contentious language issue in aviation see
      Sandford Borins, *The Language of the Skies* (Montreal: McGill-
      Queen's University Press, 1983). While the airline might not
      have gone as far or as quickly as many people would have wished
      in promoting the use of French in operations, there is little doubt
      that Air Canada was well ahead of other transportation
      companies.

26.   A leaked internal memo from a CN Rail vice-president is
      revealing in the type of political calculations which can go into
      operating decisions — even if there is no government pressure.
      The January 1988 memo suggested the possibility of an early
      election and the difficulties this would cause for any downsizing
      program and encouraged quick implementation of any programs.
      A company spokesman said: "We have to be aware at all times of
      actions that could cause problems for anybody. We have a single
      shareholder (the government) and to the extent that it would
      cause them problems we shouldn't do that." See "CN Rail told to
      move quickly on layoffs before federal election campaign starts,"
      (Ottawa) *Citizen*, (4 February 1988), p. C13.

27.   The following potted history of TCA/Air Canada is largely drawn
      from Air Canada publications, the general sources noted in note
      3 and Statistics Canada, *Aviation in Canada, 1971* (Ottawa:
      Information Canada, 1972).

28.   Air Canada, *Air Canada: 1937-77* (Montreal: Information
      Services, Air Canada, 1977), p. 46.

29.   This issue created a serious rift in Canada-UK relations when
      the British served notice that they would cancel the bilateral

agreement allowing Air Canada to provide services to the UK. The British argued that Air Canada was taking too big a share of the London-Bombay market. A last hour agreement to expand services for the airlines of both countries was reached in September 1987. Alex Binkley, "Canada's air deal with U.K. may herald lower fares," (Ottawa) *Citizen*, (19 September 1987), pp. A1,A22.

30. The airline reported that almost 70 per cent of the increase in expenses in 1987 was attributable to newly acquired subsidiaries. Air Canada, *Annual Report*, 1987, pp. 22-23. At a time when the government is trying to make the airline attractive for privatization, it is ironic that the damage caused to the bottom line is attributable to a strike over pension indexing – an issue upon which the incoming Conservative government had promised to act.

31. Garth Stevenson, *The Politics of Canada's Airlines: From Diefenbaker to Mulroney* (Toronto: University of Toronto Press, 1987), Ch. 8 and Philip Smith, *It Seems Like Only Yesterday*, pp. 325-26.

32. Stevenson, *The Politics of Canada's Airlines*, p. 159.

33. Air Canada withdrew from this partnership in 1979.

34. See Smith, *It Seems Like Only Yesterday*, pp. 339-340 for a description of the success of the GPA investment and the serendipity which led to the investment.

35. *Ibid.*, p. 342.

36. See Baldwin, *The Regulatory Agency and the Public Corporation*, Ch. 7.

37. See K.H. Laubstein "The Necessity for Advanced Booking Charters Within Canada," in *Perspectives on Canadian Airline Regulation*, ed. by G.B. Reschenthaler and B. Roberts (Montreal: Butterworth and Co. for the Institute for Research on Public Policy, 1979), pp. 85-107.

38. By the end of 1975 fuel costs had more than doubled over the beginning of 1974.

39. Davies, in reference to Australian airlines, argues strongly that "variations in performance may be attributed ultimately to differences in entrepreneurial organization". D.G. Davies,

"Property Rights and Economic Efficiency – The Australian Airlines Revisited," *Journal of Law and Economics* 20 (1977), pp. 225.

40. See J.P. Woolsey, "Air Canada Finds Improved Efficiency Best Weapon Against Spiralling Costs," *Air Transport World*, 13 (October 1976).

41. See Ashley, *The First Twenty-Five Years*, p. 59.

42. Henry Mintzberg, J. Pierre Brunet and James A. Waters, "Does Planning Impede Strategic Thinking? Tracking the Strategies of Air Canada from 1937 to 1976," draft ms. (1986), pp. 8,13.

43. This era is well documented in Canada, *Air Canada Inquiry Report* (Ottawa: Information Canada, 1975), also called the Estey Report after the commissioner, Willard Estey. See also Smith, *It Seems Like Only Yesterday*, pp. 279-95.

44. Mintzberg, Brunet and Waters, "Does Planning Impede Strategic Thinking?" pp. 14-15.

45. Smith, *It Seems Like Only Yesterday*, p. 296.

46. See the case study by John W. Langford and Kenneth J. Huffman, "The Marketing Branch is Out of Control," in *Public Enterprise: The Management Challenge*, ed. by Colm O. Nuallain and Roger Wettenhall (Brussels: International Association of Schools and Institutes of Administration and International Institute of Administrative Sciences, 1987), pp. 131-41.

47. See David Humphreys, "Air Canada shift of little concern, Mackasey insists", *Globe and Mail*, (10 January 1979), p. 8.

48. Air Canada, *Annual Report*, 1986, p. 21.

49. Smith, *It Seems Like Only Yesterday*, p. 350.

50. *Ibid.*, p. 344.

51. See Corbett, *Politics and the Airlines*, p. 170.

52. Bothwell and Kilbourn, *C.D. Howe*, pp. 109-110.

53. See *Air Canada Inquiry Report*, Chs. 5 and 13.

54. *Air Canada Act*, 1977, s. 7. Both the President and Chairman are to be members of the Board under the Act.

55. "Flying high on the Tory patronage broom," *Financial Post*, (30 March 1985), p. 11.

56. See *TCA Act*, ss. 15-17. The evolution of these contracts is more fully discussed in Corbett, *Politics and the Airlines*, Ch. 6, and forms the basis of the following account of the evolution of the government's powers up to 1963.

57. *An Act to Amend the Trans Canada Airlines Act*, S.C. 1938, c. 15, s. 2.

58. *An Act to Amend the Trans-Canada Airlines Act*, S.C. 1945, c. 31, s. 7.

59. *Ibid.*, s. 10.

60. *An Act to Amend the Trans-Canada Airlines Act*, S.C. 1952-53, c. 50, s. 7.

61. Corbett, *Politics and the Airlines*, p. 179.

62. See Stevenson for a discussion of inconsistencies in policy arising from appeals to the Cabinet, for example, the Cabinet decision to allow CP Air to compete on trans-continental routes which was effectively upset when the Air Transport Board decision which implemented the policy was overturned. Stevenson, *The Politics of Canada's Airlines*, pp. 142-48.

63. *TCA Act*, 1937, s. 13 and s. 15(f). The power to name the auditor was transferred nominally to Parliament in 1953.

64. *An Act to Amend the Trans Canada Airlines Act*, S.C. 1945, s. 10.

65. Financial Administration Act, R.S.C. 1970, c. F-10, s. 70. This aspect of the government's direct management power – combined with its critical role as a major creditor – has never been adequately documented. For a hint of the government's power see *Air Canada Inquiry Report*, p. 271.

66. Data on the losing or "social" routes are available in Baldwin, *The Regulatory Agency and the Public Corporation*, Chs. 6 and 9. Hard evidence on the degree of government "coercion" in any particular instance is lacking. See Ashley, *The First Twenty-Five Years*, p. 62. In the case of the route extension to Trois Rivières, Gordon McGregor hoped for some sort of "reciprocal understanding" from the government. See Smith, *It Seems Like Only Yesterday*, pp. 224-25.

67. Baldwin, *The Regulatory Agency and the Public Corporation*, Ch. 6.

68. Without citing specific examples Gillen, Oum and Tretheway state that, even after the implementation of the 1978 legislation, Air Canada was "pressured directly and indirectly to maintain jet service to some points perceived to be uneconomic." David W. Gillen, Tae H. Oum and Michael W. Tretheway, "Identifying and Measuring the Impact of Government Ownership and Regulation on Airline Performance," Discussion Paper No. 326 (Ottawa: Economic Council of Canada, 1987), p. 75.

69. Corbett, *Politics and the Airlines*, p. 283. Baldwin supports Corbett's intuitive argument on the basis of his model of public corporation behaviour, noting that "the public firm . . . is likely to find the benefits from patronizing Canadian industry far less than the benefits of being able to expand services when the most efficient aircraft is adopted. Unless the benefits of choosing less efficient aircraft are suddenly increased (via direct government order), efficient equipment will be chosen". Baldwin, *The Regulatory Agency and the Public Corporation*, p. 117.

70. Bothwell and Kilbourn, *C.D. Howe*, p. 109.

71. Baldwin, *The Regulatory Agency and the Public Corporation*, p. 110.

72. Corbett, *Politics and the Airlines*, p. 170.

73. Baldwin, *The Regulatory Agency and the Public Corporation* p. 115.

74. On the DC-9 decision, see McGregor, *Adolescence of an Airline*, pp. 134-137. The decision on the B-767 was delayed at the request of the cabinet which appointed a committee of senior officials to review Air Canada's decision. Tensions were heightened by the support of the new chairman, the very "political" Bryce Mackasey, for the European Airbus A-310 and the fundamental disagreement between the airline's chairman and president over the interpretation of the government's power under the 1978 Act to give "directions of a general nature". The issue was resolved when the government changed and the new minister expressed confidence in Air Canada making a "sound commercial decision" and the review committee reported favourably on the B-767. See Smith, *It Seems Like Only Yesterday*, pp. 328-33.

75. The choice of the Airbus was seen as a threat to the continued existence of maintenance facilities for the B-727 in Winnipeg. Canadair Ltd. of Montreal was proposed as a major sub-contractor on the Airbus which would give it a significant advantage in bidding for the maintenance contract. Geoffrey York, "Secret Air Canada embarrassing for Manitoba PCs," *Globe and Mail*, (25 April 1988), p. A5.

76. Interview, Transport Canada official. See also Stevenson, *The Politics of Canada's Airlines*, pp. 129-135.

77. C.A. Ashley and R.G.H. Smails, *Canadian Crown Corporations: Some Aspects of their Administration and Control* (Toronto: Macmillan, 1965), pp. 320-23. The facility was, in the event, sold to CAE Industries Ltd. in 1969.

78. Baldwin, *The Regulatory Agency and the Public Corporation*, pp. 116-7.

79. The guarantee also ensured the preservation of maintenance facilities in Montreal and Toronto. Canada, *An Act to provide for the continuance of Air Canada under the Canada Business Corporations Act and for the issuance and sale of shares thereof to the public*, s. 6(1)(c) and s. 7(b). (Legislation henceforth cited as Bill C-129.)

80. Ralph F. Harris, "The Regulation of Air Transportation," in *The Regulatory Process in Canada*, ed. by G. Bruce Doern (Toronto: Macmillan, 1978), p. 224. The airline was also expected to be a "model" corporation in other areas; for example, in 1980 the government prevented the airline from distributing bonuses to employees in order to further its anti-inflation goals. See Gillen, Oum and Tretheway, "Identifying and Measuring the Impact of Government Ownership and Regulation on Airline Performance," p. 76.

81. Air Canada, *Annual Report*, 1979, p. 16.

82. *Air Canada Act*, 1977, S.C. 1977-8, c. 5.

83. *Ibid.*, ss. 8 and 9.

84. *Ibid.*, s. 15.

85. "*An act to amend the Financial Administration Act in relation to Crown Corporations and to amend other Acts in consequence*

thereof," passed as Bill C-24 by the House of Commons 28 June 1984.

86. See Canada, Royal Commission on Financial Management and Accountability, *Final Report* (Ottawa, Minister of Supply and Services Canada, 1979), Ch. 19; and John W. Langford, "Crown Corporations as Instruments of Policy," in *Public Policy in Canada: Organization, Process and Management,* ed. by G. Bruce Doern and Peter Aucoin (Toronto: Macmillan, 1979), Ch. 9.

87. The links to CN continued until 1981 when Air Canada finally established its own medical department to conduct physicals on pilots and other employees. Smith, *It Seems Like Only Yesterday,* p. 172.

88. Canada, House of Commons, *Debates,* 12 April 1988, pp. 14362-63.

89. For discussion of these rationales see John W. Langford, "Privatization: A Political Analysis" and John Baldwin, "The Privatization of Air Canada," in *Papers on Privatization,* ed. by W.T. Stanbury and Tom Kierans (Montreal: Institute for Research on Public Policy, 1985).

90. Minister of State (Privatization) and Minister responsible for Regulatory Affairs, "Statements Made by the Honourable Barbara McDougall on the Reasons for Privatization", 1 May 1987. The reasons given are: changing economic environment, effectiveness, public funds, management styles, and fairness and equity.

91. See W. T. Stanbury, "Privatization in Canada: Ideology, Symbolism or Substance," draft paper prepared for the Conference "Privatization in Britain and North America: Theory, Evidence and Implementation," sponsored by the Bradley Research Center, University of Rochester, held in Washington, D.C., 6-7 November 1987, sec. 9, pp. 3-4.

92. Lawrence Martin, "PM says CBC, Air Canada not for sale," *Globe and Mail,* (15 January 1985), pp. A1-A2. Most papers, with the exception of the Montreal *Gazette* and *La Presse,* failed to report another statement by the prime minister that he did not rule out selling a minority interest. Other chronological material in this section is from W.T. Stanbury, "The Struggle to

Privatize Air Canada," in *Reducing the State: Privatization in Canada* (forthcoming 1988), Ch. 8.

93. "Public split over Air Canada sale, poll shows," *Toronto Star*, (12 March 1987), p. A2. It is worth noting that twice as many people favoured the privatization of Air Canada as supported the prime minister's leadership.

94. Cecil Foster, "Air Canada sale won't fly," *Globe and Mail*, (22 August 1987), p. B1.

95. The exposure of Canadian brokerage houses in the sale of British Petroleum shares resulted in the embarrassing spectacle of the brokers convincing the federal minister of finance to plead their case before the British chancellor of the exchequer.

96. For statements of Air Canada management on these issues see "Air Canada chairman urges quick privatization of airline," *Globe and Mail*, (13 January 1987), p.B1 and "Federal government urged to meet capital needs of Air Canada," (Ottawa) *Citizen*, (24 December 1986). The latter article was the first statement by Air Canada that the government needed to choose between new equity or private participation if "good service" was to be maintained.

97. Economic Council of Canada, *Minding the Public's Business* (Ottawa: Supply and Services Canada, 1986), p.66.

98. G. Bruce Doern and John Atherton, "The Tories and the Crowns: Restraining and Privatizing in a Political Minefield," in *How Ottawa Spends, 1987-88: Restraining the State*, ed. by Michael J. Prince (Toronto: Methuen, 1987), p.130.

99. Bill C-129, s. 10.

100. John R. Baldwin, "The Privatization of Air Canada," in *Papers on Privatization*, ed. by Stanbury and Kierans, pp.145-146.

101. The federal government has used similar instruments to subsidize ferry services and other transportation links in eastern Canada, primarily through CN Railways.

102. Air Canada commissioned polls showed 75-90 per cent favourable to share offerings, James Bagnall, "Air Canada may get cut if share-issue proceeds," *Financial Post*, (13 July 1987), p. 3. This approach seems to have succeeded, in political terms, as opinion polls which indicated 35 per cent favourable in February

1988 have been transformed to a majority of 60 percent favourable in April, with even NDP supporters showing significant levels of support (49 per cent). Juliet O'Neill, "Six in 10 support partial Air Canada selloff: poll," (Ottawa) *Citizen*, (23 April 1900), p. A01.

103. "Bear market could hurt TCPL's $250 million issue," (Ottawa) *Citizen*, (9 February 1988), p. B6. Only two major issues had gone to Canadian equity markets between October 1987 and February 1988.

104. See *Globe and Mail*, (13 June 1984), p. B2 and "Federal gov't urged to meet capital needs of Air Canada," (Ottawa) *Citizen*, (24 December 1986).

105. Baldwin, "The Privatization of Air Canada," p. 162. See also Economic Council, *Minding the Public's Business*, p. 85.

106. Economic Council of Canada, *Minding the Public's Business*, p. 66.

107. Bruce Little, "Auditor General urges MP input on Crown asset deals," *Globe and Mail*, (30 October 1985), p. A8.

108. Stephen Brooks, *Who's in Charge? The Mixed Ownership Corporation in Canada* (Halifax: Institute for Research on Public Policy, 1987), pp. 110-111.

109. Bill C-129, s. 6. Section 7 of the bill prohibits future amendments to the airline's articles of incorporation or bylaws which are inconsistent with the conditions imposed in section 6.

110. Excluding the sale of the investment in the CDC, the total book value of the assets sold to the end of 1987 was $2.1 billion. Air Canada's assets are $3.1 billion. See Stanbury, "Privatization in Canada," sec. 2, p. 5.

111. Roger Buckland, "The costs and returns of the privatization of nationalized industries," *Public Administration*, 65 (Autumn 1987), p. 255. The first day gains on the six big British privatizations averaged 60 per cent, "British Petroleum: For Pete's sake," *The Economist*, (24 October 1987), p. 80.

112. W.L. Mackenzie King in Canada, House of Commons, *Debates*, 2 April 1943, as quoted in Harris, "The Regulation of Air Transportation," p. 221.

113. See the detailed account of the new initiatives based on the Wheatcroft Report in Corbett, *Politics and the Airlines*, pp. 172-77.

114. R. Harris, "The Regulation of Air Transportation," p. 225.

115. See Corbett, *Politics and the Airlines*, pp. 175-177.

116. Baldwin, *The Regulatory Agency and the Public Corporation*, Ch. 9.

117. *Ibid.*, Ch. 11 and D.W. Gillen, "Bill C-13: The New Air Canada Act," in *Perspectives on Canadian Airline Regulation*, p. 195.

118. See the number of excellent essays on this subject in *Perspectives on Canadian Airline Regulation*.

119. Wardair, the most important charter operator, was allowed entry to the domestic charter market by a further cabinet intervention just prior to the demise of the Clark Government. See Stevenson, *The Politics of Canada's Airlines*, Ch. 3.

120. For a fuller account of the regulatory process see Lucinda Vandervort, *Political Control of Independent Administrative Agencies*, Study Paper prepared for the Law Reform Commission of Canada (Ottawa, Minister of Supply and Services Canada, 1979), pp. 79-90.

121. Stevenson, *The Politics of Canada's Airlines*, pp. 132,136.

122. *Ibid.*, p. 169.

123. See Vandervort, *Political Control of Independent Administrative Agencies*, p. 90.

124. Transport Canada, Information Release, 27 June 1980 and Stevenson, *The Politics of Canada's Airlines*, pp. 142-144.

125. See Stevenson, *The Politics of Canada's Airlines*, chs. 7 and 8 for a discussion of the role of the Air Transport Committee of the CTC.

126. G.B. Reschenthaler and W.T. Stanbury, "Deregulating Canada's Airlines: Grounded by False Assumptions," *Canadian Public Policy*, 9 (June 1983), pp. 214-215.

127. *Ibid.*, p. 219.

128. See John Christopher, "Domestic Airline Policy in Canada," Current Issue Review No. 82-14E (Ottawa: Library of Parliament, April 1982, revised March 1987) and Gillen, Oum and Tretheway, "Identifying and Measuring the Impact of Government Ownership and Regulation on Airline Performance", pp. 19-20.

129. Transport Canada, *Freedom to Move: A Framework for Transportation Reform* (Ottawa: Supply and Services Canada, 1985), p. 4.

130. "Freedom to Move in Canada's new transportation environment," (Ottawa: Supply and Services Canada, 1988).

131. Vladimir S. Slivitzky, "Air Canada and Airline Regulation," Working Paper No. 1984-35 (Montreal: McGill University Centre for the Study of Regulated Industries, 1984), p.5.

132. Calculated from "World airline statistics – 1986" and "The world's top 25 airlines in 1986", *Air Transport World*, (June 1987) pp. 58-59, 68-71.

133. Derived from "Interavia's Review of World Airlines," *Interavia*, 34 (November 1979), pp. 1055-59.

134. W.A. Jordan, *Performance of Regulated Canadian Airlines in Domestic and Transborder Operations* (Ottawa: Ministry of Consumer and Corporate Affairs, 1982).

135. Treasury Board, "A Study of Air Canada's Operating Performance," (1986).

136. Treasury Board, "Airline Cost Comparison," (1986).

137. Treasury Board memo, "Air Canada Management," (1986), p. 1.

138. Gillen, Oum and Tretheway, "Identifying and Measuring the Impact of Government Ownership and Regulation on Airline Performance", pp. 74,78-79. The Swiss loan is in "perpetual bonds" which the airline chooses to exclude from long-term debt because they are not payable except upon break-up of the corporation. Air Canada also does not account for changes in value of this debt due to currency fluctuations, carrying the item on the balance sheet at historic cost. In the two years that the bonds have been held, the Canadian dollar has lost about one-third against the Swiss franc; thus, any notion of a "low rate" is illusory, in the short run.

139. Ashley, *The First Twenty-Five Years*, p. 56.

140. Baldwin, *The Regulatory Agency and the Public Corporation*, pp. 104-105.

141. See Gillen, "Bill C-3: The New Air Canada Act," pp. 194-95.

142. Reschenthaler and Stanbury, "Deregulating Canada's Airlines," p. 216. Jordan suggests that in the late 1970s international routes were being cross-subsidized at the expense of domestic. If this is still the case it gives added weight to the arguments in favour of privatization. Wm. A. Jordan, "Canadian Airline Performance Under Regulation," Working Paper No. 29 (Ottawa: Economic Council of Canada, March 1982), Ch. 13.

143. Gillen, Oum and Tretheway, "Identifying and Measuring the Impact of Government Ownership and Regulation on Airline Performance," pp. xix,127-129. The authors note that the increasing market orientation of Air Canada since 1981 means that the gains would be lower, possibly below 6.7 per cent. The earlier study by Jordan, "Canadian Airline Performance Under Regulation", p. 187 found that "factors other than ownership account for the variations in operating expenses per RTM among the federally-regulated airlines."

144. Carey French, "The Sky's the Limit," *Report on Business Magazine*, (August 1987), p. 20.

145. Cecil Foster, "CAIL to buy new aircraft for $2 billion over five years," *Globe and Mail*, (15 March 1988), p. B1-B2.

146. Cecil Foster, "Wardair will buy planes but keep cash balances high," *Globe and Mail*, (12 April 1988), p. B8.

147. Acquisitions in 1987 totalled $157 million, of which the courier companies accounted for about half. The takeover of Gelco Express has led to a dispute over the value of the assets. Air Canada, *Annual Report 1987*.

148. Jordan, "Canadian Airline Peformance Under Regulation," p. 166.

149. Cecil Foster, "Combatants in reservations system fight lining up supporters to go to Ottawa," *Globe and Mail*, (16 March 1988), p. B8 and "European airlines expand booking system," *Globe and Mail*, (14 August 1987), p. B19. See also Bron Rek, "Computer

reservations controversy spreads," *Interavia*, 42 (August 1987), pp. 819-820.

150. Calculated from *Air Transport World*, (June 1987), p 64

151. Heini Nuutinen, "BA/BCal Merger: On the horns of a dilemma," *The Avmark Aviation Economist*, 4 (August 1987), p. 3.

152. Gordon McGregor, *The Adolescence of an Airline*, pp. 239-40, describes some "inept" negotiations in the 1950s when Canadian negotiators obtained a fifth freedom right to go on from Paris to Rome which could not be exercised because TCA served Paris and CPA served Rome.

153. "Rival says deal with U.S. keeps Air Canada on top," (Ottawa) *Citizen*, (6 May 1988), p. D7.

154. Treasury Board, "A Study of Air Canada's Operating Perform-ance," Table 5.26.

155. See Val Udcarhely, "Why should the public buy shares in some-thing it already owns?" *Globe and Mail*, (14 April 1988), p. A7.

Chapter IV

Petro-Canada

Larry Pratt*

This chapter analyses the origins and twelve-year development of Canada's national petroleum company, Petro-Canada. This Crown corporation, which did not exist in 1973 when the first energy crisis erupted, is now Canada's second largest oil and gas company (behind only Exxon-controlled Imperial Oil Ltd.), the only Canadian-owned enterprise operating coast-to-coast on a fully integrated basis within the petroleum industry, and Canada's eleventh largest non-financial corporation. With assets in excess of $8 billion, annual revenues of more than $5 billion, the industry's strongest landholding position, and more than 20 per cent of Canada's refining capacity and gasoline retailing, Petro-Canada now occupies a strategic position as one of four dominant companies, or integrated 'majors', that lead the Canadian petroleum and natural gas industries at the close of the 1980s. Controlled by a small group of senior corporate officers, it carries on two principal activities: upstream, the exploration for and the production of hydrocarbons, through its Petro-Canada Resources Division; and downstream, the refining and marketing of petroleum

*   I wish to thank Liz Alexander and Elaine Frank for their help with research on Petro-Canada; Allan Tupper, Alain Noel, and Tricia Smith provided much-needed criticism and advice. I am very grateful to Ruth Koenig for her excellent assistance in producing this article.

products, through its Petro-Canada Products Division. Petro-Canada was established in 1975 as a proprietary Crown corporation and it remains under the exclusive ownership of the Canadian government, notwithstanding the efforts of the company's management and of right-wing Conservatives to sell all or part of it to private investors. Partly because of the privatization issue but also because of Petro-Canada's growth and its role in the interventionist National Energy Program, the national oil company has periodically been a factor in Canadian politics.

Established, at least in part, to address some of the problems created for Canada by the oligopolistic structure of the international oil industry, Petro-Canada succeeded within a decade in becoming an oligopolist itself, its remarkable growth and vertical integration through acquisitions financed by taxpayers and legitimized by Canadian nationalists; an oligopolist, moreover, with diminishing accountability to anyone besides its own top corporate officers, particularly since its mandate was revised by the Conservatives in 1984 to emphasize commercial goals rather than public policy. This Conservative revision completed the removal of the shareholder from Petro-Canada's boardroom — at least until the next energy crisis, and possibly for good. For even without privatization, it is the company's own interests in autonomy, growth, and market share that determine Petro-Canada's corporate strategy; it has no public purpose and can no longer be understood as an instrument of national policy. Adept at manipulating nationalist distrust of multinational oil companies in its strategy of capturing a bigger share of Canada's energy market, Petro-Canada's management has successfully asserted its independence from Ottawa by becoming larger, integrated, and less financially dependent at a moment when energy supplies are in abundance and there is much less public support for government ownership of the petroleum industry. Far from being an instrument of the Canadian state operating in the energy sector, Petro-Canada under the Conservatives has become a management-controlled partner as well as rival of the few other interdependent firms that make up Canada's oil oligopoly in the late 1980s. Aside from the obvious difference that it is state-owned and the multinationals are not, the great distinction between them is that Petro-Canada is still in its first generation while the others are the by-products of the first great era of oil a century ago.

Students of public enterprise or the modern corporation are unlikely to be surprised by the fact that Petro-Canada is very large and difficult to control, though they may be impressed that this happened so quickly and with so little comment. To some extent, Petro-Canada's drive for oligopolistic status was predicted in the original version of this chapter, written in 1980-81. We analysed several influences that pointed in the direction of Petro-Canada's continued growth and concluded that "it may not be unrealistic to predict that Petro-Canada will become the dominant corporate actor in the Canadian oil and gas industries by the middle or late 1980s;" we also added the cautionary note that such dominance would give the state company a choice between its own priorities and Ottawa's conception of the national interest; and we suggested that as Petro-Canada became financially independent of the government in the mid-to-late 1980s, "Ottawa could gradually lose its effective control over Petro-Canada as an instrument of national policy."[1] That much was already clear. But what we did not predict was that Petro-Canada, together with the rest of the industry, would be confronted by 1982 with a deep recession and a growing worldwide oversupply of crude oil and other energy forms, with consequent weakness in prices throughout the decade. Nor could we foresee how Petro-Canada and its relationship with the Canadian government would be affected by changes in the world oil market, as perceptions of scarcity gave way to the realities of glut. The new, constrained economic conditions in which the international oil industry finds itself at the end of the 1980s were not part of the conventional wisdom about the future when we first analysed Petro-Canada at the beginning of the decade — our long-run expectations, as Keynes pointed out, are often based on nothing sounder than a shared delusion that an existing state of affairs will continue indefinitely.

Our purpose in this chapter is to explain Petro-Canada's origins, to review the corporation's legislative charter, and to account for its rapid growth to the present as well as its equally rapid passage from strong arm of the state to oligopolist. The focus is on the relationship between policy and commercial goals in Petro-Canada's strategy since 1976, and on how an ambitious management has been able, in part by design but also by improvising and reacting to opportunities, to build the largest Canadian-owned oil company in little more than a decade. How well have Petro-Canada's oil and gas investments served national interests? Given the aforementioned constrained economic circumstances, how has Canada's national oil company managed to survive and, indeed, expand in the 1980s? Why has the federal government encouraged the independence and commercialization of Petro-Canada, and how likely is it that the state company will be privatized? Finally, we intend to address the issue of harnessing Petro-Canada's ambition and linking it once again to the public interest. The problem here, as with so many other Crown corporations, is not so much that Petro-Canada is powerful and ambitious as it is that the government that owns it is extremely weak; there is no countervailing ambition. When legitimate government is weak, as the saying goes, it is the feudal lords who wield the real power.[2]

Part I of the chapter reconstructs the origins of Canada's national oil company. Part II examines the legislative framework of Petro-Canada and focuses on its policy mandate up to the period of the National Energy Program — roughly from 1976 to 1981. Part III examines the state company's growth and drive for managerial independence from its owner government, particularly since the mid-1980s. The conclusion argues that Petro-Canada should be kept up in the public sector rather than privatized or broken up. The powers of the government should be used to counteract, not to emasculate, Petro-Canada's ambition. The point is to reconcile the interests of the enterprise with the public interest: not profit *or* the national interest, but profit *and* the national interest.

I.   Origins: The Quest for Control

Petro-Canada is a recent addition to a now-crowded world of national oil companies, the great majority of which were established well before the onset of the energy crisis in 1973.[3]

Until 1973, Canada followed the American example, albeit with some growing reservations, of relying on the private sector to provide the country's oil and gas requirements from domestic and foreign sources, with government contributing the necessary regulatory framework, infrastructure, and fiscal regime, but moving directly into the market-place only as a last resort. North of Mexico — where the nationalization of oil occurred in the late 1930s — the North American continent was, from the days of John D. Rockefeller until the era of Sheik Yamani, an exclusive preserve of private oil.

Canadian governments, of course, have a lengthy history of direct involvement in the energy sector of the national economy. Ottawa has been active in the production and marketing of uranium, in the production of atomic energy, and in the coal industry; the provinces have been predominant in hydroelectric power. Yet until the early 1970s, both levels of the Canadian state abstained from direct participation in the oil and gas industries. There were one or two exceptions: in 1956, Ottawa agreed to invest government funds in the uneconomic section of the Trans-Canada natural gas pipeline crossing the Canadian Shield; and in the late 1960s, the federal government began investing with privately owned companies in exploration for hydrocarbons in the eastern Arctic Islands through the vehicle of Panarctic Oils. But these were classic cases of "last-resort" intervention, undertaken at the behest of private capital, and both were sharp departures from normal practice. The government-held share of Canadian oil and gas industry investment stood at less than one per cent as late as 1973.[4]

In the early 1970s, however, the world energy market and the climate of Canadian political opinion both underwent an abrupt change. Overseas, the member-states of OPEC had initiated a chain of structural alterations in the relationships between oil companies and oil-producing states; ultimately, these would radically change the entire world oil production and marketing system, leaving no country untouched by the consequences. Before the autumn of 1973, however, Canadians were less preoccupied with the changing world oil market than with the role of energy in Canadian-American relations and the relationship between energy and national economic development. After 1970, energy — especially oil and natural gas — became the focal point of a broad debate between the Liberal government of Prime Minister Pierre Trudeau and an assortment of critics. Trudeau's government was attacked for its policies relating to the conservation of non-renewable resources, the sovereignty of the Canadian North, the export of natural gas and petroleum to the United States, and the foreign ownership and control of Canadian resource industries. Much was made politically of the fact that the oil industry was dominated by the affiliates of the major American companies, and that, by Ottawa's own estimate, over 91 per cent of the assets in the oil and gas industries were under foreign control by 1973. The "Waffle" faction of the New Democratic Party (N.D.P.) proposed to halt the further sell-out of Canadian oil and gas resources by nationalizing the petroleum industry. Less radical groups, such as the Liberal-leaning Committee for an Independent Canada, argued that the alternative to such Draconian action lay in increased regulation of the industry, tax incentives promoting "Canadianization," and perhaps in limited state participation in the key energy sector. The idea of such participation would not be to displace the foreign-controlled companies, but to create a parallel Crown company that could operate alongside the private firms, particularly in sensitive regions such as the Arctic Islands or the Mackenzie Delta.

Trudeau's Liberal party narrowly escaped defeat in the 1972 federal election (the Liberals won 109 seats; the Conservatives, 107; the N.D.P., 31; and the Social Credit, 14) and managed to hold onto power only by forging a working parliamentary alliance with the N.D.P., whose leader, David Lewis, and energy spokesman, Tommy Douglas, advocated a far more interventionist role by the national government in the energy sector of the economy. When the N.D.P.'s energy policies were stripped of rhetoric, they came down to a couple of essential points: consumers must be protected from profiteering and price-gouging by the multinational oil companies, and the state must play an expanded role, not simply as a regulator but as the

dominant and controlling force within the industry. A minimal
N.D.P. agenda would thus have to include, first, government
regulation of oil and gas prices and, second, the creation of
government-owned corporations of sufficient size and power to
compete on an equal footing with the largest private firms. Such an
approach was not radically dissimilar from the policies favoured by a
growing number of influential Liberals, to whom the notion of calling
on the powers of the state to offset and balance large agglomerations
of corporate power was neither alien nor, in the context of minority
government, politically unappealing. As the N.D.P. drew closer to the
exercise of power between 1972 and 1974, the distinctions between its
own Fabian-oriented philosophy of government planning and public
ownership and the neo-Keynesian interventionism of the governing
Liberals became increasingly academic.

Significantly, one of the first initiatives of the minority Trudeau
government was to order a major review of Canadian energy policies.
The policy review, which was tabled in Parliament in June 1973, and
published in two volumes under the title *An Energy Policy for
Canada — Phase I,* was a wide-ranging effort to analyse the physical,
economic, and political determinants of Canadian energy policy. The
report raised a number of important questions about the government's
future conduct of national energy policy, including the question of
additional state participation:

> The time is shortening for government to decide whether
> there are reasons of public policy for either some additional
> participation, or quantum change in participation, in the
> development of the energy sectors of Canada. It is clear
> that enormous growth will take place in all aspects of the
> energy sector. Are additional public funds required to
> assist in the channelling of this growth, in its stimulation,
> in its sensitivity to environmental and social issues, to
> counteract foreign investment, for international relations
> purposes and for many other issues of public concern? Must
> any decision by government to participate be based solely
> on economic critieria or should government become
> involved for reasons relating to the development of the
> Canadian political community, accepting commercial
> returns of a lower scale?[5]

The specific issue of participation raised in *Phase I* — whether the
moment had arrived for Canada to establish its own state petroleum
company and, if so, whether such an entity could serve both national
interests and commercial goals — had been under official consideration
for some time. Should the Canadian government follow the lead of the

oil-producing countries and of most of the nations of Western Europe and move directly into the oil and gas sector with its own state company, using such a vehicle to capture economic rents, to control the rate of use of non-renewable resources, or to accelerate the timing of frontier exploration? Would the government's entry into a foreign-dominated industry permit Canadians to capture a larger share of the technological spin-offs, or would the high costs of such a strategy create inefficiencies in the energy sector that would have to be borne by the taxpayer? Should a national oil company be an instrument of public policy, or should it be encouraged to seek the most profitable investments and to maximize its commercial returns? Could it combine these roles and still be efficient?

It was the latter issue that preoccupied the Trudeau government in its initial deliberations, and caused it in the summer of 1973 to defer any decision on a state oil company. The Department of Energy, Mines and Resources had in 1971 commissioned the American consultants, Arthur D. Little, to prepare a study of national petroleum companies, a topic of growing interest among the department's top officials. The author of the Little study was Wilbert (Bill) Hopper, a Canadian with an energy background who had joined Arthur D. Little in 1964: Hopper was later to play a major role in designing federal energy policies from 1973 until early 1976, when he departed for Calgary as Petro-Canada's first president, later becoming its chairman. Ironically, the man who was to become the driving force behind Petro-Canada was no enthusiast of state oil companies, a number of which he had served in a consulting capacity during his years with Arthur D. Little. What he had seen had made Hopper sceptical of the idea of marrying public policy objectives and commercial interests within a single corporation. Typically, governments insisted on using their national oil companies to pursue vaguely defined political goals, and succeeded only in lowering their commercial efficiency. For example, Italy's state company, Ente Nazionale Idrocarburi (E.N.I.), had become a major force within the international oil industry through the drive of its ambitious and nationalistic founder, Enrico Mattei (of whose career Hopper has been a careful student); but the Italian government subsequently had forced E.N.I. to serve regional development goals and to locate its new refining capacity in the depressed South – a policy that reduced E.N.I.'s financial performance as well as its capacity to organize Italy's fuel market on a rational least-cost basis. While Hopper was careful to point out that such a company could not be evaluated by the same criteria used to assess private-sector oil companies, in general terms, he argued, it was most unlikely that a state oil company could achieve the efficiency of a profit-maximizing firm: it followed that any decision to establish such a vehicle should be made on other than grounds of economic efficiency.[6]

Some of Hopper's scepticism concerning the cost and efficiency of public oil companies was reflected in *An Energy Policy for Canada — Phase I*. The document was neutral on the question of whether Canada should establish such a company — ten arguments in favour, eight against were discussed — but a good deal of emphasis was given to the high costs of entering the oil industry and to the inherent problems of reconciling policy goals with commercial norms. A national petroleum company could contribute better information and knowledge to guide policy; it could improve Ottawa's capacity to collect economic rents; it could — at a cost — stimulate exploratory work in areas deemed too risky or marginal by the private sector; and it might be a useful vehicle if government-to-government arrangements increased their share of world oil trade. But assuming that the government opted for a fully integrated company operating in all phases of the industry on a nation-wide basis, the costs of such intervention, whether accomplished via acquisition or built up gradually, would be very high. If the company managed to attain a dominant role, it might attempt to use its leverage with government in such a way that public officials would place its interests above those of the government's regulatory agencies — thereby leading Ottawa into compromising conflicts of interest. The foreign-controlled integrated companies, who contributed most of Canada's high-cost exploration investments in areas such as the North or offshore, might react to the formation of a state oil company by reducing such investment, the cost of which action would have to be borne by the taxpayer. And finally, because of the diverse goals and interests it would be called upon to serve, a national oil company would almost certainly be less commercially efficient than its private-sector competitors. In all, it was a fairly convincing argument *against* a state petroleum company, and one that would be frequently made against Petro-Canada in the years ahead, but it undoubtedly reflected the cabinet's doubts on the eve of the energy crisis.

Reducing Uncertainty

In the event, this initial scepticism was rapidly overtaken in 1973 by the changing political economy of international oil. A long period of relative equilibrium in world and domestic energy matters was coming to a sudden close. Within months of the publication of *An Energy Policy for Canada — Phase I*, most of the business-as-usual assumptions underpinning federal policies had been vitiated by circumstances beyond Canadian reach, and the minority Trudeau government, driven along by events and by parliamentary pressures from the N.D.P., began dismantling the National Oil Policy through a number of *ad hoc* interventions, all of which expanded the central government's control of the energy sector.

The new federal oil management regime, involving price regulation, control over crude exports to the United States, and a contentious tax on exports, evolved in piecemeal steps as Ottawa reacted defensively to outside events. Aside from a consistent pressure to expand political and bureaucratic control over an unstable energy market, there seems to have been little grand design and much incrementalism behind federal policy. In March of 1973, the National Energy Board was empowered to begin regulating crude oil exports to the United States, such exports having increased by 83 per cent since 1970. In September, one month before the outbreak of war in the Middle East, a "voluntary" six-month freeze on domestic oil prices was announced as part of a federal anti-inflation package (though it could not have been anticipated, this was the beginning of oil price controls that are still in place). Shortly thereafter, a new federal surcharge was placed on crude oil exports. These measures, the last of which precipitated a political row with the western oil-producing provinces, were essentially consumer-oriented steps designed to protect Canadian energy users from the effects of a rapidly changing world market.

The decision-in-principle to establish a national oil company, proposed by the Minister of Energy, Mines and Resources in late October, adopted by the Liberal cabinet in November, and announced to Parliament in early December by Prime Minister Trudeau, was part of the same federal response to crisis and uncertainty: the government was attempting to tame a highly unstable energy market by extending its control over and *into* the petroleum industry. Professor Aitken's concept of "defensive expansionism"[7] — the Canadian state involving itself directly in economic development in response to threats from the external environment, typically from the United States — explains something of Ottawa's interventions in late 1973, except that in this case it was the Arab oil producers and the multinational oil companies that were deemed to be menacing Canadian security and independence. Confronted with a deteriorating international situation whose economic and political effects were unpredictable, the minority Liberal government scrapped the framework of the National Oil Policy and began to intervene in the oil market to reduce uncertainty and to increase its own control of events. The decision to establish a publicly owned oil company was only one element in this pattern of state intervention.

Of the numerous functions that a national oil company might perform, two above all preoccupied the Trudeau administration in late 1973. First, a state corporation might be required to assure the security of imported oil supplies. Second, the government's "need to know" the extent and cost of Canadian oil and gas reserves was in conflict with the normal commercial behaviour of the private oil sector; a national oil company under government control could discount the future differently and thereby satisfy the goals of public policy. Each of these requires some explanation.

In the initial stages, the oil crisis was above all one of supply. The Yom Kippur War and the ensuing Arab oil embargo brought to a boil a number of trends that had been building up steam in the world energy market over the previous two decades, and the net result was to underline the industrialized West's dependence on a non-renewable resource whose sources of supply were insecure and for which there were no short-term substitutes. The crisis involved the use of the "oil weapon" for political purposes, yet its underlying causes were technical and economic. The growth of low-cost Middle East oil in the world energy market and the decline of other fuels; the increased dependence of the United States on imported oil; the tendency after 1968 for new additions to world reserves of crude oil to lag behind annual consumption; and the low responsiveness of oil supply and demand to changes in price were among the factors that underlay OPEC's new bargaining power. What one writer has called the "first oil regime" – a regime of abundant, low-cost petroleum supplies, declining real prices related to historical costs of production, and terms of trade favouring energy consumers – was in the process of giving way to a very different regime of sharply rising marginal costs, oil prices reflecting the costs of substitutes, and terms of trade heavily favourable to producers. The basis for control of the oil industry was also changing with this historical shift: "in the first phase the control of the market is important, and in the second phase it is the control of supplies that matters."[8]

As the distribution of bargaining power among oil consumers, the international oil companies, and oil producers shifted in favour of the latter after 1970, the long-standing predominance of the large Anglo-American companies in the world petroleum trade came to an end. In several fundamental respects, the structure of the existing international oil market began to erode. First, the old system of oil concessions, inherited from an era of colonialism collapsed as the multinational companies had their networks of jointly owned producing consortia either nationalized or bought out in "participation" agreements with the governments of the producing countries; in effect, the companies lost control of the "upstream" extractive stage of the oil industry to OPEC governments. The vital function of determining the rate of development of world oil resources, heretofore performed by intercompany production-sharing arrangements, now passed into the hands of sovereign states. Second, the system of marketing crude oil, long dominated by the pools of the multinational companies, began to change with the entry of the OPEC national companies into international petroleum trading and the growth of bilateral state-to-state arrangements. Third, control of world oil prices passed from the companies to producing governments determined to set prices that would preserve the real purchasing power of oil revenues, encourage efficient intertemporal use of scarce resources, reflect the non-substitutable or "noble" use of petroleum in certain sectors, and also reflect the marginal costs of producing substitutes such as synthetic oil from tar sands.

For a nation such as Canada, which depended on the local affiliates of the global companies to assure the reliability of its imported oil supplies, these changes in the world market were bound to be disturbing. In 1973, Canada imported about 750,000 barrels of oil per day, or close to 50 per cent of its daily consumption, albeit these were still more than offset by its exports of oil to the United States. As a (temporary) net exporter of oil, Canada was in a far better position than most of the advanced capitalist states to manage the economic effects of the crisis – indeed, it stood to be a net beneficiary on a short-term basis – but the provinces east of the Ottawa Valley Line were in a position of acute vulnerability. With between 70 and 84 per cent of the region's energy requirements supplied by overseas oil, eastern Canada's exposure to interruptions in the world market was bound to preoccupy the federal government – especially a minority government whose precarious hold on office added a certain immediacy to its perceptions of the energy crisis.

Although Canada had not been directly embargoed by the Arab exporters in October 1973, the national government was pessimistic concerning the long-term reliability of imported oil. Canada was certain to be affected by cut-backs in world oil production, and by late November, the government was making contingency plans for the loss of 20 per cent of oil imports. The security of the foreign-sourced oil supplying the eastern Canadian market was subject to a number of influences over which the government had little political control: the distribution policies of the international companies, the non-arm's length arrangements between these companies and their Canadian subsidiaries, the relations of the companies and the OPEC suppliers, and the susceptibility of the companies to powerful pressures from "home market governments" such as the United States. Ottawa suspected that the Canadian-based affiliates of the majors lacked the autonomy and bargaining power to assure the continuity of supply in the event of a serious shortfall in world supplies. International supply was also likely to be constrained by political decisions of the OPEC states affecting the rate of expansion of production and by the increasing shift away from an open market in petroleum. The growing "bilateralization" of the world oil trade via government-to-government sales was a source of special concern, since it was not clear that such arrangements improved the security of offshore oil supplies.

Security of supply concerns, not price, dominated political debates over Canadian energy policy in late 1973. The N.D.P. energy critics attacked the National Oil Policy as "archaic" and demanded new steps to protect the eastern Canadian market. Replying in emergency debate in the House of Commons on 25 October to an N.D.P. motion urging the establishment of a national oil company and other measures "to ensure a continuity of supply at fair and just prices to all Canadian consumers," the Minister of Energy, Mines and Resources, Donald S. Macdonald, remarked that "we are at the moment in the process of changing from the oil structure we had known before, not only nationally but internationally." Macdonald, recently returned to Ottawa from bilateral oil talks in Caracas, noted that Venezuela, Canada's traditional offshore supplier, was "interested in negotiating a long-term contract, but indicated that the primary vehicle for this purpose should be a national government entity rather than an affiliate or affiliates of various corporations in Canada." The government was not yet decided on the proposal, but Macdonald, who implied strong personal preference for a state oil firm in this debate, saw such intervention as a hedge against uncertainty as well as a way of gaining "increased leverage" over an unstable market. "I think the real question to be decided in our mind," he added, "is whether we need to put the national corporation to work at all the levels of the highly vertically integrated industry, or whether there are some levels . . . in which a national corporation could operate most effectively."[9]

Autarky and the "Need to Know"

Security of supply considerations also led the government's energy planners to the early conclusion that Canada required a higher level of self-sufficiency in energy supply. This decision was reached in the opening days of the Arab oil embargo, and it marked a further departure from the international/continentalist framework of the National Oil Policy. Henceforward, the direction of Canadian energy policy was to be decidedly autarkic — Canadian energy requirements should be met through the exploitation of indigenous resources. That this might be a costly policy goal ripe with potential for the inefficient allocation of resources did not, of course, discourage its prompt acceptance by all the national political parties: the appeal of self-sufficiency lay mainly in its perceived *political* advantages, not in the dubious economics of "home production." Macdonald and his advisers, for example, advocated a higher level of self-sufficiency because they gave high priority to the goal of increasing the state's control over the supply of energy to Canadian users. A heavier reliance on indigenous energy resources would reduce Canadian dependence on OPEC suppliers and corporate intermediaries, thereby permitting the national government to expand its own control over the vital energy sector, and particularly over the petroleum industry. Such control was deemed essential if Ottawa hoped to reduce the political costs of dependence on foreign oil; or if it wished to support new energy-intensive industries with the assurance of supply; or if it wanted to regulate domestic energy prices beneath world levels. Little attempt was made to weigh these against the costs of an autarkic, dirigistic policy.

Governments in many jurisdictions have found the international oil industry exceedingly difficult to control. Even today, when the world oil market is increasingly subject to the decisions of states and their national oil companies, the largest multinational firms continue to hold a number of advantages that translate into bargaining leverage. The highly capital-intensive nature of the petroleum industry, its above-average levels of profitability, and the technical barriers to entry into the oil sector have continued — despite government intervention — to promote concentration and vertical integration, rendering the industry surprisingly resistant to outside interference. Not even the governments of the most powerful industrial countries — the United States, Japan, France, Britain, Italy — have felt able to exercise effective control over the international companies. (One reason why the British government created the British National Oil Corporation in 1975 was that it had been unable to exercise effective control over British Petroleum, a company partially owned by the British state since 1913).

The oil industry's world-wide political leverage has derived, in part, from its exclusive control of critical information and data concerning petroleum reserves, costs, and so on. In the early 1970s, the Canadian government's heavy reliance on information reflecting the corporate objectives of the American oil industry was notorious, and by late 1973, the government's energy advisers were pressing for the establishment of a state oil company as a way of slaking their thirst for better information. Canada's "most apparent need at the moment" was for a better and more complete assessment of its energy resources, particularly its recoverable oil and gas reserves. The capacity to manage these resources was "critically dependent" upon knowledge of their extent and the timing and cost at which they would become available to the market. The definition of Canadian energy resources was important (1) to assure adequate supplies for Canadian requirements; (2) to permit the development of policies concerning the rate of use of Canadian resources for domestic and export markets; and (3) to establish appropriate policies for the collection of economic rents. The major areas of uncertainty affecting policy included the real costs of extracting and upgrading oil from the tar sands and heavy oil deposits of Alberta and Saskatchewan, the extent and cost of recoverable oil and gas reserves in northern Canada and in the offshore areas, the cost and lead times of proposed transportation systems to connect frontier resources to markets, and the degree to which technological constraints might impede a policy of self-sufficiency.

These uncertainties created a "need to know," which, it was argued, could not be satisfied through an exclusive reliance on market forces. Government placed a higher value on acquiring information about energy stocks than the private sector could be expected to do. Operating under standard commercial norms, the petroleum industry would be unwilling to invest heavily in high-risk frontier exploration or the development of new extractive techniques in the tar sands unless assurances were given that discoveries, once made, could be quickly brought into production; and such assurances typically implied a willingness to permit large new exports. Ottawa was under constant pressure in the early 1970s from oil and gas producers to guarantee the rapid exploitation and export of any commercial discoveries that might be made in frontier regions. This commercial link between privately determined exploration rates and development pressures (described by federal officials as "the exploration-production nexus") created a difficult policy dilemma for a government interested in speeding up the pace of exploration while simultaneously restricting production. Left entirely to market forces, exploration rates and investments in new tar sands technologies were likely to be less than socially optimal, while the rate of development of Canadian resources might be faster than national interest would dictate. Cabinet was, however, given no empirical studies to support this claim.

To redress this market bias — that is, high private-sector discount rates resulting in an under investment of resources in those areas where the "need to know" was greatest — the Trudeau cabinet concluded in November 1973 that supplementary public investment via a state oil company was necessary. The Liberals never seriously entertained the idea of setting up, or acquiring, a fully integrated Crown corporation operating in all phases of the industry on a national basis — as assumed in the *Phase I* policy review: this was then regarded as prohibitively expensive and redundant. While the option of moving later into refining and marketing was not ruled out, the corporation sketched out by Liberal energy advisers in late 1973 was not intended to displace the private oil sector. Nor was its principal objective to "Canadianize" the oil industry. Its main function would not be that of a rent collector, since to be an efficient rent collector it would have to hold a monopolistic position in the industry—and this had been rejected. Rather, its initial mandate would be to pursue self-sufficiency by accelerating the *timing* of high-risk exploration and development; by supplementing the market-generated rate of frontier exploration and by encouraging joint ventures with private capital, the national oil company would attempt to redress the problem of underinvestment caused by the excessive discount rates of the petroleum industry. Because a Crown corporation could afford to use a lower rate of discount than a private enterprise, its investments in exploration and research could be undertaken without a commitment to the early production of discovered reserves. By thus severing the commercial link between exploration and production, it was hoped to increase the domestic reserves-to-production ratio, giving Canada an increased capacity to withstand a shortfall in world oil supply.

Bureaucratic and Parliamentary Politics

In light of all this, it would be plausible to interpret the Liberal decision to establish a state oil company as merely another policy undertaken by government to subsidize the risks and costs of private captial. We shall see, when we review Petro-Canada's pattern of expenditures and its heavy emphasis on high-risk frontier exploration, that this interpretation contains an element of truth. But it is only a partial explanation because it ignores the largely autonomous forces of bureaucratic politics and parliamentary coalition building which shaped the energy policies of the Trudeau government in 1973 and after; and on a more fundamental level, it seriously exaggerates the extent to which the state's behaviour can be reduced to the interests of a single class, let alone to the preferences of particular business groups. For one thing, it is rather difficult to divine the preferences of Canadian business toward a state oil company. The oil industry was, at best, unenthusiastic about the idea, some segments of the industry bitterly opposed it, and all oil spokesmen attacked the notion of giving such a company preferential rights—this in spite of government assurances that the private oil sector stood to gain, and that, as Petro-Canada's first chairman later pointed out, Canada's national oil company "was created as an alternative to nationalization rather than as an instrument of nationalization."[10] One must of course distinguish between the objective interests of a class and the ideological representation of those interests by particular groups within that class; yet even after making due allowance for ideology and granting the state enough autonomy and foresight to be able to serve the interests of a "class against itself," the idea that Petro-Canada was established simply to subsidize the oil industry is nonsense. More credibly, the decision to create a state oil company can be seen as a step to protect the interests of oil-dependent manufacturers and other industries concerned over the security of their fuel supplies. But it must also be interpreted, first, as a strategy by bureaucratic actors to extend their control over the energy sector and to expand their departmental influence and, second, as a political decision timed by a minority government to shore up its hold on office.

The federal Department of Energy, Mines and Resources (E.M.R.) seems to have viewed the 1973 energy crisis as both a difficult challenge and an opportunity to expand its own influence and jurisdiction. The crisis had opened the door for the national government to increase its control over the energy industries; if Ottawa failed to act, the provinces would quickly assert their constitutional prerogatives and occupy the vacuum. Department officials, aware of the need to co-ordinate federal energy initiatives, recommended the creation of a national *energy* company to oversee the activities of a number of Crown-owned interests and producers, such as Dominion Coal Blocks and Eldorado Nuclear: the proposed national petroleum company would be established as an operating subsidiary of the national energy company, and both would be accountable to the minister. The Trudeau cabinet turned down this broad proposal, but it agreed to give the state oil company a wide-ranging mandate (discussed in Section II).

Had the government merely wished to set up a "last-resort" vehicle with the task of subsidizing exploration risks, it could have done so without creating a new Crown corporation. But Macdonald and his advisers saw the state company beginning with a limited role and resources, and expanding in size and influence as the years wore on. Once it became a significant player, it would strengthen Ottawa's capacity to manage Canadian energy resources, and particularly to control rates of exploration and development and the timing and extent of energy-related capital investments. Summing up his case for "a new agency of government" in his submission to cabinet in late October 1973, Macdonald outlined an ambitious set of functions for the proposed national petroleum company:

> It would explore in Canada's frontier areas for various energy resources; research the problems of tar sands and heavy oil development and perhaps into further uses of petroleum; acquire existing production capacity that comes available; seek to establish reliable import supply links; and potentially enter the downstream activities of refining

and distribution. In doing this it would enhance the degree
of governmental control over the rate and pattern of the
development of Canadian energy resources; back up the
revision of other policies such as land tenure and rent
collection by giving the government the operating capacity
to fill any undesirable gaps, take direct steps to improve the
security of the supply of energy to Canadian markets;
provide a more significant Canadian presence in a foreign-
dominated industry; co-ordinate the diverse operational
activities of the federal government in the various energy
industries, and provide an instrument through which the
government might participate with provinces, foreign
governments and private sector firms in direct energy
industry activities in stimulating further developments.

These functions require a separate body — and one
which can adapt readily to the commercial and industrial
environment in which it would operate. In fact, the foreign
governments with which discussions would be sought would
prefer to deal with a publicly-owned company. It is for
these reasons that a corporate form is suggested.[11]

In addition to extending Ottawa's control over the energy
industries, the new state company would increase E.M.R.'s authority
in the vast federal territories north of the 60th parallel — an area run
like a colony by a paternalistic Department of Indian Affairs and
Northern Development (D.I.A.N.D.). Bureaucratic resistance to
E.M.R.'s empire-building quickly developed. Macdonald and his
advisers were openly critical of the existing northern oil and gas
regulations — which were administered by D.I.A.N.D. — and argued
that as part of the overhaul of the land tenure system in the North, the
new Crown oil company must be given preferential rights to federal
lands. All unallocated or surrendered Crown reserves in the North
and offshore could, for example, be offered to the state company for
first refusal in order to accelerate exploratory work and to force the
large private oil companies either to work their lands or give them up.
Never a foe of the oil industry, D.I.A.N.D. viewed this proposal with
alarm: the effect on petroleum investments in the North would be
drastic. Even worse, the national oil company and E.M.R. would, in
effect, take over control of the resource. Once the company had built
up a position, it would be difficult for D.I.A.N.D. to control the
management of northern oil and gas resources.

Parliamentary politics, always a factor in the decisions of a
minority government, also played some part in the Trudeau
government's policy toward a state oil company: in explanations of
government behaviour, the priority of retaining power should never

be underestimated, but in this case, the threat of parliamentary defeat seems, at most, to have reinforced a decision already taken for other reasons.

In early December 1973, the N.D.P. caucus threatened to defeat the Liberals unless the cabinet agreed to make certain specific commitments on energy issues: the list included a single oil price for all Canadian consumers, the creation of a national oil company, the guaranteed extension of the Interprovincial oil pipeline into the Montreal area, and accelerated exploitation of the Alberta tar sands. The Liberals had already implemented, or publicly discussed, all of these – the cabinet had discussed and approved in principle Macdonald's paper proposing a national oil company a month earlier – but the political negotiations reportedly came close to an impasse over the interprovincial oil pipeline extension. Ultimately, however, the Liberals accepted the N.D.P. list. Accordingly, Trudeau rose in the Commons on 6 December to announce "proposals which will set the basis for a new national oil policy. The objective of that policy, to be reached before the end of this decade, is Canadian self-sufficiency in oil and oil products."[12] Among other matters agreed to, Trudeau's speech confirmed the government's intention to create a "publicly-owned Canadian petroleum company principally to expedite exploration and development." The company might choose to hold part of its reserves "for the long term security of the Canadian market," a function private investors found difficult to perform but which the government regarded as important. The government-owned company was not "intended in any way to displace the private sector," added Trudeau.[13] The speech, which delighted the N.D.P., purchased five more months in power for the minority government.

The N.D.P. has often cited Trudeau's speech as evidence for its claim – frequently made in the 1979 and 1980 election campaigns – to have fathered Petro-Canada: had the N.D.P. not threatened to bring the government down, the Liberals would not have agreed to create a state oil company. But this is a parental claim with little basis in historical fact. The N.D.P. pressures certainly influenced the timing of the decision, yet it seems probable – given the internal bureaucratic pressures operating on the cabinet – that a majority Liberal government would soon have reached the same conclusion (the Liberals certainly did not hesitate to carry through the decision after obtaining a parliamentary majority in the 1974 election).

The origins of Petro-Canada must therefore be traced to the behaviour of the state itself, and especially to the tendency of its executive branch, to react to external threats and instability by expanding its own domain of bureaucratic control. The concept of a national oil company found its strongest advocates *within* the government, notably in an Energy Department attempting to extend its control over the petroleum industry. Large permanent bureaucracies crave predictability and stability. Confronted in late 1973 with an international energy supply crisis whose outcome it could not determine, and lacking influence over a multinational business notoriously resistant to political interference, Canada's federal bureaucracy sought to reduce uncertainty and to increase its knowledge of, and control over, the petroleum industry. Petro-Canada was created as an *entreprise temoin* − a bureaucratic device to witness what actually happened and why.

II. The Mandate Years

What is it that the state wants to derive from becoming an entrepreneur? What is its yardstick of success or failure? Does it want to have efficiently managed state companies that can stand on their own feet, or does it prefer to have them further national interests and to perform solely as instruments of policy? The answer of course is that the state usually wants it both ways.

National oil companies (NOCs), like all state enterprises, have a dual nature in that they are required to operate in a commercial environment while − in theory − carrying out certain services for their owner governments. What are these services? Comparative studies of some of the larger NOCs have shown that governments create and use these state corporations for a variety of motives − to enhance the security of national energy supplies, to reduce the government's dependence on the multinational oil companies by increasing its knowledge and control of the petroleum industry and resources, to capture economic benefits, and to carry out other domestic policy goals. And the truth seems to be that in many cases, national oil companies have been expected to do all of these things *and* to turn a profit.[14]

Having taken the easy first step of outlining a mandate, governments then must face up to the formidable cost of implementing it. To carry out their various tasks and to operate alongside the established multinationals, the newer NOCs require plenty of government assistance. Barriers to entry can be very high in the oil industry, and the government that wants to put its own national company on a competitive basis with the integrated majors can expect to pay a large price with little hope of early shareholder dividends. It is costly to compete with an Exxon. This is especially the case for the late entrants, such as Petro-Canada, that have had to build up their organizations in the post-1973 era of high costs. Probably it is true, as L.E. Grayson argues, that "direct intervention is more costly than indirect regulation. One must understand that NOCs cannot be launched, nor survive, nor prosper without consistent and sizeable governmental assistance. How long such assistance must be sustained depends on how rapidly the particular NOC manages to gain access to low-cost crude and significant market share in its home country."[15] State support may come in the form of equity funds, government backing of NOC loans, preferential access to land and resources, a right of participation in all production, and so forth. These are the privileges of growth enjoyed by state oil companies, and no government can afford to neglect their political and financial implications. No politician who wants to go into the oil business should take the first step without considering the last one.

The evidence cited in the previous section shows that policy-makers had a number of objects in mind for a Canadian national oil company. There was no single goal, although the desire to effect a greater control over the rate of domestic exploration and the need to acquire knowledge about the extent and costs of frontier oil and gas were pre-eminent. Control of national energy supply in an unstable world was the underlying motive of most of Ottawa's defensive interventions (though not, it must be said, of its decision to freeze domestic oil prices). What drove Canadian energy policy in an autarkic or mercantilistic direction was an external threat, not nationalist beliefs. In late 1973 the availability and price of future energy supplies were matters of great uncertainty, and Canada's minority government was under political pressure to intervene in ways that would reduce the country's reliance on the world oil system, particularly on the pools of the great transnational oil companies. As we have noted, the Trudeau government believed — correctly — that the entire structure of the international industry was in the process of decomposition and that the strategic position of the integrated major oil companies was being eroded by the takeover of petroleum resources by the state in virtually all exporting jurisdictions. Access to overseas oil was no longer assured through the private multinational systems — at any price. Yet if Canada wished to reduce its dependence on insecure imported oil, it must still rely on these same few powerful corporations, all foreign-controlled, to accelerate the rate of exploration and development of Canadian resources; alternatively, it could go into the oil exploration business itself. Without the option of public ownership and development of resources such as the tar sands, the state would find itself without bargaining leverage in negotiating with a few multinationals who enjoyed the power to veto important new energy projects. This was not a philosophical point; it was a matter of power politics.

There was of course an element of nationalism in the cabinet's policy, but it should not be overstated. Canada's new state oil company — which Prime Minister Trudeau himself had named 'Petro-Canada' — was part of a worldwide transition from multinational to national oil: it was not a creation of ideological conviction but a limited institutional response to a threat to supply originating in the unstable world oil market. Petro-Canada's policy mandate can only be understood against this background.

When the Liberals returned to power with a majority in the 1974 federal election, the cabinet gave high priority to its new energy legislation. The Petro-Canada Act was introduced in the House of Commons in October and debate on second reading was held in March and April 1975. The legislation was referred to committee for detailed study, and after an unusually long and acrimonious debate – the result of a determined filibuster by right-wing Conservatives – the Petro-Canada Act finally received third reading on 10 July. Royal Assent was granted on 30 July 1975.

Energy Minister Donald Macdonald, introducing the debate on second reading of the legislation in the House of Commons on 12 March 1975, referred to the proposed state oil company as "a most important element in the government's long-term planning to secure adequate supplies of energy to meet our national needs."[16] Petro-Canada's principal mandate, Macdonald said, would be to contribute to national energy supply by supplementing and stimulating the activities of the privately owned oil and gas industries. The government did not feel assured "that the private sector can be relied upon to mobilize all of the enormous amounts of capital which will be required to secure energy development consonant with Canada's needs over the longer term." Nor did it feel certain that the international oil industry would be willing to concentrate as much on Canada's hydrocarbon prospects as would be needed in the decades ahead. There were uncertainties as well concerning Canadian oil imports. It was plausible that in the future it would be more advantageous to arrange these via a national petroleum company than to reply on multinational subsidiaries.

Macdonald's speech was by far the best statement of Petro-Canada's mandate. Both it and the company's legislation were unambiguously clear that Petro-Canada's most important functions would lie in oil and gas exploration and development, particularly in the frontier areas, and in direct involvement in synthetic fuel projects from the Alberta oil sands. The best way to secure a Canadian presence in the oil sands, a rate of development consistent with the national interest, a proper share of the rents generated, and full access to new technology was through "direct government involvement in key ventures through a corporation which can develop the necessary expertise. Our national petroleum company would then be in a position to act as a catalyst for succeeding projects, assisting in their planning and financing as well as participating ultimately in their revenues."[17] The orientation of Petro-Canada's business would not always be short-term profit maximization, Macdonald stressed, because its mandate was to promote the "interests of long-term future energy supply for Canada". While the legislation provided powers for Petro-Canada to move into downstream refining and marketing, Macdonald's "present view" was that this was both unnecessary and prohibitively expensive.[18]

Section 6 of the Petro-Canada Act sets out five broad objectives of the company: (1) to undertake exploration and development of hydrocarbons and other types of energy; (2) to carry out energy research and development; (3) to import, produce, transport, distribute, refine, and market hydrocarbons; (4) to produce, distribute, transport, and market other fuels and energy; and (5) to engage or invest in ventures or enterprises related to the exploration, production, importation, distribution, refining, and marketing of fuel, energy, and related resources.

The Act gives the Crown corporation and its shareholder plenty of scope and powers for broad intervention in the Canadian energy industries. Nevertheless, the focus of its mandate is to secure energy supplies for Canadian users. Petro-Canada's *raison d'être*, its charter, is to find, exploit, research or acquire petroleum and other fuels in the longer-term national interest of Canada. To pool risks and costs, it is to act, where feasible, through joint ventures with private firms; yet it is plainly expected to carry out proportionately more of the longer-term, higher-risk exploration, research, and development than would those firms. The mandate is broad and of indefinite duration. "We are not incorporating this for a single or passing transaction", Energy Minister Macdonald scolded his critics, implying that they suffered from myopia while the government had a longer time horizon. Petro-Canada would be investing "patient money", carrying out exploration and research and development on its own if commercial returns were too distant or uncertain to justify private investment. In short, it would have a different view of the future, a different way of discounting the value, say, of energy research or *in situ* oil sands extraction than those used by the private sector. It will be seen that the Petro-Canada Act provides a good balance of financial powers and governmental controls over the enterprise to ensure that it could and would perform its policy role.

We have stressed the *long-term supply* focus of Petro-Canada's mandate because the company itself and its owner, the Canadian government, have by and large abandoned it in the 1980s. A policy role that clearly was expected to last for several decades was discarded long before any long-term supply was developed. Since 1984, Petro-Canada has argued that it carried out its mandate in the first seven or eight years of its operations, and that it was necessary for the company to operate in a private-sector fashion thereafter. It may be useful for Petro-Canada, a corporation with a strong interest in the early generation of cash flow to support its rapid growth, to attempt to bury its own costly mandate in favour of the virtues of the boardroom — efficiency, productivity, market share etc. — yet this is hardly *prima facie* evidence that the company has completed its policy role, let alone that it should be privatized.

Controlling Petro-Canada

In early January 1976 a handful of newly-appointed Petro-Canada officers, led by Maurice Strong, the company's first chairman, arrived in Calgary to set up the Crown corporation. Operating from a suite of rooms in a downtown hotel with a rented typewriter and an expense account for taxis, these "few brave souls with an entrepreneurial spirit," as Bill Hopper, its president, called them, were mostly federal bureaucrats expected to do the government's bidding. Initially, that meant that they would negotiate some exploration deals with the major landholders in the frontiers and try to accelerate the pace; in the name of the national interest, Petro-Canada would pay the multinational oil companies to work their Canadian lands.

How did Ottawa propose to keep its oil company faithful to its mandate? The Trudeau Liberals had conceived Petro-Canada as an arm of the state operating within the energy industries; and while they intended to build it with financial and legislative support, they had worried from the outset about losing control over it. The cabinet memorandum of 31 October 1973 proposing a national oil company had ruled out any offering of its shares to the public "since this firm is to be an operating arm of the government and, as such, an instrument of public policy. Those public policy objectives should not be constrained by the profit motives of private investors." And it cautioned that "Crown corporations, once launched, do develop a degree of independence from government which can complicate governmental attempts to direct its activities. If the firm were to operate simply as another private firm would, it is of limited value as an instrument of public policy." The same memorandum contained a sensible warning about how such an entity would view profits:

> Directing the NPC to earn a profit could lead it to operate in much the same way as any private firm would — i.e., to maximize its profits consistently with long term market position. If this were to occur, it would not stimulate the industry competitively and might help support higher prices to generate a cash flow the reinvestment of which is less completely scrutinized ... In general, the corporation might be more likely to seek the highest prices for its sales

since this will appear to be a measure of its success and a source of funds which is less controllable by the budgetary authorities.[19]

State petroleum companies operate alongside the multinationals in one of world's most costly and complex industries, and there is no doubt that they can be hard to control. To create dynamic NOCs, governments have tended to select very forceful and dynamic personalities to run their enterprises — Enrico Mattei of Italy's ENI, Arve Johnsen of Norway's Statoil, Lords Kearton and Balogh of Britain's BNOC. These men and their successors sought to create commercially viable companies independent of government control, to expand their shares of the market, to pursue vertical integration and diversification, to expand internationally, and above all to generate their own funds for growth. There is nothing irrational in such a strategy. Indeed, it closely follows the path taken by most of the multinational oil companies decades ago. The search for ways of spreading the risks and reducing the company's vulnerability to external events leads logically to a self-contained strategy of generating and reinvesting its own funds, controlling its own supply of oil as well as downstream refining and marketing through vertical integration, and strengthening its capacity to control its environment by acquiring oligopolistic market power. It is these things and not its role in public policy that can give the national oil company's operations the continuity, stability, and autonomy every management desires.

Conceiving Petro-Canada as something of a test-case in its efforts to bring federal Crown corporations under a new regime of accountability, the Trudeau cabinet had built in unusually strong controls over its state oil corporation, but balanced these by giving its board and management a broad range of powers, especially financial powers. The company was given an initial appropriation of $1.5 billion, extensive powers to raise debt capital as "an agent of Her Majesty" — which has the effect of lowering Petro-Canada's cost of capital — and access to the same range of tax incentives available to private sector oil companies. But while the Liberals wanted Petro-Canada to become a going concern, they also intended that it would be available to the federal government as a policy arm. Under the provisions of Petro-Canada's own legislation, the Crown as shareholder is empowered to exercise control over the company in several ways. The architects of the Petro-Canada Act wanted a corporate instrument faithful to its policy mandate, thus they had specified certain checks on managerial ambitions: Petro-Canada is required to get *prior* approval of its capital budget every year before it obtains authority to spend monies; the government can also give policy directives to the company via published orders in council (such directives have been issued since 1976 to direct Petro-Canada to take Ottawa's 17 per cent share of the Syncrude oil sands project, to import crude oil from Mexico, to establish Petro-Canada International Assistance Corporation, and to construct a demonstration plant for upgrading heavy residual fuel oils at its refinery in Montreal); and the government also appoints Petro-Canada's board of directors and approves the appointments of the company's chairman and president. Of these, it was the control over Petro-Canada's annual capital budget, including any future expenditure commitments and its plans to finance its growth, that gave Ottawa real, as opposed to nominal, authority to shape the corporation's strategy. Since Petro-Canada was not expected to be self-financing for at least its first decade and would be dependent on the government for much of its funding, there was reason to hope that its broad corporate strategy in the late 1970s and the 1980s would attempt to integrate the policy aims of the state with the interests of the enterprise itself.

Hard Frontier

The best way to gain a perspective on Petro-Canada's early activity may be to link it to the 'staples' school of Canadian political economy, and particularly to the work of H.A. Innis. It was Innis who described Canada as a "hard frontier": the development of its resources involved large accumulations of capital, state support, and monopolistic forms of business enterprise. Innis argued that the inaccessible environment, the high-cost nature of frontier resources, the distances and costs of transportation, and the lengthy periods from the initial discovery of resources until profits were taken discouraged private capital and induced the growth of monopolies and of "state capitalism" in Canada. The types and forms of capitalist enterprise and the role of governments in the development of Canada were profoundly shaped by the country's geography and its place in international trade. The rise and fall of staple industries, the wide swings in Canadian development in response to changing world markets, moulded Canada's political system and the interventions of its government in production and trade – interventions which might be debated in the language of political ideologies but which, in Innis's universe, were actually determined by the invariants of climate, distance, and cost. Public ownership was typically a governmental response to shifts in world markets and to the costs and dislocations occasioned by the decline of older staple products or the appearance of new ones; Innis also said that government ownership in Canada was "based on a hard core of defence against the United States."[20]

In its origins and formative years, Petro-Canada was a good illustration of Innis's explanation of the underlying motives of public enterprise in the Canadian economy. The company was a by-product of the disintegration of the international oil system in the early 1970s and of the rising price of all energy forms. It was set up to help bridge the transition from lower-cost petroleum and natural gas, located in western Canada, to higher-cost substitutes, such as offshore oil and gas in the Arctic and the Atlantic coast or non-conventional petroleum from the tar sands and heavy oils of the western plains. The new replacement energy staples were remote and risky from the standpoints of environment and economics, and the very long lead times between exploration and commercial payout meant that only the largest players could operate in the frontiers. It also meant that the state would of necessity be involved, if not as a direct partner then certainly in subsidizing private investment. Syncrude Canada Ltd., the multi-billion dollar joint venture of multinational oil companies and the Canadian state for tar sands development, was to be a prototype of the post-1973 shift to the new energy staples. The basic premise of the strategy was that low-cost oil would be scarce and that real energy prices would rise through the 1980s and beyond. The federal authorities assumed that the western Canadian sedimentary basin, which has been in commercial development since the late 1940s, was unlikely to contribute large new additions to oil and gas supply; they were unsure of the security of oil imports; and they therefore felt justified in using special incentives and direct public investment via Petro-Canada to accelerate exploratory activity on the "hard frontiers" — the tar sands and heavy oils, the Mackenzie Valley and Beaufort Sea, the Arctic Islands, and offshore Nova Scotia and Newfoundland. Given the forbidding environments, the distances to markets, and the very high finding and extraction costs, a forced transition to the frontier energy staples would involve a mix of political centralization, quasi-monopolistic enterprise, and the socialization of risks by the state.

Petro-Canada's immediate priority in 1976 was to launch a seven-to-eight-year frontier exploration programme in partnership with the multinational subsidiaries in order to determine whether significant quantities of hydrocarbons, especially oil, could be developed in any of the major sedimentary basins in the North and offshore at prevailing world prices. The "need to know" the full extent of Canada's energy resource base had, as we have seen, played an important part in the cabinet's initial decision to establish a national oil company; drilling in the frontier areas was essential so that federal energy policy planners could determine whether or not major geological structures in the Beaufort Sea, the Arctic Islands, the Labrador Shelf and so on actually contained oil and gas resources that could come to markets on a competitive basis. Private sector rates of exploratory drilling were deemed to be inadequate – between 1972 and 1977 there was a sharp decline in the amount of frontier exploration undertaken in Canada – and the federal government moved to augment activity in the north and the offshore through three policy measures which, taken as a package, could be interpreted as a precursor of the 1980 National Energy Program. First, the government sought to force the major oil companies to work their idle lands by changing its land tenure policies; the changes included provision of a controversial "back-in" right for Petro-Canada on lands surrendered to the Crown. Second, it altered its fiscal treatment of the petroleum industry in an attempt to encourage the reinvestment of cash flow in new exploration. Here Ottawa and the western provinces were in effect bidding against one another for exploratory dollars, despite much evidence that tax incentives had little to do with the allocation of the industry's overall exploration budget. So-called 'super-depletion', an extraordinary allowance on very costly exploration wells, reduced the after-tax cost of a $40 million well, such as the Hibernia discovery, to just $4 million. Super-depletion was introduced by the Liberals in 1977 and phased out by the Clark Conservatives three years later when it became clear that it was so rich that it was virtually financing all of Dome Petroleum's drilling in the Beaufort and inefficiently attracting some investment to the highest-cost alternatives. And finally, Ottawa had recourse to direct public investment in frontier drilling via Petro-Canada. Here it is important to note that it was never intended that the state oil company would act as a solo operator in its high-risk exploration activity; rather, Petro-Canada would pool risks by entering into farm-in agreements with the leading private sector oil companies, thereby getting access to land and technology and some leverage over the rate of exploration in key areas. Petro-Canada's policy role was fundamentally to *accelerate* the pace of exploration, to be a catalyst to the industry as a whole and not to displace private capital. Thus its first major initiative was to arrange some farm-in deals with Mobil Oil in order to revive drilling on the Scotian Shelf.

Petro-Canada also had its own commercial interests at stake in the frontier areas. The company was not simply the passive instrument of the national government, nor was it, as some critics had charged, a "bird-dog" for the multinationals in the north and the offshore. Bill Hopper, who succeeded Maurice Strong as the company's chairman in 1977 after a brief power struggle, had his own ambitions for Petro-Canada: frontier energy projects, such as the Arctic Pilot Project (discussed below), offered an opportunity for the state company to bring about a synthesis of private and public sector interests. He was derisive about the 'catalyst' role: it wasn't ambitious enough. "I like to win," Hopper would say of his relations with the major companies. "I want to be out front." He was fascinated with the frontier regions and fully behind the government's "need to know" mission of discovering how much oil and gas they held and how costly it would be to develop these resources. So enthusiastic did Petro-Canada become in its promotion of the east coast and of Arctic gas exports that energy planners in Ottawa came to accuse Hopper of trying to "out-Dome Dome," a reference to Dome Petroleum's flamboyant lobbying and use of government funds to advance its interests in the Beaufort.

The Arctic and the east coast represented Canada's future as an energy producer, and for Petro-Canada they offered the opportunity to be in the ranks of the biggest international players and operating in the world's toughest environments. Thus, as Hopper saw it, if important discoveries were made in the Arctic or on the east coast, and provided world oil prices stayed high enough to warrant development, Petro-Canada was positioned to be one of the main beneficiaries. He had a mandate plus the strong financial backing of the state to acquire an important interest in many of the nation's future energy developments; as Petro-Canada moved up the learning curve by assuming an operator's role in the frontiers, many of the spinoffs, such as control of offshore technology and the timing of development, would accrue to it rather than to the government.

Petro-Canada's multi-year appraisal of the frontier basins commenced in 1977 and began to wind down about 1984, the year it received a new commercially-oriented mandate from its shareholder. Because other companies were active in the Beaufort, its drilling programme was concentrated on the various offshore basins along the Atlantic coast—the Labrador Shelf, the Scotian Shelf, the Grand Banks of Newfoundland and, through its involvement in Panarctic Oils Ltd., the Arctic Islands. According to the state corporation's own internal planning documents, the *policy* interest behind the push to the frontiers was primarily to acquire intelligence about the relative economics of the various supply alternatives open to Canada, and to give federal planners enough information on which to decide by the mid-1980s whether or not to commit massive public resources to all-out development of the Alberta oil sands—a known but extremely costly source of supply. A premature decision to exploit the oil sands might impose far heavier costs on the economy than would the limited monies expended over several years on frontier drilling. It is also true that Petro-Canada's activity in federally-owned lands in the north and the offshore, combined to Ottawa's generous tax incentives, was designed to compete with the provinces for oil industry exploratory dollars; and ultimately to give the national government a larger share of the overall "take" from the oil and gas industries as well as a stronger influence over the rate of development of Canadian energy resources.

An analysis of Petro-Canada's capital expenditures after 1976 confirms the disproportionate emphasis given to frontier exploration, oil sands mining, and heavy oil development. The national oil company participated in two-thirds of the exploration wells drilled in the east coast and high Arctic between 1976 and 1981; it invested 60 per cent of its five-year exploration budget and in some years as much as 35 per cent of its total capital budget in the frontiers — whereas the industry as a whole allocated less than 10 per cent of its upstream expenditures to the north and the Atlantic coast in these same years. Petro-Canada concentrated on the offshore basins off Nova Scotia, Labrador and Newfoundland; and through its own activity, farm-ins and back-in rights, Petro-Canada became the largest landholder in the frontier regions. Driven by its policy mandate and its own interest in growth, assisted by government funding and attractive fiscal incentives, the state company participated in 114 wells off the east coast and spent about $2 billion (of which the real cost to Petro-Canada, net of government grants, was closer to 25 per cent of the total) up to and including 1985. For the period 1981-1985, while federal Petroleum Incentive Payments (or PIP grants) were available, Petro-Canada spent $2.2 billion ($775 million net of grants) on exploration in all frontier regions.[21]

The pace of frontier exploration picked up sharply after 1979 for several reasons. First, world oil prices, which had declined in real terms up to 1978, began to rise late that year in response to the political crisis in Iran; fears that the whole Persian Gulf area might be threatened by revolution and war triggered panic buying by the oil-consuming states, and the price jumped from about Canadian $13/barrel to nearly Canadian $40/barrel in a few months. The new price, though not based on any underlying *economic* scarcity of oil, did reflect the insecurities of the industrialized states of Europe, Japan, and North America over whether they would have ready access in future to the enormous reserves of low-cost crude oil in the Gulf. If not — and here was the second reason — the clear signal to states such as Canada which had the potential was to accelerate through policy the push to become self-sufficient in energy through the exploitation of high-cost alternatives to imports. Third, thanks to the spending of Petro-Canada and a few other companies in the frontiers, some important discoveries of oil and natural gas had been made by 1979, in particular near Sable Island and on the Grand Banks of Newfoundland; the much higher world prices would make it attractive to bring these to development, and they also were a strong inducement to further exploration of all of the frontier basins.

Nevertheless, it was still the Canadian state that carried most of the risks in the frontiers, and much of the risk was internalized in Petro-Canada's own operations. By 1981, Petro-Canada's frontier drilling programme accounted for 17 per cent of the $1.3 billion spent by the oil industry on federal lands. In contrast, in the same year Petro-Canada contributed just three per cent of industry spending on exploration in western Canada. "In 1981," the state company remarked in its capital budget for that year, "industry is expected to spend 77% of its domestic exploration dollar in western Canada; for Petro-Canada the figure is 37."[22] This was representative of Petro-Canada's activity in the years before 1984, and from the standpoint of the state firm it was a cause for much anxiety. Its own prospects depended too much on an uncertain future. To compensate for the industry's risk-averse, short-term orientation, Petro-Canada allocated fully 30 per cent of all capital spending to frontier exploration from 1976 to 1981. But it lacked its own cash flow-generating base in the west or in downstream activities, and this left it highly dependent on the government for funds and also vulnerable to the whims of electoral change and new government policies. The absence of cash flow meant that Petro-Canada, a company with large expenditures and a tax-deferred status, was unable to benefit from the federal-provincial fiscal regime to the extent that the major oil companies did; this was a significant factor in Petro-Canada's policy of corporate acquisitions. Before its purchase of Pacific Petroleums in late 1978, however, Petro-Canada was able to finance only 30 per cent of its capital spending from internal sources; by the early 1980s, the figure was 50 per cent but this was expected to decrease as costly new frontier projects came to development. The integrated major oil companies were by contrast funding up to 80 per cent of their capital expenditures via their own deferred taxes and cash flow.[23]

Petro-Canada would never have survived the vagaries of Canadian politics had its management not decided to link its mandate to the corporation's expansion and autonomy. In a society in which commercial success or failure is defined exclusively according to capitalist norms, a public enterprise that confines itself to the unattractive, higher-risk functions expected of it will have many detractors and few allies in Parliament or the media; as a charge on the public treasury it may even lose its supporters in government. One of Petro-Canada's internal Corporate Strategy documents, written in October 1980, noted rather tartly that the corporation could not perform its role in energy policy unless it was also a "viable business entity" able "to ensure a corporate operating and technical base from which to undertake its various ventures *and to be financially healthy so that political and public support for the institution will be maintained.* Petro-Canada has not been and cannot be expected to act exclusively in pursuit of specific projects of a public sector nature, but must strive for realistic balance in its activities in order to hold people, build skills, maintain respect and credibility, and minimize its financial needs from Government funds."24

These words were written in the aftermath of Joe Clark's attempts in 1979, not to "privatize" Petro-Canada, but to liquidate it as an entity. Clark did not want to sell Petro-Canada; his first preference was to disband and dismember it, and this was how his policy was interpreted by the company's management. Management was not opposed to privatization; what it feared was the dissolution of Petro-Canada. The Clark government's obsessive attacks on Petro-Canada, which went as far as encouraging senior executives within the company to lead a *coup* against Hopper — it failed, they were fired — strengthened public support for the company over the longer run; it would be Clark, not Bill Hopper, who would lose his job. Hopper, who had appeared to some federal energy officials not to be in control of the demoralized Crown company during part of Clark's minority government, was a beneficiary of its defeat and the return of the Liberals in February 1980. But the harsh attacks from Ottawa also taught its management that the corporation's survival could not be entrusted to the whims of partisan politicians or governments that came and went. The company was neither big enough nor sufficiently in control of its fate to shape its environment. If Petro-Canada was to survive, it must grow; if it was to have bargaining power in dealing with its masters in Ottawa, it would need its own independent funds and a strong base of political support; if it was going to carry out its mandate, it must be profitable. The organizational imperative to be profitable "so that political and public support for the institution will be maintained" might be called the first law of survival for state enterprise managers. Petro-Canada chairman Bill Hopper, a survivor, put it in his own prosaic language:

> You know the notion that we should go up and spend our total exploration budget on the frontier and go belly up in five years and have people shooting at us because it's all red ink below is just a lot of nonsense. We've got to concentrate as much as we can on the frontiers but at the same time develop the cash flow in order to fund that long-term frontier development.25

It was this conception of a need for balance that had led Petro-Canada to acquire Pacific Petroleums in late 1978 for $1.5 billion. Pacific had an excellent position in western Canada, including a small refinery and a regional marketing network, and its assets would produce cash flow which could be used by Petro-Canada to support its

high-risk activity in the frontiers. To the managers of the state
company, the real importance of the Pacific acquisition was that it
gave them independent control over their own stream of income,
thereby reducing their dependence on the federal treasury. "The
feudal barons," Paul Frankel observes in his study of Mattei and ENI,
"were strong as long as they were sustained by their own local wealth
and not dependent on favours bestowed upon them by the king."[26]

Henceforward, Petro-Canada's strategy would be one of
averaging results and balancing risks—the frontiers against the
currently-producing plains of western Canada; longer-term investments versus short-term cash flow needs; the upstream policy
mandate versus the logic of integrating upstream production with
downstream refining and marketing; the requirements of government
policy against the interests of the enterprise in survival, stability, and
its own independence. These were the antitheses that underlay Petro-
Canada's corporate strategy after 1979. There was no master plan, no
grand design to take over all or part of the Canadian petroleum
industry, no inexorable process leading to some predetermined
outcome. On the contrary, Petro-Canada *lost* more autonomy than it
gained under the National Energy Program, it improvised when the
planning process failed, it trimmed when its assumptions about the
world oil market were proven wrong, it adapted to new governments
and politicians and made the best of its opportunities to expand. It
could hardly be blamed for doing so if, when it looked to Ottawa for
guidance, it found confusion, impolicy, and, finally, a total void.

The Uses of Nationalism

Petro-Canada grew but also came under much closer governmental
control during the implementation of the Liberals' 1980 National
Energy Program. This was one of the most comprehensive and
ambitious economic interventions undertaken by any peacetime
Canadian government, and Petro-Canada was designated to play
several key roles in its realization. The national oil company had been
created, as we saw earlier in the chapter, with a developmental
orientation. Its principal mandate was to increase energy supply for
Canada and to improve the government's understanding of the oil and
natural gas industries; it was not set up to collect economic rent or
Canadianize the petroleum industry. But the N.E.P. implied that
Petro-Canada was increasingly to have a redistributive
impact—shifting industry activity from the provinces to the frontiers
and redirecting the benefits from new energy development from
foreign investors to Canadians. In what almost appeared to be a
scaled-up version of Petro-Canada's own strategy, the Trudeau
government intended that some of the income generated from current

oil and gas production in western Canada would be taxed away and re-directed through grants (tied to levels of Canadian ownership) into frontier exploration and development. This is not the place for another critique of the N.E.P., but we are interested in its impact on Petro-Canada.

Growth can come with autonomy; it can also come in fetters. Under the Liberal energy plan, Petro-Canada's mandate was expanded, the corporation's funding and access to incentives were greatly expanded, but it also found itself under a regime of increasing political supervision. While the N.E.P. promoted Petro-Canada in many ways, it also imposed on it a number of potentially-conflicting obligations. For each step that Ottawa took to expand Petro-Canada in size and significance, it took another that added something to its mandate. It was now expected to perform not only as a catalyst by accelerating the pace of frontier exploration and oil sands development, it was also required to help restructure and Canadianize the oil and gas industries, to be an instrument to collect economic rents and industrial benefits; to provide information and insights into the industry, and, in Petro-Canada's own words, to be "a federal presence to understand and influence the timing and priority of projects in a number of the industry's spheres of activity, for example, upgrading of heavy fuel oil in Montreal, new tarsands plants, and East Coast development."[27] The government was even creating a new subsidiary, Petro-Canada International, to assist Third World nations in their search for petroleum resources. There was no hierarchy of objectives: was Petro-Canada to develop new energy sources on a timely, cost-efficient basis or capture industrial benefits or be an instrument of regional growth on the East Coast – or all of these? And who would set the priorities? Would the tradeoffs among the goals not have a negative impact on Petro-Canada's bottom-line? And who would pay the bills?

Because Petro-Canada was 100 per cent Canadian-owned and its capital spending was skewed toward frontier exploration, it potentially stood to be a large winner from the N.E.P. mix of taxes and exploration grants. What it surrendered to new energy taxes it would more than make up in incentive payments. In addition, the Liberal government had agreed to double Petro-Canada's capital budget to $900 million in 1981, and to fund more than half of its expenditures (including incentive payments) annually. Further, the government committed itself under the *Energy Security Act* to a new appropriation for the Crown company of $5.5 billion to help it meet its funding requirements in the next few years. A new Canadian Ownership Account, comprised of revenues raised by a special levy on all oil and gas consumed in Canada, would be used to facilitate the purchase of one or several large oil companies; this implied, of course, that Petro-

Canada's further growth via acquisition would be financed without using its own sources or working itself more deeply into debt. If it overpaid, the costs would have to be absorbed by taxpayers.

For Petro-Canada and its management, the National Energy Program was a mixed blessing that offered growth in fetters, an expanded role without the autonomy to choose the corporation's priorities. The rigidity of the government's assumptions and of many of its new policies and regulations was soon reflected in Petro-Canada's own strategy. For instance, Petro-Canada would quickly become the biggest beneficiary of N.E.P. incentive payments; these P.I.P. grants were strongly tilted in favour of frontier exploration and levels of Canadian ownership, and they were paid for out of revenues raised from new energy taxes. By 1982 Petro-Canada was using nearly $475 million in grants, more than a quarter of its total capital funds, to finance its offshore and northern exploration. Because of its fully Canadian-owned status, it was thereby able to mount a larger program of capital spending than companies with far more assets and resources, such as Imperial Oil Ltd. But the P.I.P. grants (which Petro-Canada officials reportedly helped federal energy planners design in the summer of 1980) were a classic demonstration of Liberal paternalism: they were far less flexible than tax expenditures, they centralized decision-making, they were based on a single scenario about future oil prices, and they were intended to make the petroleum industry dependent on the federal bureaucracy. In effect, the grants tended to make clients out of those firms – Dome and Petro-Canada, for example – that chose to rely heavily on them; in the frontiers at least, their exploration programmes were entirely grant-driven. Whether such an expensive system – paid for out of new taxes on current production – could be sustained over the longer run would be decided in large part by economic and political factors over which Petro-Canada's managers had little control; any significant decrease in oil prices would quickly affect Ottawa's capacity to fund the costly programme. The sensitivity of Petro-Canada's financial position and its exploration and development plans to changes in its environment was, in fact, unjustifiably high during the N.E.P.

Nationalists supported the shift to incentive grants linked to Canadian ownership, but without critically studying how they were actually used by the industry. Typically, one of the multinational oil companies, holding good prospective lands but unable to get the maximum P.I.P. incentive, would arrange a farm-out to a qualified Canadian interest on a "two-for-one" basis – i.e., the Canadian to put up 100 per cent of the funds for drilling and to receive 50 per cent interest in the well; Ottawa to cover up to 80 per cent of the exploratory wells via P.I.P.; the multinational to get its lands drilled for nothing. By 1985 nearly $7 billion had been paid to Canadianize some of the world's costliest dry holes.

If growing control over one's own funds and a steady reduction in external financing are good indicators of a corporation's autonomy, then Petro-Canada anticipated *less*, not more, autonomy throughout the 1980s as it supported N.E.P. goals. From their standpoint as of 1980, the company's officers estimated that they would be able to cover close to half of capital spending in 1981 from internal funds; thereafter, as Petro-Canada faced massive expenditures on the development of Arctic, east coast, and oil sands projects to be undertaken in the national interest, it would only be able to fund about 25 per cent of its capital spending until late in the decade—and this assumed rising oil and gas prices. Petro-Canada's future strategy of spending in support of the N.E.P. goals was entirely based on the premise that increasing levels of federal equity funds and incentive grants would be forthcoming. To be precise, it was anticipated that Petro-Canada itself would be able to fund $2.76 billion of a total $9.34 billion in total capital spending in the 1981-85 period; the remainder would come from incentive payments of $1.8 billion, equity infusions totalling $2.2 billion, and new debt of $2.5 billion. This would leave Petro-Canada marginally profitable, but also highly exposed to changes in the political and economic environment.[28] In no sense, then, did the N.E.P. offer Petro-Canada's management an autonomous future.

What did Petro-Canada want? The only way it could reduce its level of risk exposure in these straitened circumstances was through further growth. "Growth is required not only to realize economies of scale, but to exercise control over the social, political, and economic environment in which the firm operates. The assumption here—a plausible one—is that the larger the firm, the better its ability to influence its external environment."[29] If Petro-Canada could not have profits or autonomy, it would require growth; for the government could not hope to achieve its energy goals without a greatly expanded national oil company—especially in view of the petroleum industry's bitter opposition to the redistributive thrust of the N.E.P. We cannot reconstruct the bargaining process between Petro-Canada and the Liberal government at the moment of the National Energy Program, but it seems reasonable to assume that Bill Hopper let it be known that in return for the corporation's aggressive support for the N.E.P., management would expect Petro-Canada quickly to become one of the major players in the Canadian oil industry. Two months before the publication of the October 1980 Liberal energy policy, Hopper said in conversation with the present writer that his goal was to make Petro-Canada a coast-to-coast integrated company in the shortest possible time. The corporation remarked in an October 1980 strategy document that "if Petro-Canada is to perform its role of representing national and public sector interests in the energy industry and of assisting in the promotion of Canadian participation in this essential sector, the Corporation must be as significant a player as any company in the industry. This will require a substantial operating capacity with a rapidly growing cash flow and a strong land position. Attainment of this major position in the industry will require further acquisition by Petro-Canada of other companies or their assets."[30]

Of course, Petro-Canada also wanted strong state backing for its large portfolio of upstream investments, especially for the rapid exploitation of the 1979 discoveries of oil and natural gas at Hibernia on the Grand Banks and Venture near Sable Island respectively. It also needed financial and political support for the controversial Arctic Pilot Project to bring gas exports from the Arctic Islands via LNG tankers—a concept that had little support from federal energy planners who viewed the APP as an export project that would add nothing to Canada's energy self-sufficiency.[31] However, Petro-Canada's primary goal was to secure a much larger share of downstream refining and marketing across Canada. Its first limited entry into marketing in the west via Pacific Petroleums had shown an excellent consumer response, but the state company could not expand until it owned much more refining capacity (as of 1980, Petro-Canada depended on one of the majors, Gulf, to supply 40 per cent of its products). Petro-Canada's initial demand (modest when compared with what it later obtained) was a 12 per cent share of the western region and 6 per cent of the eastern market: this would require acquisition of 100,000 to 120,000 b/d refining capacity in both regions.[32]

A further expansion into the downstream could not be justified on any serious policy grounds—though on *political* grounds the government was eager to get Petro-Canada gas stations into eastern Canada to build support for the N.E.P.—yet the economic logic of vertical integration, the desire to have full control over the phases of the industry and thereby to assure maximum efficiency and continuity in operations, applies as much to national as to multinational oil companies. For those companies that can afford the very large costs, integration is a way of spreading risk and reducing uncertainty: a producer of crude seeks a secure outlet by buying refinery capacity; the refiner needs an assured supply of oil and a distribution system to reach the final consumer. In addition, further expansion downstream would hopefully establish a firm cash flow base for pursuing the more expensive and risky frontier ventures, and stabilize Petro-Canada in the event of unexpected changes to upstream prices. In one of his annual appearances before the House of Commons Standing Committee on Natural Resources and Public

Works to discuss the company's capital budget, Hopper emphasized the generation of cash flow, not the profitability of the corporation, as the key interest:

> We are in the downstream of refining and marketing activity and our role in that activity is to be as competitive as we can and to take a bottom-line approach to that activity so as to contribute, over time, as much cashflow to the corporation generally in order to carry on our prime mandate of exploration and production. In many discussions we have had with the government, our refining and marketing activity has not been seen as an instrument of national policy, but as a commercial activity carried on by the corporation in a competitive climate in order to provide cashflow for our mainline of exploration.[33]

Expanding into refining and marketing was a way of reducing the government's direct control over Petro-Canada and its internally-generated funds; as the state company's upstream role came under closer supervision by Ottawa, Petro-Canada's logical response was to pursue growth and market share in the downstream. In the long run, the decision was bound to strengthen Petro-Canada's autonomy.

Those were the considerations that underlay Petro-Canada's acquisitions of Belgian-controlled Petrofina Canada in February 1981 for $1.6 billion and the downstream assets of BP Canada in 1982 for $425 million (Petro-Canada later estimated that two-thirds of the value of the Petrofina purchase lay in its upstream assets). The Petrofina deal was ultimately paid for by the Canadian Ownership Special Charge, a federal levy on all natural gas and oil products sold in Canada. The BP purchase was paid for by Petro-Canada itself. After these two acquisitions, Petro-Canada controlled about 12 per cent of the gasoline market in the country. While it expected its share of the market to grow because of consumer loyalty to its Canadian ownership — a point heavily stressed in its advertising — profits in the downstream were already seriously depressed in 1982 because of recession, weak demand for products, and excess refining capacity. Petro-Canada was moving into the downstream of the Canadian petroleum industry in the midst of that sector's deepest crisis, and simultaneously dedicating a full 35 per cent of its capital expenditures to high-risk frontier exploration.[34]

Petro-Canada's mandate had been recast and broadened by the National Energy Program. It was now expected to help Canadianize the oil industry, to collect economic rents and other benefits, to advise the government, and to accelerate the pace of exploration and development in areas such as the frontiers, the oil sands, and heavy oil. In the main, it was economic nationalism — the policy of redistributing the gains from ownership and control of the Canadian petroleum industry in favour of Canadian interests — that was, together with the older supply mandate, pushing Petro-Canada's upstream expansion. But management's drive for growth and greater cash flow in downstream activities was no less significant. Consequently, the company was badly overextended, only marginally profitable, and extraordinarily dependent on government funds and policy as it concluded its mandate years.

III: The Drive for Autonomy
Long-run expectations/Short-run realities

Keynes showed in *The General Theory* that investors cope with uncertainty and "the extreme precariousness of the basis of knowledge" on which most investment decisions are made by falling back on a psychological *convention* — the essence of which "lies in assuming that the existing state of affairs will continue indefinitely."[35] Keynes argued that the resort to such a convention, based on ignorance of the future, leads to private decisions oriented to short-term speculation rather than to longer-term investments. "When the capital development of a country becomes a by-product of the activities of a casino, the job is likely to be ill-done." His answer to this was to replace the casino with the state, for only the latter institution was capable of far-seeing investments. "I expect to see the State," he wrote, "which is in a position to calculate the marginal efficiency of capital-goods on long views and on the basis of the general social advantage, taking an ever greater responsibility for directly organizing investment." The rationale for public enterprise — and Petro-Canada's original mandate to develop energy supply in the public interest was a good illustration — was the need for far-sighted investment based on society's longer-term needs and general advantage. "The social object of skilled investment should be to defeat the dark forces of time and ignorance which envelop our future," Keynes insisted.[36]

That the state will actually invest for society's advantage cannot however be assumed. Unfortunately, there is nothing to prevent the enterprises of the state itself from falling back on a "convention" and assuming that the existing state of affairs will continue indefinitely — particularly when it is in their own interest to do so. State enterprise is capable of making far-sighted investments on the basis of societal interests; and it is also capable of acting in ways and for purposes that are indistinguishable from those of private enterprise. Which way it will act in practice cannot be determined from some fixed pattern or causal law, such as the Marxian position that the state serves the interests of capital; or the thesis of 'managerial capitalism' — that there is an inexorable flow of power away from those who own toward those who manage the modern corporation. How a state enterprise will act can only be determined by looking at the actual circumstances in which it finds itself, the resources at its disposal, the personalities, outlook, the policies of the government that owns the enterprise, the ambitions and skills of its management and so forth. If a public enterprise such as Petro-Canada ceases to invest "on long views and on the basis of the general social advantage," the explanation must be sought empirically in the particular weight of these and other factors, not in determinist theories which eliminate any notion of individual responsibility or any possibility that things might have been done differently.

Perhaps because the success of its own strategy was so dependent on a future regime of tight supplies and rising energy prices, Petro-Canada's forecasting about the world petroleum market in the 1980s was fundamentally wrong. It was not alone in this, of course; most oil companies and western governments failed to anticipate the coming oil glut. But Petro-Canada's analysis was especially interesting because of what it conveyed about management's perception of what made prices go up and down — state power. Its long-run expectations about the world oil system were based upon mercantilist assumptions that emphasized the primacy of geopolitics and downplayed the role of economic factors in determining demand and supply. Oil was a strategic commodity, Bill Hopper was fond of saying; and this meant that national governments would control supply. In particular, the state corporation attributed to the OPEC group of countries a unity and ability to regulate production levels and prices that had never existed in the past, and ignored the impact of growing non-OPEC production on oil prices. Petro-Canada's analysts, like too many of their counterparts in the private sector, erred badly in their estimation of world oil demand after the second oil price shock of 1979-80, even though the federal government's macroeconomic modelling in early 1981 showed world economic growth declining sharply in response to the very large rise in oil prices.[37] These analysts assumed that energy demand would be unresponsive to changes in price. What determined the price of oil was simply OPEC's capacity to control the market. Looking ahead to the 1980s, Petro-Canada said:

> The crucial role of OPEC in terms of oil supply is not likely to diminish in the next decade. The oil supply prospects of the major oil consumers are poor . . . . The OPEC countries have shown an ability to control production levels, maintain cartel discipline and extract higher prices for

their oil resource . . . the outlook is that oil prices will increase in real terms through the 1980s. A key element in keeping supplies tight and thus maintaining upward pressure on oil prices is the probability that OPEC production in the 1980s and 1990s will be maintained at a level close to the 30 million b/d achieved in 1978.[38]

Well into the worsening glut of the 1980s, Bill Hopper and Petro-Canada's other top executives implied by their public utterances that the key to market stability still lay in OPEC's hands, or rather in the hands of Saudi Arabia and a few other Gulf producers. In its 1987 Amended Capital Budget, which was based on an average price over the year of US $18/bbl rather than US $15/bbl as assumed in the original Capital Budget, Petro-Canada noted only that OPEC had agreed to abandon its market share strategy (under which prices had collapsed to less than US $10/bbl) and to return to production quotas and a target price of US $18/bbl: "There seems to be considerable non-OPEC support for the $18/bbl price and, at present, Saudi Arabia appears willing to play a limited *de facto* role as swing producer to defend the new fixed-price regime."[39]   But if anything should have been plain by 1987, it was that economic forces, not producing governments, determine how much oil can be produced at what price. Perhaps because Hopper himself was trained as a geologist and was (not without reason) skeptical of the work of many academic economists, preferring to acquire most of his intelligence about the oil market through his travel and his worldwide network of political and business contacts, or perhaps because Petro-Canada itself is an offspring of power politics, the company seems to have had a difficult time accepting that the international oil system no longer had a centre of power that could restrict output, match supply to demand, and hold prices up; or that OPEC and the Persian Gulf were much less important than they had been, say, in 1978. The diminishing significance of Mideast oil, reflected in the persistent weakness of crude oil prices despite a cruel, protracted war between Iraq and Iran since September 1980, meant that there was no 'swing producer,' no single state or group of states strong enough to regulate supply and stabilize prices.

Whatever the reason, Petro-Canada's premises and forecasts were disastrously wrong — and to repeat, they were by no means alone in this. As it turned out, the 1980s were to witness the petroleum industry's worst crisis in 50 years, a crisis of overproduction, falling oil prices, internecine competition over shrinking markets. The world price of oil has fallen steadily in real terms since 1981, (from about $47 to $17 in $US 1985), OPEC has struggled to keep its total production at about half of Petro-Canada's prediction of 30 million barrels per day, and petroleum companies world-wide have wrestled with the effects of crude oversupply, weak product demand, and surplus capacity downstream on their profitability and structure. In the main consuming states of North America, Western Europe, and Japan, oil demand was cut sharply by the world recession of 1981-82 and by consumers switching to other fuels. Moreover, economic recovery did not bring with it the anticipated increases in energy use. The historically close relationship between growth rates of energy use and of GNP had been terminated by price-induced conservation. The long-term effects of conservation measures taken in response to the 1973-74 price increases were only starting to show up in the early 1980s.[40] At that point, a massive and painful contraction and rationalization of refining capacity had to be undertaken world-wide to accommodate the changes in demand.

Thanks largely to its own pricing policies in the 1970s, OPEC's share of world production of oil slumped dramatically, from 54 per cent before the 1973 oil shock (and 48 per cent before the second) to just 32 per cent of total world oil production in 1987 – a loss of 40 per cent of its market share since the 1970s. Other producers, such as the UK, Norway, Mexico, Egypt, Angola, Brazil, India, and Australia, held 41 per cent of world production by 1987; China, the USSR and other socialist states have also increased their shares of world oil output – to 27 per cent of the total. While OPEC still controls about half the world's exports of crude and 80 per cent of the non-Communist total of proved reserves, neither it nor the leading Gulf producers in the organization have been able to reduce the massive surplus capacity that has depressed world oil prices since 1981. When OPEC tried in 1986 to drop its fixed-price strategy in favour of increased market share and opened up the taps, it saw the price of oil plummet to less than US $10 per barrel in a few months before it retreated to its previous system of quotas and official prices.[41]

The rationale for government-controlled oil companies in the new market structure was anything but clear. In the old world oil system, assurance of crude oil supplies had been an article of faith, the real *raison d'être* of the globally integrated markets of the multinationals. Then nationalizations had destroyed the majors' integrated supply systems, and the structure lost its centre and fragmented. National oil companies had been established before and after 1973 to assure oil supplies, to reduce the role of the multinationals, and to collect economic rents. So vital was energy supply assumed to be in national economic and power-political terms that governments were willing to pay a very high price to have their own 'national champion' directly engaged in the oil business. But the emerging structure of the international oil industry after 1981 was not one in which it appeared to make any sense for either the big oil

companies or consuming governments to pay a high price for the long-
term assurance of the supply of crude petroleum. With downstream
markets shrinking and refinery utilization rates well below the break-
even point, the only factor that counted in acquiring crude oil was
price. Accordingly, term, or official, prices fixed by OPEC at levels
higher than spot, or market, prices on the basis that this was the price
for security of supply, found few takers. State-to-state trading in oil,
popular in the aftermath of the Iranian crisis, was deemed too costly
by most consuming states. Futures trading in oil and gas became a
commonplace, domestic regulation of the petroleum industry
unravelled in many jurisdictions, but not because of ideology. The
new market structure was increasingly characterized by short-term
contracts, reliance on spot markets, and a shift toward oil companies
as traders rather than owners-and-developers of resources. Petroleum
was no longer the "noble" commodity:

> Security of supply has now become less of a problem
> because of production overcapacity and refinery flexibility
> that has opened wider doors to poorer grades of crude.
> Increasingly the industry's focus is short-term, the objective
> being to average down acquisition costs in order to achieve
> positive netbacks from downstream markets that remain
> below parity with OPEC-set prices. In response to radically
> changed operating conditions, and reflecting the view that
> the weakness of recent years will continue in the
> foreseeable future, the oil industry has begun to restructure
> along trading lines. The extent to which individual
> companies have made the shift varies, but most if not all of
> the majors and independents buy and sell much of their
> oil—both crude and products—in the same way that the
> more traditional commodities like coffee and copper are
> traded.[42]

The restructuring of the world oil industry in the direction of
fast-moving, short-term flexibility, with decreasing emphasis on
traditional security of supply concerns, meant that it would be more
difficult for government to regulate and also that there would be less
intervention by the state in the industry. The inevitability of state
involvement in different aspects of the industry could be—and
was—more easily challenged in the new environment of overcapacity,
falling prices, and weak demand. Success no longer required the
involvement of state oil companies in acquiring crude supplies and
establishing guaranteed markets; now the emphasis was far more on
rapid technical innovation, adapting to shifting market possibilities,
rationalizing capacity. National oil companies could survive in the

new structure only by making the same adaptations to markets, i.e., by acting on a strictly commercial basis; or by becoming a drain on the government purse. In downstream jurisdictions, the intervention of importing governments in crude supply arrangements, deemed expedient when supplies were tight and prices were escalating, made much less sense on any policy grounds in the face of these changes. The exploitation of domestic high-cost alternatives to oil — perhaps the strongest reason for state involvement in the oil industry — was abandoned by most countries. In the upstream, most oil producing governments have responded to the conditions of oversupply and declining prices by lowering marginal tax rates, offering incentives to oil companies for new petroleum investment, and deregulating the oil and gas industries. By one estimate, this has made it possible for some companies to earn better returns in a $15-per-barrel environment than they had earned in a $28-per-barrel environment.[43] The question in both producing and consuming jurisdictions is whether the shifting structure of the oil industry away from its long-term supply focus has not weakened the rationale as well as the capacity of governments to intervene in and regulate this sector of western capitalism.

John Zysman has shown how the post-war French state attempted to insure a structure of ownership and production that would allow national control over the operations of the oil, steel, and electronics industries.[44] It succeeded, first, in the cases of oil and steel, according to Zysman, because these were technically stable, capital-intensive, production-oriented industries in which technological evolutions were slow; the heavy investments locked the firms into long-term choices, brokered by governments, having to do with secure supplies of materials and protected markets. But in the second case of electronics, a technically unstable, market-oriented industry that was under extraordinary international competitive pressure and forced to adapt and innovate rapidly, a policy of national intervention failed. It was the structure of the industry, not the strategy of the state, that determined whether intervention succeeded or not. The post-1981 structure of the international oil industry more closely resembles Zysman's second case than the first; and it seems reasonable to argue that for similar reasons — its fast-changing, short-run orientation, the impact of international competitive pressures, the absence of integration — it has become much less susceptible to government intervention and control. This is the broader context in which we now propose to discuss Petro-Canada's transition in the 1980s from arm of the state to an enterprise oriented to short-term cash flow, autonomy, and growth.

The Stimulus of Crisis

We have described a classic petroleum industry crisis of over-production of crude oil, excess capacity in refining and marketing, and falling profits. Such crises have usually been caused by a falling off of demand for refined products and/or by the uncontrolled production of new sources of oil, and they have only been resolved when the major integrated oil companies, assisted by producing governments, have managed through prorationing and other measures to regulate the output of crude to demand — even going so far as imposing martial law and sending in troops to shut-in excess supplies. Crises similar to that of the 1980s occurred in the American oil industry in the late 1920s and during the Great Depression, when the great new fields of Oklahoma and Texas were brought in without controls and threatened to flood the market with cheap oil, prompting the major companies to lobby state and federal authorities to intervene to regulate production. The large integrated firms are the only ones capable of reorganizing the industry in its different segments, and they are driven to do so by the threats and opportunities posed by the qualitative changes posed by the great crises, the perennial gales of creative destruction — to use Joseph Schumpeter's words[45] — that sweep through capitalist industries when new technologies, new commodities, or new sources of supply revolutionize the existing economic structure from within, forcing each business concern to adapt, innovate, or disappear. The problem that is usually visualized, Schumpeter remarked by way of criticizing orthodox economics, "is how capitalism administers existing structures, whereas the relevant problem is how it creates and destroys them."[46] In the conditions of the perennial gale of overproduction and contracting demand that overtook the world oil industry after 1981 the old structure we described earlier collapsed completely. How would Petro-Canada adapt?

Petro-Canada, as we stressed earlier in the chapter, was already in an exposed position and highly dependent on government financing for its operations when the world oil market began to reveal the effects of lowered demand for products and an oversupply of crude. In the near term, it is quite true, Petro-Canada enjoyed extraordinarily good relations with the key Liberal cabinet minister on matters dealing with the National Energy Program, Marc Lalonde, Minister of Energy, Mines and Resources, and it had received many benefits from the N.E.P., including large increases in equity infusions, incentive grants for its ambitious frontier exploration programme, a new tax to pay for its Petrofina purchase, support for its deeper involvement in downstream activities, and Lalonde's personal commitment — backed by Prime Minister Trudeau — to make Petro-Canada as big as any of the Canadian subsidiaries of the major oil companies. Support of the

Canadian government meant that Petro-Canada was in a far better position to survive the gale of creative destruction when it struck than were many of Canada's over-extended oil and gas businesses.

Survive, but not necessarily adjust to the new order of things; for Petro-Canada's access in Ottawa and its high levels of funding depended on it loyally pursuing its frontier strategy in the name of the N.E.P. and also promoting the development of non-conventional sources of oil in western Canada. The risks it was running in frontier exploration — more than 80 per cent financed from new equity infusions and PIP grants — were minimal when weighed against the massive commitment of resources that would have to be made in the face of many uncertainties to bring an offshore or oil sands megaproject into production. For the restructuring of the world oil industry away from high-cost projects for long-term assurance of supply threatened the viability of Petro-Canada's entire strategy; the collapse of the Cold Lake and Alsands oil megaprojects in 1981 and early 1982 because of falling world oil prices ought to have signalled a shift away from the frontier toward less costly, smaller-scale energy production. No such shift occurred. The terrible loss of life in the sinking of the *Ocean Ranger* drilling rig on the Grand Banks in February 1982 demonstrated that the federal government and its national oil company were attempting to push the pace of offshore drilling in the name of self-sufficiency before an adequate regulatory regime of offshore safety was in place. Petro-Canada's own safety record in the offshore is not at issue here; the point is rather that it and other agencies of the Canadian government were incessantly pressuring the major oil companies to accelerate the activity off the east coast.

Petro-Canada and the Liberal government were convinced that a great bonanza, another North Sea, lay beneath the waves off Canada's east coast. Offshore oil and gas developments would not only contribute to domestic energy supplies, they would generate large economic spin-offs that would develop the entire Atlantic region. These "Canadian benefits" or industrial linkages in the offshore would have to be captured by state agencies such as Petro-Canada operating directly within the industry. Much the same type of strategy would be applied in the massive non-conventional oil projects of the west. The push for speed was motivated by more than an interest in domestic oil self-sufficiency; self-sufficiency was rather to be used as a way of steering the Canadian economy into an era of resource megaprojects.

For reasons already cited, this *dirigiste* megaproject strategy was uneconomic. The very long lead-times, large capital expenditures, and marginal economics of frontier projects made these high-risk propositions, while the sheer scale, capital-intensity, and vulnerable technology of tar sands plants ("brute force and ignorance", as Bill Hopper ungenerously referred to Syncrude, in which Petro-Canada held a lucrative 17 per cent interest gifted to it by the federal government in 1976 and 1981) have virtually rendered these obsolete — at least on the scale of Syncrude.

A final word needs to be said on the *politics* of Petro-Canada's frontier strategy. Petro-Canada's promotion of the resources of the north and the east coast offshore was part of a longstanding strategy by the federal government to shift exploration activity (and eventually production) from the lower-cost regions of western Canada to the higher-cost frontier areas. Tax expenditures, such as super-depletion, the PIP incentive grants, and Petro-Canada's heavy focus on frontier exploration in its capital expenditures all were designed to reallocate the oil and gas industry's exploration budgets toward the federally-controlled Canada Lands. These extraordinarily rich enticements lowered the net cost of exploration in the frontiers, and at a very high cost they did attract investment away from western Canada. But the question we wish to raise here is whether in focussing on the economic costs of this induced inter-regional shift of activity we may be missing the real point — namely, the domestic politics of energy.

Petro-Canada was legislated into existence in order to strengthen the capabilities of the federal government in the energy sector. Part of Ottawa's difficulty in dealing with the first energy crisis was that so much of the jurisdiction over the oil and gas industries rested with the producing provinces, especially Alberta; the provinces were busily extending their powers, collecting the economic rents, and fiercely resisting any federal interventions. The architects of federal energy policy in the 1970s, among them Bill Hopper, appear to have believed that in the longer run the Canadian petroleum industry would reduce its spending in the west — a mature producing basin which had yielded no significant oil discoveries in years — and that this process ought to be encouraged in the interest of federal-provincial balance and financed through part of the funds generated from current production in the west. Petro-Canada itself remarked at length in its 1978 corporate strategy document that governments everywhere had assumed a much greater role in controlling the oil industry, and that the government of Alberta's financial position "has improved enormously as a result of higher oil and gas prices and it has shown a determination to play a greater role, indeed a dominant role, in energy decisions both through its legislative and regulatory powers and more recently through the investment decisions of corporations over which it has control or influence." The oil industry was "watching to see which level of government will play the principal role," noted Petro-Canada; moreover, those companies which had been active on the frontiers were moving back to Alberta once again:

> With few exceptions, the industry has shifted the emphasis of its efforts to the western Canada basin due to the recent exploration successes and fiscal incentives. The development of production capacity in the frontier basin should be actively pursued and it is premature to downgrade the longer-term supply potential of the frontier basins. The development of the frontiers can serve to balance the dominant role of Alberta in the energy industry since this production will be on federal lands.[47]

Of course, the same concerns about the growing wealth and power of the oil-producing provinces were enlarged by the second oil shock in 1979-80 and underlay much of the National Energy Program's mix of prices, grants, and taxes. One of the real continuities we can find in Canadian energy policy going back to the early 1970s is how the federal-provincial struggle for power and jurisdiction has involved governments in very costly competitions for exploration investment and control over production. Petro-Canada has had other important motives for investing so heavily in the frontiers, and yet there is no doubt that an unstated *political* purpose in its capital spending has been "to balance the dominant role of Alberta"; unquestionably, Alberta has used its own energy corporations (see chapter 5) for similar political objects. A real irony in this for Petro-Canada of course is that much of its own land base, proven reserves, and oil and gas production is located in Alberta.

Turning to a review of Petro-Canada's capital expenditures in the 1980s, Table I shows that the state oil company maintained a very aggressive and costly frontier exploration programme until about 1986, when the federal PIP grants were terminated. It was the PIP incentive and annual equity infusions from the government (the last equity funds were paid in 1984) that paid for Petro-Canada's frontier drilling; once it was forced to carry these from its own cash flow, it prudently reduced spending and shifted to lower-risk activities. Its reinvestment of internally-generated funds sharply declined after the mid-1980s. The frontier expenditures also reflect the downward path of world oil prices in the 1980s, especially after the failure of OPEC to defend the price in 1986, as Petro-Canada slashed its long-term speculative investments in favour of projects capable of generating early cash flow (see Table II).

Petro-Canada thus remained in the frontiers long past the point of commercial prudence, but it ought to be remembered that the

Table I
Petro-Canada: Capital Expenditures, 1981-87
($ million)

Resources	1987	1986	1985	1984	1983	1982	1981
Exploration
Frontier	41	245	442	601	581	371	207
Western Canada	101	62	145	128	123	143	108
Foreign	12	11	19	30	6	1	5
Development
Western Canada	108	99	166	104	127	156	116
Foreign	--	1	6	6	--	2	15
Oil Sands
Syncrude	44	47	60	31	22	30	16
Other	35	17	30	53	5	20	15
Total Resources	341	482	868	953	864	723	482
Products
Refining	49	55	115	90	49	142	50
Marketing	73	57	50	33	49	62	30
Total Products	122	112	165	123	98	204	80
Corporate Admin.	25	20	26	55	35	43	35
Direct Capital Expenditures	488	614	1059	1131	997	970	597
PIP grants	(5)	(166)	(349)	(380)	(469)	(300)	(139)
Net Capital Expenditures	483	448	710	751	528	670	458
Reinvestment ratio	0.62	0.63	0.86	0.87	0.85	n.a.	n.a.

Source: Petro-Canada, *1981-7 Annual Reports*.

company was mostly spending what Dome Petroleum used to call O.P.M. — other people's money — in doing so.   In other ways, Petro-Canada began to detach itself from the government purse and agenda in 1982 and 1983 — both extremely hard years for the petroleum industry and for the wider economy.   Although the Canadian oil and gas industries were heavily regulated and therefore did not experience the full, immediate effect of the crisis in world oil, any shelter was temporary.   The downstream operations of the industry now felt the depression in demand from recession and conservation; oil and natural gas were being shut-in in western Canada; the big energy megaprojects were being shelved.   Oil industry profits fell off dramatically.

Table II
Petro-Canada Canadian Exploration Expenditures

	Western Provinces		Frontier		PIP Grants	PIP Grants
	Total	Per cent of Total	Total	Per cent of Total		Per cent of Total Exploration
	$ millions		$ millions		$ millions	Expenditures
1987	101	71.1	41	28.9	5	3.5
1986	62	20.2	245	79.8	166	54.1
1985	145	24.7	442	75.3	349	59.5
1984	128	17.6	601	82.4	380	52.1
1983	123	17.5	581	82.5	469	66.6

Source: Petro-Canada, *1987 Annual Report.*

The 'policy' side of Petro-Canada depended on the company's special access in Ottawa, and this was cut back in 1982 with the departure of Joel Bell, Executive Vice-President, from the company; involved in the corporation's earliest operations and the man responsible for its finance and capital budgets, Bell was a Trudeau-era intellectual manque who seemed to spend most of his time in Ottawa working on energy policy questions.   Then Marc Lalonde, Petro-Canada's powerful patron in the Trudeau Cabinet, was shifted from Energy to Finance, a clear sign that the government's priority was no longer to be the N.E.P. but the worsening economy. At the same time Petro-Canada was being informed that its annual equity allocations were being cut. All of which suggested that Petro-Canada's status as a well-financed but tightly-controlled agent of policy was no longer viable: Petro-Canada must look to its own resources.

At least a year-and-a-half before the election of the Mulroney Conservatives in September 1984, Petro-Canada had begun to shift its own strategy and structure in response to the world oil crisis. Strategy began to seek a better balance between short-run opportunities to generate cash and the more promising longer-term investments. Petro-Canada continued to rationalize its downstream assets as a way of gaining efficiencies. It emphasized natural gas production and exports. It wrote-off some of its more dubious investments. It increased its exploration activity overseas. To reduce its dependence on federal government funding, it began to cut costs and high-risk ventures such as the Arctic Pilot Project and to stress increased production from western Canada.   It restructured its operations into three groups: Petro-Canada Resources, the upstream; Petro-Canada Products, the downstream; and the Corporate Division. The company's five senior executives, led by Bill Hopper, formed the Executive Council, the central decision-making body. Hopper noted in March 1984 that the rapid growth and complexity of Petro-Canada led him to recruit senior managers from outside the corporation; for the most part, these have been Canadians formerly employed by multinational oil companies. These were executives oriented to the commercial, "bottom-line" culture of the oil industry, not to the grey ambiguities of a state oil company.

The remarkable growth of Petro-Canada's refining and marketing (shown in Table III) through the 1980s is perhaps the most important feature of its post-1981 development. Partly because weaker growth in product demand and overcapacity forced the Canadian oil industry to close eleven refineries and carry out large rationalizations of marketing operations, those companies that have had integrated operations have been less vulnerable to an unstable world oil market. In a fully deregulated oil industry, upstream revenues and earnings are largely driven by world prices; if the price collapses, as it did in 1986, producers have little protection except for government fiscal relief. On the other hand, an integrated firm can receive a strong counter-cyclical boost from the lower cost of crude oil to its downstream refineries and marketing: thus in 1986, when the world price of oil fell from $US 31/bbl to $US 10/bbl, upstream revenues and rates of return in the Canadian oil industry completely collapsed; whereas cash flow and net income increased sharply in the downstream. Petro-Canada's upstream earnings declined from $197 million in 1985 to $57 million in 1986, but its increased earnings downstream (from a loss of $22 million to $115 million) more than offset these losses.[48] These results partly reflected the fact that Petro-Canada had moved, just before the world price began to slide in late 1985, to make its fifth takeover — Gulf Canada's downstream assets west of Quebec, including its major Edmonton refinery, for $875 million. The Gulf acquisition, paid for with debt and internally-generated cash, was a very attractive commercial proposition for Petro-Canada — the assets were reportedly sold below book value — and it was encouraged by the Conservative government as a way of permitting the takeover of Gulf Canada's upstream assets by the Reichmann-owned Olympic and York of Toronto. With Gulf's downstream assets, Petro-Canada now controlled better than 20 per cent of Canadian refining and gasoline marketing, second only to Imperial Oil Ltd.. Concentration in the Canadian petroleum industry increased significantly; but the takeovers and dis-integration of Gulf — part of the consequences of the restructuring of the world oil industry — were hailed by Prime Minister Mulroney as a victory for Canadianization. In fact, the further expansion of Petro-Canada into the downstream divided the Conservative caucus, and the cabinet reportedly made it a condition of its approval of the takeover that Petro-Canada itself would be privatized.[49]

The Gulf acquisition, like many of Petro-Canada's opportunistic investments, was both an aggressive strategy to increase its market share at the expense of the remaining integrated companies — Imperial, Shell, and Texaco — and a defensive move designed to increase Petro-Canada's capacity to withstand the cycles of the world oil market and to generate much more of its own operating funds. It was the deteriorating business environment — unstable oil and gas prices, weak demand, a continuing surplus of natural gas in North America — and the end of government equity funding of Petro-Canada (negotiated with the outgoing Liberal government), and *not* the election of the new Conservative government in September 1984 that led Petro-Canada to adopt a much more conservative strategy of optimizing existing assets for cash flow and shifting from the frontiers to conventional oil and gas properties in the west. As an increasingly autonomy-oriented enterprise capable of generating a significant share of its working capital from its operations, Petro-Canada was re-orienting itself away from its old long-term assurance of supply mandate and learning how to adapt to deregulation and a market-driven energy policy. It announced in its 1984 *Annual Report* that its early phase of building up the company and investing for energy security was over. The corporation, stated Bill Hopper, "has now been given a new mandate by its shareholder — to operate in a commercial, private sector fashion, with emphasis on profitability and the need to maximize the return on the Government of Canada's investment. In this regard, Petro-Canada is not to be perceived in the future as an instrument in the pursuit of the Government's policy objectives."[50] This of course was intended to signal the forthcoming privatization of the state oil company (which had not occurred by mid-1988).

Table III
Petro-Canada: Downstream Operations

Refining	1987	1986	1985	1984	1983
Refinery crude capacity (thousands of m³ per day)	64.0	64.0	46.2	31.6	31.6
Crude oil processed by Petro-Canada (thousands of m³ per day)	48.4	47.2	34.2	27.6	25.3
Refinery utilization (per cent)	76	74	78	86	78
Marketing					
Retail and whole-sale outlets	4,268	4,344	4,620	2,716	3,107
Products Sales (thousands of m³ per day)	45.6	44.4	35.5	29.8	27.1

Source: Petro-Canada, *1987 Annual Report.*

Petro-Canada's "new mandate" to operate in a purely commercial fashion, never published and only given verbally by Conservative Energy Minister Pat Carney, was highly convenient to the company: in effect, it meant that management would now have full control of all of the assets of Petro-Canada — including the paid-in equity of the government, valued at $6.6 billion in 1984. The statement that it was not to be perceived as a policy instrument would make it politically impossible for government not only to use the corporation, but perhaps even to control it. It gave Petro-Canada *carte blanche* to write-off many of the high-cost, risky frontier assets it was carrying on its books (in 1985 Petro-Canada wrote-off $865 million in frontier oil and gas properties). And it also strengthened the corporation's hand in bargaining over the terms of development for frontier oil supply projects such as Hibernia or its own Terra Nova discovery: in the upstream, as in the refining and marketing sector, Petro-Canada would now be negotiating as an oligopolist — one of four or five dominant firms without whose concord major oil and gas projects in Canada do not proceed.

In early 1986, the world oil crisis of overproduction struck with full fury and the price fell below US $10/bbl before recovering to somewhat higher values. Petro-Canada now recognized that the price drop was not an aberration, but a fundamental reaction to supply and demand imbalances. Management assumed that "a low and unstable crude oil price environment" would prevail, and began a drastic contraction of the corporation: two thousand employees, or 23 per cent of Petro-Canada's work-force, were fired in early 1986, capital expenditures were cut back, and all the emphasis shifted to upstream production and downstream profit margins.[51] Petro-Canada slashed its research and development programme and many other longer-term investments in energy in order to generate higher cash flow and "to maintain the integrity of its financial structure" and its fixed financial obligations.[52] In a word, Petro-Canada's response to the crisis was shaped by the need to demonstrate to the banks and financial markets that the corporation enjoyed autonomy *vis-à-vis* the government and was suitable for privatization. One of Petro-Canada's stated objectives for its 1986-1990 planning is: "To develop and manage a Corporation that is judged by the financial investment community to be financially sound and self-sustaining, through an appropriate mix of upstream and downstream activities and short and longer-term investments and prudent financing thereof."[53]

However, large oil companies have to plan beyond the short run. Even if oil prices are low and the future is uncertain, they must replace the oil and gas reserves they are using up or they deplete their capital. An integrated oil company with downstream assets as large as Petro-Canada's will strive to keep its market share upstream as well — e.g. in conventional oil production — and increase it in, say, the *in situ* oil sands; for Petro-Canada is a crude-short company, it refines four times as much crude oil as it produces. Because productive capacity from reserve additions of conventional light oil is inadequate to replace the oil reserves now being used up, it is expected that Ontario refineries will be importing some of their oil requirements in the early 1990s. Petro-Canada and the industry in general have a strong commercial interest, despite current low oil prices, in bringing on new production from Hibernia, the Beaufort Sea, and in upgrading heavy oil and bitumen. What government needs to understand is that Petro-Canada's commercial interests are not necessarily incompatible with the national interest. In Petro-Canada's own words:

> For much of its ten year existence, Petro-Canada has been a leading explorer in Canada's frontier areas, especially the East Coast and the Arctic. The Corporation's success in these areas has established a significant inventory of resource prospects. Consistent with its commercial orientation, Petro-Canada is moving toward developing its most attractive resources, specifically Hibernia, offshore Newfoundland .... The Corporation's current Plan also envisions future participation in a second mineable oil sands project in the Province of Alberta and the Venture gas project offshore Nova Scotia ....

> Petro-Canada's decision to emphasize early development, when weighted against the depressed outlook for oil prices and the Corporation's finite funding capability, has significant implications for the strategic directions established for the rest of the Corporation's exploration and development activities. First, is the major reduction in frontier exploration activity after 1986. Second, in order to facilitate the transition from short-term lower risk projects in western Canada to long-term, high risk offshore projects, and also to compensate for declining western Canadian conventional oil production, the Corporation has increased its involvement in staged *in situ* oil sands development.[54]

The antitheses which we earlier noted in Petro-Canada's strategy are still present today: the long run opportunities versus the need for short run profits; the frontiers versus the west, etc. If the Canadian government still has an interest in the development of some of these oil supply projects, then it should participate in their financing via Petro-Canada. This means giving the corporation new equity funding, but it would have to be contingent on its application only for the specific projects (and not for use, say, in marketing). Petro-Canada should also be using some of its own cash resources in these risky projects, but the company has a legitimate point when it argues that its participation requires new equity funding. Because we do not favour the privatization of Petro-Canada and want to hold it in the public sector as insurance against an uncertain future, we would argue that there is room for negotiation on the issue of financing the company's capital needs on specific oil supply projects.

Conclusion

Our principal theme in this chapter has been the role of a changing international environment in Petro-Canada's origins and development. Among Canada's federal Crown corporations — of which it is now the largest — Petro-Canada has undoubtedly been shaped the most dramatically by the impact of external forces. In the first phase of the energy crisis, Petro-Canada was conceived and began its operations. In the second phase of the energy crisis, the corporation was expanded and turned into the direct arm of the state. And in the third phase, which has truly been the industry's real energy crisis, Petro-Canada improvised its autonomy and further growth.

Yet there was no inexorable process at work; no hidden hand was pushing the actors in an inevitable direction. More than external forces were at play. Politics — domestic Canadian politics — played an important part in every phase of Petro-Canada's development. Nationalist pressures to reduce Canada's reliance on the multi-national oil companies and to protect consumers from the instabilities of world oil helped to support Petro-Canada's expansion. The rivalry between Alberta and the federal government over control of the oil industry reinforced Petro-Canada's shift to the frontiers in the late 1970s and early 1980s. And the role of individual personalities, especially that of Petro-Canada chairman Bill Hopper, has sometimes overridden everything else: without Hopper's ambition, his knowledge of the international oil system, and his capacity to play the game of power politics, it is most unlikely that Petro-Canada would have become the force that it is today. Whatever one may think of it, it was Bill Hopper's accomplishment that he seized the potential of the world oil crisis, tied the growth of his corporation to the policy of the state, and through a peculiarly Canadian combination of enterprise and public interest built it into an autonomous corporate empire.

Can Petro-Canada's own interests and ambitions be linked again to the public interest or is it now too large and independent to control? If the company is partially privatized and turned into a mixed enterprise on the model of, say, British Petroleum or the French group of national petroleum firms, then it will be very difficult, if not impossible, for the government to have influence in its decisions or investments; moreover, management would have little accountability to either the private investors or the state. Would a mixed enterprise be more efficient? It may be less prone to risk-taking (Petro-Canada is already less prone to take risks), but it would be unlikely to maximize profits: rather, the managers would run it to increase their own autonomy, internal cash flow, and market share. It would be little different than it is now except that it would be beyond government direction in another crisis.

Petro-Canada should be kept in the public sector and expected to operate on a normal commercial basis, using its own earnings and its access to debt capital to finance its operations. For its much larger and riskier oil supply projects, such as Hibernia, there is a good case for additional equity; just as there may be a good case for the government to take dividends when the oil begins to flow offshore. In the interim, Petro-Canada's strategy of developing medium-sized *in situ* oil sands projects, such as Wolf Lake, is a good one; but federal subsidies will probably be needed to build the upgraders which are required to turn the bitumens and heavy oils produced in such ventures into oil that can be used in Canadian refineries.

Petro-Canada is not at present an instrument of policy, but we have argued that its own commercial interests are not necessarily incompatible with national interests. Assuming that the company is not privatized, how can its owner shareholder keep it accountable? We have no simple answer to that question: Petro-Canada is now a very large, complex oil company capable of generating much of its own funds. Attempts to force it to act so as to foster increased competition in the downstream have already been resisted; state oil companies are notoriously poor instruments to promote competition and efficiency in refining and marketing, and tend to behave like any private oligopolist. But in upstream operations and investments, there is a good deal more latitude for the government to exercise control: this will be especially the case if oil prices are high enough to bring on the development of, say, Hibernia and Petro-Canada's nearby Terra Nova discovery. Petro-Canada's enacting legislation, as we have shown, contains enough controls and accountability measures to permit a government to protect its interests in the corporation without impairing it with too much partisan supervision and intervention. It is a question of balancing power with power; interest with interest. In a very different political context, James Madison remarked in *The Federalist Papers* that in framing a government of men over other men, the great difficulty lay in the need to oblige government to control itself. Only by giving each department the power and the motive to prevent encroachments by others, by forcing "ambition to counteract ambition", could this be assured, said Madison.[55] It remains a good principle. If there is a problem in regulating and directing Crown corporations such as Petro-Canada, surely the answer is to supply the ambition in Ottawa to do so. When legitimate government is weak, it is the feudal lords who wield the real power.

Notes

1. Larry Pratt, "Petro-Canada", in *Public Corporations and Public Policy in Canada*, ed. by Allan Tupper and G. Bruce Doern, (Montreal: Institute for Research on Public Policy, 1981), pp. 95-148.

2. P.H. Frankel, *Mattei: Oil and Power Politics* (New York: Frederick A. Praeger, 1966), p. 26.

3. Canada, Department of Energy, Mines and Resources, *An Energy Policy for Canada--Phase I*, Volume 1 (Ottawa: Information Canada, 1973), pp. 18 and 184.

4. *Ibid.*, p. 192.

5. Interviews, and *An Energy Policy for Canada--Phase I, op. cit.*, Volume 2, pp. 242-47.

6. *An Energy Policy for Canada--Phase I*, op. cit., Volume 1, pp. 183-93.

7. *The State and Economic Growth*, ed. by H. G. J. Aitken, (New York: Social Science Research Council, 1959), pp. 79-114.

8. O. Noreng, *Oil Politics in the 1980s: Patterns of International Cooperation* (New York: McGraw-Hill, 1978), p. 11. On the changing structure of world oil, see also F.J. Al-Chalabi, *OPEC and the International Oil Industry: A Changing Structure* (London: Oxford University Press, 1980); *Petroleum Economist* 47 (August-September 1980), pp. 329-32; and J.E. Hartshorn, "From Multi-national to National Oil: The Structural Change," *Middle East Economic Survey* (28 April 1980).

9. Canada, Parliament, House of Commons, *Debates*, 25 October 1973, pp. 7220, 7222. (Hereafter cited as *Debates*, date, page).

10. Maurice F. Strong, "Canada's Energy Future: The Role of Petro-Canada," Speech to the Canadian Club, Toronto, 18 April 1977, p. 9.

11. Hon. Donald S. Macdonald, "A National Energy Company," Memorandum to Cabinet, 31 October 1973, p. 34.

12. *Debates*, 6 December 1973, pp. 8478-82.

13. *Ibid.*, p. 8479.

14. L.E. Grayson, *National Oil Companies* (Chichester: John Wiley and Sons, 1981); L. Pratt, "Nationalised Oil Corporations and the Changing World Industry", *Transnational Corporations Research Project*, University of Sydney, 1983.

15. Grayson, *National Oil Companies*, p. 8.

16. *Debates*, 12 March 1975, p. 4036.

17. *Ibid.*, p. 4040.

18. *Ibid.*, p. 4041.

19. "A National Energy Company," Memorandum to Cabinet, 31 October 1973, p. 24.

20. H. A. Innis, *Problems of Staple Production in Canada* (Toronto: Ryerson, 1933), p. 80.

21. Petro-Canada, *Prospectus*, 28 April 1986.

22. Petro-Canada, *1981 Capital Budget Annex B*, October 1980.

23. See Larry Pratt, "Petro-Canada: Tool for Energy and Security or Instrument of Economic Development," in *How Ottawa Spends Your Tax Dollars 1982*, ed. by G. Bruce Doern (Toronto: James Lorimer, 1982), pp. 87-114.

24. Petro-Canada, *Corporate Strategy*, October 1980, pp. 1-2.

25. "The Watson Report," 21 February 1979, CBC transcript.

26. Frankel, *Oil and Power Politics*, p. 167.

27. Petro-Canada, *Corporate Strategy*, October 1980.

28. Petro-Canada, Memoranda re. revised 1981 Capital Budget, 26 November 1980.

29. Grayson, *National Oil Companies*, p. 250.

30. Petro-Canada, *Corporate Strategy*, October 1980.

31. See Jennifer Lewington, "Lessons of the Arctic Pilot Project," in *Politics of the Northwest Passage*, ed. by Franklyn Griffiths, (Kingston and Montreal: McGill-Queen's, 1987), pp. 163-180.

32. Petro-Canada, *Corporate Strategy*, October 1980.

33. Canada, House of Commons, Standing Committee on Natural Resources and Public Works, *Minutes of Proceedings and Evidence*, 14 February 1984, p. 1:10.

34. Petro-Canada, *1982 Annual Report.*

35. John Maynard Keynes, *The General Theory of Employment, Interest, and Money*, (New York: Harbinger, 1964) chapter 12.

36. *Ibid.*

37. G. Bruce Doern and Glen Toner, *The Politics of Energy* (Toronto: Methuen, 1985), p. 58.

38. Petro-Canada, *Corporate Strategy* October 1980.

39. Petro-Canada, *Summary of the Petro-Canada Capital Budget for the 1987 Budget Year.*

40. On demand, see *BP Statistical Review of World Energy* June 1987.

41. See *Petroleum Economist,* January 1988 for a useful overview.

42. *Petroleum Economist,* January 1984, p. 13.

43. Panos Cavoulacos, "Upstream investment strategy urged," *Petroleum Economist,* February 1987, p. 66.

44. John Zysman, "The French State in the International Economy," in *Between Power and Plenty: Foreign Economic Policies of Advanced Industrial States* ed. by Peter J. Katzenstein (Madison: University of Wisconsin Press, 1980), pp. 255-294.

45. Joseph A. Schumpeter, *Capitalism, Socialism and Democracy,* London: George Allen & Unwin Ltd., 1976, pp. 81-106.

46. *Ibid.,* p. 84.

47. Petro-Canada, *Corporate Strategy 1978,* October 1978.

48. Canada, Petroleum Monitoring Agency, *Canadian Petroleum Industry 1986 Monitoring Survey* and Petro-Canada, *1986 Annual Report.*

49. R. Gwyn, "Carney Still Eager to Privatize PetroCan," *Toronto Star*, 7 February 1986.

50. Petro-Canada, *1984 Annual Report*, p. 2.

51. Petro-Canada, *1986 Annual Report*.

52. *Ibid.*

53. Summary of the Petro-Canada Corporate Plan for the 1986-1990 Planning Period and the Capital Budget for the 1986 Budget Year.

54. *Ibid.*

55. James Madison, "Federalist No. 51", in James Madison, Alexander Hamilton and John Jay, *The Federalist Papers*, (Penguin: Harmondsworth, 1987), pp. 318-322.

Chapter V

Alberta Energy Company

Allan Tupper

This essay examines the Alberta Energy Company (AEC) as a case study in mixed enterprise and as an instrument of public policy in a resource-based economy. The firm certainly provides students of such issues with a treasure trove of information. Since its inception in 1973, the AEC has aroused considerable debate and controversy. Scorned by the right and some elements of the oil industry as an unnecessary intervention into the market and denounced by the left as an inferior instrument to a Crown corporation, the firm has often charted a difficult course.

My theme is that in creating the AEC the Progressive Conservative government of Alberta Premier Peter Lougheed seriously underestimated the problems created by state ownership of oil in the Alberta economy. Further, the contradictions induced by such ownership were actually magnified in this case by the mixed enterprise format embracing as it does a sometimes tense combination of public and private capital. This having been said, I also warn readers to be wary of sweeping generalizations about the behaviour of mixed enterprises. For the AEC, for most of its history, seems to have balanced satisfactorily the interests of both its state and private shareholders.

The rationale for the AEC is probed in some detail as is the corporation's mandate, structure, and legislation. I examine

Lougheed's arguments about the need for the creation of Alberta-owned firms and his related ideas about Crown corporations. In particular, I note the government's initial edict that the AEC not compete directly with the conventional oil and gas industry in the province. Then I point out how the issue of competition between the AEC and private firms quickly emerged as a major political issue as did the perennial problem of the accountability of "quasi-public" firms. Then I explore the AEC's behaviour paying particular attention to its role as an instrument of provincial policy. The firm's apparently growing independence from the government is explored as is the possibly related commitment of the province to reduce its equity in the enterprise. I conclude with an overall evaluation of the AEC as an instrument of intervention and ask whether its further "privatization" is warranted or desirable.

The Origins of Intervention

The AEC is best understood as a product of Alberta's radically changing political and economic landscape in the early 1970s. First announced by Premier Lougheed in a province-wide television broadcast on 18 September 1973, the AEC was heralded as a unique partnership between government and citizens in the development and ownership of Alberta's valuable natural resources.[1] Ownership of the new corporation would be shared between the provincial government which would hold at least 50 per cent of the shares and individual Canadian investors with priority being given to Albertans. At the time government spokespersons spoke glowingly of the various investment opportunities available in the province and the need for vehicles that enabled provincial residents to participate in profitable activities. The AEC was to be a primary vehicle for such participation particularly in the massive Syncrude project at Fort McMurray, a project that lay at the heart of the Lougheed government's emerging economic vision.

In defending his government's involvement, Lougheed argued that a direct, substantial, and enduring provincial government role was required lest control of the new corporation fall into extraprovincial hands as had happened in the case of the Alberta Gas Trunk Line (now Nova, an Alberta corporation). As he put it: "... I think it's essential that we set up a vehicle like the AEC to give the citizens an opportunity to in fact invest; it's important that the government have a partnership role because the experience in Alberta has been, for example with the AGTL, the ownership is not in the hands of Albertans, even though the majority of the shareholders in number reside in Alberta."[2] As well as stressing the need for local control, Lougheed emphasized the AEC's role in allowing individuals, ideally those with little experience in financial affairs, to become involved in the stock market and to thereby gain a better appreciation of the virtues and complexity of corporate capitalism. In his initial guidelines to the AEC's president, Lougheed portrayed his scheme of "people's capitalism" in the following way: "Modern society is challenging the concept of private investment and, sometimes with justification, the behaviour of corporations. It may well be that the Alberta Energy Company, by creating widespread ownership and corporate participation in the province, will foster better understanding between our citizens and our economic system."[3]

If intervention was necessary to protect provincial interests, why was a potentially more flexible instrument like a wholly-owned state firm rejected? In answering this question Lougheed advanced the conventional argument that a wholly-owned state enterprise at the provincial level was simply too expensive and too risky. But other reasons are probably more important. For while Lougheed was clearly a "strong state Tory", one willing to employ provincial government power where necessary, he was also aware of the concern in his own party and among Alberta capitalists that his appetite for intervention might be excessive. Moreover, the provincial NDP clearly favoured Crown corporations as policy instruments and it was thus tactically important for the Conservatives to differentiate themselves while not appearing wedded to outmoded laissez-faire concepts. Finally, Lougheed and his senior ministers were undoubtedly aware of developments in Ottawa where plans to establish a large, potentially aggressive, wholly government-owned national oil company were under review. For obvious reasons, such a firm might be very unpopular in Alberta, a fact that gave Lougheed further incentive to develop a distinctive vehicle and one that differed from the proposed national oil company.[4]

Analysis of the AEC's legislation, articles of association, and initial assets reveal several important themes. First, the government had no precise goals for AEC, although it is clear that it expected the firm to grow quickly and to concentrate on investments in Alberta. Second, while it is an exaggeration to suggest that the government saw no role for the AEC in risky ventures, there is also little doubt that it was committed to establishing a company with significant growth and profit potential. Finally, the AEC clearly enjoyed a special status with the provincial government, notwithstanding the government's refrain that the AEC was "just another company".

As passed in 1974, the Alberta Energy Company Act established the company's ownership structure but said little about the firm's objectives or its relationship with the government or the provincial legislature.[5] Salient features include the provision that the provincial government must retain 50 per cent ownership and that no other shareholder could acquire more than 1 per cent of the voting shares. Given the wretched state of relations between Ottawa and Edmonton at the time, it is not surprising that the statute *explicitly* applies the 1 per cent rule to the federal Crown and its agents. Moreover, three quarters of the directors are to be Alberta residents and four of these may be appointed by the provincial government. Preference must be given to provincial residents in all share-offerings. The province may guarantee the corporation's debts and may transfer or sell provincial properties to the firm. All shareholders must be either Canadian citizens or residents of Canada. The act is silent on the mechanisms of control that the government might exercise over the firm as it is on the question of legislative oversight.

More information on the relationship between the province and the AEC is found in an October 1974 letter from Premier Lougheed to the AEC's president David E. Mitchell.[6] Here Lougheed maintained that the provincial government would be involved in the *ownership* not the *management* of the firm and that neither members of the Legislative Assembly nor civil servants would sit on the AEC board. The AEC would be fully taxable once a public share offering was made. The company would be apprised by the government of "investment opportunities" that are available to the province when these "appear adaptable to public equity ownership". The firm's board, moreover, should exhibit a "particular awareness" of the public interest of Albertans and the firm should yield "good" returns to its shareholders. Like the governing statute, Lougheed's letter fails to spell out any mechanisms of provincial control or legislative oversight. By implication, the message is that the former are informal and that the latter are non-existent.

The AEC's 1973 Memorandum of Association outlined the firm's objects very broadly. In support of its central goal of encouraging Albertans to invest in provincial resource industries, the firm was empowered: "To take part in the management, supervision, or control of the business or operation of any company."[7] And as well as granting the AEC a broad, almost open-ended mandate, the government also conferred a number of significant, and potentially profitable, investments on its new creation. Noteworthy among these initial opportunities were several undertakings at the Syncrude plant including an 80 per cent interest in the Edmonton-Fort McMurray pipeline and a 50 per cent interest in the Syncrude power plant. Moreover, the AEC was given an option to acquire up to a 20 per cent interest in the main Syncrude plant at any time before the production of 5 million barrels of synthetic oil. At the same time and much more controversially, the company was allowed to purchase the natural gas rights to the "Suffield Block", a relatively undeveloped 1,000 square mile tract of land north of Medicine Hat. Estimated to hold reserves of up to 4 trillion cubic feet of natural gas, the Block created development problems. The Alberta government owned more than 95 per cent of the mineral rights but the federal government owned the surface rights and leased the area to the British army as a training site. AEC's place in the provincial energy infrastructure was further enhanced by the government's decision to have the company become a partner with the Alberta Gas Trunk Line in Pan-Alberta Gas Ltd., a fledgling firm designed to market Alberta natural gas beyond provincial boundaries.

In the development of these and other opportunities, the AEC was to labour under a sole, but major, constraint. It was to develop its investments in concert with private enterprise and was forbidden, to employ Lougheed's phrase, "to engage in exploration in the conventional oil and gas industry in Alberta."[8] Such restrictions were motivated by political considerations, notably Lougheed's desire to quell criticism about his government's "socialist" tendencies and to further differentiate the AEC from Petro-Canada. As we shall see such an ambiguous guideline neither limited conflict about the AEC nor clarified the corporation's position within Alberta's oil and gas industries.

The upshot of this description is that, notwithstanding the government's contrary claims, the AEC was indeed an energy company "pas comme les autres." Created by provincial statute, half owned by the province, and blessed with valuable assets and access to political elites, the company was positioned as a "major player" in future resource development projects in Alberta. Indeed, the AEC's privileged position led some oilmen to argue that the company was more akin to a public utility than a conventional oil company.

The creation of the AEC evoked a vigorous debate whose themes about the proper role for the company and the government persist to the present. The notion of a "mixed" ownership energy company was greeted with skepticism by Alberta's two major opposition parties in 1973, the Social Credit and the New Democratic Party, but for different reasons. The NDP, led by the late Grant Notley, saw the AEC as a timid and circumscribed instrument of intervention. For Notley who favoured a Crown corporation, the AEC might become little more than a "glorified service company" for the multinationals who dominated Alberta's oil patch.[9] What was required was a firm with a broad mandate to compete aggressively with the private sector in all phases of the industry. Interestingly, Notley sensed that the AEC's structure might impede its usefulness as a policy instrument. He was concerned that the need to satisfy private shareholders might lead the firm to eschew important, but risky, projects. A Crown corporation would be free from such a constraint and hence would be better placed to advance provincial interests. Notley also argued that the AEC, by creating a large new cadre of Albertan investors, might create a political base for the too rapid exploitation of Alberta's valuable, non-renewable resources. The fledgling firm might also give the provincial government an interest in a rapid pace of resource development.

The Social Credit party, as the Official Opposition during the 1971-1975 period, was also concerned about the AEC but for different reasons than the NDP. Its concern was that the new company, far from being too timid, might be too aggressive thereby causing "unfair" competition between a public firm and the private industry. The party's initial position called for a reduction of government equity to 25 per cent and the imposition of strict legislative prohibitions on AEC's capacity to compete with private companies. Spokespersons insisted that the government must refrain from "political" interventions into AEC's operations.

Public opinion is difficult to gauge on such a topic, although the overwhelming response to AEC's first share offering suggests the concept struck a responsive chord. Editorial writers in Alberta's major dailies generally endorsed the idea of a "hybrid" firm, although they called for a more precise corporate mandate. The *Edmonton Journal* endorsed the concept, in a manner remarkably similar to much of the debate about "privatization" in the 1980's, by arguing that the AEC allowed for state intervention while preserving freedom of choice for citizens.[11] Like the NDP, the *Calgary Albertan* noted the potential for the private shareholders to restrain the government's capacity to intervene, although unlike the NDP it applauded such a restraint.[11]

At the time of its establishment in 1973, Alberta's oil and gas companies were lukewarm about the AEC but adopted a "wait and see" attitude. G.W. Cameron, general manager of the Independent Petroleum Assocation, expressed anxiety about the expansionary tendencies of government firms and their capacity to compete with private firms.[12] But he also expressed confidence in the abilty of the Lougheed Tories, unlike other governments, to resist political interventions into AEC's affairs.

The Contradictions of Public Intervention

It must be remembered that when it created the AEC in 1973, the Lougheed government was very inexperienced, yet very ambitious. Moreover, it began its tenure in an environment of major change in the domestic and international energy markets. For these reasons, it is hardly surprising that the Conservatives' original "model" for the AEC seems remarkably simplistic in hindsight. Two key dimensions of the initial grand-design now appear particularly naive and lacking.

First, the government's claim that, despite its 50 per cent equity, it exercised no role in AEC decision-making caused enormous skepticism and aroused a decade long debate about the proper relationship between the firm and the provincial state. The investment of substantial public monies in the AEC and the mere existence of a political opposition, however weak, forced the government to the defensive and mocked its claim that it invariably eschewed any involvement in AEC decisions. Second, the government's vague prohibition of competition between the AEC and private firms was inadequate to the task of accommodating an interventionist state with the needs of a private sector long accustomed to a passive state presence. Here we note how the government's need to insure the success and rapid growth of its own enterprise led it to undertake a series of policies detrimental to private interests at least in the short-term.

The Dilemma of Accountability

In creating the AEC, the provincial government was determined that its company not be confused with a Crown corporation, either in structure or behaviour. And to this end, it resolutely maintained that it was not involved in the management of the firm. The AEC was free from government direction and in its operation commercial principles were to be paramount. Moreover, the government would be satisfied if the company abided by its legislation and pursued profitable investments. And in repeatedly rejecting opposition demands for greater information and debate about the AEC, the government stressed that the best test of accountability was the "bottom line".

The government's simple formula for the AEC's accountability soon broke down. For armed with the claim that the legislature, as guardian of the public purse, must be allowed to scrutinize all expenditures, the opposition parties repeatedly raised questions about the AEC's behaviour and performance. Their zealous pursuit of the high-road of political accountability and legislative oversight was further inspired by baser political motives. Both the NDP and the Social Credit sensed that the obvious popularity of most of Lougheed's policies was undercut to a degree by public concern about governmental secrecy and aloofness.

Throughout the 1970's the opposition bombarded the government with requests for information about its involvement in AEC affairs. Indeed, shortly after the company's establishment, rows erupted about whether the president's salary was a matter for the public record and about the appropriateness of stock options for senior officers in a "quasi-public" firm. A more profound controversy emerged in 1976 when a well known, non-union, Alberta contractor claimed that his firm lost a major contract for the Syncrude pipeline even though his bid was the lowest.[13] The implication was that the AEC, *possibly* operating at the government's behest, awarded the contract to a unionized firm in order to avert a general strike at the main Syncrude plant over the issue of non-union labour. In the face of much controversy, the government maintained that it had not intervened with AEC. But it was defensive and was forced to endure a prolonged public debate and business criticism for its handling of the affair.

Throughout the 1970s the opposition demanded greater accountability for the AEC. Several private members' bills were introduced and routinely defeated by the government's massive post-1975 legislative majority. And while the government gave no ground, it provided the opposition with a further avenue for attack when it transferred the province's equity in the AEC to the Heritage Savings Trust Fund whose operations were annually scrutinized by a select standing committee of the legislature. In all of this it is difficult to state precisely the impact of the opposition's attacks. For in refusing to answer queries about routine matters, the government was merely following the time-honoured path trodden by most Canadian governments when accounting for their entrepreneurial activities. But the government's claim that such crucial questions as the exercise of AEC's Syncrude option were simply "management" decisions began to wear thin after frequent repetition.

In November 1974, an *Edmonton Journal* editorial sensed the importance and difficulty of integrating a firm like the AEC with responsible government. In pointing out the dilemmas it argued: "It is vital at this early stage to establish the principle that the elected representatives of the people should be able to ask for and receive a considerable amount of information about the affairs of AEC, in order to exercise on behalf of the public the scrutiny that is healthy, but can be difficult, in respect of bodies like the AEC."[14] The Lougheed governments' stubborn resistance to proposals to increase AEC's accountability is difficult to justify. For one thing, it put the government in a position where every controversial action of the AEC was interpreted in one of two very critical ways. On one hand, a school of thought emerged that the government, as AEC's principal shareholder, frequently intervened in AEC's affairs to the possible detriment of private shareholders while avoiding accountability for such interventions. On the other hand, another viewpoint accepted the government's claims of non-involvement but reviled it for too passively guarding a major public investment. Implicit in this view is the notion that certain forms of public debate and discussion, far from impeding government firms, might enhance the quality of the decisions by broadening the range of debate and by keeping management on its toes.

A revered theme in the study of public enterprise is the tensions between political control, legislative accountability and corporate autonomy in the administration of state firms. The imperatives of public debate and the disclosure of information often conflict with the need for commercial freedom particularly when Crown firms operate in competitive markets. Mixed enterprises, the AEC being no exception, raise particularly vexing problems as the general dilemma is compounded by the specific problems posed by the existence of private shareholders. In all of this, the Lougheed government added further confusion and controversy by amending the AEC's legislation in 1975 to allow members of the Legislative Assembly to hold AEC shares without being in a conflict of interest. The rationale for this measure was never made clear except that senior government spokespersons implied that their non-participation in AEC ownership might be interpreted as a lack of confidence in the firm. While acknowledging that the government had a capacity to determine the AEC's prospects, they claimed that AEC ownership should not be seen as different from owning shares in any other firm operating in the province.

Debate about the propriety of this practice became an ingrained part of broader discussions of the AEC's role. And by 1979, 18 of 29 cabinet ministers held AEC stock with only 8 of them conferring these on a "blind trust".[15] The always simmering controversy boiled over in that year when opposition members noted that AEC was one of several firms bidding for valuable provincial timber leases and that the ultimate decision was in the government's hands. Government spokesmen proclaimed their neutrality and stressed that the AEC operated at a very long "arm's length" from the government. Moreover, proof of conflict of interest demanded the establishment of *direct* links between political intervention and personal gain. Critics remained skeptical and advanced the obvious counterclaim that in a democracy even the appearance of conflicts of interest must be avoided. While rejected by the government, such a view is sensible. The government's decision to allow ministers to hold AEC shares simply added another complex problem to an already lengthy list.

Public-Private Sector Competition

The expansion of the state into new areas often evokes conflict between government and business even when state intervention may enhance the profit-making capacity of elements of the business community. This general statement is particularly true of an industry like oil which rhetorically worships the free enterprise ideal and in a province like Alberta where until the 1970's the government played a passive role in resource development.

As noted earlier, a concern for maintaining harmonious relations with the oil and gas industry led the Lougheed government to prohibit competition between the Alberta Energy Company and the private sector. But in assessing the relationship between the firm, the government, and the private sector, it becomes apparent that such a prohibition is vague and subject to competing interpretations. Indeed, in industries as complex and specialized as oil and gas, it is difficult to imagine any role whatsoever for a state-sponsored firm that was literally bound by such a prohibition. Moreover, the Alberta government on several occasions unrepentingly conferred "preferential treatment" on the AEC even in the face of angry opposition from the private sector. Such policies were undertaken because the government had distinct political interests in the AEC's success and in their pursuit was sometimes willing to challenge the private sector.

Despite the provincial government's contrary wishes, tensions quickly emerged between it, the AEC, and the private sector over the Suffield Block. At issue was the price paid by the AEC for the asset. Noting that it had been denied the opportunity to bid on Suffield leases, the industry maintained that the problem was compounded by the $54 million price tag which was said to be far too low. Such concerns were fuelled by "rumours" in Calgary that the AEC planned to purchase its own rigs and explore the area on its own. These allegations were denied by the province and the AEC and the area was indeed developed through a series of "farm-outs" from the AEC to the private sector. But in acting to advance quickly the prospects of its own creation, the province firmly established the image of the AEC as a firm whose well-being was guaranteed by the province and which hence might be a threat to the well-being of the private sector. The emerging view of the AEC in 1975 was neatly captured by Horst Heise when he remarked: "AEC is possibly the most pampered investment vehicle to hit the Canadian investment scene for many years. If a purely private company had ever received the preferential treatment in sugar-coated acquisitions and sure-fire options the public would have a right to cry bloody murder."[16]

As if oblivious to the dispute about the Suffield Block, the government generated an identical controversy when in 1978 it granted the AEC development rights to the Primrose Lake Block. This land, comprising more than 1.25 million acres, straddled the Alberta-Saskatchewan border. As in the Suffield Block, the province owned the resources but leased the area to the federal government which employed the virgin lands as an air weapons range. In transferring the lands to the AEC the government argued that the unique development problems at Primrose called for intergovernmental collaboration and that an agency like the AEC was better equipped to respond than the private sector. And in further defending the transfer, Don Getty, then minister of Federal and Intergovernmental Affairs, added that the province had an "obligation" to consider the AEC because "it was there".[17]

This repeat performance of the Suffield episode further angered the oil and gas industry. For while the AEC had not yet provided direct competition in the exploration phase of the industry, its presence had certainly made access to potentially valuable lands much more difficult. Moreover, industry spokesmen resented what they believed were absurdly low transfer prices. In the Primrose case, the AEC allegedly paid $20 per acre ($45 per acre after other obligations were worked in according to government figures) when industry sources estimated that a "realistic" price was $150 per acre.[18] According to some estimates, the Primrose transaction cost the provincial Treasury at least $150 million in lost bonus payments. And in rejecting the AEC's claim that the cost correctly captured the area's risk potential, the industry noted that adjacent lands had recently brought bids in the $200 to $600 range. It was hard therefore to accept the AEC's claim that it was buying a "pig in a poke". The AEC's decision to award "farm-outs" at Primrose to its most vocal private sector critics lessened the private sector's animosity, but only to a degree. The AEC's government-led emergence as a significant firm had soured relations between government and business.

What explains the repeated tendency of an avowedly "pro-business" government like the Lougheed Conservatives to confer special status on a quasi-public firm in the face of private sector opposition? First and perhaps most obviously, government firms in the oil industry, to be effective, must generally be large and must become large quickly. Such rapid growth usually requires state assistance and such assistance will often be seen by private firms as discriminatory.[19] The AEC is no exception to this general problem. Second, while Premier Lougheed saw the AEC as a vehicle for instructing Albertans in the dynamics of a capitalist economy, it is difficult to imagine that he intended his electorate to suffer personal financial loss through their AEC investments. The company's preferred access to valuable lands, for example, allowed it to establish quickly a basis for profitability while still maintaining that it was subject to the rigours of market discipline. Moreover, AEC, with its close links to the provincial government and with its almost exclusive focus on investments within the province, was a barometer of sorts for the health of the provincial economy. As one investment analyst described an investment in AEC: "It's almost like investing in the province of Alberta."[20] The significance of such perceptions was probably not lost on the premier or his associates. Finally, the Primrose deal was probably related to the Alberta government's deep commitment to the Syncrude venture. For if the AEC was to exercise its option for 20 per cent of the entire venture, it would have to borrow extensively. Its credit-worthiness and investor appeal would be further enhanced by the addition of another rich asset to its collection. For the government of Alberta, some hopefully short term conflict with elements of the private oil and gas industry was a modest concern compared to the ultimate success of Syncrude.

The Primrose and Suffield examples show how the AEC enjoyed a special relationship with the provincial government. But in other areas, notably petrochemicals, complex political and economic circumstances prohibited any special status for the firm. Like many energy companies, AEC saw enormous opportunities in the expansion of Alberta's petrochemical industry in the late 1970s and early 1980s. The industry was potentially profitable and was heralded as a means of "diversifying" Alberta's economy. But lacking the expertise to become a major petrochemical player on its own, the AEC was forced to enter consortia with established firms. One of these was a proposed joint venture with Dupont Canada for the construction of a major polyethylene plant in the province. Other forces were at play, however, notably the emergence of rival projects and an acute shortage of ethylene, a petrochemical building block. In the early 1980s, Alberta's sole ethylene plant was owned by Alberta Gas Ethylene, a Nova subsidiary. This plant's output was entirely consumed by Dow Chemicals and in response to the shortage AGE proposed a trio of new plants. One of these, AGE 2, was nearing completion. But even before the plant was completed, it was obvious that demand for its output far exceeded the plant's capacity. This difficult problem was compounded because Nova itself had further ambitions in petrochemicals including a joint venture polyethylene plant with Shell Canada. The AEC-Dupont consortium and the Nova-Shell venture both coveted the same scarce commodity.

A classic dilemma emerged for the Lougheed government in 1981. Its widely discussed commitment to a major expansion of Alberta's petrochemical industry was stalled by a lack of ethylene. But more fundamentally, the ethylene shortage evoked intense rivalry between business factions. And one of the most troublesome feuds was between the AEC and Nova, Lougheed's "chosen instruments" and the crown jewels of Alberta's new business establishment. Both firms enjoyed close relations with the government, but now both sought, in concert with Canadian subsidiaries of international firms, the same scarce resource. This rivalry was dramatized when the two Alberta firms traded insults in hearings before a provincial regulatory board. In opposing the AEC-Dupont polyethylene venture, AGE denounced Dupont as an enemy of Alberta business because of its parent's alleged campaign to block entry of Alberta petrochemicals into American markets.[21]

The provincial government sensed that emerging tensions in the provincial petrochemical industry were too serious to be resolved by the firms themselves. And in a classic example of the use of government power to maintain order in a key industry, it issued an order in council stating that the allocation of AGE ethylene required the approval of the Minister of Economic Development.[22] Given this intervention, the AEC argued that AGE must be ordered by the province to allocate ethylene to its joint venture with Dupont. In bolstering its case, AEC claimed that its proposal boasted the greatest Alberta ownership even though Dupont Canada was a wholly-owned subsidiary of its American parent. Such proposals fell on deaf ears with the result that the AEC-Dupont proposal failed to receive ethylene from AGE 2.

In this case of "zero-sum" intra-capitalist rivalry, the winner was Nova not the AEC. And while the government was silent on its reasons for not intervening on AEC's behalf, it is likely that Nova's pioneering work in petrochemicals was the decisive factor. In this industry, the AEC was the newcomer, Nova the established force. The key point emerges that the state faces limits in its capacity to favour particular firms whether "chosen instruments", mixed firms, or Crown corporations. The well-being of an important *industry* must sometimes prevail over the interests of particular firms however well-placed.

Alberta Energy in Action: Policy Goals and the Bottom Line

The recent proliferation of mixed enterprises in Canada has raised questions about their effectiveness as policy instruments. A particular concern is whether the combination of public and private capital within a firm can be readily wedded. Compelling work by Stephen Brooks suggests that mixed enterprise seldom works and that tensions often arise between the state and private participants.[23] The resolution of such tensions may result in either the withdrawal of private capital or an increasingly passive state role as government, in the face of shareholder resistance, becomes unwilling to employ the firm for policy purposes. At best, mixed firms are blunt and inflexible policy instruments.

What lessons does the AEC hold for students of mixed enterprise? Have its operations been plagued by tensions between the state's interests and those of the company's private shareholders? Such questions are more easily asked than answered for several reasons. First, the government never established precise goals for the firm and hence its intentions do not provide clear criteria for evaluation. Second, public conflict between the firm and the government over major policy questions has not occurred. Observers of the AEC are thus denied episodes of visible conflict from which generalizations about mixed enterprise are frequently derived. Finally, assessments of the determinants and motivations of corporate decision-making are necessarily subjective. Indeed, to assess accurately the impact of various ownership forms one would have to examine, for example, the behaviour of almost identical public, private, and mixed ownership energy firms under like circumstances. Social scientists are seldom provided with such laboratories.

All this having been said, I argue that the AEC has followed a corporate strategy broadly congruent with the main policy thrusts of successive Progressive Conservative governments in modern Alberta. This implies neither that the firm is under the direct control of the government nor that its management is unconcerned with the company's growth as an end in itself. As in all such firms and Crown corporations, successful managers pursue strategies to maximize their own autonomy.

Before investigating AEC's behavior as a mixed enterprise, some data and commentary on the company's growth are necessary. The Lougheed government's goal of quickly establishing a substantial Alberta-based resource company has been achieved. The company's net revenues, amounting to $479.7 million in 1987, have grown substantially from their 1978 total of around $55 million. The *Financial Post* now ranks the AEC as Canada's 182nd largest firm by revenues and it has been among the country's top 200 in this category since 1982.[24] Its asset growth has been even more impressive. For 1987 AEC's assets total slightly less than $2 billion leading to a *Financial Post* ranking of 56th. In 1978, total assets amounted to only $500 million. While tiny when compared to Petro-Canada, AEC is a major company in Alberta where it is the 28th largest firm as measured by assets and revenues.[25]

AEC is a major producer of natural gas in Alberta, production having increased from a 1978 total of 27 billion cubic feet to present volumes of slightly over 85 billion cubic feet.[26] And it is an increasingly significant producer of conventional oil particularly since its controversial 1982 acquisition of Chieftain Development Co. Ltd., an episode discussed in detail below. In 1987, the firm produced 2.4 million barrels of conventional oil up from 1 million barrels in 1985 and a mere 100,000 in 1982. Such conventional output is dwarfed, however, by synthetic oil output of 5 million barrels in 1987. The bulk of AEC's earnings are derived from gas and synthetic oil sales, although the company is also a coal producer. In 1987, coal production was 475,000 clean tons down notably from its 1981 high of 754,000 tons. AEC is a major landholder in Alberta having acquired petroleum or natural gas rights to more than 4 million acres. It now employs 485 persons.

Diversification and the Syncrude Option

The preeminent theme of the early Lougheed governments was the urgent need to diversify Alberta's economy away from its dependence on depleting non-renewable natural resources. And while the AEC was created as an energy company without an explicit mandate to pursue diversification, it is noteworthy to observe its actions in this area. Its first controversial acquisition was a 70 per cent interest in 1977 in Willowglen Industries, a Calgary-based manufacturer of specialized electronics equipment for the petroleum industry.[27] At the time the firm was financially troubled and owed large sums to the Alberta Opportunity Company, the government's "lender of last resort". As a result, the acquisition was denounced as a politically inspired intervention and evidence of the AEC's lack of corporate independence. In defending the purchase, AEC management asserted that it had acted autonomously and that the Willowglen's growth potential made it an attractive investment for both government and private shareholders. Such was not the case, however, and Willowglen collapsed in 1980 amidst lawsuits and further controversy with cumulative losses for AEC of $5 million.

Such losses, while relatively small for a firm like AEC, and the attendant public debate clearly took the wind out of the AEC's early entrepreneurial sails. Indeed, the company never again exhibited interest in a firm engaged in any sort of secondary manufacturing and opted instead to invest exclusively in resource-related industries. Such an outcome implies that mixed enterprises are inappropriate vehicles for high-risk investments. But the AEC's loss of interest in various forms of diversification is consistent with the provincial government's declining enthusiasm for the notion in the 1980s. It is thus difficult to divine whether AEC's almost exclusive focus on resource-related activities in the 1980s is a function of its structure *per se* or of a general sense of the course of provincial government priorities.

If Nova and the AEC were the chosen instruments of intervention in Alberta in the 1970s, petrochemicals was a chosen industry for that intervention. The Lougheed government saw petrochemicals as an opportunity for industrial diversification and as an industry where Alberta, by virtue of its proximity to secure feedstocks, enjoyed some comparative advantage. Such views have been debated and challenged in the province since the 1970s, but there is little doubt that the AEC undertook vigorous, albeit less than successful, efforts to participate in the petrochemical boom. As a company lacking the resources to mount "world scale" projects independently, AEC entered into a series of joint ventures generally with more experienced partners. But for one reason or another, all of AEC's major proposed undertakings fell apart often because the Alberta firm was jilted by a partner. This problem, as well as the complex struggle over ethylene supplies described earlier, caused AEC's petrochemical plans to falter. Such setbacks notwithstanding, the company, like the government, remains committed to petrochemical expansion within the province.

AEC's most important decision of the 1970s concerned its exercise of an option, granted by the province in 1973, to acquire a 20 per cent interest in the Syncrude oil sands venture. The option was to be exercised before the plant produced 5 million barrels of synthetic crude oil, probably in 1979. To many observers, AEC's decision would be revealing of the company's true nature, particularly the extent of its independence from the Lougheed government.[28] The success of the Syncrude plant and the expansion of oil sands developments generally were basic commitments of the governing Conservatives. And as the *Edmonton Journal* mentioned in a 1979 editorial, AEC's refusal to exercise its option would be a vote of "non-confidence" in the Syncrude plant and key Conservative resource policies.[29] On the other hand, some analysts wondered whether a profit-seeking enterprise would devote such attention to oil sands given the prospects for profitable, conventional oil and natural gas developments.

To the surprise of few observers, the AEC exercised its Syncrude option in August 1979 for $570 million making it the second largest shareholder next to Esso which had a 25 per cent stake. Prior to and after this decision, concerned interests, including the Social Credit and NDP oppositions, wondered whether the government had bullied AEC into picking up the option thereby mocking its public commitment to an independent, entrepreneurial company. In response, both the government and the AEC denied the exertion of political pressure and claimed that the option had been exercised for exclusively commercial reasons.

A concern with whether the Syncrude option was undertaken because of direct political pressure, while interesting, overshadows the broader point that the government had *structured* the AEC with a view to ensuring its commitment to the tar sands. The Syncrude pipelines and power plant were key parts of AEC's operations which contributed to corporate cashflow, allowed it to undertake other ventures, and kept it dedicated to the continuing success of the entire project.[30] It must also be recalled that the AEC was forbidden to compete directly with the conventional oil and gas industry. This prohibition obviously limited the firm to oil sands investments.

Moreover, the government, in granting the AEC exclusive access to the lucrative Suffield and Primrose developments, had proven a friendly master and one that ought not to be challenged unnecessarily. When in a position to start a mixed firm from scratch, governments may thus be able to arrange assets so as to almost guarantee particular outcomes. Such a structuring also lessens the need for subsequent "political interventions" that may be seen by private shareholders as detrimental to their financial interests.

While the AEC exercised its Syncrude option as expected, it turned many heads by selling, a mere two weeks later, half its Syncrude interest to a consortium comprising Petrofina and Hudson's Bay Oil and Gas. This $365 million undertaking, described by some companies as "a most unusual business practice", netted AEC a handsome $80 million profit and evoked no rebuke from the province.[31]

Competition and Acquisition

As noted earlier, the AEC was prohibited by the provincial government from competing directly with the private oil and gas industry in Alberta. Such a prohibition was important for both the government and the firm. For the province, the restriction was an important political compromise – one that it allowed to intervene while also acknowledging the preeminence of private enterprise. But as the AEC expanded, the prohibition grew onerous and was seen by management as an obstacle to the pursuit of corporate strategy. What was the future of an energy company whose oil and gas activities were restricted to oil sands ventures and two military ranges in Alberta?

In late 1980 the AEC seized the moment and requested that the Alberta government remove the restrictions on its commercial activities. The company's timing was tactical, for in the aftermath of the National Energy Program (NEP) a spate of firms left the western sedimentary basin, citing the superior fiscal conditions for exploration in the United States and in riskier Canadian areas. Under these circumstances, the AEC played its trump when it argued that the combination of the NEP's incentives and the restrictions on its activities in Alberta would force it to mount major activities outside the province if the company was to remain profitable.[32] In the absence of major policy changes by the provincial government, AEC's exclusive focus on Alberta would increasingly be an abdication of its duty to shareholders.

In responding to the AEC's request, the government faced a dilemma. If it refused, AEC might indeed begin to move out of Alberta thereby causing the province acute embarassment in the complex politicking of the immediate post-NEP period. And in the event the government then tried to block AEC, the situation could escalate into a crisis which pitted the government's interests against those of the shareholders. Further, the removal of restrictions on AEC's commercial activities would rob the firm of much of its distinctiveness, enhance its commercial freedom, and speed it on the road to orthodox corporate behaviour. On the other hand, a vigorous and visible AEC presence in Alberta's oil patch fitted the government's political strategy of maintaining "investor confidence" and stimulating exploration activity in the aftermath of the NEP's devastation. Accordingly, a compromise was reached when the premier lifted the restriction on AEC's exploration activities within Alberta while prohibiting any acquisition activity. Lougheed's explanation of his "direction" to the AEC is interesting and worthy of lengthy quotation:

> . . . because of the important lessor/lessee relationships of our oil and gas leases, we said to the Alberta Energy Company that we did not want them, at least in their initial period, to become involved in the conventional oil and gas industry. We excluded the Suffield and Primrose areas, which were special circumstances, and we excluded the oil sands and related activities.
>
> As a result of the decline in drilling activity that has occurred since the federal energy program of October 28, 1980, we were approached by the Alberta Energy Company as to whether or not they could be relieved from that constraint of becoming involved in the conventional oil and gas industry. We considered that matter in the spring in a very long and difficult way, and considered it in relationship to service, drilling, and supply companies that were under such strain within the province, and are as well today, and felt that it would be useful to at least have the Alberta Energy Company move into that position of being involved in the conventional oil and gas industry. That position was made clear by the president of the Alberta Energy Company at its annual meeting in April. It was a decision that we felt could be taken without upsetting the investment climate that is so essential and so delicate, if you like, with the conventional oil and gas industry. And it has proved, I think, since that decision to be working out properly.
>
> But in our direction to the Alberta Energy Company, we did make a clear constraint upon them that they would not pursue a program of attempting to acquire other petroleum

companies. That's very important in the investment climate of the conventional oil and gas industry. It would be folly in the extreme for the government of Alberta or any entity controlled by the government of Alberta at this time, after all the history we've had to lessor/lessee relationships, to be both the lessor for everybody and compete with the lessees in Crown lease sales or compete in a direct way. I can't think of a more foolish course of action for the government to take.[33]

The deal having been struck, the AEC, armed with important new powers, mounted a major exploration program in Western Canada principally in concert with Gulf Canada.[34] And in outlining the company's new horizons to shareholders, AEC's president David Mitchell noted how his firm eschewed the short-term lure of extra-Alberta locations opting instead to remain in the province where the long-term action allegedly lay.[35] The vote of confidence had been given.

This important episode gives some feel for the bargaining that occurs between mixed firms and their state shareholders and suggests why the advantage probably lies with the firm. Generalizations about relative power must be approached cautiously, however, for it is impossible to state categorically whether AEC was really willing to leave Alberta had its bluff been called. In a crisis, would the government or the firm have blinked? The particular point notwithstanding, the general point is that the AEC has undertaken *no* major activities outside of Alberta in its fourteen year existence. This obvious, yet crucial, fact must be constantly borne in mind. For it is difficult to imagine any private firm, or indeed a "commercialized" mixed enterprise or autonomous Crown corporation, being so wedded to a particular territory. To be sure, calculations of whether AEC's territorial commitment has reduced private investors returns, as compared with other hypothetical strategies, would be enormously complex. But whether costly or not, AEC's exclusive focus on Alberta may *in itself* satisfy the interest of its principal shareholder. To date, AEC management has given no indication that this expectation is too onerous.

Premier Lougheed's 1981 "direction" seemed to deny categorically to the AEC the option of acquiring privately-owned oil and gas companies. His political motive in so doing was to distance himself, his government, and the AEC from the "confiscatory" elements of the NEP and particularly from the heinous favouritism allegedly heaped by Ottawa on Petro-Canada. As such, the AEC direction was part of the bitter post-NEP feud between the federal and Alberta governments. But less than a year later AEC acquired for

$168 million a majority interest in Chieftain Development Ltd. a stable, medium-sized, Edmonton-based oil and gas exploration company.[36] The takeover bid was "friendly" having been recommended by Chieftain's directors and involving a premium for the shares acquired. Moreover, both firms declared themselves winners. For AEC's part, Chieftain was a major asset because of its growth potential, proven track record, exploration expertise, and high quality reserves and land holdings. On the other hand, Chieftain's Canadian ownership jumped to 75 per cent thus making it eligible for Petroleum Incentive Payments under the NEP. It welcomed the stability provided by association with a larger firm.

The Chieftain acquisition raised a brief, but intense, political storm which passionately brought to the fore the prevailing viewpoints about the AEC. The NDP argued that by paying a premium for Chieftain shares the AEC had redistributed taxpayers' monies to Chieftain shareholders.[37] Moreover, while other provincial firms floundered, the AEC made a costly acquisition of an already strong firm. In a very different vein, William Thorsell in a long editorial in the *Edmonton Journal* used the occasion to denouce Lougheed and the company.[38] His thesis was that the "no acquisition" edict (although patently violated in this case) was a terribly incorrect policy whose impact was to sacrifice the interests of AEC's private shareholders on Lougheed's political altar. Further, the policy was short-sighted and actually detrimental to the long-term provincial interest. For while Alberta's conservative political elite fretted about free enterprise ideology and bargaining with Ottawa, the federal government through Petro-Canada was extending its ownership of petroleum and gas assets. Finally, some editorialists and business writers, reaching new dimensions of hyperbole, assailed AEC's actions as no better than Petro-Canada's, labelled Lougheed a hypocrite, and raised the spectre of wholesale nationalizations.[39]

In all of this, little was said about the AEC's seemingly blatant defiance of a direct order from its major shareholder. And to the extent that this issue was raised, observers simply rejected Lougheed's claim that he had not been consulted by the AEC and mocked his explanation that his directive applied only to hostile takeovers of the sort practiced by Petro-Canada. The possibility that AEC management had acted independently in pursuit of growth and consciously in defiance of the government was never mentioned. But such an explanation is plausible when one ponders the likelihood of Lougheed having, for *unspecified* reasons, approved the Chieftain acquisition in advance given its obvious contradiction of his public position and its impact on his negotiations with Ottawa about the NEP. Noteworthy too is AEC's subsequent disinterest in the acquisition of other oil and gas firms.

The Drift to Privatization

The cost of the Chieftain acquisition and other business developments caused the AEC to take a hard look at its finances in 1982. As a result, the firm decided to make an offering of common shares with a view to raising capital for debt reduction. Such an undertaking had direct implications for the provincial treasury as the province was bound by AEC's act to maintain a 50 per cent stake in the venture. The upshot of this provision was of course that the province would normally assume half of any AEC issues. But a provincial election had intervened. And although the Lougheed Conservatives were returned with another overwhelming legislative majority, there had been a noteworthy change in the party's rhetoric. Such issues as expenditure cuts in some areas and the need for greater reliance on private enterprise had crept into Alberta's political discourse. The now vogue notion of "privatization" also emerged with respect to provincially-owned Pacific Western Airlines. Such political developments and AEC's proposed share offering led the province to reconsider its relationship with the company in the fall of 1982.

In December 1982 the government announced that it would not take up half of AEC's impending share offer.[40] Accordingly, legislation was introduced in the spring of 1983 that allowed government ownership to fall below 50 per cent. Hereafter the province would make investment decisions in the AEC on a case by case basis. In outlining this policy change, government spokesmen advanced three arguments. First, AEC was now an established force in the provincial resource industries and no longer required the initial degree of government support. Second, a reduced ownership in AEC would reinforce the government's "signals" to the private sector that it was lessening its role. Finally, the province's fiscal position was changing as the resource revenues that had fuelled past expenditure budgets dried up. As the province considered tax increases and expenditure cuts, further investments in the AEC became a low priority.

Two interesting sidelights emerge from this policy change and the ensuing debate. First, while the reduction of provincial ownership in the AEC was not a major controversy among Conservatives, a number of senior ministers noted publicly that the action might *inhibit* not encourage individual investors. For example, John Zaozirny, Minister of Energy, noted how shareholders take "comfort" in the large state shareholding.[41] His view corresponds with the notion expressed by some investment dealers that AEC shares are sometimes perceived by investors as the equivalent of savings bonds. And while this viewpoint did not prevail, its articulation led the government to stress repeatedly that its action must not be construed as evidence of a lack of confidence in the firm. Second, while the government allowed its AEC stake to drop, it rejected the argument that it should also remove the restriction against private holdings in excess of one per cent. The province wanted a major ownership role in the AEC and the potential for control.

The 1980-1982 period was one of major change for the AEC. During that time the corporation achieved new commercial freedom including a capacity to compete directly with other oil and gas firms in Alberta. It also acquired another oil company possibly in direct defiance of a provincial government edict. And for its part, the government was more remote from the AEC than it had been previously. In the struggle for petrochemical expansion and forestry leases, the company received no special treatment. It is tempting to interpret these developments and the ensuing reduction of government ownership as evidence of yet another failure of mixed enterprise and the triumph of commercial principles over government policy. But a suitable interpretation is both more subtle and more complex.

For one thing, the government's primary intention in establishing the AEC was to create *quickly* a vigorous, Alberta-based and owned resource company. And as noted several times earlier, the firm commenced operations with a rather vague and open-ended mandate. It seldom faced direct political "interventions" that might harm its profitability. Under these circumstances, the state's partial withdrawal from the AEC is as much a reflection of the achievement of the government's key goal as it is of any inherent problems of mixed enterprise. Alberta's modest withdrawal from the AEC was on its own terms.

The provincial government's growing passivity toward the AEC must also be seen in context with broader political forces in the 1980s notably the demise of the Lougheed government's "province building" strategy and the increasingly managerial stance of the Progressive Conservative regime. Viewed from this angle, changes in the government-AEC relationship are as much a function of Alberta's changing political economy as they are of problems associated with mixed enterprise *per se*. The Lougheed government of 1982 was a pale imitation of the ambitious regimes of the 1971-1979 period. The rhetoric of privatization and fiscal restraint replaced the 1970s heady talk of building a new Alberta and aggressively extending provincial sway over the course of economic development. And with the advent of the 1980s the once revered goal of provincial economic diversification was seldom discussed publicly. The Trust Fund would soon become a source of short-term revenue for the Provincial Treasurer and Pacific Western Airlines, acquired by the province in 1974 in a dramatic takeover, was on the block. Mr. Trudeau's constitutional proposals and a defensive reaction to the NEP had replaced the "eastern establishment" as objects of Lougheed's wrath.

Several factors combine to explain the growing conservatism of the governing Tories. Most obviously, a decade of governing had taken its toll. Moreover, much had been accomplished including the unquestioned elevation of Alberta as a force in national resource policy-making. Other goals, notably economic diversification, proved much more complex in implementation than was imagined in the early 1970s. In these circumstances, the government's relative disinterest in the AEC in the 1980s is thus more easily grasped when one notes the general disfavour into which interventionist strategies had fallen. A government with an increasingly conservative posture in economic matters is unlikely to have a strong interest in the manipulation of a successful mixed enterprise.

Conclusions

Between 1983 and the present, the AEC's operations have faded as a provincial political issue. The government is preoccupied with its fiscal position and the company is, like all resource firms, obsessed with the problems posed by the decline of prices. Indeed, the government sold a portion of its AEC shares for $125 million in 1985 simply as a means of reducing a potentially large deficit.[42] Its stake in the firm is now around 37 per cent.

The spectacular drop in oil prices in late 1985 posed serious problems for the AEC but the firm has since rebounded. During the downturn, it pursued a relatively active exploration program in Alberta but was forced to sell some of its assets, most controversially its 18 per cent share of British Columbia Forest Products. This interest, acquired by AEC to gain access to timber reserves, was sold at a loss. Critics portrayed the undertaking as evidence of both bad management and the company's less than successful record in ventures unrelated to oil and gas. In a somewhat related vein, the company's affiliation with the government, although more distant than in the past, once again proved valuable. A highlight in the otherwise dismal 1985-1986 period was the conclusion of a deal with the province for the Suffield Block.[43] In a complex arrangement struck at the time of the Block's transfer, the province was able to take up to 50 per cent of the production revenues from the Block three years after the AEC recovered its development costs. A negotiated payment of $51 million was ultimately agreed on and analysts suggested that the provincial levy could well have been much higher. In investment circles, the province's perceived generosity to AEC was seen as a positive factor in an otherwise bleak short-term environment.

The AEC's brief life highlights the problems posed by mixed firms for democratic government. In particular, the interests of private shareholders may well conflict with the public's right to information and discussion about the expenditure of public monies and the purposes pursued. This general problem was compounded by the Lougheed governments' stubborn refusal to consider the AEC as a public body whose relationship to the government and the legislature merited clarification and debate. The constant refrain that the AEC was merely another provincially based oil and gas company worked against a solution. Unnecessary controversy was added by the government's steadfast defence of its suspect practice of allowing ministers to hold AEC shares without being in a conflict of interest. The AEC has not therefore been a happy experience for those concerned with the control and accountability of public institutions.

Nor was the AEC uniformly the "model" for a new partnership between the public and private sectors as envisioned in the early 1970s. While the firm did embrace a relatively harmonious relationship between its public and private shareholders, its operations and development were frequently stressful for the private sector and for more than simply ideological reasons. The government's commitment to quickly establishing the AEC as a major actor caused it to confer special benefits on its new creation much to the chagrin of elements of the private sector. The government's original edict that the AEC not compete directly with the conventional oil and gas industry was thus inadequate to the task of regulating relations with the industry. On the other hand, the firm successfully worked with the private sector on many projects and as best illustrated by the petrochemical experience the province sometimes eschewed preferred treatment for the AEC.

As noted many times already, the AEC's experience has been devoid of overt conflict between its public and private owners. And armed with the advantage of hindsight we can isolate some of the reasons for such harmony. One essential condition was the simplicity and generality of the government's original purpose in investing in the AEC — to establish a prominent firm capable of pursuing broad provincial interests in the resource boom. The firm's original assets and mandate virtually compelled it to follow a course of action acceptable to the province. Second, the province's support for the firm was aggressive and visible particularly in the 1973-1980 period. Indeed, unlike the experience of other mixed enterprises, the affiliation with the state in AEC's case was almost invariably seen as a positive force by *private* investors. For its part, the AEC remained committed to projects in Alberta even under circumstances where conventional firms looked farther afield. Such a territorial focus might have reduced the firm's profitability thereby penalizing its private shareholders. But such calculations are remarkably complex and perhaps more importantly, the company's essentially Albertan operations have not evoked much criticism either from shareholders or from investment analysts. The firm's greater independence from the government in the 1980s is more a product of changing political circumstances than a triumph of managerial quests for autonomy and commercial freedom.

The paramount question about the AEC is the future role of the provincial government, its principal shareholder. In this vein, only one thing can be said confidently — the Conservative government of Premier Don Getty has little interest in an active policy role for the AEC. Elected with a reduced majority in 1986, the government has lurched from crisis to crisis as it struggles to cope with serious economic problems. If any theme characterizes the Getty government, it is deficit reduction. The flames of government entrepreneurship, flickering under the later Lougheed governments, have been extinguished completely under Getty's orthodox administration.[44] The AEC is thus entering an extended period of relative independence from government.

Under these circumstances it will probably be difficult for future governments to extend their sway over the AEC. For example, the provincial New Democrats profess a more interventionist resource policy and if elected might look upon the AEC as a vehicle for the pursuit of various ends. But as Larry Pratt has effectively argued, a firm with substantial private ownership will resist explicit government policies that might lead it down less profitable and secure paths.[45] Risky undertakings like further oil sands developments and heavy oil ventures would be particularly suspect and are better pursued by a Crown corporation. An extended period of relative political neglect would thus magnify the already inflexible nature of a mixed firm like the AEC.

If I am broadly correct and circumstances preclude the emergence of a more active governmental role toward the AEC, should the province retain its extant interest? Put differently, should the province see its stake as an investment or should it completely "privatize" the firm? Political preferences will loom large in any answer. But my view is that in the absence of a precise governmental statement about the relationship between it, the AEC, and the legislature, the province should sell its stake in the AEC. The present circumstances might thus be profitably employed to clarify the AEC's place in Alberta's changing political economy. The firm should be removed from its longstanding position in the no-man's land between the public and the private sectors.

Notes

1. For details see "Text of Premier's T.V. address," *Edmonton Journal* (19 September 1900), p. 6.

2. *Ibid.*

3. Hon. E. Peter Lougheed, Premier of Alberta, to David E. Mitchell, President, Alberta Energy Company (9 October 1974), p. 2.

4. Premier Lougheed and senior ministers often contrasted the AEC and Petro-Canada. See for example Mr. Lougheed's remarks in Alberta Legislative Assembly, *Debates*, 3 May 1974, p. 1686 (hereafter referred to as *Debates*, date, page).

5. Alberta, Laws, Statutes, etc., *The Alberta Energy Company Act*, 1974, Chapter 6.

6. Peter Lougheed to David Mitchell, (9 October 1974).

7. Alberta Energy Company Ltd., *Memorandum of Association*, 18 September 1973, p.1.

8. Peter Lougheed to David Mitchell, (9 October 1974), p.3.

9. "Notley warns Albertans on investing in energy firms," *Calgary Herald* (10 December 1973), p.8.

10. "Sharing in AEC," *Edmonton Journal* (22 October 1973), p.6.

11. "State Capitalism?" *Calgary Albertan* (12 December 1973), p.6 and "Hybrid Enterprise," *Calgary Albertan* (2 May 1974), p.6.

12. "Petroleum industry welcomes new plants," *Edmonton Journal* (19 September 1973), p.6.

13. For details see "Kow-towing": Syncrude opts for better labour relations over a cheaper contract," *St. John's Edmonton Report* (3 January 1977), pp.22-23.

14. "Proper Scrutiny," *Edmonton Journal* (11 November 1974), p.4.

15. For details see Doug McConachie, "18 cabinet ministers own AEC shares," *Edmonton Journal* (7 July 1979), p. B-3.

16. Horst Heise, "Alberta's favored firm goes to the public well," *Financial Post* (8 November 1975), p.17.

17. Thomas Kennedy, "Producers are miffed about AEC land deal," *Globe and Mail* (28 April 1978), p. B-1.

18. *Ibid.*

19. For an excellent overview of issues surrounding the growth of state oil firms see Larry Pratt, "Nationalised Oil Corporations and the Changing World Industry," Occasional Paper 5, Transnational Corporations Research Project, University of Sydney (Sydney: Australia, 1983).

20. John Schreiner, "AEC rated as a chunk of Alberta," *Financial Post* (19 March 1977), p. 25.

21. For details see Tom Campbell, "Companies wave Alberta flag," *Edmonton Journal* (9 July, 1981), p.C-1 and Michael Cornell, "Ethylene issue forces government hand, "*Financial Post* (3 October 1981), p.20.

22. Terry McDonald, "Dupont denied feedstock," *Financial Times* (31 August 1981), pp. 1 and 4.

23. For details see by Stephen Brooks, "The Mixed Ownership Corporation as An Instrument of Public Policy," *Comparative Politics* 19 (January 1987), pp. 173-191, "The state as entrepreneur: from CDC to CDIC," *Canadian Public Administration* 26 (Winter 1983), pp. 525-543 and *Who's in Charge? The Mixed Ownership Corporation in Canada* (Montreal: Institute for Research on Public Policy, 1987).

24. *Financial Post 500* (Summer 1987), pp. 78-79.

25. "Alberta's Top 50," *Alberta Business* 4 (July/August 1987), pp. 18-19.

26. The following data are derived from Alberta Energy Company, *Annual Report 1987*, pp. 38-39.

27. For overviews of the Willowglen debate see "Alberta Energy Corp: Willowglen's rescuer," *St. John's Edmonton Report* (24 October 1977), p. 27 and Thomas Kennedy," Rivals questioning recent acquisition by AEC," *Globe and Mail* (18 October 1977), p. B-1.

28. For details see John Howse, "AEC faces moment of investment truth," *Financial Times* (6 November 1978), pp. 11-12.

29. "Buying Syncrude," *Edmonton Journal* (31 August 1979), p.4.

30. Geoff White, "Intimacy between AEC and Tories suggests enterprise in Alberta is not free from government influence," *Calgary Herald* (21 July 1979), p. A-7.

31. Thomas Kennedy, "AEC expected to disclose plans for Syncrude option," *Globe and Mail* (30 August 1979), p. B-6.

32. Jim Lyon, "Alberta Energy plays for big stakes, "*Financial Post* (13 March 1982), p. W-11.

33. Alberta, Legislative Assembly, Standing Committee on the Alberta Heritage Savings Trust Fund Act, *Transcript of Proceedings and Evidence* (26 August 1981), p.117.

34. For details see "AEC to lay out $100 million on oil exploration, "*Edmonton Journal* (2 December 1981), p. G-1.

35. "AEC decides to keep base in the West," *Calgary Herald* (9 April 1981), p. 9.

36. For details see Anthony McCallum, "Price of Chieftain shares jump $3 after AEC announces plans for bid," *Globe and Mail* (18 June 1982), p. B-1 and Jane Becker, "Chieftain directors to tender 30% of holdings to AEC," *Globe and Mail* (18 June 1982), p. B-14.

37. Dennis Hryciuk, "AEC deal a free lunch, opposition charges," *Edmonton Journal* (18 June 1982), p. 12.

38. William Thorsell, "The chairman/premier of the board," *Edmonton Journal* (22 June 1982), p. 6.

39. See for example Tom Kennedy, "Double standard and double talk," *Calgary Sun* (25 June 1982), p. 7.

40. For details and background see Geoff White, "Provincial ties with energy firm on the line," *Calgary Herald* (19 November 1982), p.7 and Sheila Pratt, "New AEC offer too rich for province," *Calgary Herald* (4 December 1982), p.1.

41. Sheila Pratt, "Alberta Energy issue PC priority," *Calgary Herald* (2 December 1982), p.1.

42. For details see Duncan Thorne, "Province selling $125 million in AEC shares," *Edmonton Journal* (23 February 1985), p. B-1.

43. Dennis Slocum, "Province proves a generous pal during Alberta Energy's travails," *Globe and Mail* (18 December 1985), p. B-4.

44. For details see Allan Tupper, "New Dimensions of Alberta Politics," *Queen's Quarterly* 93 (Winter 1986), pp. 782-792.

45. Larry Pratt, "Energy sector warrants Crown agency," *Edmonton Journal* (5 October 1986), p. A-7.

Chapter VI

The Potash Corporation of Saskatchewan

Maureen Appel Molot and Jeanne Kirk Laux

Introduction

The resounding election victory of the Progressive Conservatives in
1982 ended eleven uninterrupted years of New Democratic Party
(NDP) rule in Saskatchewan. Immediately, the new government
proclaimed the province "Open for Business" and established a
commission to inquire into all "investments of the Government of
Saskatchewan in Crown Corporations and other businesses." Arguing
that corporate mandates were often unclear, that boards of directors
were often subject to political interference, and that the holding
company, Crown Investments Corporation (CIC), had excessive
powers, the Wolff Commission invited the government to formulate an
overall policy on the very "purpose, necessity and long term future of
Crown Corporations."[1]

By calling into question the role of public enterprises, the
Conservatives challenged not only NDP doctrine, but also longstanding traditions of Saskatchewan political economy. For the NDP,
the *a priori* acceptability of public enterprises as vehicles to achieve
economic development goals is part of a longstanding heritage. In the
1940s, its predecessor, the Co-operative Commonwealth Federation
(CCF) had formed a government which used state ownership to
provide infrastructure (Saskatchewan Power) and salvage jobs by
taking over small manufacturing plants. By the 1980s, when the

Conservatives gained power, the Crown Investments Corporation oversaw more than a dozen commercial Crown corporations, centered on the resource and energy sectors, including several major corporate players created by the NDP government in the mid-1970s: Saskatchewan Mining Development Corporation (SMDC), Saskatchewan Oil and Gas (Saskoil) and the Potash Corporation of Saskatchewan (PCS). For Premier Grant Devine, free enterprise, not public enterprise was the order of the day: "The general philosophy is that the resource companies should be in the hands of the public, through public share offerings .... We wouldn't have nationalized them in the first place."[2]

The Potash Corporation of Saskatchewan, a wholly government owned world scale mineral producing enterprise, competes directly with multinational corporations in Canada for sales in the United States and combines with them in an exporters' association — Canpotex — for offshore sales. Originally set up in 1975 as a small Crown corporation charged with exploring different avenues for state participation in the potash industry, PCS was transformed into the world's second largest potash producer (after the USSR) when the NDP government chose to resolve its dispute over resource rents with private companies through nationalization. By 1978 PCS had purchased four mines and the majority interest in a fifth from U.S., French, German and South African corporations, with the result that it controlled approximately 40 per cent of Canada's potash capacity. Thanks to an aggressive marketing strategy and rising world prices PCS was a commercial success by 1980, making profits and paying dividends to the government-as-shareholder. From the perspective of Conservative doctrine, what more suitable candidate for privatization could exist than a competitive, profitable public enterprise producing a commodity almost exclusively for the export market?

How effectively did the Conservatives implement their 1982 commitment to reduce the role of government and to privatize public enterprises in Saskatchewan? By early 1988, it can safely be said that the PC government has indeed introduced several changes in the spheres of administrative controls and appointments and most significantly in the ownership structure of Saskoil which has issued shares to the public. More striking, however, when viewed against initial policy intent, is the lack of radical change. For example the Crown Investments Corporation, renamed the Crown Management Board, remains in place. Nor has the government sold or relinquished control of its major commercial Crown corporations.[3] As regards the Potash Corporation of Saskatchewan, the Conservative government, as owner, adopted the language of corporate jingoism. In his 1986 message the Chairman of the Board of PCS, a former cabinet minister and a dedicated proponent of free enterprise, Paul Schoenhals, spoke not of privatization but heralded the challenge "to build a stronger and more productive company" and of the "need to turn the Corporation around and head it towards a successful and profitable future."[4]

The Argument in Brief

Our analysis of the Potash Corporation of Saskatchewan seeks to explain this disparity between rhetoric and reality — between policy intent and policy outcomes — in the sphere of commercial public enterprise. Our method is comparative, juxtaposing the five years of NDP direction of PCS (1977-82) with five years of Conservative control (1982 to 1987). The framework for comparison comprises the following variables: ideology; government finance; market conditions; stage of corporate development; and policy agenda. Let us summarily indicate the contrasts between the two periods for each of these variables.

Until the defeat of the NDP government in 1982, official ideology expressed social democratic precepts and the policy agenda centered on economic development through diversification, using state ownership where necessary. The Saskatchewan Conservative party espoused a belief in the virtues of the market and proposed a policy agenda to reduce state ownership in favour of private investment. For most of the NDP tenure, the government's financial wherewithal was impressive, as witnessed by the growth of the Heritage Fund and the province's ready access to international financial markets for funding public enterprises. Just as the Conservatives came in, the province ran its first budget deficit in 20 years and fiscal constraints became central to policy-making. Market conditions, that is, levels of demand and prices in the international markets for potash, were buoyant in the first period making it plausible for a state enterprise at the entry stage to target larger market shares and expand capacity. In the second period, reduced demand in the U.S. market and falling world prices obliged a now established state enterprise to assume a defensive posture, trying to rationalize production and at the same time to protect its market share.

Despite these dramatic contrasts, a common theme emerges from our analysis — the adaptation of ideology to market realities. Conservative as well as NDP governments deferred strategic goals in order to meet second order commercial imperatives. Each thus revised its policy agenda. Their reasons for doing so point us to two powerful factors which continue both to incite and limit governments in Canada in their efforts to use public enterprises for industrial development: regionally based economies and market forces. As we argue, the NDP government turned to state ownership when it became convinced that multinational firms' strategies were inimical to the province's development priorities. It then overcame barriers to government entry into a competitive, oligopolistic industry by reopening the ground rules of corporate capitalism. Only thereafter, and in modest fashion, would the public enterprise be used to advance broader policy objectives. On the other hand, the Conservatives confronted "barriers to exit" in the face of weak private investment in Saskatchewan and ultimately acknowledged that Crown corporations had a role to play in the provincial economy. They further recognized that with poor market conditions compounded by U.S. protectionism, if either PCS or its private counterparts were to make money, government regulation of the potash industry was required. Accordingly, the theory of privatization has not been readily transplanted to the harsh realities of the Canadian prairies.

The NDP and Public Ownership

In spite of NDP policy that committed the party to reclaim ownership and control of foreign-owned resources where feasible, and to consider bringing the potash industry under public ownership, the Blakeney government moved cautiously in its resource policies after its first election in June 1971. In its early years, it preferred collaborative forms of statism notably joint ventures. The government did not set out to nationalize potash mining companies but by 1975 saw itself with no alternative after a long and acrimonious battle with the industry which included companies withholding resource tax fees, refusing to submit financial statements, postponing the expansions of mines despite rising demand and — following the NDP's re-election in 1975 — challenging provincial legislation in the courts. At this point, a bureaucratic task force went into action to devise means of state participation in the industry without which, it was now believed, government could neither influence the pace of resource development nor garner a greater share of the economic rents.

The November 1975 Throne speech proclaimed the Saskatchewan government's intention to intervene in the potash industry — either by the purchase or the expropriation of existing companies — and radically changed the nature of the state's relationship with the mining companies. The Potash Corporation began to implement the government's nationalization policy early in 1976 — contacting all potash companies in the province and then negotiating a purchase price with the parent companies of those which were willing to consider a buy-out. An important condition of acquisitions was that purchased firms withdraw from the ongoing legal challenge to the government's regulatory and tax regimes. Within two years, PCS had purchased four mines, and the majority interest in a fifth, to become Canada's largest potash mining company.[5] No longer would the government and the private sector find themselves on opposite sides of the table bargaining over industry development. Henceforth they would compete with each other in the production and sale of potash on world markets.

The purpose of taking on the role of state-as-producer was clearly more than punitive. The importance of the potash industry to the province of Saskatchewan as a source of revenues and as a route for diversification of a wheat dependent regional economy were key factors underlying the escalation of government-industry conflict. Potash ranked third, behind wheat and petroleum, in terms of its contribution to the provincial gross domestic product. The NDP government created PCS alongside Saskoil and SMDC as part of a strategy to assume greater direction over resource development. Yet if the nationalization of hydro-electric power or automobile insurance find their rationale for social democrats in the provision of essential services to the people at a low cost, the take-over of potash mines did not offer so obvious a social benefit. Fertilizers are of course essential to a farm-based economy, but the low potash requirements of prairie soil and the enormous excess of production beyond local or even Canadian needs means that 95 per cent of Saskatchewan's production is exported.

The social benefit that state ownership may contribute therefore comes mainly indirectly from its control over the distribution of earnings generated by sales which can be allocated to social or industrial programs, as well as directly from its control over corporate decision-making, assuming that a Saskatchewan based head office and local directors have greater incentives to promote, for example, innovation in products, processes or work-place conditions. In the view of then Minister of Mineral Resources, Jack Messer, PCS was expected to advance the two basic aims of general NDP resource policy: "We want to be certain there will be sufficient returns through the development of that resource going to the people of Saskatchewan. We also want to provide spin-off from the development of that resource in the Province of Saskatchewan benefiting Saskatchewan people."[6] To what extent did the Potash Corporation of Saskatchewan prove to be an appropriate instrument of policy thereby enabling the NDP government to meet these goals?

Once the government had decided upon takeover, the immediate challenges presented to PCS managers were those of successful entry through careful acquisition of existing mines; dissipation of opposition to government intervention; and actual operation of the newly purchased mines — in short, survival! It was not after all obvious that a state owned firm could compete with established corporations in world markets and make a profit. Skepticism about the entrepreneurial abilities of bureaucrats, and about the ability of nationalized companies to survive in a global economy dominated by the more flexible, transnational firms, then prevailed among businessmen and economists in North America.

The Saskatchewan government succeeded in entering the potash industry and running companies for profit thanks to three factors: the nature of the commodity, a cautious corporate strategy, and favourable market conditions. As we have argued elsewhere, there were at the time of nationalization few readily accessible alternative sources of supply for North American consumers of potash and no substitute for potash as a fertilizer; potash mining technology was stable and the companies nationalized were not vertically integrated.[8] As long as the new state enterprise had the requisite financial wherewithal and the qualified personnel – as PCS did – it would be well positioned to take its place among the oligopolists.

Making Money and Making Policy

The PCS represented an enormous investment of political and financial resources by the provincial government. Hence the state's early guiding strategy was to demonstrate that it was capable of running mines for profit by playing according to industry ground rules.[9] And since the take-overs resulted from revenue disputes, continued profitability under state management was vital to avoid a political fiasco. As the minister responsible for PCS put it, in the early years the Crown corporation was asked to behave "by and large like a private company," with its main objective being "profit maximization."[10] One key decision ensuring a smooth transition to state ownership was the retention of experienced industry personnel. PCS sought to keep all mine supervisory staff and plant managers as part of the acquisition package negotiated with each of the transnational corporations. This conservative approach to management was paralleled in the approach to industrial relations. Faced with an anomalous situation in which a social democratic government found itself the owner of a non-unionized mine, no effort was made to reconsider the results of the miners' referendum which opted for a non-union affiliated workers' association; nor did PCS deviate from the wage scales prevailing in the private sector.

By 1980, PCS had demonstrated that it was an aggressive competitor by competing directly with the five Canadian and American controlled transnational companies operating mines in the province. Moreover, it embarked on an ambitious marketing strategy to increase its share of North American sales including innovations in transportation and acquisition of warehouses in the U.S. to improve product delivery and reduce costs. PCS also pushed to capture more of the overseas market and was successful, notably in China and Brazil, to the point that it decided to opt out of the producers' exporting agency, Canpotex. Fortuitously for the NDP government, until at least 1980, world market conditions were highly favourable: demand was on the increase and prices for potash were rising.

To follow up these bold marketing policies, PCS managers sought to ensure continued competitiveness by adding to production capacity. Because the government had claimed in its dispute with the potash industry that private enterprise was unwilling to expand and hence the state was foregoing potential economic rents, ministers were receptive to the Crown corporation's expansion plans. In the first instance, expansion merely entailed "de-bottlenecking" or improving efficiency (for example, increasing the hoist speed of existing shafts). Then, in 1979, the cabinet authorized a $2.5 billion capital plan as requested by the Crown holding company CIC to permit PCS to undertake a ten-year investment program involving major expansion projects at two existing mines and also the development of a new mine. The first phase of the program, completed in 1980, increased the Crown corporation's production capacity by 23 per cent.[11]

In pursuing commercial success, did the public enterprise also serve the government's stated purposes, that is to earn revenues which would go from the state "to the people" by way of social/economic programs and also to generate spin-offs for economic development in the province? In the early years of NDP stewardship, PCS plowed most of its earnings back into the corporation rather than paying dividends to the government which might have served to finance budgetary expenditures on social programs. Once cabinet agreed that the huge new capital outlays to expand potash capacity would be financed mainly by borrowings undertaken by the Minister of Finance on behalf of the Crown Investments Corporation, PCS retained enough earnings to pay a $50 million dividend to its holding company, the CIC, in 1980 and 1981 as well as to pay mining taxes to the provincial government (on the same basis as the private companies).[12] The decision as to how to allocate much of PCS's profits — the dividend payments — thus resided with the board of the holding company (which included cabinet ministers as directors). On the whole, revenues generated by PCS ended up either being reinvested in the potash industry or being reallocated by CIC to other state corporations to help make up their operating deficits.

Although an immediate benefit "to the people" from reinvesting corporate earnings in social programs cannot be demonstrated in the case of PCS, it could be argued that by building up a viable commercial public sector, the NDP government was creating a reliable source of revenues over time. Unfortunately, to achieve stable earnings in the resource sector requires stable market conditions. Instead, just as PCS was engaged in phase II of its major expansion, potash demand slumped. The fall in prices from $142 per tonne to $100 in the 1981-82 fertilizer year reflected conditions well beyond the corporation's or the government's control. A world wide recession constrained both farm incomes and Third World governments' budgets while a new U.S. "payment in kind" program reduced crop acreage. Faced with these market adversities, a state owned enterprise looks particularly vulnerable as compared to a more footloose transnational corporation – especially without diversified product lines and when exploiting a resource which does not create forward linkages. As a result, PCS's net income dropped from $147.7 *million* in 1981 to $607 *thousand* in 1982. Intent on holding employment steady in a sensitive pre-election period, management announced a "no lay-offs" policy in December 1981 and proceeded to build-up inventory.[13] By March 1982, however, just before the NDP's defeat at the polls, the state enterprise was obliged to switch miners to refurbishing work as production was curtailed for six months.[14]

The NDP government's objectives for its public enterprises like PCS in the resource sector looked beyond financial returns to future economic development. Both government officials and the corporate executives they appointed emphasized that by locating the head office of a potash company – one which was part of an established public sector guided by social democratic principles – in the province for the first time, managers' cost-benefit calculations would come to include broader social considerations. Compared to private sector managers, their time frame for a return on investment could be longer as they had a vested interest in the stable development of the industry. And some social costs would be seen as necessary capital costs by PCS because its sole shareholder was a government sensitive to its constituents.

Following the acquisition and consolidation period, PCS budgets and public relations efforts after 1980 expressed management's concern to generate spin-offs through research and development, local sourcing, and diversification. PCS committed at least one per cent of sales to research and development and focussed these funds on research to eliminate the vexing problem of "soil leaching" caused by the salt wastes resulting from potash refining. Purchasing by the five PCS mining divisions was centralized to facilitate an active policy to identify and use Saskatchewan suppliers.[15] Finally, to promote diversification, the government announced the establishment of a potassium sulfate pilot project plant.[16] Having put aside such industrial development initiatives so that PCS could confront immediate commercial challenges, the NDP government ran out of political time. For the Crown corporation, two radical changes redefined corporate strategies and possibilities – notably a severe market downturn and the election of an ideologically distinct Progressive Conservative Government.

The Conservative Party and Privatization

The Progressive Conservative government of Grant Devine assumed office in 1982 determined to restructure the state sector and to terminate what it saw as the "politicization" of Saskatchewan's Crown corporations. Long vocal about political interference in the operations of Crown corporations, the Conservative party made the size and character of the public enterprise sector a central theme during the election campaign. Once in power, the new PC government appointed a review commission to examine the government's investments and to make recommendations for revised mechanisms of accountability and control. The Wolff Commission report criticized "the heavy emphasis on political control mechanisms at the expense of corporate autonomy"[17] and recommended more dramatic restrictions on political involvement in state enterprises than the Devine government was prepared to accept. Although committed to a "free enterprise" philosophy and desirous of a private sector mentality in the day-to-day functioning of Crown corporations, the Devine government refused to remove all political influence from the state enterprise sector. It retained the holding company for Crown corporations, the Crown Investments Corporation, but changed its name to the Crown Management Board (CMB) and replaced ministers as chairmen of Crown corporation boards with private sector nominees. Nonetheless, ministers would henceforth be vice-chairmen of Crown corporation boards and would continue to sit, along with appointees from the public, on the board of the CMB. Saskatchewan's commercial state enterprises were directed to make a profit and to be attentive to bottom line considerations.[18]

For PCS the change of government meant the immediate imposition of constraints. PCS's president, David Dombowsky, who had directed the corporation since its establishment in 1975 and who was closely identified with the NDP, was replaced. The company's decision, taken prior to the election, to withdraw from Canpotex was reversed. In 1983 the corporation announced that PCS International, a subsidiary created in 1981 to handle PCS's offshore sales following its anticipated withdrawal from Canpotex, and PCS Transport, created at the same time to provide central co-ordination of transportation and distribution services for both domestic and international sales, would be disbanded and their functions amalgamated with those of an existing subsidiary, PCS Sales.[19] Under the Tories PCS did what its private sector counterparts had been doing since the beginning of the market decline in 1981 and what the NDP had avoided – lay off workers to reduce inventories. All but one planned mine expansion was cancelled (its completion schedule was lengthened) as were plans to construct a new mine at Bredenbury.[20]

The impact of harsh market realities made very difficult the Potash Corporation's adherence to the government's performance criteria of profitability and return on the state's investment. The demand for potash, buoyant when the NDP government moved into the industry, began to fall in 1981. And by the time the Conservative government came to power the downturn in global demand for potash was clearly evident. This weak market continued for most of the 1980s with only intermittent increases in overall sales. The U.S. market, which traditionally absorbed some 60 per cent of Saskatchewan's potash output, went particularly flat. Overall North American potash consumption fell from an average of slightly more than 5.4 million metric tons in 1981 to 1985 to an estimated 4.7 million metric tons in the 1987/88 fertilizer year. Offshore sales have also fluctuated since 1980 approximating in 1986 the level (1.7 million tons) previously attained in 1984 and 1981. World supply of potash currently exceeds demand by some 20 per cent.[21]

This situation of surplus capacity has its roots both in increases in potash production and in fluctuations in potash consumption. Internationally, potash producers in Jordan, Israel, the United Kingdom and the Soviet Union have all expanded output capability.[22] Within Canada there has been considerable expansion in capacity since 1980 as producers completed expansions that were triggered by the strong market of the late 1970s. In Saskatchewan, PCS added to the output capacity of four of its mines while three private firms also increased capacity. Two mines came on stream in New Brunswick in the mid 1980s.[23] The combination of mine expansions and openings and reduced demand has meant that Canadian mines functioned in 1985 and 1986 at about only 63 per cent of capacity.[24] Despite the problem of surplus capacity, a third Canadian province wants to produce potash. The Manitoba government has not only taken a 49 per cent interest in the Manitoba Potash Corporation formed in May 1986 (Canamax Resources has 51 per cent), but it has also provided the funds to complete the surveying, exploration and feasibility study for the mine and has pursued sales and equity participation with potential consumers.[25]

Surplus capacity has translated into lower potash prices and thus declining corporate revenues. By 1986 potash prices were almost 50 per cent lower than at the beginning of the decade.[26] From a company which had a healthy annual income up through 1981 PCS has become one with large losses ($49.6 million and $103.4 million in

1985 and 1986 respectively) and an accumulated debt of some $810 million. In fact, by 1986 PCS's total losses had exceeded total profits. And although PCS paid dividends to the Crown Management Board from 1982 to 1984 (despite a weak balance sheet), in 1985 and 1986 it declared no dividends.[27]

Overall employment in the government-owned mines has decreased by over 600 since 1982. Although part of PCS's original mandate was to generate employment for Saskatchewan, like the privately owned companies it has been forced by market conditions to schedule mine closures from time to time, thus temporarily laying off workers. At the same time, cognizant of the potential political costs of lay-offs, PCS has attempted to equalize down time across its mines, rather than drastically reduce production at its least efficient locations and operate the most efficient ones at full capacity.[28] For the first time PCS is "seriously studying the possibility of closing down a mine."[29] Mine closure presents an extremely complex problem, particularly if the government foresees a subsequent re-opening – there are concerns about maintenance of mine shafts and equipment and the prevention of flooding (already a problem in Saskatchewan potash mines) – but that it is under examination attests to the cost implications of over capacity.

For a provincial economy as dependent on staple commodities as Saskatchewan's, the depressed potash market illustrates the problems of regionally based resource economies. Jobs were lost in the industry and private investment did not take up the slack. Moreover, government revenues from potash royalties decreased. Two other important Saskatchewan resources (in which the state also has a share in production) – oil and uranium – have similarly declined in price in recent years, a function of changing global economic conditions. Government revenues from these three resources have thus fallen significantly, from approximately one third of government revenues in 1981 to only 13 per cent in 1987.[30] This decline in resource prices and government income stands in sharp contrast to a decade earlier when price rises led to expenditure decisions based on the expectation of continuing price increases. With extensive fixed and growing expenditure commitments, the combination of weak agricultural prices and loss of resource revenue has meant provincial budget deficits annually for the Conservatives since their election to office in 1982 (and an accumulated deficit of $3.4 billion over five years).[31]

Clearly there is a qualitative difference in the environment in which PCS has operated as an established corporation over the last five years compared to the years following its entry into the industry. As we will argue below, the state's goals for its potash producer had to be revised to adapt to the new environment. Following the Devine government's re-election in October 1986, we see a change in the government's priorities as the state as manager confronted deteriorating conditions in the market place and the state as regulator reacted to American protectionism. Privatization remained on the agenda but became secondary to such goals as streamlining PCS to improve its competitive image, absorbing debt to assist corporate survival, and providing overall industry support in the face of protectionism.

The State as Manager and Regulator

The re-election of the Conservative government in 1986 led to a new relationship between the government and the PCS. Gary Lane, the Minister of Finance and the minister responsible for PCS, announced in 1987 that PCS would henceforth have a full-time chairman of its board. Paul Schoenhals, a former Conservative minister defeated in the previous October elections, was appointed to the position with a mandate "to streamline efficiencies and downsize the Corporations's structure".[32] Lane explained that "given the serious financial problem in PCS, the government had no choice but to take a more active role in the day-to-day operations of the Potash Corporation."[33] Schoenhals wasted little time in implementing an internal restructuring at PCS which resulted in the dismissal of the president and a number of senior executives and the release of 115 employees.[34]

The most important change at PCS was the appointment of Charles Childers as president. Childers, an American who has spent most of his career in the potash industry, was a senior executive with a major PCS competitor, International Minerals & Chemical Corporation (IMC), prior to joining the Crown corporation. He moved quickly to replace personnel and to alter PCS's image within the industry. After bringing in a new president for PCS Sales, Bill Doyle (also an American and a colleague from IMC), Childers sought to make PCS the industry leader by raising prices, thereby prompting the private sector to follow suit. Moreover, the Crown corporation embarked on an aggressive marketing program to woo new U.S. customers and began to work more closely with its present customers. As offshore marketing takes place within the bounds of Canpotex pre-apportioned shares, it is only the U.S. which offers hope for increasing a company's market share. To facilitate this, PCS Sales, the North American marketing subsidiary, moved its headquarters from Saskatoon to Chicago. Finally, there has been some rethinking of the previous emphasis on research and development and product diversification and a reduction in research personnel. Although R&D remains important, in a situation of ongoing losses allocating money for research has lower priority. Once again, PCS should, in the view of its new chief, emulate its private sector competitors all of whom spend some funds on R&D but who keep the need for R&D in a mature industry in perspective.[35]

To assist Childers in his task of turning the corporation around, the Tories decided to restructure PCS's finances. By mid-1987 PCS had a very large accumulated debt, the result of financing expansion and the losses of recent years. In announcing the government's decision, the Minister of Finance claimed that his government had "no choice but to write off the $810 million debt. The corporation simply can't survive in a very competitive market with low prices carrying that level of debt. . . ."[36] The decision to write off the Potash Corporation's debt suggests that the state as manager may expect its executives to run the company's operations, but that it remains attentive and protective when major issues of corporate viability arise.

Under the Conservative government, managers of Saskatchewan Crown corporations continue to execute their responsibilities within a bureaucratic structure which has evolved over more than forty years and which was established to provide direction for state-owned corporations. The key organization in this structure is the Crown Management Board, the former Crown Investments Corporation. Although the Wolff Commission recommended the exclusion of ministers from the board of the Crown Management Corporation, ministers continue to sit on the board of the CMB as they did under the NDP. The CMB, itself a Crown corporation, acts as "the holding company responsible for overseeing the operations of Saskatchewan's commercial Crown corporations" and manages the province's equity in other corporations.[37] Like its predecessor, the CMB remains accountable to its "shareholders" — the people — through the provincial legislature to which it submits its own annual report and those of each of the statutory Crown corporations.

The role of the CMB has been evolving under the Tories but the differences between it and the CIC are cosmetic. The major change was the appointment of private sector/citizen members to the CMB's Board of Directors. All Crown corporations continue to submit their capital and operating budgets to the CMB which examines both before compiling the projected financial requirements of the state sector for presentation to the government. Before presenting a budget to the CMB, each Crown corporation's Board of Directors has the opportunity to evaluate and approve the predicted financial picture. The CMB remains primarily interested in strategic decisions — new Crown investments or fundamental changes in marketing plans — rather than day-to-day operations of state enterprises and to this end has policy meetings with each enterprise annually. In an effort to engage in long-range planning, the CMB tried to persuade all Crown corporations to articulate a basic strategic direction, including an investment profile with respect to expansions, against which budget submissions could subsequently be judged. Although many corporations responded to this request, the exercise was not successful with PCS and reinforced the perception on the part of both the government and the CMB that PCS's management was weak.[38] The state therefore stepped in, as noted above, to ensure a corporate reorganization. Clearly the Conservative government, while asking its private sector appointees to run the business, has not refused to exercise its powers as shareholder, but rather made critical decisions in the areas of corporate organization, financial structures and strategic planning.

Although the Conservatives propounded a free market philosophy there were clear limits to it as strikingly revealed by the Devine government's response to accusations of dumping levelled against Saskatchewan potash producers. Two small U.S. potash producers filed allegations of dumping against Saskatchewan firms before the U.S. Department of Commerce in February 1987 and charged that Canadian potash was being sold in the United States below "fair market value." They claimed that this practice was causing injury to U.S. producers. Potash has long been mined in New Mexico, but the declining quality of the New Mexico output was a major factor in the decision by a number of U.S. mining multinationals in the 1950s and 1960s to invest in production in Saskatchewan.[39] Canadian potash now supplies more than 80 per cent of the needs of U.S. farmers while domestic production accounts for approximately 3 per cent.

In 1985 two newcomers to the industry, Lundberg Industries Inc. and New Mexico Potash Corp., purchased operating mines at cut rate prices from corporations anxious to sell their potash assets. Both mines currently produce at half their former capacity and have only a few years reserves.[40] It was these newcomers, supported by the town of Carlsbad, the unions, the state of New Mexico and one of its federal Senators, *not* the long time potash producers, who alleged that Saskatchewan potash was being sold in the United States below the costs of production in Canada and demanded punitive tariffs.[41] A preliminary finding in August 1987 upheld the charges and Saskatchewan potash producers were assessed duties varying from 9 to 85 per cent, with that on PCS potash placed at 51.9 per cent. Following this announcement, PCS raised the price of its potash sold in the U.S. by 60 per cent, or 7 per cent more than the assessed duty.[42]

With one of the province's major industries under attack the government stepped in to regulate production in the interests of preserving the potash sector. Its response to the charges was to introduce legislation which allocated output quotas to each company producing potash in Saskatchewan. From Premier Devine's perspective, with everybody in the industry already "losing lots of money," intervention by the state was justified: "We're like OPEC.... We're the big player in potash and we're prepared to take that leadership role."[43] Concerned as well that the variation in duties would alter the competitive balance within the industry because companies assessed lower duties might then decide to increase production levels in anticipation of greater sales in the U.S. market, the government drew on its augmented powers under the 1982 Constitution Act which enables provinces to make laws relating to the "development, conservation and management of non-renewable natural resources."[44]

The Potash Resources Act, proclaimed in early October 1987, builds on the management power afforded by the Constitution and gives the provincial cabinet far greater direct influence over the potash industry than existed previously using such indirect regulatory mechanisms as taxation. The legislation enables the cabinet to determine total potash production levels within the province for a specific period, to approve (or not) any additions to production capacity within the province and to establish the Potash Resources Board to apportion production levels amongst the mines.[45] In the view of PCS's president, prior to the introduction of the Potash Resources Act the government had no authority to regulate production; had the producers attempted to do so on their own, they would have violated federal anti-combines laws.[46] With the legislation the government can control potash output and penalize companies that fail to adhere to the production quotas.

An extraordinary coalition of interests resulted in the removal of the U.S. duty threat when, on January 7, 1988, Saskatchewan companies signed an accord with the United States government agreeing not to sell potash in the U.S. at prices below that which the Department of Commerce deemed fair market value. The agreement effectively suspends the trade case against Canadian potash for five years and includes all potash producers, not only those cited in the original dumping action.[47] Although the companies were pleased with the resolution of the contentious issue, their acceptance of what is in effect an administered price system (*one* price was not established—rather the companies agreed not to sell below a minimum price set in Washington) may leave them vulnerable to offshore competition for U.S. customers which they would be unable to match in price without contravening this agreement.[48] At the same time, as long as the minimum price is higher than it was during the depths of the demand slump, profits will rebound to the Canadian mining companies and indirectly to the provincial government as owner and tax collector.[49] The Saskatchewan government is not itself a party to the agreement. Relieved that the dumping case has been resolved, the government's concerns about the health of the potash industry nonetheless remain and it will continue to monitor all developments in the industry closely.

What is interesting about the government's response to the dumping duties is the similarity between its behaviour and that of previous Saskatchewan governments, both Liberal and NDP, which took steps to preserve the province's potash industry when it was threatened. Once again, we see how the need to protect a key industry took precedence over ideology. Although the regulatory legislation ran counter to the Tories' free market philosophy, the government's purpose was to preserve jobs and protect investment in a troubled, resource dependent regional economy.

Conclusions: Business and Politics

By reconsidering the Potash Corporation of Saskatchewan in terms of the policy agenda set by two successive governing parties with opposed philosophies about the economic role of the state and the function of the public enterprise, we have stressed how ideology and market realities combine to reorder priorities in a provincial economy reliant on commodity exports. Certainly there were dramatic differences in PCS's operating environment as an established oligopolist during the five years since the Conservative government assumed office compared to the years following nationalization by the NDP government. A depressed industry replaced a growth industry; government deficits replaced surpluses, and U.S. competitors sought protection via government action in the anti-dumping case. The ways in which the provincial state—as manager, as shareholder, and as regulator—adapts to and seeks to alter these conditions is the subject of our chapter. To date, the Conservative government has had to modify its objectives and focus on streamlining PCS to improve the company's competitiveness as well as intervene to regulate production in the industry as a whole. Corporate survival and the health of the provincial economy became paramount while thoughts of full-scale privatization receded. What then does the future hold?

The future for the Potash Corporation of Saskatchewan is linked to the political business cycle. As long as the Conservative party remains in power, a formal commitment to privatization will prevail. Betwixt ideology and practice, however, intervene pragmatic considerations notably the limitations on free market philosophy in a resource dependent regional economy. Here policy-makers recognize that public sector enterprises represent jobs (direct and indirect) and a discretionary instrument (eg., through their purchasing policies). This recognition, in the absence of massive job creation by private investors, dampens their incentive to relinquish full control over the major corporations. As a senior bureaucrat at the Department of Energy and Mines put it, "philosophy doesn't put bread on the table."

At the same time, the broad public support for provision of essential services by Crown corporations in a rural economy is well known to the Conservatives who see no political gain from a wholesale disposal of government-owned utilities. In the resource sector, the government has sought to reconcile ideology and political realism by reconsidering "its position on holding such investments *as an exclusive owner*." Rather than full-scale divestment, the preferred alternative, in the Premier's words, is "a sharing of risk and investment opportunities through public participation in such enterprises."[50] Thus, in contrast to Quebec or Ottawa which have named ministers of privatization, the new Saskatchewan minister responsible for implementing the privatization program holds the title of "minister of public participation."[51] This populist approach to neo-conservatism enables the government to show dedication to the principle of privatization and bring in supplementary funds to the public sector while also retaining government as the major share-holder.

PCS, however, does not appear to be a likely candidate for this method of "semi-privatization". Here the Conservative government confronts a second pragmatic consideration – the limitation on policy implementation imposed by the market. Simply put, the state as seller has to find a buyer. As a single product company in a volatile international commodity market, PCS does not have obvious appeal to the public, a public which is extremely prudent about investing, and a province which lacks a stock exchange.[52] To give shares in the potash venture an attraction equivalent to Saskoil shares (offered before the full extent of the drop in world oil prices was known and before the October 1987 stock market crash), the government would have to wait for a market upturn and a new record of profitability on the part of PCS. And yet the dialectics of power within the party are unpredictable. Should it be that those more dedicated to the free market doctrine dominate, an asset sale to another large corporation cannot be excluded. Indeed, a number of the changes in PCS management and financial structures undertaken by the Conservatives can be interpreted as prerequisites to a purchase of the state enterprise by International Minerals & Chemical Corporation (IMC), the giant U.S. transnational corporation which already operates potash mines in the province.

What is the evidence behind this speculation? Specifically, the government's decision to absorb PCS's outstanding debt in order to give it a debt:equity ratio akin to private companies makes the corporation highly saleable.[53] The appointment of a president and CEO from IMC; his subsequent appointment of the former vice president, International of IMC as president of PCS's subsidiary, PCS Sales and his hiring of IMC's public relations officer for Canada; the relocation of the sales office to Chicago, site of IMC's head office – all create a convenient administrative network. The two companies, IMC and PCS, although direct competitors, have a longstanding cooperative relationship. When PCS originally purchased the potash reserves owned by Amax Corp it negotiated a 42 year service contract with IMC to mine and deliver a set volume of ore to PCS annually. Although there is overcapacity in the industry generally, IMC has been obliged to operate at half capacity much of the time since 1985 due to severe flooding in one of its two Saskatchewan mines. As an integrated fertilizer company without reserves elsewhere, IMC might have an interest in acquiring other mines, if the price were right. In a time of market downturn the price a government could propose for selling the Potash Corporation of Saskatchewan might indeed be right for the buyer, if not for the taxpayer. The commercial and the personnel links are thus in place should the ideological agenda of the Conservative government and the business agenda of the U.S. corporation coincide.

Notes

1.   Crown Investments Review Commission (The Wolff Commission), *Report to the Government of Saskatchewan* (December 1982), p. 47.

2.   Cited in the *Globe and Mail* (21 July 1987) p. A5.

3.   A novel privatization proposal for the Saskatchewan Mining Development Corporation (SMDC) was announced in February 1988. SMDC was to be merged with the federal government's wholly owned Crown corporation, Eldorado Nuclear Ltd, and the new company is to be 61.5% controlled by the Saskatchewan government. The two governments agreed in principle to offer shares to the public representing 30% of the corporation's equity within 2 years and to fully privatize by 1995. See "Ottawa will sell off new uranium giant," *Financial Post* (23 February 1988), p. 1. For a more detailed discussion of the provincial Conservative government's privatization program see Maureen Appel Molot, "The Provinces and Privatization: Are the Provinces *Really* Getting Out of Business?", this volume, chapter X.

4.   PCS, *1986 Annual Report*, p. 3.

5. PCS acquired the assets of the Vada Mine from U.S. Duval Corp, a subsidiary of the Pennzoil Co. ($128.5 million), the Sylvite Mine owned by Hudson Bay Mining and Smelting which was then controlled from South Africa ($144 million), the Alwinsal Mine – a joint venture owned by French and German interests ($86.5 million), and a 60 per cent interest in the Allan Potash Mine as well as the potash reserves previously owned by U.S. Amax Corporation ($85 million).

6. Cited in the *Globe and Mail* (19 March 1979), p. B2.

7. For a detailed analysis of the opposition to government intervention, see Maureen Appel Molot and Jeanne Kirk Laux, "The Politics of Nationalization," *Canadian Journal of Political Science* 12 (June 1979), pp. 227-58.

8. Jeanne Kirk Laux and Maureen Appel Molot, "Multinational Corporations and Economic Nationalism: Conflict Over Resource Development in Canada," *World Development* 6 (1978), pp. 837-49.

9. For greater detail and further documentation on NDP strategy and PCS performance prior to 1980 readers should consult the first edition of this collection: Laux and Molot, "The Potash Corporation of Saskatchewan," in *Public Corporations and Public Policy in Canada*, ed. by Allan Tupper and G. Bruce Doern (Montreal: Institute for Research on Public Policy, 1981), pp. 189-220. The financial cost of take-overs was some $444 million in current (1976, 1977) Canadian dollars – see note 5 above for details.

10. Personal Interview, Regina, Saskatchewan, 1977.

11. PCS, *Annual Reports* 1977, 1978, 1979 and PCS *News Release* (7 October 1980).

12. *Ibid.*, 1980 and 1981.

13. PCS, *News Release* (10 December 1981).

14. *Ibid.* (8 March 1982). At year-end 1981, the last year of NDP government direction, PCS employed 2,267 persons. Since then, under the Conservative government, the Crown corporation has reduced employed every year to 1,668 at year-end 1986. PCS *Annual Report* (1985 and 1986 "Five Year Review").

15. PCS, *1981 Annual Report,* p.11. For example, PCS began to purchase its conveyor belts (which carry ore from the mine head back to the shaft) from a Regina firm rather than the original U.S. supplier after the province's Department of Industry and Commerce encouraged the local company to manufacture the belts. See "Leonard Industries just rolling along," *Financial Post* (3 October 1981), p. S5.

16. PCS Press Conference, Regina, 6 May 1980. Potassium chloride is the standard product. Potassium sulphate is a specialty fertilizer and has potential industrial applications. The sulphate of potash demonstration plant at the Cory mine was completed in January 1986.

17 Crown Investments Review Commission, *Report to the Government of Saskatchewan* (December 1982), p. 15.

18. Attentiveness to considerations of profit is one characteristic of what we have described as the trend to commercialization of state enterprises in Canada and Europe. See Jeanne Kirk Laux and Maureen Appel Molot, *State Capitalism: Public Enterprise in Canada* (Ithaca, N.Y.: Cornell University Press, 1988), especially chapter 3.

19. PCS, *1983 Annual Report,* p. 6. When PCS rejoined Canpotex, two private companies did the same, thereby giving the exporters' association control of 100 per cent of Saskatchewan's offshore potash sales. "Canpotex gets important boost," *Northern Miner* (8 July 1982), p. 3. Canpotex then relocated its head office from Toronto to Saskatoon.

20. *Ibid.* 1984, p. 6 and 1985, p. 6.

21. PCS, PCS Sales, *The Potash Letter* 9, 2 and 3 (Spring and Fall 1987); PCS, *1986 Annual Report,* inside cover; *Ibid.,* (1985), p. 16, *Ibid.,* (1984), p.16; and G.S. Barry, "Potash", *Canadian Minerals Yearbook* (Ottawa: Supply and Services Canada 1986), p. 49.1.

22. Barry, "Potash", pp. 49.3-49.7. Flooding in a major USSR mine in 1986 temporarily reduced overall Soviet potash production.

23. Three companies hold mining leases in New Brunswick, Potash Company of America (PCA), Denison-Potacan Potash Company and BP Resources Canada Limited (Selco Division). Only the first two are producing potash. Although exploration of the New Brunswick deposits preceded the NDP government's entry into the potash industry, the Potash Company of America, saw its

eastern venture as securing for it long term flexibility should operating in Saskatchewan become less attractive. PCA's Saskatchewan site had water problems in 1986 resulting in the mine's closure for 3 weeks and again in 1987 when the mine was forced to close for far longer. Ironically, PCS has supplied PCA with potash to allow the latter to meet its sales commitments.

24. Barry, "Potash" (1986), p. 49.1.

25. Canamax Resources Inc. is a subsidiary of the Amax Corporation which had mined potash in Saskatchewan until its reserves were purchased by PCS in 1978. At the end of 1986 India's Minerals and Metals Trading Corporation was reported interested in up to a 30 per cent equity investment in the Manitoba mine. *Ibid.*, p. 49.3; "Manitoba potash mine woos Indian investment", *Globe and Mail* (24 December 1986) p. B4 and "Countertrade may be answer to potash woes," *Financial Post* (24 May 1986), p. 17. A recent study confirms the viability of the Manitoba potash deposits. The Saskatchewan industry, and in particular the president of the exports' association, Canapotex, is unhappy with the prospects of additional Canadian competition and has warned Manitoba that the market is not big enough for another player to enter, at least not before 1995. "Manitoba potash venture must include private funds," *Globe and Mail* (25 November 1987), p.B11.

26. Minister of Finance, *Saskatchewan Economic and Financial Report*, March 1987, p.2.

27. PCS, *1986 Annual Report,* inside cover and Hon. J. Gary Lane, Minister of Finance, Province of Saskatchewan, *Budget Address* (17 June 1987), p.19. The payment of $62,000 in dividends in 1983, a year when PCS lost $18 million, can only be seen as dividend stripping to help defray a provincial budget deficit.

28. The only exception to this policy is the Rocanville mine which makes a different potash product than the other divisions and which has lower inventory. "Union protests layoff of 700 at Potash Corp.," *Globe and Mail* (19 September 1987), p. B6.

29. Statement by PCS President Charles Childers quoted in "PCS puts New Game Plan in Action," *Farm Chemicals* (June 1987). See also Endnote 14 above.

30. Hon. Gary Lane, Minister of Finance, Province of Saskatchewan, *Budget Address* (June, 1987), pp. 2-3.

31. "Saskatchewan assumes Potash Corp.'s woes," *Financial Post* (13 July 1987), p.32.

32. PCS, *1986 Annual Report,* p. 3.

33. PCS *News Release,* (2 January 1987).

34. *Ibid.,* (17 March 1987).

35. Interviews with officials of PCS and the government of Saskatchewan, Saskatoon and Regina, September 30 and October 1, 1987 and Childers, "PCS puts new game plan in action."

36. *Financial Post,* (13 July 1987), p. 32. At the time of writing the Tories had decided to remove the debt from the corporation's books, but had not yet determined how would this be done. The most likely scenario would be for it to be absorbed into the province's cumulative debt (thereby pushing it up to some $11.8 billion).

37. Crown Management Board of Saskatchewan, *1986 Annual Report* p. 4. Saskatchewan currently has thirteen commercial corporations and equity in a few others, the most important of which is Saskoil in which the government's share has gone from total ownership (i.e., a Crown corporation from 1973 to 1985) to current state ownership of less than fifty per cent. For details on the change of Saskoil's status see Molot, "The Provinces and Privatization" this volume, chapter X.

38. Interviews with officials of PCS and the Government of Saskatchewan, Saskatoon and Regina, September 30 and October 1, 1987.

39. Jeanne Kirk Laux and Maureen Appel Molot, "Potash" in *Natural Resources in U.S.-Canadian Relations* Volume II, ed. by Carl E. Beigie and Alfred O. Hero Jr. (Boulder: Westview Press, 1980), pp. 153-155.

40. Barry, "Potash" (1986), p. 49.6.

41. *Ibid.,* p. 49.7 and interviews with officials of the Potash Corporation of Saskatchewan and the government of Saskatchewan, Saskatoon and Regina, September 30 - October 1, 1987. See also "Canadian potash blamed for U.S. cities' woes," *Globe and Mail* (7 April 1987), p. 83. In 1984 Amax Chemical Corporation and the Kerr-McGee Chemical Corporation (which

subsequently sold its mine to New Mexico Potash Corp.) filed dumping petitions against potash producers from Israel, the German Democratic Republic, Spain and the USSR. The U.S. companies lost these cases. G.S. Barry, "Potash", *Canadian Minerals Yearbook 1985* (Ottawa: Supply and Services Canada 1986), p. 48.7.

42. "Potash Corp. increases U.S. prices 60 per cent," *Globe and Mail* (5 September 1987), p. B13.

43. "Saskatchewan potash bill sets $1 million fine," *Globe and Mail* (2 September 1987), p. A1.

44. Section 92A (1) Department of Justice, *The Constitution Acts 1876 to 1982* (Ottawa: Supply and Services 1983).

45. Government of Saskatchewan, Bill 36 of 1986-87, *The Potash Resources Act.* Although similar in spirit to the 1969 Potash Conservation Regulations introduced by the then Liberal government to avoid cutthroat pricing in an era of surplus capacity, the current Act has a broader constitutional base and does not establish a floor price for potash which the earlier legislation did. Analysis of the earlier regulatory regime is found in W.E. Koepke, *Structure, Behaviour and Performance of the World Potash Industry*, Mineral Bulletin MR 139 (Ottawa: Energy, Mines and Resources, 1973).

46. "Saskatchewan potash bill . . ." *Globe and Mail* (2 September 1987), p. A1. Because PCS had expanded its market share in the U.S. just prior to the anti-dumping case, the Saskatchewan government's power to regulate production levels from that point in time effectively freezes PCS's relative advantage.

47. "Settlement ends threat of penalty for potash," *Globe and Mail* (8 January 1988), p.B1. Those who would have been most hurt by the dumping duties were the U.S. farmers. Both PCS and private sector spokesmen had foreseen that the U.S. farm lobby would be their strongest ally in opposing the duty. In the words of John Van Brunt, vice-president of Cominco Fertilizers, ". . . I don't think the Commerce Department has realized the immense lobby American farmers can launch. Compared to the influence of farmers U.S. potash producers are insignificant in this battle." Cited in "Potash producers caught in border war crossfire," *Financial Post* (7 September 1987), p. 1.

48. Telephone interview, Department of Energy and Mines, Regina, 14 January 1988.

49. "Potash deal cheers Canadian producers," *Financial Post* (11 January 1988), p.4 and "Removal of duty unlikely to lower potash prices," *Star Phoenix* (8 January 1988), p. 1. Following the signing of the suspension agreement PCS announced that it would provide rebates to its U.S. buyers equivalent to the $35 (U.S.) per tonne price increase implemented to reach the effective floor price set by the U.S. Department of Commerce. "Potash producer to give rebates to U.S. customers," *The Citizen* (12 January 1988), p. B3. This decision suggests that maintaining its market share over time is more important to the state enterprise than reaping all the windfall profits.

50. (Emphasis added) Crown Management Board, *1986 Annual Report* p. 4. The Premier's statement was made in his capacity as Vice-Chairman and Minister Responsible for the CMB.

51. The new department, headed by the former Small Business minister, is intended to "facilitate the public being involved. That is, owning shares or being part of government operations financially" according to Premier Devine cited in the *Star Phoenix* (16 January 1988), p. 1.

52. Interviews, Regina, 1987. The market situation may of course change. Settlement of the dumping charges, we have noted, permitted a healthy boost to Canadian companies' revenues derived from U.S. sales while international markets have started to improve again with 1987 export sales up 18% in volume over the previous year. "Saskatchewan Potash," *Globe and Mail* (27 January 1988),p. B6.

53. In terms of public finance, such transfer of liability from a Crown corporation to government makes little sense. PCS is not looking to borrow directly on private financial markets (needing therefore a debt:equity ratio which appeals to commercial bankers) — the debt absorption rather appears as a clean-up to enhance PCS's appeal to a private buyer.

Chapter VII

Hydro-Quebec*

Philippe Faucher and Johanne Bergeron

Introduction

The recent debate about state enterprise is characterized by a false ideological polarization between the public and the private sector. This artificial premise has given rise to the growing clamor for privatization of public corporations in Canada and abroad.

Intellectual liberalism, currently the dominant school of economic thought, sees government intervention as an obstacle to the optimum utilization of productive factors in a market economy. But in our opinion, economic policy, including regulation, plays an important role in defining economic space, and in many circumstances substituting for a lack of private sector initiative. It also plays a key role in maintaining market stability and business confidence.

* This paper is primarily based on our book: *Hydro-Québec; la société de l'heure de pointe*, (Montreal: Les Presses de l'Université de Montréal, 1986). Part 2.6 uses material published in *Recherches sociographiques* 28, 1, (June 1987), pp.9-28, in a paper written jointly by Ph. Faucher and J. Niosi entitled: "Les marchés publics comme instrument de développement industriel: le cas d'Hydro-Québec." Part 3 is entirely new material. We want to thank Kevin Fitzgibbons for the translation and for proving, against the authors' pretension, that bilingualism is a life achievement. Our sincere thanks to Allan Tupper for his comments on an earlier version and the thoroughness of his editorial work.

Contemporary debate often focuses on the performance of particular firms, but also on the broader role of public enterprise as an instrument of economic policy. Canadian public enterprise is often controversial, either because of perceived inefficiencies, or conversely because of profitability and the resulting envy of the private sector.

Narrow economic criteria seldom provide a solid justification for nationalization. Inevitably, ideological and political reasons come into play. In Canada, given our emphasis on private initiative, the passionate ideological debate, that had so shaken the European countries, has remained placid. In this respect, it is surprising that the state has such a large and important role in the domestic economy. In our opinion, this is the result of a purely practical view of economic development. Basically, the state filled a vacuum left by private enterprise. This was the case with the creation of Air Canada and the Canadian Broadcasting Corporation in the 1930s.[1]

The key question today is whether extensive public ownership is still justified. Thus stated, it seems to us that the only possible answer is no. The old instrument, and the mandate it has been given, may not be today the most adequate form of intervention. But this does not mean that the instrument is necessarily obsolete. For this to be determined, prior questions must be asked: through a change in mandate and/or behavior, could public enterprise fulfill current needs and contribute to the dynamism of our economy? We believe there is strong evidence to support the case.[2]

The alternative, privatization, is not satisfactory from the point of promoting growth and structuring markets. For it does not generate wealth, it merely redistributes assets within the economy. This may, in certain circumstances, have a stimulating effect, but it is not necessarily the solution to the problems in specific sectors. It would be naïve to claim that poor profit performance is the result of inefficient civil service management and that dynamic management can revitalize an industry. It is more a question of different management strategies. There is no such thing as "spectacular recovery" without a "skimming off" of services and manpower. In reality, the private sector cuts services and adds to unemployment for costs that it is unwilling to absorb.

Hydro-Quebec, like any public enterprise, is an organization that operates in the nebulous area between the public and the private sectors; as such, it is subject to both economic and political constraints. As an enterprise abiding by the demand and supply of market forces, it seeks greater organizational autonomy by defining its own objectives and management rules. In this lies the specificity of state enterprises in relation to both the private sector and public administration. Because state enterprise is in permanent relation with both government bureaucracy and the private markets without being completely influenced by either, and because both sectors can finance as well as legitimate its activities, state enterprise can enjoy an important degree of autonomy. This autonomy is significant in its control of financial (self financing, financial performance), economic (strategic economic sectors, competition with private enterprise, size) and political factors (links with specific public policy objectives, legal arrangements).

Twenty-five years have passed since the second wave of nationalization that gave Hydro-Quebec its actual form. More than a mere enterprise, it is a symbol of national affirmation and economic achievement. But this should not mean that the enterprise should escape any serious analysis of its operations, accomplishments and problems. This chapter advances such an analysis.

Moreover, this assessment of economic and political performance of Hydro-Quebec rests on more general considerations about the role of state enterprise in economic development, state control and the autonomy of the enterprise. This complex problem of political accountability of state enterprise has led to a wealth of literature. Hydro-Quebec's experience tends to demonstrate that in the absence of government frameworks and directives, state enterprise will tend to fill the gap by defining its own management criteria and rules.

Managerial autonomy gives state enterprise large discretionary powers if its activities are not guided by government control. This political control must be conducted by in-depth reflections about the role and functions of state enterprise in the national economy and include considerations of financial management, price, procurement and energy policy. If we agree with the basic idea that state enterprises are instrumental for the achievement of economic, social or political goals, then the most important question is whether or not Hydro-Quebec can be considered as a tool of Quebec's public policy. This question rests upon the state's willingness to control its enterprise according to its policy objectives and the exercise of its powers.

Insofar as Hydro-Quebec is concerned, this is a two-fold issue. The first mandate requires Hydro-Quebec to produce and distribute electrical power. Therefore, after a survey of the historical background of the nationalization, which will allow us to understand the main objectives that have been entrusted to Hydro-Quebec from the beginning, we can examine the way in which the company has managed the collective resources, development projects, planning, supply and demand management policies. But as a public enterprise, Hydro-Quebec has a second mandate which is to maximize the economic impact of its activities. We must therefore consider pricing, financial and procurement policies.

We show that Hydro-Quebec has entered the privatization era in its own peculiar way. The serious constraints coming from the evolution on the energy and financial markets have forced an ongoing reorientation of the firm's perspectives. Indeed, it is probable that, after ten years of introspection, Hydro-Quebec will be in the 1990s a very different organization.

1. Hydro-Quebec's First Challenges

1.1. The Incomplete Nationalization

Hydro-Quebec's origins can be traced to 1944 and the creation of the Quebec Hydro-Electric Commission following the state acquisition of the Montreal Light Heat and Power Consolidated and its subsidiary, the Beauharnois Light, Heat and Power. Initially, Hydro-Quebec served the Montreal area. This first nationalization, initiated by the Liberal government of Premier Godbout, occurred in a tense climate. The owner's resistance to nationalization obliged the government, after several unsuccessful attempts to negotiate an agreement, to resort to expropriation, which took until 1953.

The debate over nationalization of Hydro erupted in 1925 when a campaign started against the "unfair practices of the monopolies". The debate gained momentum in 1934 with the creation of the Lapointe Commission[3] which was charged to inquire into the pricing practices of the private utilities. The report accused the Montreal Light, Heat and Power Company of profiteering with a minimal capital outlay and hence redistribution of excessive gains to its shareholders.[4] The report also demonstrated more generally that the electrical companies were guilty of overcapitalization, of an artificial division of capital/shares, and of profit accumulation at the expense of its consumers.

In 1938, the provincial Electric Board was empowered to investigate electrical rates. Its report confirmed previous observations and asserted that the Montreal Light, and Power Company's accounting did not conform with the normal rules: its book value was artificially inflated which in turn overstated its share value. From 1939, the provincial Liberals argued that this poorly managed enterprise should be nationalized. The war interrupted this project which was eventually put into effect in 1944.

In order to respond to Montreal's needs, the newly formed Hydro-Electric Commission had to assure energy production, transmission and distribution and to develop new hydro potential. Development was urgent because of burgeoning post war demand for electricity. The Commission had therefore to engage in major capital construction.

The 1944 nationalization involved four plants, the most important being, the then unfinished Beauharnois. Initiated soon after the nationalization, the second phase of Beauharnois was completed in 1953. Then two plants were built on the Bersimis River and went into service in 1956 and 1959 respectively. By 1960, a third section of Beauharnois had been completed and the Carillon facility had been installed on the Ottawa River. The Manicouagan site was experiencing its first activity and teams had been sent to James Bay for preliminary studies.

Outside the Montreal region, the Quebec Hydro-Electric Commission began its rural electrification programme and extended service to Abitibi and the Lower St. Lawrence. Relying on the metropolitan market, the Commission was in a position from 1944 on to reduce its prices and offer its consumers the lowest rates in the Province.

The Hydro-Electric Commission was thus dynamic in the 1944-1962 period. In 1960, in order to assure the rational development of hydro-electric resources, the state corporation was empowered to develop all the waterways for which exploitation rights had not already been granted. All these factors, along with the fact that Hydro-Quebec had already initiated the gigantic Manic-Outardes project which could generate power far greater than the needs of the Montreal region, contributed to the eventuality and even the certainty of government control over the whole of the production, and distribution of electrical energy in Quebec. Against all expectations, Hydro-Quebec had proven that public enterprise could be efficient.

The debate over the second nationalization began in 1961 in the middle of "la Révolution tranquille". But this debate was strongly influenced by French-Canadian nationalism. Hydro-Quebec was a modern and positive example of Quebec's accomplishments and potential. Electricity became the symbol of economic, social and technological progress. The Liberal government of Jean Lesage, very much aware of this sentiment, stressed nationalization in his 1962 election campaign.

The 1963 nationalization process cannot be understood without being linked to the entire economic and social disruptions of the "Révolution tranquille". This period is characterized by a twofold process of state restructuring and collective affirmation of Quebec society. At the public policy level, this movement led to a set of nationalizations in the finance (SGF, CDPQ, SDI), and natural resource sectors (electric power) and also steel, mines, petroleum, forests, agricultural products. It also led to numerous social reforms (in education and health systems) and to significant increases in government assistance to French-Canadian businesses.

Although the specific orientations assigned to state enterprises can vary from one to the other, all public enterprises created in that period were driven by the general objective of promoting Quebec's

economic power. The state, through its enterprises, had to take on a
role of economic and social leadership. J. Niosi suggests that this
process of state restructuring acted as a means of consolidation of the
French-Canadian bourgeoisie. This nascent and weak regional class
needed the state to reinforce its economic position in order to compete
against Anglo-Canadian and American capital.[5] In Quebec, the state
took control of this movement, by initiating an important programme
of reforms and nationalization, including hydro-electric power.

The main instigator of the nationalization process was René
Lévesque, former Minister of Natural Resources in Jean Lesage's
Liberal government. Technically and financially, the operation was a
success in spite of intense debate emerging from two series of
oppositions. On the one hand, at the social level, the project drew
criticism from the Canadian and foreign bourgeoisie, embodied in the
Quebec Board of Trade and the Montreal Board of Trade, whose
membership included shareholders of the private electrical
companies, the Union Nationale, as the official opposition party, being
their representative in the political arena.[6] But the project also
received support from the majority of the population, including the
unions and the French-Canadian bourgeoisie, as revealed by the
conclusive result of the November 1962 election.

On the other hand, the Liberal Party itself was divided on the
nationalization issue[7]. In the beginning the project was conceived by
René Lévesque and his small team of close advisors, without
consultation with the executive of the party or the Prime Minister.
Lévesque announced his idea in a public speech in front of
representatives from the electrical industry in February 1962,
astonishing his own party and Mr. Lesage. The ministers and the
Prime Minister were profoundly shocked by Lévesque's attitude that
placed the party in front of a "fait accompli". Tensions developed over
the issue in a cabinet dominated by moderates. After a stormy
reunion at the Lac-à-l'épaule government lodge in the Laurentide
National Park, the cabinet endorsed Lévesque's project, ready to
launch an electoral campaign on the issue.

Nationalization can be defended on technical and economic
grounds[8]. For example, the integration of private networks was an
attempt to resolve the problem of several competing networks
operating in the same area. This strategy reduced service costs and
allowed for a better utilization of resources by unifying tariffs,
eliminating redundant production and distribution facilities, reducing
management and administration costs and rationalizing plants.
Nationalization also allowed for partial tax rebates from Ottawa
based on the principle that one level of government cannot tax
another.[9] At the time, this represented consumer savings of close to

$15 million annually as well as a further $20 million of shareholder profits.

The directors of these firms, mostly Anglophones, were strongly against nationalization and maintained that the provincial administration was using nationalism as grounds for socializing the economy. More specifically, the companies claimed that they were not monopolies because of strong regulatory control from the Ministry of Natural Resources and the Electricity and Gas Board. They justified rate increases by pointing to growing production costs and maintained that their profits were not excessive. They also blamed the French universities for failing to produce engineers—hence the almost exclusive Anglophone presence in senior management.

In 1963, Hydro-Quebec bought out the remaining private producers and distributors of electricity in Quebec. The nationalization involved initially eleven private companies for a total cost of $611 million. The purchase included a net payment of $359 million for stocks and bonds. The covering of long-term debts represented an additional expenditure of $249.8 million while miscellaneous expenditures amounted to $2.6 million. The second phase of acquisition involved the buying out of co-ops and municipal networks at a cost of $27 million.[10] The overall transaction was financed through bond issues on the U.S. market for a value of $300 million.

As a result Hydro-Quebec doubled its assets and number of customers. A rate standardization policy was implemented and from 1963 onward, the majority of domestic consumers paid the same rates as those in Montreal. An ambitious reform was also initiated, with the objective of rationalizing the tariff grid and eventually standardizing the 85 domestic rates and 80 user rates in effect. In order to standardize the network Hydro-Quebec converted its frequency from 25 to 60 cycles for its northwestern consumers and agreed to absorb the conversion cost of its users' appliances. Finally, its network was fully integrated and its transmission lines were standardized and updated. The large majority of personnel became, with a minimum of layoffs, government employees. Now that Hydro-Quebec was responsible for the largely increased consumer demand it had to implement a large scale equipment upgrading programme. The Manic-Outardes project, started before nationalization, continued and became one of several significant technological achievements.[11]

A general misconception is that nationalization, and the resultant monopoly, meant that the province's hydro-electric production capacity had been put entirely under government control. But in fact at least 40 per cent of production capacity, which belonged to self-producers, was not affected. By "self-producers", we mean those companies whose electrical generating facilities are operated for their own use.   Self-produced industrial hydro-electricity is mostly used in pulp and paper and in primary metal transformation such as aluminium.

There were two forms of exemption to nationalization: the non electrical commercial assets of the nationalized firms and the electrical assets of industrial companies.   The first case primarily concerned the Shawinigan group.   Only its electrical assets were obtained by the government and transferred to Hydro-Quebec, while its diversified interests in chemicals, engineering and construction were untouched. The second case is much more significant in that it excluded from the public sector almost 40 per cent of the province's installed capacity.

The companies affected by the nationalization (Shawinigan, Gatineau Power, Northern Quebec Power, etc.) only accounted for 23.2 per cent of the production capacity even though they supplied almost half of the consumer market (47 per cent).   With these acquisitions, Hydro-Quebec controlled 59 per cent of the installed power capacity and 90 per cent of the consumer market.

Such limitations to nationalization meant that a large portion of rent from hydro development remained with the self-producers. Two studies estimate that the rent value that Quebec extracted from its hydro-electrical resources was between \$880 million and \$1,292 million.[12]   If we take into account that self-producers generated 14,222 million kwh[13] we can then estimate that if the rent is somewhere between \$140.8 million and \$277.3 million following the most conservative estimates.   In other words, the self-producers controlled between 16 per cent and 21.5 per cent of the province's hydro-electric rent.

Among the thirty or so self-producers, Alcan of Canada Corporation controlled 27.5 per cent of the province's installed capacity in 1962: twice that of the nationalized Shawinigan Water and Power Co. Other exempted sectors were in metallurgy (Canadian British Aluminium), pulp and paper (C.I.P., McLaren, Eddy, Consolidated Paper, Price, Donohue, etc.), and mining (Asbestos, Iron Ore, Quebec Cartier Mining).

In 1962, industrial enterprises produced 27.3 per cent of the electricity in Quebec but with the growth of the public network this proportion had fallen to 18 per cent in 1982 (18 billion kwh.). Notwithstanding a loss of \$ 360 million in potential revenue for the government corporation, this represents 75 per cent of the electricity purchased from Hydro-Quebec by large industrial consumers in the manufacturing and mining sectors.

The self-producers' activity was 1/3 of the energy consumed by the mining and manufacturing sectors.   In 1983, their facilities represented 10.7 per cent of the province's installed capacity and 16.6 per cent of total electrical production.[14]

The importance of electricity as a force in industrialization was widely discussed after the nationalization. Electrical energy consumption was concentrated in six sectors of the economy (80 per cent of the consumption for industrial use): pulp and paper, steel making, smelting and refining, cement, oil refining and chemicals. The self-producers were naturally very active in these sectors, which in turn restricted the government's capacity to intervene. As a result, the government's ability to promote industrialization through the supply of cheap energy was limited. It was not until recently that energy consuming investments were carried out with the construction of the aluminum refinery at Bécancourt and the magnesium refinery, Norsk-Hydro.

Contrary to the general conception, the 1963 nationalization did not give Quebec the power to fully control the hydro-electric resources or to use them to simulate industrial development. We have an example of truncated nationalization.

1.2. The Building Era

The second nationalization began a period of spectacular growth for Hydro-Quebec. Once this was completed, the company decided to put into practice a management policy that emphasized demand promotion and mega-projects that would secure future expansion. From 1964, the company embarked on a programme of construction of dams, plants and reservoirs and the expansion of its distribution and transmission network. These projects satisfied consumer demand which Hydro-Quebec stimulated through a marketing strategy. In this sense, the enterprise played an important role in the expansion of its own market. Hydro-Quebec's development strategy was thus two fold: network expansion and an aggressive commercialization strategy. Insofar as production had to respond to consumer demand, it was also important that consumer needs adjust to the new production capacity in order to generate the revenue necessary for expansion. At this stage in the firm's development, supply ("produce for consumption") and demand, ("consume for production") were interrelated.

Following the nationalization, Hydro-Quebec's total assets were $2,351 million, with an installed power of 6,572 megawatts. Sales were at 35.2 billion/kwh for a revenue of $269 million. Twenty years later, total assets were $27,129 million. Sales rose to 123.8 billion kwh, and installed power was 24,475 megawatts.[15] The two mega-facilities at Manic-Outardes and James Bay account for the immense hike in installed capacity.

Despite this production increase, Graph 1 shows that from 1972 on there was a growing tendency of confirmed sales to be more important than Hydro-Quebec's actual production. This generally Indicates a deficit. On the other hand, the total energy curve shows a significant surplus in relation to sales. The reason for this is that the first supply curve shows only nationalized production while the second takes into account energy purchases from neighbouring networks and from self-producers in Quebec.

Total energy supply then is the key indicator for the scope of surplus at Quebec's disposal. Essentially, Labrador was the source of this surplus. An agreement reached in 1969 with the Churchill Falls Labrador Corporation authorized Hydro-Quebec to purchase virtually all the electricity produced there in return for substantial participation in the conception, construction, and financing of the project. The conditions of this contract were particularly advantageous for Hydro-Quebec: guaranteed access to between a minimum of 31 and a maximum of 43 of the 45 billion kwh produced by the plant over the next 65 years, at a fixed price of 3.5 mils/kwh (0.35 cents) for the following 45 years and a lower negotiated price for the remaining two decades. Hydro-Quebec distributed this energy through the internal market at an average standard rate of 36.27 mils/kwh in 1985[16]. For years, Newfoundland has struggled to modify the terms of the agreement in order to obtain a more favorable price for its energy.

1.3. Growth Stagnation

Hydro-Quebec's development in the 1960s and 1970s was stimulated and maintained by demand growth. Between 1964 and 1970, sales increased by 44 per cent and in the following three years (1971-1974), grew to 48 per cent. After a slow-down in 1975, demand again grew and by 1980 total sales had grown 38 per cent over 1975 totals. Demand stagnated between 1980 and 1983 and has since settled to an annual average of around 7 per cent. Today the Quebec market is saturated and no one believes that growth will return to the levels of fifteen years ago. Current forecasts by Hydro-Quebec see demand growing at 2.7 per cent annually over the next 20 years. The forecasts for domestic and agricultural consumption, which historically provided the bulk of demand growth, are a low 1.9 per cent.[17]

After 25 years (1950-1975) of remarkably stable growth, Hydro-Quebec took almost ten years to adjust its forecasting to new market conditions. Indeed, as time went on, the gap between forecasts and reality pushed the government to take a special interest in the Crown

Graph 1

Hydro-Quebec: total sales and disposable energy, 1962-1986

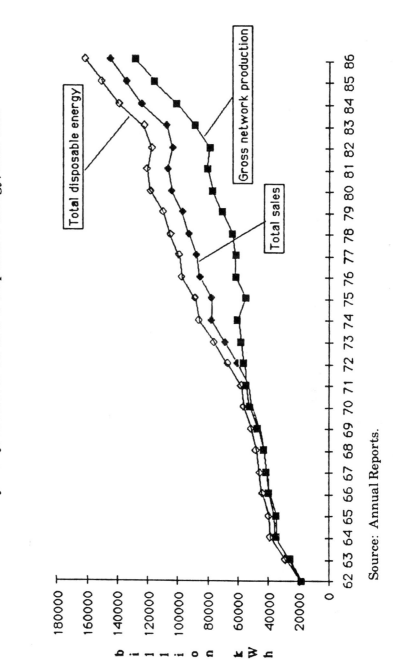

Source: Annual Reports.

corporation's forecasting system. In the early seventies, according to the most optimistic forecasts from Hydro-Quebec's planning department, the potential exploitable hydro-electric resources would be exhausted within the foreseeable future and the need for nuclear technology would be imminent. Given its expertise, Hydro-Quebec totally ignored the forecasts provided by the Energy Division of the Ministry of Natural Resources between 1972 and 1978.

In 1974 the Crown corporation's forecasts were subject to discussion before a parliamentary committee where they were challenged by the Ministry's estimates[18]. The government study foresaw an inevitable decrease of the annual demand growth rate from 1975 to 1990 based on the observation of several determining factors for the future: limited population growth, a transition in growth from manufacturing to services, and a drop in consumption and better conservation after the oil crisis. The government concluded that the rate of demand growth would decrease progressively until the end of the century with an average annual increase rate of 6 per cent until 1980 and then a drop to 3 per cent by 1990. Hydro-Quebec's own estimates over the same period of time were 8 per cent annually. The government's estimates now seem more accurate.

Demand forecasting had serious implications for the enterprise's development programme. For instance, at the beginning of 1985 Hydro-Quebec's total installed capacity was 28,705 megawatts of which only 21,760 were required at annual peak.[19] The resulting power surplus of 24 per cent was equivalent to the capacity of its two largest power plants at James Bay: LG-2 and LG-3. Unfortunately for Hydro-Quebec, the drop in demand coincided with the opening of the massive hydro-electric plants and therefore resulted in serious financial difficulties for the company.

1.4. Hydro-Quebec and Energy Policy

Hydro-Quebec is often mistakenly assumed to be responsible for the establishment of provincial energy policy and the general economic development of the province. This widely held misconception has significant consequences.

It is a fact that given free rein Hydro-Quebec would take advantage of its position to reinforce its institutional autonomy. But the interests of the Crown corporation are not always compatible with the best interests of the community. The claim that Hydro-Quebec is a "state-within-a-state" points to the government's failure to impose a clear policy orientation on the firm.

Hydro-Quebec was originally responsible to the Ministry of Natural Resources and since 1977, to the Ministry of Energy. For the greater part of the past 20 years the government has been reticent to exert its controlling power. The Crown corporation has enjoyed remarkable autonomy in the management of its affairs and only recently has the government begun to enforce its will and to take control of its corporation.

This renewed state interest in the Crown corporation is indicative of a broader interest in the energy policy as expressed in recent policy statements. Insofar as electricity is the resource central to Quebec's energy self-sufficiency, it is a key element in Quebec's "post-oil crisis" energy strategy.

Although Hydro-Quebec is a key economic force, the government by the 1970s had not yet developed a policy capable of overseeing its expansion for two reasons. First, energy policy was not a central preoccupation in any western economy prior to the first oil shock. Energy was generally considered a stable, permanent resource available at a fixed price. Second, Quebec had created a powerful instrument, with a mandate to satisfy, without restriction, the whole of the population's electrical needs at the lowest conceivable price. For these reasons, Quebec, proud of its accomplishments, seldom seriously questioned the validity of its energy policy.

The creation of the Ministry of Energy by the Parti Quebecois in 1976 marks a new era of state intervention and reflection in energy policy. The first document, published in 1977, is simply an overview of the problems and challenges facing the province in the energy sector[20]. Such problems as supply guarantees and waste were partially dealt with in the policy statement "Assurer l'avenir" published in 1978[21].

Energy policy was presented as a key element in the province's economic development strategy. Its primary objective was to increase the province's self-sufficiency in energy. "Assurer l'avenir" proposes three measures for achieving self-sufficiency:

— the promotion of energy efficiency and conservation;

— the doubling of Quebec's energy resources within twelve years;

— the insurance of stable energy imports.

The first two elements of this policy were basically incompatible with Hydro-Quebec's logic, dynamics and primary objectives. Encouraging energy efficiency implied energy conservation, which in turn had to be taken into consideration as a key variable in forecasts and investments. Hydro-Quebec, on the other hand, based its development strategy on constant demand and revenue growth as a financing factor for investment and production.

Furthermore, doubling the supply of Quebec's energy resources implied that the government was promoting the replacement of oil by electricity while supporting the introduction of natural gas. This strategy was incompatible with Hydro-Quebec's traditional

philosophy. In a medium-range perspective, such measures would
hinder the company's growth.

However, the policies put forth also included measures which
could benefit the Crown corporation. The export of excess power was
seen as an excellent means of disposing of surplus electricity. The
document even suggested selling a portion of the regular energy
production to foreign customers and amending the corporation's
mandate to enable it to do so.

The document, "Bâtir le Québec," also addressed these questions
from the Ministry of Industry and Commerce's point of view[22]. The
significant investments required for the production, distribution and
transmission of electricity, the reliability of resources, the abundance
of power and the practice of preferential rates were all factors which
were considered likely to attract industry to Quebec. Government
intervention could take the form of rate-setting and of controlling the
economic impact of new facilities. The document suggested that
surplus energy be used in Quebec, rather than exported, and that this
could be achieved by offering preferential rates to new businesses
entering the province. The views on uses of surplus expressed in this
document reflected divergent viewpoints. On the one hand, the
Ministry of Energy and Hydro-Quebec supported the export of surplus
energy while the Ministry of Industry and Commerce hoped that new
investments would increase energy consumption. But this conflict
was resolved by other developments in the economic situation. For
Quebec's surplus is now such that it allows for both exports and very
low industrial rates. The implementation of these policies led to
legislative changes which redefined Hydro-Quebec's mandate and
management. These laws purported to help the Crown corporation
adapt to changing markets while increasing the government's
jurisdiction.

Bill 41, passed in June 1978, was consistent with the new energy
policies. It dealt with at least two major aspects of Hydro-Quebec's
administration. The law abolished the Hydro-Electric Commission of
Quebec, which comprised five senior company executives, and set up
in its place, an administrative committee, made up of eleven
members, eight of whom (including the chairman) would be appointed
by the government. The new law also altered the Crown corporation's
mandate. Article 8 stipulated that Hydro-Quebec's plans and
forecasts be subordinate to the government's energy policy.

Bill 16, passed in December 1981, went further. It radically
altered the corporation's financial structure by making Hydro-Quebec
a limited liability corporation (as was already the case for other
commercial or industrial Crown corporations) and requiring it to pay
annual dividends and a tax on capital, on the same basis as privately
owned companies. The corporation's fifty million shares were held by

the Ministry of Finance. It was expected that the firm would pay dividends to the government out of its profits.

Bill 16 reduced the corporation's financial independence, as it allowed the state to claim a portion of surplus funds; this in turn enabled the state to exert a coercive power over the company. The government felt that Hydro-Quebec had a financial surplus which it did not require for financing. This new policy had a two-fold purpose: to deter energy waste by extracting higher rates and to collect "excess financial surplus". This logic was dubious since, regardless of the government's wishes to reduce waste, rate increases would undoubtedly increase the Crown corporation's revenue. This, in turn, would create a considerable "surplus". It is easy to see that, at a time when the budget showed a deficit, Hydro-Quebec's income was a kind of gift from heaven for the government.

In 1983, the government passed Bill 4, which set operating standards for the Crown corporation and amended energy export laws. Restrictions on exports were lifted, although all contracts were subject to government approval. More than any other legislative measure, Bill 4 points to a significant shift in the role and mandate of Hydro-Quebec. The Crown corporation is no longer the "great builder" it once was: it is a commercial operation, whose main purpose is to sell power on all fronts and to derive commercial benefits from any technological advantage it may have. It had taken the government a full ten years, since the oil crisis, to change the utility company's operating standards and to respond to market changes.

Although the government had committed itself to promoting electricity as alternative energy, it did very little toward fulfilling this mission. Even during the energy crisis, the ministry responsible for this task failed to issue guidelines for the sale and marketing of electricity.

It has been commonly voiced that Hydro-Quebec enjoyed so much autonomy that it acted as a "state within the state". This opinion is not based on fact. The government enjoys extensive powers over its firm. The government is responsible for the designation of the members of the board of directors and all tariff changes. Major contracts are all submitted for approval. A Parliamentary Committee is annually informed of the firm's perspectives. On this occasion Hydro-Quebec publishes its Development Plan presenting the firm's analysis of the short and medium term perspective of its market as well as its development projects. Over the past years this publication has turned into an opportunity for the media and the general public to get a closer look at Hydro-Quebec's performance.

Any provincial administration, given that it has a clear set of intentions, has the authority and the means required to have its orientations understood and followed. With the obvious exception of the anticipation by the Liberal administration of Premier Bourassa of the James Bay project, the government has made very little use of its powers. For lack of orientation the firm has grown accustomed to make full use of its managerial discretion in increasing its autonomy. As an enterprise Hydro-Quebec believes in growth; it is no surprise that over the years demand has been overestimated, and investment exaggerated, producing excess capacity as result.

The legal tightening that is found in bills 41, 16 and 4 can be interpreted as a manifestation of the government, under the Parti Québécois, making better use of its privileges as the firm's owner. This is no occasion for confrontation, rather the new legal framework can be understood as the necessary adjustment to the drastic changes that occurred in both energy and financial markets.

Given the energy shocks experienced, it is quite reasonable for the state to insist on a clear definition of lines of authority over matters of energy policy. Likewise, the tight financial conditions and serious credit constraints (the fiscal crisis) can help us appreciate why the government tried to impose stringent performance goals and limits on the financial autonomy of its firms by defining better the conditions under which it is required to operate. The opening of the mandate towards the liberalization of exports should be placed in a context of large excess capacity in a situation of high prices for energy. Finally it should be noted that the government has proceeded with caution, making statutory changes, using a technocratic approach in a conscious effort not to politicize the debate in a partisan mode. This apparent neutrality is also an indication of the limit of the control capacity of the government over Hydro-Quebec.

There is a distinction to be made between formal and real power. The literature on managerial discretion suggests that the nomination of administrators is not necessarily an efficient instrument of control since once nominated, administrators have a tendency to identify with the interests of the enterprise and to pursue particular objectives that differ from those of the owner[23].

Until recently, government approval of tariffs and supply contracts was basically a formal exercise. Hydro-Quebec was required to publicly justify its propositions, rarely running up against firm opposition. And finally, if in principle, Bill 16 has reduced Hydro-Quebec's financial autonomy by diverting part of its profits back to the state, the actual tax rate of the enterprise remains inferior to the 1963-1975 period[24]. Moreover, Hydro-Quebec paid no dividend in either 1985 or 1986.

Hydro-Quebec has therefore shown a tendency to resist government attempts to control it through the use of its economic and financial resources. The enterprise's position is more stable than that of the government. It is desirable that it should be sheltered from the priorities of partisan politics. Its long-term production mandate is linked to markets and thus necessitates a degree of managerial coherence and rationality. But as a state-owned organization it cannot decide its major orientations. The main company-government issue is the extent of corporate freedom within a framework of greater political control. It is in this sense that one can understand the intervention of the Parti Québécois.

1.5. Trends in demand and the firm's strategy

Rate schedules were divided into four categories: residential, general, institutional, and industrial. Residential consumption rose rapidly during the 1960s and 1970s, due to the greater use of electrical appliances in homes and the massive introduction of electrical heating. But the rate of increase in demand dropped suddenly in 1978. Whereas the annual increase rate averaged 10.6 per cent from 1970 to 1977, it fell to 3.9 per cent for the 1978-1983 period. From 1981 to 1985, the growth rate was an even 4 per cent[25].

Conditions had changed drastically: residential consumption was no longer encouraged through the practice of low rates. Rather, Hydro-Quebec took advantage of the high prices of other forms of energy to request and obtain considerable yearly rate increases. From 1978 to 1983, six successive authorized raises amounted to a cumulative 80 per cent increase, or a 13.4 per cent average increase per annum. These raises helped Hydro-Quebec maintain a 16.6 per cent annual growth rate in residential sales, in spite of the comparatively slow demand growth rate.

The growth of commercial demand dropped even more dramatically. This decrease can be linked to an overall slow-down in economic activity. But this situation did not prevent Hydro-Quebec from increasing its sales. Although regular electricity sales rose an average of 2.8 per cent each year from 1978 to 1983, sales revenue increased an average of 16 per cent per year during that same period.

In the industrial sector this tendency was even more pronounced. From 1978 to 1983, 13.3 per cent average annual rate hikes resulted in a 102.9 per cent increase in Hydro-Quebec's sales revenue. Thus, on the average, sales revenues went up 14.7 per cent every year, while sales volume decreased 0.3 per cent annually.

This pricing policy had the following consequences: on the one hand, electricity sales went up only 12.7 per cent from 1978 to 1983, while sales revenues doubled. On the other hand, the growth rate of electricity sales was beginning to drop off just as the James Bay facilities were going into operation.

Electrical energy had become expensive. Rate-setting policies reduced electricity's competitive edge over gas and oil. This is reflected in the slower replacement of oil heating equipment and in the growing popularity of gas. Accustomed to a certain level of demand, Hydro-Quebec could not come to terms with the current energy situation. Faced with shrinking demand, the company increased its rates, jeopardizing the relative competitiveness of electricity. This kind of "sound management" prevailed over an optimum use of our energy resources. By setting rates comparable to those of oil and gas (which were being manipulated by the Federal government), Hydro-Quebec influenced consumer behavior. By increasing its sales revenues, it has actually contributed to a decrease in demand.

The Crown corporation had neither the power nor the motivation to implement any other policy. In this regard, it fulfilled its original mandate, which was to produce and supply electrical energy at a rate consistent with sound financial management. It would not be fair to hold the company entirely responsible for its surplus. It is up to the state to define objectives, to issue guidelines and to provide arbitration if necessary. Hydro-Quebec is not to blame for taking the initiative to implement a policy which would bring profit at a time of economic uncertainty.

2. The Economic Performance of Hydro-Quebec

In a period when many companies are being privatized, analyses concur in asserting that the public sector must have operating standards different from the private sector. This is why the public enterprise's contribution to the community's distinct socio-economic development must be considered. If Hydro-Quebec's rates, and its financial and procurement policies, do not distinguish it from a comparable private company, what is the use of nationalization? This question is not merely a rhetorical one. More than management style, the fundamental issue is the appropriation by the private sector of the benefits derived from collective resources.

2.1. Pricing

Hydro-Quebec's pricing was based on simple principles. According to its mandate, which consisted until 1981, in "supplying energy at the lowest rates consistent with sound financial management"[26], Hydro-Quebec set its rates according to the average cost of producing electricity so that it could cover its financing. It tried to maintain a net operating income equal to at least 100 per cent of the interest it had to pay, and a 25 per cent capitalization rate.[27] By law, Hydro-Quebec had to sell its power at prices which covered all operating costs, interest on its debts, and amortization over a maximum 50 year period.

Since it was created, Hydro-Quebec has not lost sight of its plan to standardize rates throughout the Province. This means that rates for a given user category must be the same throughout Quebec. Geographical discrepancies still apply to outlying areas which are not connected to the main system and which rely on oil generators. These areas include the Magdelene Islands as well as communities located north of the 53rd parallel. In addition to standardizing its rates, Hydro-Quebec has also endeavored to simplify them, by doing away with categories for specific uses of electricity (heating, cooking, lighting, etc.), and keeping only major distinctions between user categories. For instance, before nationalization, there were 85 different residential rates, 80 commercial rates and 70 industrial rates. In 1967, these categories were reduced to 7, 7 and 3 respectively. At present, the rate schedule comprises three major categories — residential, general and public lighting — and lists a total of ten different rates.

As for pricing, the company usually appears before a Parliamentary Committee in order to discuss rates and operations. Rates are agreed upon, and are automatically approved by the Minister's Council. The rates of major industrial customers, however, are negotiated separately.

2.2. Preferential Rates.

One social and political consideration which arises in pricing is the practice of preferential rates, whose purpose is to stimulate local or regional industrial development. The question of rates as a factor in the establishment of industry and in regional development has sometimes led to controversy since 1967. Government and opposition members alike have requested that Hydro-Quebec grant major energy consuming businesses a preferential rate and that it thus take an active part in industrial policy. But until Bill 41 in 1978, the government did not have the jurisdiction to take part in the pricing process.

Until quite recently, Hydro-Quebec had vehemently opposed any government intervention in this regard and it was not to be swayed. The company felt that electricity was a factor in economic development merely because it was available, whatever its cost. It also argued that Hydro-Quebec's mandate was not to provide subsidies.[28] According to Hydro-Quebec, a reduced rate amounted to a subsidy to a business; therefore, it was up to the Ministry of Industry and Commerce to establish the criteria, measures and instruments required to attract business and stimulate regional development.

In support of this position, Hydro-Quebec pointed out that for most of the province's manufacturers, electricity comprises only 1 or 2 per cent of production costs.[29] In relation to added manufacturing value this percentage reached 4.4 per cent for the year 1979. But it is considerably higher in certain industries: 21.6 per cent for steel-making; 24.1 per cent for metal refining and smelting; 21.6 per cent for pulp and paper; 20.5 per cent for industrial chemicals; 13.6 per cent for cement; and 10.7 per cent for plastics, all sectors in which self-producers are present.[30]

Due to government pressures, economic developments and the presence of surplus following the opening of the James Bay installations, Hydro-Quebec revised its position. In 1978, Bill 41 greatly undermined the company's financial independence. The law stated that Hydro-Quebec's activities had to follow all energy policies approved by the cabinet. This policy left the door open to coercive measures by the government during the negotiations of supply contracts with customers.

In order to sell off surplus energy, commercial programmes, aimed at businesses, have been regulated since 1981. The conversion programme for industrial boilers, for instance, not only provides financial assistance for businesses replacing or acquiring electrical boilers, it also ensures lower rates than those of the energy form being replaced. A rate reduction programme has been in force since 1983. Reductions, of up to 50 per cent, are offered to businesses investing in installations which will increase their electricity requirements. Individual contracts have also been drawn up for businesses with special needs. These programmes have been successful. The average annual increase of electricity sales between 1981 and 1986 has been in the order of 44 per cent; revenues which were only $20 million in 1982 reached $135 million in 1986.[31]

Rates have also been negotiated on the basis of "shared risk and shared benefit". Contracts take into account the way customers operate, the amount they must invest, the phasing-in period and economic cycles.[32] This is how contracts were drawn up for the Reynolds and Bécancourt and for the Norsk Hydro project, from Norway.

2.3. Rate schedules and subsidies

The rate schedule is divided into two main rate categories[33]: residential and farm rates, (Rate D), and the general rate, which is subdivided into three classes:

— the low-power rate applies to installations consuming less than 100 kilowatts. These include small industrial or commercial operations as well as small-scale non-profit organizations. This rate is further broken down into five sub-rates: Rate G, which accounts for the bulk of sales, and Rates G-9, E, P and T;

— the medium-power rate (Rate M) includes all customers, other than residential consumers and public lighting equipment, whose power requirements are listed between 100 and 5,000 kilowatts;

— the high-power rate (Rate L) applies to customers in the 5 000-150 000 kilowatt bracket.

Contracts for requirements above 150 000 kilowatts are not bound by these rates and are negotiated on an individual basis.

Selling prices are calculated on the basis of the revenue generated for the company by the sale of one energy unit (the kilowatt per hour) at the rates provided in the rate schedule. As seen in Table 1, the basic high-power rate (L) is substantially lower than the average rate, although successive increases have brought it closer to residential rates. Whereas in 1973, Rate L was 63 per cent lower that Rate D, (Residential and Farms) by 1978, the discrepancy was only 49 per cent and by 1984 the gap had narrowed to 40 per cent. Low and medium-power rates (G and M) have also increased considerably. This is especially true of Rate M which caught up to Rate D in 1979 and then exceeded it.

One widespread belief is that higher domestic rates enable Hydro-Quebec to offer its business customers better rates. This view implies that when a consumer pays his electricity bill, he is actually subsidizing multinationals which take advantage of Quebec's national resources. But this analysis is based on two erroneous premises. First, it considers rate levels only as inferred from Hydro-Quebec's sales to each category of customers, without finding a way of calculating the "subsidies" that could be transferred from one category to another. Secondly, the analysis rests on the equally false assumption that all electricity is identical, in other words, that the power sold to enterprises and that which is sold to individuals is of a comparable nature.

This is clearly not the case. Each rate category has specific criteria concerning connection to the system and conditions under which power is used. For instance, high-power customers receive high-voltage power directly from the transmission network, which virtually eliminates distribution costs and losses. Residential customers, on the other hand, entail more expenses for the company, due to losses incurred through low-voltage distribution, expenditures involved in distribution equipment (transformers, meters, etc.) and to the handling of over two million accounts.[34] Furthermore, businesses and homes do not use the same kind of energy. The rate of power use

Table 1
Revenues from Regular Sales
¢ per kWh

Year	Residential (D)	Low power (G,G-9,T)	Medium power (M)	High power (L)	Public lighting	Mean rate
1973	1.55	1.84	1.1	0.57	2.86	1.13
1974	1.56	1.91	1.15	0.61	3.07	1.17
1975	1.68	2.12	1.38	0.71	3.39	1.34
1976	1.74	2.31	1.51	0.8	3.84	1.43
1977	1.89	2.57	1.71	0.91	4.24	1.59
1978	2.14	2.99	2.08	1.09	5.31	1.85
1979	2.43	3.41	2.44	1.3	5.96	2.15
1980	2.78	3.81	2.87	1.47	6.56	2.45
1981	3.05	4.08	3.16	1.69	7.02	2.74
1982	3.54	4.64	3.72	2.09	7.49	3.25
1983	3.84	5.01	3.95	2.28	7.87	3.51
1984	3.94	5.16	4.1	2.37	8.09	3.61
1985	3.99	5.24	4.2	2.31	8.35	3.63
1986	4.2	n.a.	n.a.	n.a.	8.7	3.72

Source: Hydro-Québec; Statistiques, ventes et revenues, années 1984, 1985, service Tarification, groupe Marchés internes.

in industry is fairly constant, from 80 to 95 per cent; but residential customers use only 40 to 50 per cent of their power supply. Thus, the demand for electricity in business varies little, whereas residential customers only use their full power supplies for a few weeks each year, mainly because of the seasonal demands. In reality, the transfer of funds from one rate category to another can only be calculated on the basis of the difference between the cost and the selling price of services to each user category.

Statistics reveal that customers in the residential category actually derive the greatest benefit from this transfer, as residential sales (in 1983) covered only 87 per cent of production costs. High-power customers may have had the upper hand in the early 1980's, but by 1983 they were paying their fair share. Overall equilibrium is maintained through rates which exceed costs in the low (124 per cent) and medium-power categories (120 per cent).[35] The average cost system shows that, contrary to popular belief, commercial customers are subsidizing residential consumers!

2.4. High-Power Contracts

Within this category (5,000 kilowatts of power) fall companies with vast energy requirements, some institutions (stadiums, universities, harbors, airports and military bases), commercial customers (shopping centers) and municipalities. Out of the 212 customers included in this category, 147 are enterprises. Industrial customers fall into four main industrial sectors: pulp and paper (38), metal and non-metal mining (24), chemicals (20) and steelmaking (14). In 1984, these industrial customers consumed 80 per cent of the power bought by all Quebec industries (only 43.5 per cent of companies who produce their own energy are included), and accounted for 67 per cent of industrial sales.

Beyond the 150,000 kilowatts requirements, the rate schedule no longer applies. In such cases, individual contracts are drawn up. At regular intervals, Hydro-Quebec calculates the opportunity cost of offering preferential rates rather than regular high-power rates. For the year 1977, the cost was $27 million. As of January 1, 1983, 21 corporate customers had special rates. In 1982, those accounts cost Hydro-Quebec $57.8 million or 10 per cent of total sales in the high-power category. Hydro-Quebec estimates that, in 1984, it helped its customers save $100 million by selling them surplus energy at reduced rates and by offering them various rate discounts.[36]

Hydro-Quebec's rate reductions were more a result of its commercial strategy than government policy designed to maximize economic spin-offs from the abundant supply of inexpensive energy. In spite of government policy statements, the aluminum works at

Bécancourt and the Norsk Hydro project have been the only cases where the rates were scrutinized by cabinet. Hydro-Quebec does not consider itself an instrument of industrial policy in this sense.

2.5. Investments and Debt

On an international scale, the mega-projects at Manic and James Bay are among the largest and the most expensive in the world. Their completion involved huge investments and loans on financial markets in Canada and abroad. Therefore, although Hydro-Quebec played an important role in stimulating and backing up Quebec's failing economy, its investments are also responsible for a large portion of the province's debt. By the end of 1986, Hydro-Quebec's debt had risen to close to $3,400 per capita or a total of over $20.3 billion.

By virtue of its investments of approximately $2 billion a year, Hydro-Quebec is the source of significant economic activity. The realization of a major project represents thousands of jobs and million of dollars in equipment supply contracts. These investments are financed through corporate revenues and loans. These revenues come primarily from the sale of electricity to industries, institutions and private consumers. The interest rate is determined by production revenue and, because it is a public enterprise, by the provincial government's credit rating. Obviously, the size of the loan depends on sales revenue. Therefore there is a direct relationship between the size of the debt, investments, and electrical rates. As a result, in order to present a better financial profile the enterprise must hike its rates in order to increase its revenues. In the end, consumers bear the burden of the debt through higher rates. Because of the scale of its operations and because of its control of the supply of an essential product, Hydro-Quebec plays a significant role in income distribution in Quebec.

The figures presented in Table 2 reflect the increase of Hydro-Quebec's activities in the 1970s. During the 1960s, growth was moderate and constant. With the exception of profits, which tend to follow their own dynamic, the principal financial indicators show a parallel evolution. Between 1973 and 1975 investments practically doubled and continued to accelerate until 1978 when they reached over $2.5 billion, a level of investment which held until 1982. As a result of this growth between 1973 and 1982, the long-term debt maintained an annual average of 17.7 per cent, while during the previous decade it was below 10 per cent. During this period, the company showed a regular profit and in some years, such as in 1982, huge gains of $800 million. But during the period 1980-1982, investments levelled off at $2.5 billion annually, long-term debt grew

Table 2
Hydro-Quebec: Major Financial Indicators
$ million

Year	Assets	Property & Equipment Value*	Value of Construction in Progress	Long-Term Debt	Reserves (or Shareholders' Assets)	Annual Investments	Sales Revenues	Net Profit
1963	2,050	1,580	346	1,409	391	193	202	44
1965	2,539	1,895	531	1,804	507	315	289	57
1968	3,387	2,328	791	2,347	712	269	390	78
1970	3,890	3,142	388	2,676	913	293	483	117
1973	5,088	3,894	752	3,360	1,260	551	662	121
1974	5,814	3,955	1,197	3,912	1,437	616	783	177
1975	7,068	4,215	1,970	4,910	1,667	1,142	904	230
1978	12,886	5,396	6,221	8,857	2,882	2,588	1,600	523
1979	15,505	7,691	6,565	10,354	3,628	2,818	1,956	746
1980	18,012	10,884	5,878	12,107	4,374	2,668	2,413	746
1981	20,730	13,099	6,075	13,713	4,926	2,592	2,770	559
1982	23,162	14,969	6,506	15,628	5,719	2,546	3,257	800
1983	25,179	19,255	4,035	16,453	6,366	2,248	3,593	707
1984	27,129	21,940	2,343	18,326	6,511	1,681	4,101	301
1985	29,183	22,948	2,469	20,123	6,720	1,615	4,423	209
1986	30,588	24,448	1,948	20,349	7,023	1,537	4,673	303

* properties and equipment in use - depreciation = net value of properties and equipment
Source: Hydro-Quebec; Annual Reports.

and an artificial increase in revenues occurred. Given these indicators, Hydro-Quebec seemed to have dug itself a deep financial hole.

Not surprisingly, the level of employment follows the same trend as investment. Between 1965 and 1982, the number of employees nearly doubled, reflecting the growth of the enterprise. This growth was particularly strong during the construction of the James Bay project, reaching a peak in 1982. From 1982 to 1986, the slow-down observed in the construction of generating facilities, in investment and in the demand of electricity resulted in a 8 per cent reduction in the number of employees (both permanent and part-time) from 19,959 to 18,470.

One can prove that Hydro-Quebec is a driving force in the provincial economy simply by comparing the relative importance of its annual investments with overall investments in the public and private sectors (Table 3). The weight of these investments remained remarkably stable in the ten years following its nationalization. In relation to public investments (federal, provincial and municipal), Hydro-Quebec's participation fluctuated between 25 and 30 per cent and between 11 and 15 per cent compared to the private sector (which includes all primary, secondary and tertiary activities), giving an average proportion in the area of 9 per cent in relation to total investments.

These ratios were brutally inflated with the construction of the James Bay project. In 1979, Hydro-Quebec's investments alone represented 57 per cent of public investment, 40 per cent of private investment or 24 per cent of all provincial investments. This proportion reflects the acute weakness of private sector initiative during this period.

In general, the public sector is more flexible than the private sector in that profit is not the fundamental criterion for investment decisions. The public sector is responsible for 40 per cent of total investment, Hydro-Quebec being its largest single contributor. These capital injections can be planned to reinforce economic activity during periods of slow-down. But a comparison of Hydro-Quebec's investments with that of the public and private sector shows no particular pattern. In fact, the mandate of the enterprise and the nature of the sector of activities make it difficult to program investments in relation to the economic climate. From the drawing board to production, a major hydro-electric project, on the scale of Manic-5, is a ten-year endeavor. In other words, one cannot simply pull a mega-project out of the closet to stimulate a stagnating economy. Equally, it is impossible to predict the economic fluctuations over such a long period of time. Finally, given the extremely high cost of such projects, it would be a

Table 3
Investment in Quebec
$ million

Year	Hydro-Quebec - 1 -	Public Investments - 2 -	Public Investments 1/2 %	Private Investments - 3 -	Private Investments 1/3 %	Total Investments - 4 -	Total Investments 1/4 %
1963	193	682	28.3	1,601	12	2,283	8.4
1965	315	1,131	27.8	2,091	15.1	3,221	9.9
1968	269	979	27.5	2,196	12.2	3,174	8.5
1970	293	1,148	25.5	2,270	12.9	3,418	8.6
1973	551	1,874	29.4	3,952	13.9	5,826	9.5
1975	1,142	3,653	31.3	5,517	20.7	9,170	12.4
1978	2,588	4,729	54.7	6,064	42.7	10,794	24
1979	2,818	4,921	57.3	6,933	40.6	11,854	23.8
1980	2,592	5,033	51.5	7,786	33.3	12,819	20.2
1981	2,668	5,123	52.1	8,616	30.1	13,739	19.4
1982	2,546	5,200	49	7,898	32.2	13,097	19.4
1983	2,248	5,258	42.7	8,689	25.9	13,947	16.1
1984	1,681	5,204	32.3	10,544	15.3	15,748	10.7
1985	1,615	5,403	29.9	13,847	11.7	19,240	8.4

Sources: Hydro-Quebec; Annual Reports.
Statistics Canada, cat. 61-205; Public and Private Investments in Canada, (selected years).

great financial risk for the company as well as for public finances to use another James Bay for the sole purpose of economic recovery without assured outlets for the energy produced.

Nevertheless, there exists a lag between the economic climate and Hydro-Quebec's rate of expansion. This lag has had a counter-cyclical effect at times. Between 1975 and 1977 and in 1978 with investment increases of 85 per cent, 54 per cent and 33 per cent respectively, Hydro-Quebec maintained its investment growth rate. Its slow-down in 1984 coincides with a slight economic recovery. But this counter-cyclical effect is accidental since the projects that were at the origin of these investments were initiated during the economic prosperity of the early 1970s.

In 1983, the government, searching for means to stimulate a weak economy, publicly asked the enterprise to re-evaluate its increasingly conservative investment programme. Since there was no room for expansion, Hydro-Quebec decided instead to accelerate its programme of modernization of its transmission and distribution network in order to satisfy government objectives. The message from the government to its enterprise is that average annual investments of at least $2 billion until the year 2000 will be needed to stimulate economic growth. But that level of investment could not be maintained and has been falling since 1982. In 1986, it was a billion dollars less than the 1982 level. Hydro-Quebec's share of public and total investment has dramatically declined in the last years. In 1985, it represented less than 30 per cent of public investment and a little over 8 per cent of total investment. Its most recent development plan, covering the period 1988-1990, foresees investments of $7,550 million which is equivalent to total investment between 1981 and 1983.

Hydro-Quebec's investments necessitated major borrowing on the Canadian, American and European markets. Such borrowing rates and the external financing conditions have a significant effect on the global financial status of the company and, by extension, on its rates. The financial health of Hydro-Quebec is based on three indicators: reserves; the covering rate on interest payments (fixed by law at 1.25 times the net exploitation revenue); and the self-financing margin. Specialized firms in financial analysis such as Moody's, Standard and Poor's, Kidder, Peabody and Co. consider Hydro-Quebec to have a very conservative management policy.

In spite of these expensive precautions in the application of these ratios, the borrowing rate is presently rather high and this can be explained by the close links between Hydro-Quebec's rate and that of the government of Quebec. Hydro-Quebec's loans are unconditionally guaranteed by the Province.[37] In other words, even if Hydro-Quebec has the necessary financial autonomy to establish its own reputation on the financial market, its borrowing rate, regardless of the quality of its own financial situation, cannot be superior to that of its guarantor[38].

The situation of Ontario Hydro confirms this analysis. The financial situation of the Ontario corporation is weaker than that of Hydro-Quebec. On the other hand, over the last several years Ontario's borrowing rate has been significantly better than Quebec's. A close examination of the average bond interest rates reveals a significant difference (up to 1.13 points in October, 1982 for an average difference of 0.75 for the period: 1982-1983) consistently in favour of Ontario Hydro.

Under these circumstances, Hydro-Quebec's strategy, which consisted in presenting a financial report far superior to what was required by its creditors, is open to criticism for two reasons. First, in order to present an exceptional financial report, Hydro-Quebec obtained rate increases from the government (there were sixteen increases between 1967 and 1987). The capacity to generate revenues was not sufficient to convince creditors of the enterprise's financial health. The borrowing rates demanded were significantly higher than the base rate, meaning that a large part of revenues was used for interest payments. The vicious circle of rate hikes then began: payment of high interest rates while maintaining the high covering rate on interest, requiring rapid tariff rate increases. Any monetary imbalance such as high inflation, a sudden interest rate hike or a fluctuation in loan exchange rates in relation to the Canadian dollar had acute repercussions on price.

Given what we have just demonstrated it is not surprising to note in Table 4 that Hydro-Quebec borrowed heavily and paid dearly. From 1974 onwards, the James Bay project pushed up the volume of loans beyond $ 2 billion in 1980, 1981, and 1982. Inflation increased construction costs and hiked up interest rates. The average interest rate on new long-term loans (1-5 years) stood at 15.10 per cent in 1981, 12.25 per cent in 1983 and 11.5 per cent in 1986. As a result, the constant evolution of interest payments since 1964 has increased dramatically in recent years (+22 per cent in 1980, +22 per cent in 1981, +15 per cent in 1982). Quebec pays close to $2 billion in interest annually or approximately $300 per capita.

If Hydro-Quebec is an ideal client for the banks, how does the general population benefit from its revenues? As is the case with all provincial Crown corporations, Hydro-Quebec is exempt from federal corporate tax. The enterprise is taxed at the municipal and provincial levels and the provincial government holds jurisdiction over the applicable tax rates.

The fiscal policy for Hydro-Quebec was modified following the 1963 nationalization. Afterwards, fiscal management changed for the

Table 4
Hydro-Quebec: loans and interest
$ million

Year	Total of Long-term Loans	Average Loan Cost %	Long-term Interest Debts Payable	Total of Interest Payable
1963	403 (1)	5.15 (3)	n.a.	n.a.
1964	210	5.33	75 (2)	82 (2)
1965	125	5.31	84	91
1966	250	5.88	93	105
1967	270	6.65	105	121
1968	185	7.44	117	132
1969	262	8.63	131	151
1970	230	9.68 (4)	148	164
1971	325	8.58	168	179
1972	377	8.5	191	197
1973	465	8.14	224	231
1974	703	9.76	259	267
1975	1,068	9.95	344	242
1976	1,718	9.49	485	494
1977	1,098	8.32	621	642
1978	1,542	9.84	785	861
1979	1,783	10.77 (2)	972	1,103
1980	2,090	12.54	1,191	1,350
1981	2,239	15.1	1,467	1,648
1982	2,290	13.47	1,807	1,898
1983	1,768	12.25	1,938	2,093
1984	1,164	12.16	2,149	2,397
1985	1,952	10.5	2,298	2,312
1986	1,259	11.57	2,373	2,417

Sources: (1) Quebec Statistics Bureau; Financement à long terme du secteur pub québécois, 1970, 73, 77, 81 and 1983.

(2) Hydro-Quebec; Annual Reports, 1963-1986.

(3) CPRN, 4th session, 28th legislature Quebec, Dec. 14, 1969

(4) CPRNTF, 3rd session, 29th legislature, May 11, 1972.

first time in 1973 and then successively in 1979, 1980 and 1981 following a series of reforms brought about by the Parti Québécois. Bill 16, passed in 1981, extended the potential for government control, already established by Bill 41, to the enterprise's finances. As mentioned before, Bill 16 obliges the enterprise to pay an annual dividend to the Minister of Finance, its sole shareholder. These annual dividends cannot exceed the "surplus susceptible to distribution" defined as equal to 75 per cent of the net investment revenue less gross interest expenditures. However, no dividend will be due if it reduces the enterprise's capitalization rate to less than 25 per cent. It is important to note that the dividends are not considered tax payments. Bill 16 also obliges Hydro-Quebec to pay a tax on its capital on the same basis and at the same rate as private sector corporations. This tax carried an initial rate of 0.30 per cent and was increased to 0.45 per cent in July, 1981. The taxable capital comprises the total of accumulated reserves and the long-term debt.

These fiscal changes brought about $106.4 million in expenditures for the 1981 financial year (the first year of the law's application), $43.4 million of which was capital tax and $63.0 million being sales tax. A $6.9 million dividend was also paid to the shareholder. In 1982, the tax grew to $98 million and to $108 million in 1983; sales tax amounting to $71 million and $83 million respectively (Table 5). The dividends which stood at $7 million in 1982, rose dramatically to $60 million and then to $156 million in 1984 because of the enterprise's excellent financial health as determined by the ratio mix.

Until 1980, the taxation scheme imposed on Hydro-Quebec in no way reflected its economic performance. The provincial tax was a fixed amount levied out of total revenues. As for school and municipal taxes, these are determined according to the local evaluation of buildings and properties. The proportion of taxes to revenue was in constant decline from 1966 to 1979 when it equalled only 2.2 per cent. The reforms brought about in 1980 and 1981 effectively link taxation to the enterprise's performance; this applies in particular to the 3 per cent tax on gross revenues originating from sales of electricity. The linking of fiscal disposition to economic performance can be verified if we consider the dividends paid in 1983 and 1984 by Hydro-Quebec. The rate of taxation rose sharply in 1981 and increased to a level of 8.8 per cent in 1984. Still, we are far from the rates of 20 per cent that were the standard during the 1960s. Nevertheless, there has been an improvement and if we include taxes and dividends, the ratio reached 15 per cent in 1984.

Table 5
Taxes and Dividends Paid by Hydro-Quebec
$'000

Year	Education Tax	Tax on Energy Produced	Real Estate Tax	Total of Paid Tax	Net Revenues Before Taxes	Tax Rate % Tax/Revenue
1963	3,577	1,513	4,604	9,694	98,756	9.8
1964		19,621	7,905	27,526	142,534	19.3
1965		19,524	9,776	29,300	145,451	20.1
1966		21,679	11,236	32,915	153,885	21.4
1967		22,179	14,476	36,655	191,904	19.1
1968		22,088	17,999	40,087	203,277	19.7
1969		23,744	18,091	41,835	218,380	19.2
1970		27,784	18,182	45,966	275,523	16.7
1971		29,057	19,070	48,127	305,821	15.7
1972		29,882	18,875	48,757	303,372	16.1
	Provincial Tax					
1973	15,000	8,222	18,783	42,005	334,597	12.5
1974	20,000		18,379	38,379	395,651	9.7
1975	20,000		18,806	38,806	464,670	8.3
1976	20,000		19,209	39,209	556,493	7

Table 5 (Cont'd)

Year	Education Tax	Tax on Energy Produced	Real Estate Tax	Total of Paid Tax	Net Revenues Before Taxes	Tax Rate % Tax/Revenue	Shareholder's Dividends
1977	20,000		20,217	40,217	685,523	5.9	
1978	20,000		20,388	40,388	939,311	4.3	
1979	5,000		20,249	25,249	1,152,487	2.2	
	3% Sales Tax	Capital Tax					
1980	51,188		6,343	57,531	1,446,737	4	
1981	63,003	43,418	8,469	114,890	1,580,660	7.3	7,000
1982	71,518	97,866	15,963	185,347	1,956,000	9.5	7,000
1983	83,272	108,236	17,514	209,022	2,193,000	9.5	60,000
1984	91,025	114,445	18,346	223,816	2,534,000	8.8	156,000
1985	102,772	123,289	19,853	245,914	2,542,000	9.7	0
1986	112,328	137,308	22,379	272,015	2,751,000	9.9	0

Source: Hydro-Quebec; Annual Reports.

2.6. Procurement Policy

With $ 1.3 billion[39] in annual buying power, Hydro-Quebec provides an opportunity to put into practice a preferential procurement policy at the provincial level.[40] It is surprising to note that Hydro-Quebec itself initiated a preferential procurement policy in 1962. This behavior is a contrast to the firm's vigorous resistance to preferential tariffs. This apparent contradiction can be understood, however, if one considers the repercussions of these practices on Hydro-Quebec's financial status, managerial autonomy, and development strategy. If the procurement policy involves costs it is conceivable that it involves definite political and economic advantages.

Given the nature of the enterprise's activities, the relationship between Hydro-Quebec and Quebec's industry takes on another dimension. The production, transmission and distribution of hydro-electric energy demands original technical solutions to the unique constraints of each site. Thus, this field of activity is susceptible to technological innovation and lays the foundation for the accumulation of significant know-how. It was partially in order to activate this technological potential that *l'Institut de recherche en électricité du Québec* (IREQ) was founded in 1967. In this same vein, the engineering consulting subsidiary, *Hydro-Québec international,* was founded in 1979 in order to sell the firm's expertise internationally.

Hydro-Quebec's preferential procurement policy was formulated in 1962 within the context of the debate which spurred the process of the nationalization of electrical power.[41] Contracts over $50,000 are awarded by tender primarily restricted to local producers when local competition seemed adequate to ensure reliable quality and service. If this condition is not met, the call for tenders is open to other Canadian and foreign producers. For contracts between $2,000 and $50,000 at least three producers are invited to bid. Finally, for small contracts, below $2,000, the company directly contracts its current purveyors.

About 5 per cent of the contracts, for 25 per cent of the total value of purchases, are publicly announced. Bids on invitation represent 75 per cent of the contracts for 72 per cent of the value. Direct purchases represent approximately 25 per cent of the orders but only 3 per cent of the monetary value of the orders.

In the case of public tenders not limited to local producers, the selection process allows for a 10 per cent preferential margin in order to help producers with high local content compete with foreign firms. But local content is certainly not the only factor determining the successful bidder. A first selection is made on the basis of the technical quality and performance of the product, on the timetable for delivery, and on the credit offered. It is only then that the lowest bid is considered and the 10 per cent preference applied.

The effect of this procurement policy seems clear. For example, a sample from the *Daily Commercial News*, shows that only local producers bid. We can safely assume that invitations to bid on smaller contracts are restricted to Quebec firms. For most years since 1967, goods and services bought by Hydro-Quebec have come in a proportion of about 75 per cent in value from local producers, 15 per cent from producers from other provinces (mostly Ontario) and around 10 per cent from foreign countries .

But the concept of *local content* as applied should be explained. For Hydro-Quebec, this does not mean the local value added as it could be expected but simply the total value of goods and services bought from firms established in Quebec. This is a rather weak definition, for it maintains the confusion between goods that are produced in Quebec and goods that are purchased from firms established in Quebec. This is a first indication that the real value of the local content, defined as it should be as local value added, may be much less than claimed by Hydro-Quebec.

This guess is confirmed by the only study that has tried, using an economic model, to operationalize the concept of value added applied to the economic activities of Hydro-Quebec.[42] The first phase of the James Bay project (La Grande phase 1) required an investment of $ 8 billion (1979) of which 76 per cent was spent on local goods and services. Out of this high percentage, 55 per cent were wages and salaries for the thousands of construction workers, heavy equipment operators and peripheral services that were paid exclusively to Quebecers.

Of the $3.663 billion paid for the purchase of manufactured goods and services, more than half, $1.669 billion (54 per cent), was spent outside Quebec. More drastically, 83 per cent of the value of the imports necessitated by the project were industrial goods. This means that most of the equipment bought or rented including trucks, cranes, fuels, tools and heavy electrical products were imported. The company explains this situation by claiming that there are no local producers for such products.

Since local producers, when they exist, are selected mainly on the basis of the conditions regulating the attribution of contracts, it is logical that the 10 per cent price preferential has a very limited impact on the cost of purchases. The additional cost fluctuates between $1.5 million and $376,000, which, besides the rather large difference, represents less than one tenth of 1 per cent of the total value of goods and services purchased or between 1 and 4 per cent of the cost of the contracts allocated under the preferential provision. The procurement policy applied by Hydro-Quebec is therefore much less effective than the company claims. It has not been applied aggressively given the small amount of monetary incentives used and the absence of local producers for most of the manufactured goods and equipment required.

Hydro-Quebec, however, has had a major impact on a few large firms in the electrical equipment industry. The turbines, alternators and water-gates complex represent between 40 and 50 per cent of the cost of equipment of a hydro-electrical plant. This is the reason why two firms established in Quebec decided to produce this equipment. They are *Marine industrie,* using French technology (bought from Neyrpic, a subsidiary of the Alsthom group), and Dominion Engineering Works (a subsidiary of Canadian General Electric). Other firms who have specialized in the production of goods required by Hydro-Quebec are ASEA Electric Ltd. (transformers), Merlin-Gérin Co., Cegelec Industries Inc., C.G.E. and Montel (insulators and circuit breakers), Westinghouse Canada (reactors, condensators), Reynolds Aluminium, Pirelli, Northern Telecom, Cable Phillips and Alcan Products of Canada (electrical cables and wires), BBC Brown Boveri Canada (heavy electrical equipment), and B.G. Checo International (construction works).

In all of these cases, where expanded facilities were required, the investment occurred between 1965 and 1970. Some firms were offered guaranteed markets (for a twenty year period in the case of ASEA) and/or preferential pricing along with other advantages (in the form of government loans, subsidies and fiscal incentives). But there were only a few such investments. The value of the goods and services purchased in Quebec has not increased since 1971. In its present design, and the way it is being applied, it seems that the procurement policy had all the effects it could on the industrial structure of the province. It is quite possible that the small dimension of the market allows only for a limited number of highly specialized producers. More generally it may also be an indication of the limits of demand-pull policy, which confirms the analysis proposed by Rothwell and Zegveld.[43]

Because of a recent downturn in investment, Hydro-Quebec has undertaken a more active procurement policy. Through the establishment of more direct links with its contractors, the public corporation is trying to have a positive impact on their growth, while at the same time using its market power to stabilize prices, control quality, stimulate R & D and promote exports.

Initially, a few measures have been considered to stimulate local production. It has been considered that production lines could be nationalized if firms, instead of competing with each other, agree to cooperate through sub-contracting. Such an agreement on inter-connecting material for instance, could increase local content from 30 to 60 per cent. When there is no local producer for the equipment needed, an exclusive procurement contract can be signed contingent upon the creation of a production facility. But Hydro-Quebec cannot always guarantee constant orders and the enterprise must commit itself to actively explore export markets. This can also be used to keep a local supplier in operation.

It also has been considered that, when the contract being passed includes little or no local content, the state enterprise can negotiate a compensating agreement with the firm. It will buy the goods against a commitment by the firm to expand its productive activities in the province. This strategy is being tried with foreign firms which are encouraged to seek exclusive production agreements.[44]

Why would Hydro-Quebec engage in such an activity? On the face of it, the enterprise, in the absence of a direct order from the minister, should have no interest in spending time and resources to help local producers if it does not find a direct advantage in the operation. The only logical reason is that the enterprise wants to secure a reliable supply for the goods it requires. This means getting proper equipment at a fair price in sufficient quantity when needed. The danger of offering a market guarantee is that the firm may fall back on competitiveness and through neglect of its R&D efforts, offer technologically obsolete equipment (talk of feather-bedding suppliers with poor records on foreign markets is already being heard). This is why Hydro-Quebec insists that its market should be used as a basis from which the firm will seek new markets. Also as a public enterprise, it does not want to be held responsible for the well-being of its purveyors.

Over the past two years, Hydro-Quebec has signed a few production agreements.[45] The enterprise has identified a limited number of "strategic" products for which its demand represents a large share of the market. Twenty eight products and 41 producers are identified as potential candidates for such agreements. Using this market power potential, Hydro-Quebec approaches the producers with conditional market guarantees. These may represent up to 80 per cent over three years of real needs for a given commodity, with a minimal guarantee of 50 per cent of forecasted needs. The enterprise has to agree to respect the technical specifications established by the user, deliver on schedule, control quality and stay within an established price range. Given these minimal conditions, three other dimensions are considered. First local content has to be improved. There is no pre-established minimal level, but the firm has to prove that whenever possible it buys parts and products from local suppliers, and that, within a negotiated timetable, production facilities will be established in Quebec. The major indicator used is the amount of investment the firm is committed to undertake. Second, Hydro-Quebec is concerned with the export capacity of its suppliers as a means to ensure their competitiveness, and as a way to avoid the state enterprise's responsibility as a monopsonic buyer. Since most producers are branch plants of foreign firms, an exclusive production mandate is considered a positive sign of the willingness of the firm to cooperate. Otherwise, export targets are set, market perspectives are discussed and all barriers to foreign trade (like restrictive patents and licences) are expected to be lifted. Third, R&D requirements are set and product specification and performance are regularly updated to create an additional incentive. The ability of Hydro-Quebec to influence technical change is limited when the technology used reaches a high level of maturity.[46] These agreements are signed for periods of three years and are regularly monitored by Hydro-Quebec. The latest available figures show that six firms are currently involved in such agreements for the production of fourteen different products. Hydro-Quebec has purchased products through such agreements for a value of $ 38.73 million.[47]

Along with this public market demand one would expect to find some indication of technological innovation. Hydro-Quebec's research center, IREQ, tests new equipment and finds solutions to problems arising from the production and transport of huge amounts of electricity under difficult geographical and weather conditions. Over the years, close to sixty innovations or adaptations were considered sufficiently important for a patent to be issued in as many as 20 countries.[48] But the commercial success of these discoveries has been slow. In fact, it is only recently that IREQ has made any effort to have its scientific prowess transformed into commercial undertakings. Some firms have agreed to produce under licence agreement new products developed and tested by IREQ. In 1985, production reached $3 million, but it is not clear at this stage if sales are only those of Hydro-Quebec, or if other clients have been successfully approached.

Another dimension of public markets associated with Hydro-Quebec is the development of local engineering firms. Around one third of the activities of these firms is directly related to energy projects in the form of feasibility and impact studies and planning power plants, dams, roads, and power lines. All such activities are related to Hydro-Quebec.

Quebec has an important engineering industry with more than 200 firms employing more than 10,000 persons, half of whom are professionals. The development of these firms can be directly linked to the major projects undertaken by Hydro-Quebec. During the fifties, the contracts for the Bersimis 1 and 2 plants were given to the Acres firm from Ontario.[49] With the change of government in 1960 and the strong nationalistic affirmation, the major Francophone firms established in Quebec have expanded directly in association with major energy projects. Of the largest engineering firms of Quebec, Surveyer, Nenninger and Chênevert (SNC) was part of the Manic 5 project that started in 1960 and was completed in 1970; Asselin, Benoît, Boucher, Ducharme and Lapointe (ABBDL) worked on Manic 2 (in association with Acres), 3, 5 and on the Outardes 2 power plants; Georges Demers was part of Outardes 3 and 4; SNC, Montreal Engineering Company (Monenco) and the Shawinigan Engineering Company collaborated on the Gentilly 2 nuclear plant; while Lavalin along with a subsidiary of Bechtel Corp. of San Francisco, were responsible for the James Bay project.

The creation and expansion of an engineering industry in Quebec is probably not the result of a conscious policy of Hydro-Quebec. Rather, it appears to be the happy outcome of a rational policy of systematically using sub-contracting instead of allowing for the expansion of an in-house engineering capacity. Difficult labor relations between Hydro-Quebec and its unionized professionals that date back to the early sixties are responsible for this decision.

Out of the need for survival, the engineering firms, unlike the equipment producers, have expanded their activities in foreign, mostly third world markets. But it is remarkable that this expansion has not given birth to an equivalent development of local equipment.[50] The reason this sector of activity has not developed into a full grown industry can be explained to a large extent by the overwhelming domination of foreign multinationals.

Finally, it is interesting to note that in 1978, Hydro-Quebec created a subsidiary called Hydro-Quebec International which, in close collaboration with the private sector, is supposed to promote local technology and expertise in matters related to electrical energy production, transport, distribution and management. It is difficult at this time to have a clear picture of the success or failure of this interesting initiative. Since 1978, Hydro-Quebec International has obtained contracts for a value of approximately $ 50 million ($ 13 million for 1985 alone). Presently, the enterprise is involved in 40 projects in 22 countries involving training, technical expertise, feasibility study and project design. In the early 1980s, the new subsidiary has been attacked by the private sector for fear that Hydro-Quebec International has an unfair advantage (by being part of a state-owned enterprise and therefore not having to meet the performance criteria of the private sector) and represents additional competition in a market already saturated. But recent developments reveal that public and private strategies of market penetration can be reconciled. Four different projects are now underway involving at least one other private engineering firm.

We have seen how Hydro-Quebec, using a broad definition of its original mandate, has contributed to the development of the province. It results in a fairly critical balance of the activities of the firm. Hydro-Quebec has tried to preserve its autonomy, and has not always been willing to bear the costs of being an instrument of economic policy. On the other hand, the procurement policy can be credited with some achievements. Now looking in the other direction, we should try to see what comes ahead, and how Hydro-Quebec is adjusting to the recent changes.

3. New Challenges in the Privatization Era

The drastic reduction in the rate of growth of demand for electricity has profoundly shaken Hydro-Quebec. Its positive public image was shattered by the huge capacity surplus that has been piling up with the expansion of the multi-billion dollar James Bay project.

The corporation's first reaction was one of total denial; the slow-down was so atypical of the trend of the past twenty years that the enterprise was convinced that demand would soon resume its historic growth rate. Then Hydro, when it was clear that the old order was not to return, entered a phase of lethargy with a sense of growing insecurity flowing through the whole structure. Profound changes were announced and/or expected but nothing happened and a paralyzing uncertainty entered the organization. Then a new Chief Executive Officer, Guy Coulombe, was nominated in 1982, someone who was not from the rank and file, and worse from a traditional standpoint, was a manager not a professional engineer.[51]

As a result, under close scrutiny from the government, the flagship of Quebec development, initiated a cautious change of direction in the murky waters of the recession. Like dominos, elements of the internal organization were tumbled and Hydro-Quebec internalized a new self-image. Taming the raw forces of the northern rivers was no longer required, selling energy was the priority. The enterprise still considers itself to be in a period of transition with a recovery being completed by the early 1990s when the huge surpluses will have been absorbed, and the tight financial period will have passed.

In the meantime, the environment continues to change. While the enterprise is still trying to adapt to changes that have occurred more than ten years ago, society evolves and new challenges emerge as new, more complex claims are voiced. Hydro-Quebec must respond to these demands if it is to regain its dynamism and leadership.

Four issues, which because they are conflicting can be considered as constraints, will shape the firm's future. First, the enterprise will be required to show a strong market orientation. Second, it will have to develop a commercial policy that allows for the export of energy. Third, it will have to adjust to the growing concern of the population for the respect of the environment and fourth, it will have to maintain an acceptable level of activity despite greater financial vulnerability. These aspects will be considered in turn.

3.1. *Playing by the Rules of the New Order*

Hydro-Quebec is certainly not a candidate for privatization,[52] but it must adapt to the government's changing perspective on economic intervention.

Hydro-Quebec is no longer the builder it once was and it is now engaged in marketing activities to sell its electricity. With the Parti Quebecois in power, the government has had a more direct concern with energy policy and given the growing public debt, for tighter financial management.

The privatization issue has never been mentioned seriously even in the context of the Bourassa government's moderate privatization drive. But it must adapt to the government's changing perspective on economic intervention. R. Parenteau, in a study prepared for the Economic Council, suggests an explanation:

> In our view, it seems out of the question that the government relinquish such an efficient policy instrument (economic and energy), an instrument which does not draw on the public budget, all of its activities including its enormous investments being covered by the payments received from the consumers of electricity.[53]

Nevertheless, there has been some talk of the government's intention to sell 10 per cent of its Hydro shares. Some have interpreted this project as the first step to privatization. We disagree. It can be seen as a financial operation whose objective is to raise revenues for the state, not for the public enterprise. But certainly, this project, if completed (although it now seems forgotten) is not relevant to the privatization issue. If it happens, it will be no more than a manipulation of the symbolism of capitalism while providing some added liquidity to the budget.

Manifestations of the changes in the rules are of another nature, and are being introduced. For instance, although it is not an item of high priority given the current electricity surpluses, efficient management of the available resources will impose a pricing policy based on the marginal cost of production. In the future, tariffs will discriminate by the type of use and the time period of utilization. Major investments can be saved if through these measures the period of daily and seasonal peak demand can be somewhat flattened. To introduce this change, Hydro will have to confront the attitude of the consumers for whom electricity is an essential good, which when used

freely can bring easy comfort at a low cost[54]. For both financial
reasons and reasons dealing with the province's energy balance, this
attitude is bound to change and for Quebecers' life-style it will be a
true revolution.

The engineers who formed the core of the firm's senior
management are being replaced by more cost conscious professionals.
The enterprise has been taking a hard look at its operating costs and
seeks productivity gains. This has an effect on the way the enterprise
is entering its new life. To have a commercial strategy requires to be
close to the market, to identify customers, to develop a strategy
adapted to segments of the market, and to require product
differentiation.

Until recently, with its price advantage and growing demand,
Hydro had a more passive marketing strategy. Its campaigns merely
told customers that electricity was safe and clean and that various
new services were available. This perspective is changing and
commercial strategy is now a priority directly related to the economic
performance of the enterprise. For example the 1987-1989
Development Plan calls for "selective market development".[55]
Programs are being created with discounts and rebates. These include
the bi-energy program for residential, commercial and institutional
clients, the risks and benefits sharing program, the interruptible
power program (comes with a 9 per cent discount), and the electro-
technology program, on which Hydro will spend $30 million in three
years. These programmes will probably multiply and change, if only
to keep customers alert and to show that new products are available.

For years Hydro has boasted that it has actively encouraged and
helped local producers of goods and services. But we have argued that
this claim is largely overstated. The real cost of the procurement
policy has always been low (2/10 of 1 per cent of total purchases in
1986). Nevertheless, buyers are frugal, more extra-province bidders
are making deals on the basis of lower prices, and traditional
suppliers are closely scrutinized.

Even the Research Institute (IREQ) has felt the pinch of the
emerging order. It is justly renowned for scientific capacity but has
had to undergo a restructuring.[56] Basic research has been reduced,
and the highest priority is now given to applied research either for
Hydro-Quebec, or to promote the use of electricity for industrial
application. Productivity gains are being looked for and sub-
contracting with industry and/or the universities is increasing. Lower
costs and immediate results are expected.

3.2. Reassessing the Market

The diminution in the rate of growth of the internal demand has had an important impact on Hydro-Quebec. Huge surpluses were generated for which there was no internal demand at any price. At the same time, the need to cover production costs and generate enough revenue to pay the debt required important tariff hikes which had the further effect of discouraging demand. New markets had to be found, both internally and externally.

This new situation will not vanish even when the surpluses are absorbed. For it is quite unlikely the the rate of growth of electricity demand will return to the pre-energy crisis level. On the other hand, electricity generation, through hydro-electric sources and given Quebec's geography, comes in lumps of thousands of megawatts at a time. Surpluses have a structural origin. To serve the local market with a reasonable margin of security, requires some unused capacity. This is why exports have been considered in the first place.

Quebec has been selling energy to the United States since 1912, although the quantities have remained small until 1978. Peak demand in Quebec occurs in winter, while such occurs in summer in the northeastern American states. On a regional basis, exchanges of surpluses make good economic sense. In 1986, total energy available amounted to 160.9 billion kwh (of which 32.8 billion were imported, from Churchill Falls). Sales in Quebec were 120.3 billion kwh, hence a surplus of 40.6 billion kwh, 1/3 of internal demand was available. Of this surplus, 26.9 billion kwh were exported mostly at a reduced rate, of which 12.6 billion kwh went to the United States.[57]

Out of necessity, Hydro-Quebec approached exports very cautiously. Large contracts were signed in the mid-1970s. In Canada, the major clients are Ontario and New Brunswick, but bigger sales are made to the New England states as shown in Table 6. In most contracts, the sale price is indexed on competitive energy sources. But this formula has shown, with the collapse of the price of petroleum, that it can be quite uncertain. This is why the latest contract with Central Maine Power uses a different pricing mechanism based on inflation indices from a 1985 base price.

The type of contract has also evolved. The first agreements were on non-guaranteed surpluses. This meant that Hydro, whenever it needed, could interrupt the supply to foreign customers to serve priority local needs. But now Hydro will supply energy on a firm basis.

At this stage the quantity of energy that can cross the border is limited by the capacity of the available transmission lines and interconnecting equipment. The agreement with Central Maine Power requires the construction of a new line between James Bay and

Table 6
Summary of Major Export Contracts

	Date of Effect	Expiry Date	Type of Energy	Maximum Annual Deliveries (billions kw/h)	Maximum Total Deliveries (billions kw/h)
Canada					
New Brunswick Hydro Electric Commission					
Interconnection Agreement	1979	--	Surplus	7	
Ontario Hydro					
Sales Contract	1982	1987	Guaranteed	2	12.5
Interconnection Agreement	1979	--	Surplus	8.7	
St. Lawrence Power Co.					
Sales Contract	1985	1990	Guaranteed	0.4	2
United States					
Central Main Power					
Sales Contract	1992	2020	Guaranteed	n.a.	122
New York Power Authority					
Sales Contract	1977	1998	Guaranteed	3	111
Sales Contract	1984	1997	Surplus	11	
Interconnection Agreement	1978	1996	Surplus	6	

Table 6 (Cont'd)

	Date of Effect	Expiry Date	Type of Energy	Maximum Annual Deliveries (billions kw/h)	Maximum Total Deliveries (billions kw/h)
Niagara Mohawk Interconnection Agreement	1982	--	Surplus	1.8	
New England Power Pool Sales Contract Interconnection Agreement	1990 1986	1997 --	Surplus Surplus	4 2	33
New England Utilities Sales Contract	1990	2000	Guaranteed	7	70
Vermont Department of Public Service Sales Contract	1985	1995	Guaranteed	1.3	13

Note: Maximum deliveries indicated are determined by the transport capacity of the lines.

Source: Hydro-Quebec; Profil financier, 1985, 1986, p. 11.

the American border. For the time being, the maximum available capacity is 5,415 MW.

Obvious progress has been made. Tables 7 and 8 show that between 1973 to 1986, the volume of sales increased by around 125 per cent, while the revenues are 1,300 per cent larger. This surprising situation is the result of sales made to the State of New York in 1979 for which the price is indexed to the cost of petroleum. This bonanza came to an abrupt stop when the barrel price dropped below $15 dollars. The unit price of a megawatt-hour declined from $27.80 to $23.95 between 1985 and 1986, a drop of 14 per cent that explains why export revenues have dropped although the quantities exported have increased.

Exports to the United States have increased while sales to the Canadian provinces have declined. Between 1981 and 1986 sales to Canada have increased by 41 per cent, while those to the south are up 52 per cent. Revenues have followed the same path (an increase of 93 per cent for American sales against 51 per cent for Canadian sales).

Finally it is worth mentioning that despite this significant increase in sales, exports as a proportion of total energy sales by Hydro-Quebec, have only increased by 1.4 per cent from 1973 levels. Although exports have more than doubled between 1980 and 1986, it is worth noting that in proportion to total sales such sales only represent a 1.5 per cent increase in revenues (Graph 2). It is true though that the impact of the export drive is yet to come. Many contracts that have been signed will only come into effect at the end of this decade.

The debate on the export of electricity has taken a different turn recently. The idea now is to export energy all year round on a guaranteed basis which requires the construction of new production facilities and transmission lines. This is a radical departure from tradition that reserved the exploitation of local resources for the exclusive use of Quebec consumers. Premier Bourassa has campaigned on the issue of energy export, promising to sell enough electricity to the United States to justify another mega-project. For this to be feasible, Hydro needs to sell an additional 12 000 megawatts. The enterprise's estimates are much more conservative. It argues that the market can only absorb a third of the government's objective, a mere 3,500 MW.[58] Even then, this potential demand assumes that the American northeastern states, Ontario and New Brunswick will not build new facilities, improve existing ones, and import exclusively from Quebec.

Does Quebec have a significant advantage in the production of electricity? Coal is a pollutant and nuclear plants are now very suspect. Moreover, flooding scarcely populated, immense territories is

Table 7
Exports of Electricity
billions of kwh

Year	United States	Canada	Total	% of Electricity Sales
1973	0.3	11.7	12	17.3
1975	0.9	14.9	15.8	20.4
1978	1.4	11.7	13.1	14.2
1980	8.1	9.3	17.4	16.7
1981	8.3	10.1	18.4	17.2
1982	8.5	9.4	17.9	17.3
1983	10.2	9.3	19.5	18.1
1984	11.2	11.7	22.9	18.5
1985	9.6	14.6	24.2	18.1
1986	12.6	14.3	26.9	18.7

Source: Hydro-Quebec: Annual Reports.

Table 8
Export Revenues
$ million

Year	United States	Canada	Total	% of Sales Revenue
1973	3	45	48	7.2
1975	16	76	92	10.2
1978	16	113	129	8.1
1980	164	136	300	12.4
1981	196	179	375	13.5
1982	294	181	475	14.6
1983	340	188	528	14.7
1984	388	258	646	15.8
1985	332	341	673	15.2
1986	378	271	649	13.9

Source: Hydro-Quebec: Annual Reports.

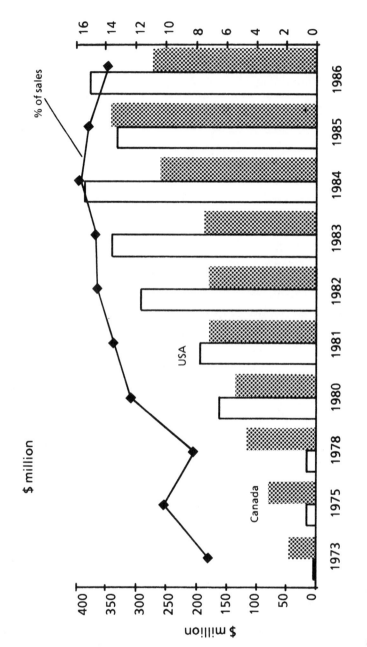

**Graph 2
Export Revenues**

% of sales

$ million

$ million

USA

Canada

1973   1975   1978   1980   1981   1982   1983   1984   1985   1986

0   50   100   150   200   250   300   350   400

0   2   4   6   8   10   12   14   16

Source: Annual Reports.

still acceptable for the time being. Through imports, the United States is reducing both its production of pollution and expensive energy. And buying Quebec's energy also means exporting the environmental uncertainties to the seller. Still, Quebec electricity is not cheap. It requires huge investments[59] that are at the total mercy of market-driven interest rates.

Americans fear another petroleum crisis. They have learned that dependence on foreign suppliers can be risky and costly and have established as a rule of thumb not to import more than 20 per cent of their consumption from foreign (and in this serious matter, friendly Canada is foreign) sources.

To this day three contracts to supply energy on a firm basis have been signed with neighbouring American states. The first, signed in February 1987 with Central Maine Power Company, involves the delivery of 400 megawatts starting in 1992, increasing to 900 megawatts by the year 2000. Concluded in November of the same year, Hydro-Quebec sold an additional (maximum) 500 megawatts to the Vermont Joint Owners and in January 1988, the New York Power Authority agreed to buy 1000 megawatts of power. Combined these agreements represent a guaranteed export of 2,400 megawatts or 70% of the official target.[60]

The market for export is still to be found. But other considerations are important. Money is to be made and the export revenues will indeed improve the profit position of Hydro-Quebec. But as always, the magic of figures should be discounted. Selling billions of dollars worth of electricity can be deceiving. For instance, a 15 billion dollar contract over a period of 29 years, represents revenues in the order of 70 million per year, or less than 1 per cent of the provincial debt. Also once the facilities are built, we know the buyer often has the stronger negotiating position. And the strategy of the potential buyer is to encourage excess capacity. This is why American predictions about the need for imports from Quebec are suspiciously high.[61] Hence, export contracts become a gamble, unless new guarantees are found. At this point, Hydro-Quebec is being very cautious, playing the market by ear, adjusting to it and to the type of agreement it is able to strike.[62]

3.3. Rethinking its relation with the environment

Until recently, Hydro-Quebec was not a major target for environmentalists. But for the last two years serious and challenging questions have been asked by various groups. Among the current issues are: the layout of the high tension line between Radisson and the Des Cantons connecting facility; the high mercury concentration in the James Bay reservoirs; the use of pesticides along transport corridors; the growing concern with the long term effects of electric fields on living organisms; and the existence of deadly PCBs in the transformers' cooling systems. The problems are not new but are being approached more aggressively and in the context of a distrust of Hydro-Quebec itself.

James Bay phase 1 required the flooding of 11 500 square kilometers for the La Grande complex and 4 350 square kilometers for the Caniapiscau reservoir. When the project was started, ecological impact was not a priority. In 1985, public health studies showed high mercury concentration among the Cree Indian population. It was found that the trees flooded were producing an acid that in reaction with the earth released mercury. The metal then enters the food chain with the result that fish and game contain more than five times the maximum allowable. As a result, Crees are strongly advised not to consume fish from Hydro's reservoirs. An ecological group presented the case in May 1986 to the World Environment and Development Commission.

Even the genius of Hydro as a builder has been shaken. Cracks were found in the Manic V dam requiring major intervention. Faulty water-gates at the Bryson and Campbell's Bay power stations were also reported. And even though the problems were solved, the confidence of many people in the safety of hydro has been shaken. On the other hand, Hydro-Quebec has been able to take the lead in the PCB issue. Faced with the need to discard some of its PCB filled transformers, the company has researched better ways to destroy PCBs. A new process has been tested, refined, and developed by a private firm. On this occasion, Hydro was an innovator.

A major public issue is the transport of large amounts of electricity. One concern is use of the right of way on agricultural lands, another issue is the health hazards of very high voltage lines and the third is the layout of Line 6. The great distances over which the electricity is transported is a great burden on our energy production system. More than 65 per cent of the energy available is produced more than 500 km away from consumers. Quebec is covered by a network of more than 10,000 km of very high voltage lines (735 kv) and about 18,000 km of 315 kv or less.

Farmers have seen power lines cross their fields for a long time. And Hydro has used its right of way without paying much attention to the inconvenience it caused. Only in 1986 did the company finally settle with the farmers' groups. Compensation will now be paid to cover losses caused by power lines, property divisions will be better respected, and towers will be installed, if possible, on low value land.

Research on the health hazards of high voltage has not been conclusive. Studies from the Soviet Union and the United States list possible causal relations that range from tiredness to leukemia.[63]

Hydro-Quebec has taken the lead, and has undertaken an important research project or the possible link between cancer and magnetic and electric fields. In itself this is certainly of great comfort. Obviously Hydro's own interest in this question is enormous and one cannot help but think that public health may be better served if an independent institution were responsible for this research.

The most important public opposition to Hydro-Quebec has been on the sixth power line between Radisson and Des Cantons, using the planned Grondines-Lotbinière route. This line is needed to enable Hydro to supply New England utilities. The project was proceeding smoothly, that is without public interference, until public hearings were held on the issue, under the authority of the *Bureau d'audiences publiques sur l'environnement* (BAPE) in 1986. On this occasion, the opposition organized itself.

Under the clever, and bilingual, name of "Contestension", citizens of Lotbinière and Grondines protested the chosen route. They objected to the line because it will alter the view, and request that it be diverted either to the neighbouring counties of Champlain and Bécancourt or be modified as a submarine line that will rest on the St. Lawrence bed. The report published in 1987, argued that Hydro did not consult the population previously and that it manipulated the government by providing no alternatives. Hydro ignored the environmental protection law by not doing feasibility studies. The BAPE recommended that the line use a submarine passage to respect the "exceptional natural beauty of the region".[64]

The BAPE position could be discussed at length. One of the proposed "Contestension" solutions consists of moving the line towards the densely populated Trois-Rivières area. A narrow regional interest group was hence able to mobilize for the purpose of sending to neighbors undesirable towers and power lines. Obviously, Hydro was caught off guard and was defeated because it had not fully respected consultation mechanisms.

But there is more to learn from this issue. Hydro-Quebec, it seems, will not have the freedom it once enjoyed. Its high credibility and citizen trust are things of the past. Environmental issues will multiply and Hydro-Quebec must take the lead and use its own resources to find solutions. Projects will require more extensive consultation, introducing delays and additional costs to already expensive undertakings.

3.4. Surviving in a tight financial environment

As already mentioned, the spectacular growth of Hydro-Quebec occurred during a period of rapid growth in the demand for electricity. This environment shaped the enterprise. In order to supply an ever

increasing demand, projects requiring large investments were
initiated. Credit was easily available and not too expensive.
Borrowers were favored by the inflation rate that lowered real
interest rates.

From 1975 to 1986, Hydro's long-term total debt more than
quadrupled from $4.9 billion to $20.3 billion. It is expected to increase
at the rate of $2 billion per year in the next two years.[65] New projects
are relatively more expensive and will require important additional
borrowing. This does not mean that Hydro-Quebec has been badly
managed or that its financial situation will necessarily deteriorate.
Hydro-Quebec is a good risk for an investor, because it has shown its
willingness to cooperate and follow a strict financial policy, which has
been mostly immune from outright political pressures. But Hydro-
Quebec is certainly more exposed than it has ever been and its
financial liberty has been seriously reduced.

This analysis can be argued as follows: the mean interest rate
over the debt has increased during the first years of 1980, reaching
15.1 per cent in 1981. Although it has declined somewhat (the one to
five year rate was 11.57 per cent in 1986), the interest is growing
faster than the debt. In 1986, $2.4 billion had to be paid in interest
alone. Hydro is therefore more exposed than ever to changes in the
interest rate.[66]

Given the importance of its needs, and because it sought to
spread the risk, Hydro issued bonds on different markets. Today 40
per cent of the total debt is in Canadian dollars, the rest in American
dollars (46 percent of the total) and European and Japanese
currencies. To the interest rate uncertainty, one must add the foreign
currency market fluctuations that directly affect the financial
strength of such a enterprise. In 1986, $43 million had to be paid in
interest to compensate for the relative loss of value of the Canadian
dollar.[67] Also, $22 million was lost on capital reimbursement for the
same reason.

Hydro-Quebec has lost the exclusive control, it once had, over its
economic performance. In this "golden age", the rate of return over the
total investment was not a major concern. It could remain low as long
as it was positive. The population and the government were satisfied
with the added comfort and the progress associated with the
availability of electricity. The debt was easily covered by the
increased revenues flowing from growing demand. But now it is a
different matter. The rate of return is now 4.4 percent, which is less
than half the interest rate on the debt. There are only two solutions
for such a situation. One is to increase revenues, which, in the
absence of a growth in demand, requires increased tariffs. The other
is to roll the debt, that is, borrow more to cover the interest due.

This is analogous to the "catch 22" situation facing all third world countries. To convince financial institutions that it is a reasonable risk, Hydro must dramatically increase its profits or accept higher interest rates which will require even more borrowing. Then it is financially less expensive for the community to accept higher electricity tariffs, which will, at this stage, slow-down any expansion in demand. How do we get out of this costly maze?

What does it mean concretely for Hydro-Quebec to be more exposed to changes in different markets? A one per cent increase in demand for regular energy means $45 million more in revenues. An increase of one per cent in tariffs represents an added $27 million in benefits. But when the price of a barrel of petroleum goes down by a dollar it means a loss of $22 million. The potential losses caused by changes on the financial market are more important. A one percent rise in interest rates means additional payments of $21 million, which is slightly less than the equivalent tariff increase. Finally, a one cent diminution of the Canadian dollar in relation to the American currency translates into a loss of $10 million.

If the current ideological drive towards privatization leaves the enterprise unaffected, it is certain that in order to maintain and preserve its financial strength Hydro-Quebec will adopt a policy that, more than ever, will follow very closely the "law of the market".

Conclusion: Hydro-Quebec in the new wilderness

Hydro-Quebec is filled with nostalgia. With age, the economic giant of the Quebec economy has lost its stamina. In the future, Hydro-Quebec should satisfy itself as just another public utility, trying to avoid premature bureaucratic sclerosis.

Exporting electricity is the major issue facing the enterprise. Hydro-Quebec is being observed with great attention by the other Canadian utilities. The contract with the Churchill Falls (Labrador) Corporation has just left the courts bound for the political arena. For more than ten years, the government of Newfoundland has tried to change the contract by which it has to sell its energy at a ridiculously low price. Politics made a remarked intrusion when Prime Minister Peckford publicly raised the issue at the First Ministers meeting held in late November 1987 when he asked for direct federal intervention to find a negotiated settlement.

The federal government is also keeping a close watch because the National Energy Board must approve all contracts for export and for the construction of international lines. The law says that the energy must be offered on a priority basis to the Canadian provinces and only if there is no local demand can the energy be exported. Also, the export price cannot be lower than the internal tariffs. Accordingly, the NEB did not approve Hydro-Quebec's contract with Central Maine Power until it satisfied the energy demand of neighbouring provinces. An agreement was eventually reached but the board's decision is a serious reminder that Quebec's energy trade policy is controlled by a powerful federal leash.

This guarantee was not considered enough by Ontario authorities. Ontario Premier David Peterson also used the Prime Ministers' conference to remind his colleagues that energy surpluses should be shared nationally before being exported and that foreign markets should be approached in a coordinated fashion. It is certain that Quebec will have to consider seriously the claims made by the other provinces and adjust its policy towards the American markets accordingly.

On the demand side, alternative energy sources are plentiful for the American northeast and a determined conservation policy makes great sense both economically and ecologically. Thermal power, using coal or gas, is certainly feasible as well as all the "alternative" sources (sun, wastes, mini-hydros, wind, etc.). In fact the only socially unacceptable alternative is nuclear power. Even there, several attempts to close the single nuclear power plant in Maine have failed. The third referendum on the issue, held in 1987, favored maintenance of the facility. Hydro-Quebec's marketing strategy will have to consider these alternatives. Very clearly, this is a market over which governments' (of both buyer and seller) hand is rather heavy. This means that considerations over price will be combined with measures of economic growth and preoccupation over national security and sovereignty, with the result that outcomes are unpredictable.

Hydro-Quebec must watch its financial situation. The firm paid no dividends in 1985 or 1986, and does not plan to do so for the next two years. Investment is at its lowest level in more than ten years[68], but debt keeps increasing. Little else can be done than hope for lower interest rates and a moderate increase in the value of the Canadian dollar. All analysts agree that demand will maintain a moderate upward trend and it is difficult to allow tariffs to increase more than inflation.

The issue of government control has never been squarely faced. Because electricity was abundant and relatively cheap, energy issues were never given a high priority and demands on the firm were kept low. The major challenge once faced by Hydro-Quebec was internal. It had, over the past ten years, changed its fundamental culture and orientation to give more space to economic efficiency. Reshuffling within the organization has been intense and open scars are still visible. Hydro-Quebec is very much like a patient that has been prescribed total rest; time is the cure.

What does this mean for government? Because the Liberal government of Premier Bourassa seems committed to mega-hydro-electric development, it will be difficult to avoid the issue. Political discourse is already filled with megawatts in a pathetic exercise of schizophrenia. The enterprise will be hard pressed to pay more than lip service to the official exuberant discourse. Tensions will arise when political voluntarism will confront the organizational resistance of its untamed creature.

Notes

1. Canada, Economic Council, *State Entrepreneurship*, (Ottawa: Minister of Supply and Services, Canada 1986), p. 15.

2. This was the basis of our argument in the article recently published in *Recherches Sociographiques*, where we look at the realizations and potential for industrial and technological development associated with the procurement policy of the state enterprises.

3. The Electric Commission known as the Lapointe Commission was mandated to look into the possibility and the effects of nationalization of the companies and the *municipalization* of the urban networks, the possibility of reducing electrical rates (considered prohibitive) as well as rural electrification.

4. Clarence Hogue, André Bolduc and Daniel Larouche, *Québec: un siècle d'électricité*, (Montreal: Libre Expression, 1979), pp. 102-5.

5. Jorge Niosi, *La bourgeoisie canandienne*, (Montreal: Boréal Express, 1980), p. 134.

6. *Ibid.*, p. 132.

7. René Lévesque, *Attendez que je me rappelle...*, (Montreal: Québec-Amérique, 1986), pp. 231-238. Also Pierre Godin, *Daniel Johnson: la passion du pouvoir*, (Montreal: Éditions de l'Homme, 1980), pp. 304-314.

8. Hogue, Bolduc and Larcouche, pp.229-36.

9. This reason was also envoked by Premier Bennett for the nationalization of B.C. Hydro. See Aidan R. Vining, "Provincial Hydro Utilities", in *Public Corporations and Public Policy in*

Canada, ed. by Allan Tupper and G.B. Doern (Montreal: Institute for Research on Public Policy, 1981), note 53, p. 185.

10.   Raoul Barbe, *"Les entreprises publiques"*, Working Paper, Régie des services publics du Québec, December 1979, pp. 189-204.

11.   Manic V was the largest single dam facility in the world. Its reservoir holds larger water reserves than the whole of all the other reservoirs in Hydro Quebec's system (2,100 km² and 23 billion m³ of water). Manic II was also the largest grooved joint heavy dam in the world while Manic III's impervious wall (which prevents water penetration into the alluvial soil) is a double concrete partition more than 130 metres deep: the deepest of its type in existence. In 1965, 735 kv high tension transmission lines, perfected by Hydro-Quebec engineers (a world first), were installed linking Manic II to Montreal. In fact Hydro-Quebec became a research leader in high tension transmission. Its laboratory, *Institut de Recherche en Électricité du Québec* (IREQ), founded in 1967, specializes in long distance high tension transmission problems.

12.   Jean-Thomas Bernard, G.E. Bridges and Anthony Scott, "An Evaluation of Potential Canadian Hydro-Electric Rents", Department of Economics, University of British Columbia, 1982. Richard C. Zucker et Glenn P. Jenkins, *L'or liquide; production hydro-électrique et rente économique,* Economic Council of Canada (Ottawa: Minister of Supply and Services, 1984).

The rent value is the difference between the cost of exploitation of hydro-electric resources and the cost of different production systems (i.e. thermal) which could substitute hydro-electric energy at a lower price. An alternative nethod, which responds more to our preoccupations and would permit us to estimate the rent value of the self-producers, is to establish the difference between the rates charged to Hydro-Quebec's large industrial consumers and the average electrical generation cost for the self-producers. Unfortunately, the latter statistic is unavailable. The rent value therefore would have been defined as the cost reduction by self-production in relation to the public network current tariff.

13.   Canada, Statistics Canada, *Electrical Energy Statistics*, volume 11, Annual Statistics, 1979, cat. 57-202, table 2.

14.   Hydro-Québec, *Statistiques, abonnements, ventes et revenus, année* 1982, Montreal, March 1983; Canada, Statistics Canada,

Electrical Energy Statistics, volume 11, Annual Statistics, 1979, cat 57-202.

15. Over and above the installed power capacity of its own plants Hydro-Quebec has access to the major part of production at Churchill Falls (5,225 megawatts).

16. Hydro-Quebec; *Statistiques, Abonnements, Ventes et revenus, année 1985*, Montreal, June 1986, p. 40.

17. Hydro-Quebec, *Plan de développement Hydro-Québec 1987-1989*, Montreal, 1987, p. 25.

18. Quebec, National Assembly, Commission parlementaire des Richesses naturelles, Terres et Forêts, 3 July 1974, no. 118, pp. B-4561-64.

19. Annual peak indicates the number of kilowatts required over a short period of time when consumer needs reach their annual peak.

20. Quebec, ministère de l'Énergie, *L'énergie au Québec; livre blanc sur la politique énergétique québécoise*, (Quebec: Éditeur officiel, 1977).

21. Quebec, ministère de l'Énergie, *La politique québécoise de l'energie, Assurer l'avenir*, (Quebec: Éditeur officiel, 1978).

22. Quebec, ministère d'État au Développement économique, *Bâtir le Québec; énoncé de politique économique*, (Quebec, Éditeur officiel, 1979).

23. Yair Aharoni, "Managerial Discretion", in *State-Owned Enterprises in the Western Economies*, ed. by R. Vernon and Y. Aharoni, (London: Croom Hlem 1981); also Herbert Simon, "Rational Decision-making in Business Organizations" *American Economic Review*, 64, (December 1974) pp. 493-513.

24. Ph. Faucher and J. Bergeron, *Hydro-Québec: la société de l'heure de pointe*, (Montreal: Les Presses de l'Université de Montréal, 1986), pp. 169-73.

25. Hydro-Québec, *Statistiques: Abonnements, ventes et revenus, année 1985*, June, 1986, Part 2, p. 8.

26. Bill 16 altered this mandate (see above); it did away with overall rate restrictions, but stated other financial obligations to be met.

27. These ratios determined in Bill 16 (Article 15.2), passed in 1981, are used to establish share prices for the company on the financial market. Market prices influence lending rates and conditions, thus, they indicate Hydro-Quebec's financial situation.

28. This argument has been brought up several times by Hydro-Quebec Parliamentary Commissions. See for example: Quebec, National Assembly, Commission parlementaire des Richesses naturelles, Terres et Forêts, 3e session, 29e législature, 11 May, 1972, no. 25, pp. B-1443-4.

29. Quebec, National Assembly, Commission parlementaire de l'énergie, 3e session, 31e législature, 28 septembre 1978, no. 164, p. B-6781; also, Quebec, National Assembly, Commission parlementaire des Richesses naturelles, 20 May 1969, pp. 2109-10.

30. Hydro-Québec, Statistiques sur l'industrie manufacturière du Québec, ratios par établissement et en dollars de valeur ajoutée pour 1979, Service des Études commerciales, novembre 1982. These sectors of acitivity make up the largest portion of regular electricity sales to industrial customers. Pulp and paper plants are the single largest customer (30%), while smelting and refining accounted for more than 17% of sales in 1986 according to Hydro-Quebec, *Plan de développement d'Hydro-Québec* 1987-1989, p. 18.

31. Hydro-Québec, *Annual Report*, 1986.

32. Hydro-Québec, *Plan de développement d'Hydro-Québec*, 1987-1989, p. 34.

33. Hydro-Québec, *Règlement 290 établissant les tarifs d'électricité et les conditions de leur application*, October 1981.

34. Quebec, National Assembly, Commission parlementaire des Richesses naturelles, Terres et Forêts, 3e session, 30e législature, 4 juillet 1975, pp. B-5433-37.

35. Hydro-Québec, *Dossier argumentaire: revenu requis par catégorie tarifaire, prévision 1983*, Commission parlementaire, règlement tarifaire no. 321, année 1983, October 1982, p. 2.

36. *Le Devoir*, 11 June 1985, p. 11.

37. This guarantee does not apply to a sum of $257 million (in 1985 dollars). Hydro-Québec: *Annual Report 1986*, Montreal, p. 64.

38. Kidder, Peabody and Co., Hydro-Québec, *Company Analysis*, November, 1983

39. Purchases are divided in goods, services and construction contracts. In the last years, the total value of procurement has been $1,025 million in 1984, $1,326 million in 1985 and $1,350 million in 1986. Hydro-Quebec, *Rapport annuel 1986: acquistion de biens, services et traveaux*, Service, Pratiques commerciales, Transport et gestion du matériel, Montreal, 1986.

40. By "preferrential procurement policy" we mean the practice by which the procuring organization accords, through a contract adjudication process, preference to certain suppliers by virtue of such criteria as the principal production site, the nationality of the enterprise's capital, the proposed technology, the number of employees, etc., which in a sense qualifies the amount of the tender. See Robert Dalpé, *Politique d'achat et développement technologique*, (Quebec: document interne no. 6, Conseil de la science et de la technologie, 1987).

41. Article 14 of the Order in Council of June 11th, 1962 defines the procurement policy as:

    The Commission (hydro-élelctrique du Québec) may accord preference to a company of which the principal place of business is located in Quebec even if its tender is not the lowest.

    Regulation relative to supply tenders and contract adjudication, (A.C. 963, June 11, 1962) article 14 in Règlements d'application des lois du Québec, vol. 2, chap. VII, August 1972, p. 2-663.

42. Hydro-Québec, direction Recherche Économique; "Les retombées économiques québécoises du complexe la Grande Phase 1", *Information Cadres*, 14, 11, (November 1981), pp. 29-38.

43. Roy Rothwell and Walter Zegveld, *Reindustrialization and Technology* (Harlow: Longman Group Limited, 1985).

44. Firms such as Canadian General Electric, Federal Pioneer, Cegelec, BG Checo International, Westinghouse, ASEA, Siemens, Crouse-Hinds, Brown-Boveri Howden and Klochner-Moeller were given such mandates. But because these production agreements concern essentially products that are of

specific interest for Hydro-Quebec or Ontario Hydro, they haven't been followed by a significant rise of the country's export of electrical equipment. Dalpé, *Politique d'achat et développement technologique*, p. 104.

45. Interview, Hydro-Québec, Service des approvisionnements, May 16, 1986.

46. "The single most important factor affecting the ability of public procurement to influence technological change was the stage of maturity of the product and the industry. It is when the industry and product are in the early stages of their cycle of development that procurement incentives have their greatest potential impact on technological change." Roy Rothwell and Walter Zegveld, *Reindustrialization and Technology* (Harlow: Longman Group Limited, 1985), p. 123.

47. The six enterprises are ASEA, Cegelec, CGE, Sangamo, Balckburn and Joslyn. See Hydro-Québec, *Évaluation des ententes particulières d'approvisionement*, vice-président finances et administration, June 1987.

48. Data on IREQ's performance are drawn from documents specially requested by the authors.

49. Jorge Niosi, Jean Dumais, Christime Médaille, "La montée des sociétés canadiennes d'ingénierie (1945-1985)", *Interface*, 11, 1 (January-February 1988), pp. 12-17.

50. This information is mentioned in the study by Major and Martin Inc., *Les activités des sociétés québécoises de génie-conseil et leurs effets d'entraînement*, Québec, OPDQ, AICQ, 1981.

51. Under intense speculation of conflicts with the Minister of Energy, Guy Coulombe has asked the government not to renew his mandate as CEO of Hydro-Quebec.

52. Privatizing Hydro-Quebec has, to our knowledge, never been mentioned seriously; it is nevertheless absolutely coherent with the argument used by the Bourassa government to explain its (moderate) privatization drive. See Comité sur la privatisation des sociétés d'État, *De la révolution tranquille. . . à l'an deux mille*, Report presented to Mr. Pierre Fortier, ministre délégué à la Privatisation, Quebec, June 1986.

53. Roland Parenteau, *Hydro-Québec, les relations entre l'État entre son entreprises*, (Economic Council of Canada, Ottawa: Minister

of Supply and Services 1986), p. 130, (our translation). Despite its obviousness, we could not come up with a more refined argument, if not the equally banal reference to the symbol (that verges on a myth) that Hydro still represents for the ruling generation.

54. This is still what the current (fall of 1987) TV advertising is presenting as the central message.

55. Hydro-Québec, *Plan de développement d'Hydro-Québec*, 1987-1989, p. 32.

56. Institut de recherche d'Hydro-Québec, *Rapport d'activité 1986*, Montreal, 1987. See also *Plan de développement 1987-1989*, p. 69. In this last document the new orientation is very openly stated: "Increase research for new technologies; continue development and demonstration of new productive processes using electrical energy; push for an increase in commercialization of the technical knowledge, the laboratories and testing facilities; better appreciate the commercial technological potential of research and technical projects. In the fields related or connected to energy, participate in industrial activities taking advantage of the technical know-how developed by the firm." We don't think it can be stated more clearly.

57. Hydro-Quebec, *Annual Report, 1986*, Montreal, p. 80.

58. Hydro-Québec, *Plan de développement, 1986-1988*, Montreal, 1986, p. 49.

59. Bourassa mentions an estimate of a staggering 25 billion dollars of 1984, Robert Bourassa, *L'Énergie du Nord*, (Montreal: Québec–Amérique, 1986).

60. Hydro-Québec, *Plan de développement 1988-1990*, Montreal 1988, p. 57.

61. The whole strategy in the commodity sector has been clearly presented by J. D'Cruz and J. Fleck. Because of the relevance of their analysis, we believe a lengthy quote is useful:

> "It is not difficult to find customers abroad who will support these projects by guaranteeing long-term contracts, technical expertise and modest financial assistance. As a momentum builds, it becomes easy to accept overly optimistic projections of demand. The inherently cyclical nature of markets for these

commodities compounds the problem of assessing demand because it is easy to mistake a cyclical upturn for long-term secular growth. Those who argue otherwise are thought to be too pessimistic and their words of caution are swept away. Operators of existing capacity are accused of self-interest when they issue warnings about the dangers of overcapacity.

Adroit customers can create a false sense of urgency, a "time-window," providing an opportunity that will be lost forever if major commitments to the project are not forthcoming. Such tactics are often successful, even though the project may take several years to complete. When it is finished and the promised increase in demand does not materialize, the industry finds itself saddled with expensive new capacity, heavily subsidized financing, and an array of expectations for new jobs, economic growth and prosperity in an economically depressed region." Joseph R. D'Cruz and James D. Fleck, *Canada Can Compete! Strategic Management of the Canadian Industrial Portfolio* (Montreal: The Institute for Research on Public Policy, 1986), p. 101.

62. Very serious concerns have emerged publicly concerning the price obtained by Hydro-Quebec for its electricity in its deals with the American power utilities. The price formula used results in transferring a larger share of the economic rent to the buyer than was initially intended. Also the contracts signed will result in the anticipation of the costly Nottaway-Broadback-Rupert project, eventually forcing Hydro-Quebec to export its electricity at a loss for some years.

63. G. Drouin, "Tension sous les lignes", *Québec Science*, July-August 1987.

64. Quebec, Bureau d'audiences publiques sur l'environnement, *Rapport d'enquête et d'audience publique: Projet de ligne à courant continu à +/- 450kv, Radisson-Nicolet-Des Cantons*, Quebec, 1987.

65. In 1986, the debt amounted to $7,800 per customer, Hydro-Quebec, *Plan de développement d'Hydro-Québec*, 1987-1989, p. 85.

66. Although expected increases in export revenues will help pay for the interest to be paid in American dollars.

67. Inversely, as the value of the Canadian dollar increases relative to the American currency, the profit rate of the export contracts when estimated against the production costs of electricity, diminishes. To supplement the low growth of the internal market by exports amounts to playing financial roulette and should therefore be restricted to a small amount of total output.

68. For 1987, Hydro-Quebec announced $1,786 million in investment; *Annual Report, 1986*, p. 68.

Chapter VIII

Teleglobe Canada

Richard Schultz

In February 1987, the federal Government announced, after a tumultuous and tortured two year process, that it had finally sold Teleglobe Canada, the federal Crown corporation engaged in international telecommunications.[1] The privatization of Teleglobe was significant for several reasons, not the least important was that it was the largest sale to date by a Canadian government. More importantly, Teleglobe was widely regarded as the most attractive Crown corporation to be put on the block: efficiently managed, highly productive and most exceptionally a consistent profit-maker. Teleglobe's sale, for our purposes, was also significant because of the nature of the privatization process. In this process private actors played an insignificant role compared to the public sector participants. Finally, the sale of Teleglobe is interesting because the successful bidder, Memotec Data, not only was one-sixth the size of Teleglobe but beat out several of Canada's corporate giants in the bidding process.

This chapter analyses the history of Teleglobe as a public enterprise and its privatization. The first section reviews the nature of Teleglobe as a public enterprise, its creation, its mandate and its relations over time with the Canadian state and the other primary components of the telecommunications sector. The second section examines the privatization process.

Two central arguments are advanced. First, for advocates of public enterprise, Teleglobe's development provides little support because throughout its history it has been without a demonstrable public purpose. Furthermore, as a public corporation for almost four decades, it operated with the maximum degree of managerial autonomy and minimal public scrutiny conceivable. Consequently, its continued status as a public enterprise, despite the tears of some when it was privatized, was difficult to justify. On the other hand, advocates of privatization, except those driven by the mindless fixation that the mere transfer of a business from the public to the private sector is an inherent gain, should be concerned both by the process and the terms of Teleglobe's sale. The process was very narrowly focussed, largely unguided by major principles and dominated by a closed, intra-governmental debate. In selling Teleglobe public officials displayed as much autonomy from social forces as Teleglobe's managers had enjoyed from public authorities. The terms of sale, furthermore, did not produce a reduction in the state or alternatively an enhancement of the market. To the contrary, by subjecting a private Teleglobe to public regulation and by entrenching Teleglobe's status as a monopoly provider of telecommunications services, if only for five years, the result of privatization, as Charles Dalfen has noted, was "an extension of monopoly and an increase in regulation."[2]

The first two sections of this chapter seek to establish the validity of these arguments while in the concluding section we attempt to explain why Teleglobe was created and allowed to operate without any public purpose and why its privatization took the form it did. Finally we address the larger issues and implications raised by the privatization of Teleglobe.

From Outsider to Cash Cow

Teleglobe Canada was created in 1949 as the Canadian Overseas Telecommunications Corporation (COTC).[3] The decision to create an international telecommunications Crown corporation while not reflecting the absence of mind said to have accompanied the creation of other public enterprises was hardly either an ideological act or the rational application of the calculus of instrument choice. Quite simply, the decision was the consequence of the Government of Canada's decision to implement the Commonwealth Telegraph Agreement of 1948 to which Canada was a signatory. This agreement required public ownership of enterprises providing overseas telecommunications services and Canada gave effect to the agreement by creating the COTC which was empowered to acquire the relevant assets of Cable and Wireless and Canadian Marconi. It should be noted that the ease with which Canada created another public enterprise reflected the Canadian cultural predisposition to accept public ownership and the extended use of such ownership in World War II and its immediate aftermath.[4]

Although the federal Liberal government of Louis St. Laurent justified its action on the grounds of "strategic purposes" and its treaty obligations, no attempt was made to specify either the nature of these purposes or the "public needs" which were invoked to defend public ownership.[5] Nor was the enabling legislation any more specific about the public policy mission of the new Crown corporation. Its statute listed five "purposes":

(a)   to establish, maintain and operate in Canada and elsewhere external telecommunications services for the conduct of public telecommunications;

(b)   to carry on the business of public communications by cable, radiotelegraph, radiotelephone or any other means of telecommunications between Canada and any other place;

(c)   to make use of all developments in cable and radio transmission or reception for external telecommunication purposes as related to public communication services;

(d)   to conduct investigations and research with the object of improving the efficiency of telecommunications services generally; and

(e)   to coordinate Canada's external telecommunications services with the telecommunications services of other nations.[6]

Three aspects of Teleglobe's creation merit comment, two that pertain to its relations with the government while the third involves its place within the telecommunications industrial structure. First, notwithstanding the absence of explicit policy objectives in its statute, the government gave itself the power to issue directives to the corporation.[7] Second, in addition to the directive power and the routine controls that the government possessed over Crown corporations such as audits and appointing directors, provision was made for control through an independent regulatory agency, the Board of Transport Commissioners, which then regulated the private telephone companies under federal jurisdiction.[8]

Despite this provision Teleglobe was never regulated because the laws which Parliament assumed to be operative – An Act respecting the Telegraph Act and An Act to Control the Rates and Facilities of Ocean Cable Companies and to Amend the Railway Act with Respect to Telegraphs and Telephones and the Jurisdiction of the Board of Railway Commissioners – were invalid. As Brownlee Thomas discovered, these two acts which would have made the activities of Teleglobe subject to regulation never came into effect because the British legislation needed to trigger them was never passed.[9]

Given the clear intent of Parliament it is particularly remarkable that no one seemed to notice that Teleglobe was not being regulated or, if they did, cared enough to want to change the situation. In the ten year period after Teleglobe was created, there was not a single question in the House of Commons about its non regulated status. In fact Teleglobe's anomalous regulatory situation only became an issue during the early stages of the privatization process when the corporation informed the Department of Communications, which thought otherwise, that the relevant statutes "did not have any operative effect."[10]

A final curious aspect of Teleglobe's creation, particularly in light of subsequent developments, was that its enabling statute did not establish Teleglobe as a monopoly provider of telecommunications services. The Act allowed the corporation to provide "external telecommunication services" but did not stipulate that it was to be the sole provider of such services. In fact, in the parliamentary debates creating Teleglobe the government insisted that the corporation was not being given a monopoly and pointed out that there remained another company that would continue to operate in this sector.[11] Within a few years, however, this company was no longer active and Teleglobe assumed a *de facto* monopoly in the Canadian overseas telecommunications market.

It is also important to note Teleglobe's place in the structure of the Canadian international market because of its implications for Teleglobe's non-regulated status and to issues that would arise when privatization was planned. The 1949 Act not only did not give Teleglobe any monopoly privileges, it did not envision such privileges for other international service providers. The Act defined "external telecommunication services" to mean "telecommunication services between Canada and any place outside Canada."[12] In other words the external service market included both overseas and Canadian-American services and Teleglobe was authorised to enter both market segments.

Teleglobe's act notwithstanding, the "external" world for Canadian telecommunications companies was indeed divided up after 1949 and *de facto* monopolies created: one for the North American market and another for the "overseas" market. The former had been created largely as a result of the integration of the Canadian and American, primarily AT&T, networks. The eight largest Canadian telephone companies had joined together in 1931 to create the TransCanada Telephone System and subsequently came to regard the North American market as their exclusive territory.[13] To the extent that the new public enterprise was prepared to accept such a claim, especially in the first five years of its operations when its business was almost exclusively telegraph-based, the domestic carriers were prepared to assign the "overseas" market exclusively to Teleglobe. It is worth noting, however, that the market shares were hardly equal. The Canadian-American traffic has traditionally represented approximately 85 per cent of the international telecommunications market while the overseas segment accounted for the balance. Teleglobe's acceptance of what was considered to be a "gentleman's agreement" to permit this form of market sharing is another example of the dominant role that the telecommunications companies have played in the development of public policies in this sector for most of the past century.[14]

Once Teleglobe's monopoly status in the overseas market had been conferred, it was free to assume the traditional "quiet life" of a monopolist. Aside from the fact that it had the best of all possible worlds as a monopolist – it was unregulated – life was particularly quiet with respect to its relationships with the Government and Parliament. Its performance was an important contributing factor. Despite its restricted market share of revenue sources, Teleglobe in its first five years was a consistent, if somewhat stolid, profit-maker. Its profit picture changed dramatically in 1956 with the laying of the first underseas coaxial cable which permitted the introduction of overseas telephone service. This produced a very significant shift in both the source and extent of Teleglobe's revenues. Figure I clearly illustrates both these developments.

Teleglobe's ability to make a regular, indeed increasingly substantial profit, was crucial because it meant that funds necessary for expansion or maintenance were internally generated thus relieving the officers of Teleglobe from making demands on the public treasury. The self-financing role of Teleglobe explains, more than any other factor, the exceptionally autonomous nature of the corporation's relationship with political authorities. Unlike some public enterprises which, it is claimed, actively seek autonomy, Teleglobe managers were able to assume such autonomy.[15] It also helped, of course, that Teleglobe reported to the government through the Minister of Transport as there was no Department of Communications for the first two decades of Teleglobe's existence. Within the priorities of the designated department, Teleglobe was largely irrelevant.

One minor measure of Teleglobe's distance from the government was the fact that the directive power was never used to shape the corporation's activities. Nor has Parliament shown any substantial or sustained interest in the corporation's affairs. A review of Parliamentary debates and committee proceedings since 1949 shows only sporadic and incidental interest in Teleglobe. From 1949 to 1984, there was less than one question a year raised in the House of Commons about Teleglobe; not one of these questions could be described, even generously, as raising a policy issue.

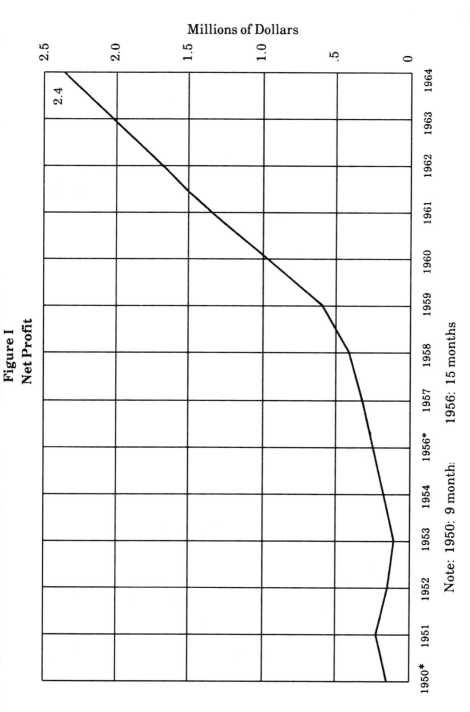

Figure I
Net Profit

Millions of Dollars

Note: 1950: 9 month;   1956: 15 months

Source: COTC Annual Report, 1964

Teleglobe's quiet life began to disappear in the late 1960s. Reference has already been made to the substantial shift that began in the late 1950s in its revenue sources from telegraph to telephone service. This shift has continued to the present such that telephone service now provides approximately 90 per cent of the revenues and telegraph less than 1 per cent, the remainder coming from telex services. As important as the shift in revenue sources were technological changes particularly the introduction of satellites for telecommunications purposes.[16] Teleglobe was an active participant and indeed played a leading role in the growth of Intelsat, the International Telecommunications Satellite Organization.

The deployment of new technology, combined with the changing nature of Canadian society as a result of immigration and relative affluence in the 1970s, resulted in a radical transformation in Teleglobe's performance. Gone were the days of stolid profit-making; Teleglobe became a veritable cash cow. One reason for this was the phenomenal growth in traffic volumes, particularly in telephone traffic. Figure II shows not only the relative shift in revenue sources but that telephone traffic grew almost geometrically since the early 1970s. The consequences of this volume growth can be appreciated by an examination of Tables I and II. Table I shows that Teleglobe's total assets from 1975 to 1985 increased by 307 per cent while its employees for the same period increased only 11 per cent. Even more spectacular, and certainly justifying the "cash cow" designation, are the figures on retained earnings. Table II shows that for the same period, Teleglobe saw its retained earnings grow by 400 per cent. Finally, for the decade 1976-1985, Teleglobe reported an average return on equity of approximately 17 per cent. At first glance, while undoubtedly impressive, this does not seem exceptional. The federally-regulated carriers, for example, were permitted to earn a rate of return on equity in 1985 of between 14 and 15 per cent. When one looks behind Teleglobe's figures, however, the true enormity of its profit-making becomes apparent. If Teleglobe had a debt-equity ratio comparable to its federally-regulated counterparts, according to industry sources, its true rate of return would have been approximately 35 per cent. Although all the carriers were making reasonable profits, for more than the past decade only Teleglobe was truly earning monopoly profits.

Despite the need to adapt technologically and to the changing marketplace, Teleglobe's relationships with the state did not change substantially in the 1970s. This is not to suggest that there were no changes. The creation of a Department of Communications in 1968 with an explicit focus on communications issues and a mandate that partially overlapped that of Teleglobe's caused some change, but

Figure II

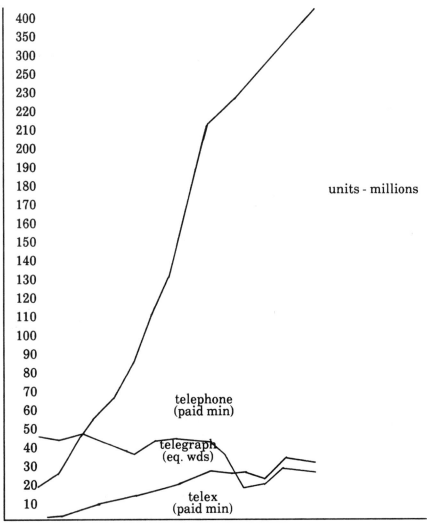

Traffic volumes, 1972-1982

Source: Teleglobe Annual Reports,

Table I
Retained Earnings (thousands of dollars)

	1976	1978	1980	1982	1984	1986
Net income	11,986	14,484	35,888	47,073	41,176	62,950
Balance, begin-ning of year	76,907	103,770	138,118	199,626	284,487	307,353
Am't remit-ted to Gov't. of Canada	-	-	3,800	7,400	-	80,000
Balance, end of year (retained earnings)	88,893	118,254	170,206	239,299	325,663	290,303
Revenues	67,879	72,844	110,370	170,162	201,613	273,790

Source: Annual Reports of Teleglobe.

Table II
Assets/Employees (thousands of dollars)

	1976	1978	1980	1982	1984	1986
Total Assets	117,719	220,081	299,592	399,424	519,959	502,423
Employees	1,037	1,218	1,347	1,391	1,356	1,110

Source: Annual Reports of Teleglobe.

surprisingly very little.[17]   The new department led to neither a radically revised role for Teleglobe nor to any significant restrictions on its autonomy.

Not surprisingly, the influence of the Department was felt in the years immediately after it was established. In one early instance the minister, Eric Kierans, in an effort to ensure that the Government's creation and partially-owned domestic satellite carrier, Telesat Canada, was economically viable, pressured Teleglobe to take capacity from Telesat to link its international gateways to its domestic terminals. Terrestrial links would have been much cheaper, and in fact were restored when the original contract expired, but Teleglobe acceded to the request. The second major instance came when the Department intervened to encourage the president of Teleglobe to take early retirement. From 1950 to 1970 Teleglobe's personnel and purchasing policies were very traditional with a preference for British staff and suppliers. The new Minister and his senior staff believed that Teleglobe should be both more explicitly Canadian and especially bilingual.[18] It is worth noting that neither of these ministerial interventions was by way of a directive.

The greatest potential change was proposed in 1977 when the Government introduced a national Telecommunications Act in Parliament.[19] Among other things, this legislation proposed to subject Teleglobe to regulation by the CRTC which had acquired jurisdiction for telecommunications regulation in 1976. This legislation caused the one occasion when it could be said that Teleglobe management actively sought to protect its autonomy. In a brief to the minister, Teleglobe executives contended that CRTC regulation was inappropriate and could have deleterious consequences on the corporation because of Teleglobe's unique international environment.[20] Teleglobe management insisted that the firm was already subject to effective public controls and to add an additional one would merely impose a further burden. The spectre of regulation disappeared, however, when the legislation failed to advance beyond first reading on three different occasions. After the failure to get the legislation passed, Teleglobe ceased to be an object of attention for either the minister or departmental officials.

Although Teleglobe ceased to be an object of departmental attentions, others in Ottawa were becoming appreciative of the corporations's financial performance. The Treasury Board, in particular, began to argue that it was inappropriate for Teleglobe to earn substantial profits and to have almost exclusive control over their use. As a result of Treasury Board pressures, Teleglobe paid a dividend of $3.8 million in 1980 and, as Table I indicates, subsequently was required, with only one exception, to pay an annual dividend until it was privatized. The one exception came in 1984 when CDIC, to whom Teleglobe reported, opted against a dividend because it would have entailed a transfer to the Consolidated Revenue Fund of the Government of Canada at the expense of CDIC.

Privatizing Teleglobe: The Gang that Couldn't Sell Straight

In the 1980s three aspects of Teleglobe's environment dominate. Two of these are of commercial significance while the other involves its status as a Crown corporation. The two commercial concerns arose from dangers that Teleglobe might have to face both international and domestic competition. With respect to the former, the corporation's traditional quiet life as a monopoly provider of international telecommunications services faced serious challenges.[21] The United States, having unleashed the forces of domestic competition, proposed to do so in the international sector. Not only did the Americans significantly restructure their portion of the international telecommunications system, they were also prepared to allow new entrants into the sector that would operate both fibre optic cable and satellite systems in direct competition with the traditional international monopoly service providers of which Teleglobe was a partial owner. These developments were particularly threatening for Teleglobe because any competition that developed would be primarily for the North Atlantic traffic that provided the bulk of its revenues. In response to such challenges, Teleglobe and its international collaborators in Intelsat developed new services such as Globesat to appeal to their large business customers and to discourage them from switching to the new entrants.

A major consequence of Teleglobe's response to the changing international environment was the emergence of tension between the firm and the Canadian domestic telecommunication companies. Globesat, for example, linked Canadian firms directly with offices in Europe and the United States thereby bypassing the Canadian domestic carriers who naturally perceived such a service as an invasion of their exclusive territory, the North American market. In any event, the domestic carriers had been critical, for some time, of the terms of their revenue-sharing agreement with Teleglobe. They thought that they should either receive a larger share of the revenues or Teleglobe should lower its rates. Although the domestic carriers had groused about their relations with Teleglobe, for the most part they kept their concerns confidential believing, in part, that Teleglobe was in a position to exploit its status as a public enterprise to their disadvantage. One important sign of the potentially antagonistic relationship occurred in 1985 when the domestic carriers rejected Teleglobe's proposal for a ten-year interconnection and revenue sharing agreement and were willing only to sign renewable one-year agreements.

One area of presumed stability was Teleglobe's relationship with the Canadian state. With respect to Parliament, despite the changes in corporate personnel and performance over the previous decade, Teleglobe remained unknown and largely ignored. Even with the government, Teleglobe's relations were tranquil and relatively benign. Treasury Board objectives were met by the commitment to pay annual dividends and the Department of Communications, to whom the corporation reported, lost any interest in the firm. Perhaps most significantly for Teleglobe's planning was that it was apparently not included in the Clark Government's list of privatization candidates in 1979 even though Teleglobe's management was beginning to favour such a course.[22] The major obstacle to privatization at this time, according to one participant, was a Department of Justice opinion that the Commonwealth Agreement which led to the creation of Teleglobe constituted a "treaty" that Canada could not unilaterally break by privatizing the enterprise. The subsequent sale of British Telecom undercut this argument.

Teleglobe's intragovernmental stability was shattered, however, in 1982 when the Liberal government established the Canada Development Investment Corporation (CDIC). Henceforth Teleglobe would no longer report to the Minister of Communications but to the Minister responsible for CDIC. Such a transfer, not surprisingly, reinforced the lack of interest in the corporation within the Communications Department and heightened it within CDIC. This is not the place to examine the role and purposes of CDIC or in particular to judge whether CDIC officers saw their task as the privatizing of Teleglobe or, as some suspect, using its substantial assets as the means necessary to underwrite further interventions in the private sector.[23] Teleglobe, perhaps more than any other CDIC asset, guaranteed both the salaries of CDIC officers and working cash without having to go before Parliament. More importantly, for our purposes, the transfer of responsibility for Teleglobe to CDIC precipitated sustained external interest in the firm. Senator Jack Austin, Minister responsible for CDIC, and Joel Bell, its president, spent a considerable amount of time assessing and analysing Teleglobe. Officials knowledgeable about this period contend that one of the consequences for CDIC of this activity was that knowledge of the policy complexities within which Teleglobe operated may have resulted in CDIC becoming bogged down in detail and hence diverted from its original objectives for the firm, whatever they may have been. For Teleglobe, the CDIC exercise was important because the scrutiny that it received significantly heightened the awareness within the firm of its relationships with the government and the need for it to interact more extensively and more regularly with other elements of the state. The CDIC experience made Teleglobe realize that it could no longer take for granted its life of "benign neglect" within the Canadian public sector.

Teleglobe did not have much time to act on its new appreciation of its governmental relationships for the 1984 general election saw a Progressive Conservative landslide victory. The significance of the change in government was immediately apparent for Teleglobe. Less than a month after the election Sinclair Stevens, the Minister for Regional Economic Expansion and CDIC's designated minister, announced that all of CDIC's assets, including Teleglobe, were to be sold to the British Columbia Resources Investment Corporation (BCRIC) which itself had only been recently privatized by the government of British Columbia.[24] Teleglobe quickly learned, moreover, that unlike the close relationship it developed with Bell and others at the CDIC during the Liberal government, it would have only a limited role in future discussions or deliberations on privatization. Stevens' announcement was interpreted as an attempt to preempt those of his cabinet colleagues who were thought to be "soft" on the issue of privatization. Given that he thought he already had a buyer, he believed it unnecessary to provide a substantial defence of either his general rationale for privatization or the sale of Teleglobe in particular. Indeed, insofar as Teleglobe was concerned, he refused to accept that there were policy questions to be resolved before the sale and also accused any officials who attempted to raise them of being "closet" Liberals. Such accusations, especially from someone who had come to be known as the "Slasher" during his term as president of the Treasury Board in the Clark government, decisively discouraged further discussions.

One of the most significant aspects of Teleglobe's privatization as initiated by Stevens in late 1984 was the acute lack of debate, within or outside of government, about the principle of the sale. Stevens invoked general arguments about "sound business principles" and a "tough international marketplace" to justify the sale of CDIC assets but he made no attempt to develop a specific case for the sale of Teleglobe.[25] Even though the sale of CDIC assets to BCRIC fell through, the principle that Teleglobe should be sold was established and even subsequent statements by cabinet members were not particularly informative about the specific rationale or justification for privatization.[26] On the other hand, except for a general rejection of privatization as being motivated by mere ideology, those who were opposed to privatization did not offer a substantial defence of Teleglobe's status as a public enterprise. Having lifted the veil on Teleglobe, it was as if everyone was surprised by, but could not think of reasons for, its presence within the public sector.

Henceforth, the debate was not whether Teleglobe should be privatized but to whom and on what terms. From this debate it became clear that, aside from a general ideological predisposition towards "shrinking the state" on the part of a minority of ministers, the privatization of Teleglobe was driven almost exclusively by the goal of obtaining the largest sale price possible in order to contribute to the government's deficit-reducing objective.

Subject to this revenue objective, the Teleglobe privatization process was dominated for the next two years by a largely intra-governmental conflict over possible purchasers and the terms for the sale. For his part, Stevens saw the issues of "to whom and on what conditions" in very stark terms. As indicated, he refused to acknowledge initially that there were substantial policy questions involved. He did not, for example, believe that there need be a concern for Teleglobe's place within national telecommunications policy nor did he feel it necessary to resolve the issue about Teleglobe's *de facto* monopoly and the related issue of regulation. For Stevens, once a sale to BCRIC was not an option, the sole issue, aside from price, and it is not clear which was more important, was very specific: anyone could buy Teleglobe, as long as no domestic telephone company participation was involved.

Stevens' position on telephone company ownership was influenced by both philosophical and idiosyncratic concerns. He was critical of the degree of industrial concentration in Canada generally and in the telephone sector in particular. Sale of Teleglobe to the domestic telephone companies would only further entrench their existing market power and reinforce their capacity for anti-competitive behaviour. In addition Stevens was not particularly responsive to a telephone company bid for personal reasons. Prior to, and especially after his appointment to the cabinet, Stevens had asked Bell Canada to provide Extended Area Service to his constituency just on the outskirts of Toronto. Such service would have enabled subscribers to make local rather than long distance toll calls to Toronto. In the 1984 election, Stevens had made such service availability a plank in his campaign and subsequently, according to industry sources, whenever he met Bell officials he refused to discuss other matters in order to press them on the service issue. Bell was opposed to Stevens' request because of its implications for other communities and its position infuriated him.

Stevens' opposition to the domestic telephone companies and towards Bell Canada in particular became an important force in the early stages of privatization. Surprisingly, neither Bell nor its associates appreciated the obstacles they faced or, if they did, assumed that they could count, as one industry participant stated, on Jean deGrandpre's ability "to call the P.M." to straighten out the situation.

The telephone companies' self confidence was shown by the fact that Bell Canada, on behalf of Telecom Canada, submitted three unsolicited bids immediately following Stevens' CDIC sale announcement for all of the federal government's telecommunications holdings.[27] It proposed to purchase Teleglobe, the 49.9 per cent holding in Telesat and the telephone companies owned by Canadian National. In terms of subsequent developments such a bid was surprising because it could only set off alarm bells within Ottawa about the threat of industry concentration and monopolization at a time when the CRTC was considering an application to introduce more competition in telecommunications and the DOC was still attempting to come to grips with the overall policy issues.[28] In addition there remained some residual opposition to the ease with which Bell Canada had reorganized itself into Bell Canada Enterprises in order to reduce the extent of regulatory scrutiny over its activities.[29] After the president of Canadian National preemptorily rejected the CN offer, a separate bid, again unsolicited, was put in for Teleglobe. When the deadline expired on this bid at the end of 1985 without a reply from the minister, Telecom Canada wrote to Stevens to extend the date an additional four months. Again, despite no reply, they made a further extension until the end of September 1986. Although the telephone companies believed their bids, however unrequited, were necessary for strategic reasons, namely to preclude a non-tendered sale, the eagerness of their pursuit caused concern among some Ottawa players who shared Stevens' opposition, if not his rationale, to a domestic telephone acquisition of Teleglobe.

Stevens may have successfully preempted his colleagues by announcing in 1984 his intention to sell CDIC assets; he could not exclude them, however, from the actual privatization process. Consequently those departments wanting a role, particularly with respect to the policy issues, insisted successfully that Stevens negotiate with them on the terms of privatization. Although a number of departments became involved, two in particular sought to play a major role, Communications and Consumer and Corporate Affairs, especially the latter's Bureau of Competition Policy.

After difficult interdepartmental negotiations, in August of 1985 a set of "policy assumptions and guidelines" was announced whose purpose was "to form the general direction for government policy with respect to Teleglobe and govern the operations of the company upon its privatisation."[30] The following were the more important considerations that prospective purchasers were asked to respect in their bids:

1. *Organizational Structure:* Legislation will be developed to reorganize Teleglobe into an appropriate corporate form which,

as a legal, accounting and operating entity will remain separate from its private owners;

2. *Control on Share/Asset Disposition:* CRTC approval will be required for subsequent transfers of effective control. The CRTC must also approve future dispositions of the substantive assets or business undertakings of Teleglobe;

3. *Foreign Ownership:* Non-resident ownership will be restricted to a minority position (e.g. twenty per cent) with the CRTC empowered . . . to approve or disallow any transfer of effective control to foreign interests;

4. *Single Interface Policy:* The government would continue its policy under existing legislation of restricting the issuance of cable landing and international earth station licences to Teleglobe for the purpose of Canada-overseas telecommunications. The government will undertake to maintain such policies in effect for at least a period of five years.

In addition the government acknowledged that some form of price and profit regulation would be likely but indicated that "a less stringent form of regulation" than that employed by the CRTC might be acceptable. Consequently, prospective purchasers were asked to "submit an alternative bid proposing a form of price regulation not tied to return on equity."

These guidelines were the first attempt to address the complex policy issues hitherto ignored by Stevens and reflected a complex set of compromises among the major departmental interests. For his part, Stevens had not focussed on the question of Teleglobe's regulation for the simple reason that he had assumed that the firm would lose, once privatized, its *de facto* monopoly status. The other extreme was the position of the Department of Communications which argued for either a statutory monopoly or a continuation for an unspecified period of a *de facto* monopoly for a privatized Teleglobe. Both Stevens and the Bureau of Competition Policy vigorously opposed either alternative and the result was the compromise: a five year protection from new entrants and the suggestion that "carrier and user access to alternative international services will remain subject to other telecommunications legislation within Canada." The latter reflected the position of the Department of Communications that a privatized Teleglobe must be given some protection from users attempting to bypass Teleglobe, that is employing alternative facilities, especially American, to complete their overseas calls while at the same time it warned Telecom Canada members that the government would not permit them to undermine Teleglobe by routing their traffic through non-Teleglobe facilities. The latter stemmed from concerns shared by Stevens and the Competition Bureau. Although the source of the threat was different for the two sets of governmental actors, both shared a common concern, namely if competition was permitted in overseas communications Teleglobe could easily be reduced from a "cash cow" to a "white elephant."[31]

The policy statement was largely silent on the issue of restrictions on possible owners. The 20 per cent maximum foreign ownership rule was a major concession forced from Stevens by the Department of Communications—Stevens had no objections to complete foreign ownership or control. Stevens, however, remained obdurate in his opposition to domestic carrier ownership and was initially opposed to allowing them even the 20 per cent available to non-residents. Although the public announcement made no reference to such a limit, Stevens took the position, and was supported by Consumer and Corporate Affairs, that if domestic carrier ownership was allowed it too would be limited to 20 per cent. In the press release accompanying the "guideline statement" Stevens hinted at his continuing opposition to the domestic carriers when he stated that the goal of privatization was "to ensure that Teleglobe remains a commercially viable and organizationally distinct company with the flexibility to respond to its rapidly changing environment."[32]

Although federal officials apparently envisioned the sale of Teleglobe by the end of 1985, the process quickly became bogged down over the role of the domestic carriers.[33] Both the Minister of Communications, Marcel Masse, and his officials continued to reject the limited ownership role being offered to Telecom Canada which was, in fact, Communications' preferred purchaser of Teleglobe. It is not difficult to explain this preference. On the one hand, the Department of Communications was concerned about the long term viability of a privatized Teleglobe, particularly if either users or especially the domestic carriers had an incentive to attempt to bypass Teleglobe. Both Masse and his officials feared that they would be left with the responsibility, and the political fallout, if Teleglobe got into financial trouble after privatization. On the other hand they were afraid that selling Teleglobe to someone other than Telecom Canada could seriously destabilize the national telecommunications market-place and consequently national telecommunications policy-making. The fear was based on the possibility that such a purchaser might actively seek to end the traditional division of international telecommunications into two markets, the overseas and the Canadian-American. If this happened, the domestic companies would naturally retaliate, possibly by bypassing Teleglobe through American networks to complete their overseas calls. In order to preclude the potential turmoil that could result from a Teleglobe-domestic carrier conflict, the department almost single-mindedly pushed for Telecom Canada's case to acquire effective control of Teleglobe.

Although almost twenty bids were received including multiple bids from several parties that were premised on alternative responses by the government to the major policy questions, the government did not respond for almost thirteen months. The reason for the delay was the debate which raged within the federal government in 1986 over the role of the domestic telephone companies. In particular, Masse opposed the condition that they were to be treated the same as foreign companies. What specifically irked him and his department was that foreign carriers, not merely non-residents, were given the same status as the domestic carriers. As a tactic in his internal battle, Masse encouraged his provincial counterparts at a February 1986 intergovernmental conference to protest the limited role being offered the domestic carriers. Provincial ministers shared the fears of Masse and his officials about the possible ramifications of non-Telecom Canada control of Teleglobe.

When provincial opposition, even in a period when "national reconciliation" was uppermost in the Conservative government's objectives, failed to persuade Stevens and his allies to alter their position, Masse employed a different tactic: he sought to derail the process by dramaticaly increasing the stakes. At a cabinet meeting to discuss the issue, Masse argued that it was inappropriate to sell Teleglobe separately. He contended that the government could obtain a much better price by selling Teleglobe and Telesat as a package. He insisted as well that any sale be conditional on keeping Teleglobe's headquarters in Montreal. It would be very damaging to the Government, he argued, if a high-technology company managed by French Canadians were to leave Quebec as a result of privatization.

Masse's arguments were successful in persuading his colleagues, if not Stevens, that a decision should be postponed. It is worth noting that, in addition to the arguments he put forward, the case for delay was strengthened by general cabinet dissatisfaction with the quality of the bids received especially the proposed purchase prices. What was also particularly notable about all the bids but one, according to knowledgeable sources, was that they called for the continuation of traditional rate of return regulation. The bid from Telecom Canada was the exception.

The privatization process was changed substantially shortly after this Cabinet meeting as a result of Stevens' resignation over conflict of interest allegations. In the first place, the privatization became less of a priority following the creation of a new portfolio — Minister of State for Privatization and Regulatory Affairs — and the need for the new minister, Barbara McDougall, to bring order to the overall approach to privatization and to hire staff. One of the important consequences of this change was the creation of a cabinet Committee on Privatization, Regulatory Affairs and Operations. This gave more of a focus to the privatization process and reinforced the position of the Minister of State who assumed the lead position in the process. Previously, the process had been rather chaotic and confused as a result of both substantive disputes such as that between Stevens and Masse but also a power struggle most notably between Stevens and Robert de Cotret, the President of the Treasury Board, over who was to control the privatization process. Finally, another major consequence of the Stevens' resignation was the related cabinet shuffle which saw Flora MacDonald replace Marcel Masse as Minister of Communications.

The significance of the personnel and process changes were felt within a few months when in November 1986 the government issued a new call for bids.[34] The second round was subject to an expanded set of conditions. Communications clearly had more impact than previously because foreign telecommunications carriers were declared ineligible although non-residents could acquire a maximum of 20 per cent of Teleglobe. Furthermore, the domestic telephone companies would now be permitted initially to own 40 per cent but this was to be reduced to 33 1/3 per cent after a share offering. Although the Communications Department had made some gains these were conditional on the acceptance of several controls to prevent the telephone companies from gaining effective, permanent control over Teleglobe. These controls included:

1.   Telephone company membership on Teleglobe's board would be restricted to one-third of the board;

2.   Teleglobe's officers could not be officers or directors of telephone companies or their affiliates;

3.   Teleglobe could not be amalgamated or wound up without Parliamentary approval;

4.   Canadian Radio-television and Telecommunications Commission approval would be required for both transfers of effective control and the disposition of the substantive assets of the firm;

5.   Teleglobe would be subject to CRTC regulation similar to that in force for the domestic carriers with some allowances made for international aspects;

6.   Teleglobe would be subject to a governmental power of direction; and

7.   Existing employee contracts and pension provisions must be respected and employees must be offered a chance to purchase ten per cent of the shares of the firm.

The government maintained its earlier commitment to protect Teleglobe's *de facto* monopoly for at least five years but refused to grant the firm a statutory monopoly. The government also clarified and expanded the original position on bypass by committing itself to use its regulatory powers to maintain the existing arrangements between the domestic telephone companies and Teleglobe. In the statement the government asserted that it would use "governmental policy direction as required . . . to ensure that established international service arrangements and practices are maintained and that Canadian telecommunications traffic is routed on Canadian facilities to the maximum possible extent."[35]

The new set of conditions, a product of intragovernmental bargaining subject to little external influence, clearly reflected compromises on the part of all the major participants. Those in the Privatization and Regulatory Affairs Secretariat and the Bureau of Competition Policy opposed to granting a dominant role for the domestic carriers were satisfied that they had won enough concessions which, even if they did not advance the cause for competition in telecommunications, seriously impeded the carriers from reducing the potential for such competition. The Department of Communications, on the other hand, which had almost single-handedly championed the cause of the domestic carriers, believed that the new terms incorporated the best deal it could gain for them.

The November 1986 call for new bids recognized that the outcome would in part be dependent on the willingness of the telephone companies to accept the conditions. Consequently they were to be given in effect a right of first refusal on 40 per cent of Teleglobe subject to the conditions described. The bidding process was structured to determine if the telephone companies would accept the terms by their deadline of December 29. Other potential bidders were to be advised of the carriers' decision to permit them to submit their bids by January 7, 1987.

Telecom Canada members were not pleased with the terms offered, particularly the condition that limited them to a one-third ownership share without knowing who the controlling shareholder might be. Their concerns were well articulated by their president who said, "It's like asking us to sign a marriage contract without seeing the bride. We might wake up the day after the wedding and get a nasty surprise."[36] After considerable debate within Telecom Canada, where unanimity is required for decisions, the carriers opted to ignore the official conditions and to submit a bid that, if accepted, would ultimately give them control. This was done on the last day possible.

Within 24 hours the carriers were informed that their bid did not comply with the specified conditions and consequently had been rejected. Government officials were offended by what they considered to be the carriers' arrogance. Even their advocate, the Department of Communications, felt betrayed especially because the carriers' bid was perceived to be premised on the threat to bypass Teleglobe if it were not accepted.

Although the carriers denied this publicly, they had indeed considered the possibilities including giving the required one-year notice of termination of their agreement with Teleglobe and "repatriating" the Caribbean countries into the Canada-U.S. market. This option was possible because the Caribbean could be reached by the North American Numbering Plan and, if exercised, would reduce Teleglobe's revenues by ten per cent. An additional move would be to make arrangements with American carriers to complete overseas calls for them. As for the government's contention that it could prevent such an action, Telecom Canada strategists thought the government was bluffing. They noted that federal jurisdiction did not extend to the provincially regulated carriers and in any event such an action might be politically difficult to enforce if the carriers were able to reduce significantly overseas rates for both residential and business customers.

With the rejection of the Telecom Canada bid, offers to purchase from Power Corporation, Inter-City Gas of Winnipeg, and First City Financial remained. Prior to the January 7 deadline three additional bids were received, two of which were the consequence of the failure of the telephone companies to make an offer within the terms and conditions. One involved Telecom Canada with the Caisse de Dépôt et Placement du Québec and Spar Aerospace of Toronto while the second came from a newly created company financed by Gordon Capital of Toronto. This last company, not insignificantly, believed it had an informal understanding that, if it were successful, Telecom Canada would purchase one-third of the privatized Teleglobe at Gordon's cost of acquisition prior to taking the remaining shares public.

Review of the final bids by the CDIC, its financial advisers and government officials was rather hasty in large part because it was driven by a commitment to complete the sale in time to include the sale price in Finance Minister Wilson's February budget. The objective was to apply the revenue received against the deficit. Even in the final stages, the telephone companies were subject to intense scrutiny. In particular, the Bureau of Competition Policy suggested that if the Telecom Canada bid, supported by the Caisse and Spar, was chosen there might be need for an independent review by the new Competition Tribunal created under the *Competition Act*. If such a review was undertaken, it raised the possibility that, even if successful in the bidding process, the decision could be overturned on the grounds that it significantly lessened competition. Bureau officials were concerned that Telecom Canada's partners would be passive thereby allowing them to dominate Teleglobe.

Although there was considerable speculation about which bid would be chosen no one predicted the winner which was announced one week before budget day: Memotec Data, a company one-sixth the size of the firm it was to acquire.[37] When CDIC officers responsible for assessing the bids and making a recommendation to the government raised questions about Memotec's ability to complete the deal, Memotec brought in acknowledged Toronto and Montreal financial heavyweights to reassure them that the money was available.[38] Once this obstacle was removed, Memotec was recommended by CDIC and received the highest ranking in the subsequent memorandum to cabinet for one primary reason: it offered the government the best price. The sale price satisfied the government's stated objective of approximately $600 million based on $488 million paid by Memotec, the government receiving $102 million in accumulated cash in Teleglobe and a special dividend of $18 million to be paid by the end of 1987. The sale met all the conditions set by the government including a share purchase option for employees, acceptance of the terms of the employee pension plan and existing collective agreements, no worker layoffs and a reduction in overseas telephone and telex rates by 13.5 per cent and 10 per cent respectively on January 1, 1988.

Although the decision had been made, the drama (trauma?) of privatization was not quite complete. Shortly after the deal was announced, sale of Memotec shares was stopped because of concerns about insider trading. Subsequently, seven individuals, including a former president of the Progressive Conservative Party, were charged with offenses under the *Quebec Securities Act*.[39] The former president was acquitted of all charges in April 1988, however, and no decision had been taken on whether to proceed with the remaining charges.

Perhaps the most important post-bidding development was the May 1987 announcement that Bell Canada Enterprises (BCE) had acquired one-third of the equity in Memotec thereby making it Memotec's largest single shareholder.[40] Such a move made sense for BCE because of Memotec's obvious need for money to complete the deal and the danger that a firm potentially hostile to the telephone companies such as Power Corporation or First City Financial would acquire control of Memotec. Moreover, the president of Memotec acknowledged that, prior to Memotec's submission of a bid to purchase Teleglobe, discussions about a possible partnership with BCE had been held.[41] Although some federal officials believed that the purchase violated the spirit, if not the terms, of the government's conditions especially because of the assumption that all the members of Telecom Canada would acquire the percentage open to them, thereby diluting the influence of any particular domestic carrier, neither the Privatization Minister nor the Minister of Communications shared such concerns.[42] In response to questions about the purchase, a spokesman for the former stated that "it's out of our hands and our job is just to sell the corporations."[43] Following an exchange of letters and requests for information, the CRTC indicated that the purchase was not in contravention of the conditions established under the Teleglobe Canada Reorganization and Divestiture Bill.

Conclusions

We have concentrated, for the most part, on describing the origins and evolution of Teleglobe as a public enterprise and the process by which it was privatized. Our objective in the first section was to establish that Teleglobe was created and operated as a Crown corporation without a public mission. Until it was privatized, except for the episodic imposition of a specific task by its public masters, Teleglobe had no more public policy purpose than the domestic telephone companies. In fact, to the extent that its monopoly profits accrued largely to the firm and were not used as part of the system of cross-subsidies associated with domestic telephone pricing, it could be argued that Teleglobe had even less of a public mission than Canadian private telephone companies.

We have also described how Teleglobe left the public sector almost in as much of a muddle as it entered. Teleglobe's privatization was not based, especially in the early stages, on any clear principles. There was no claim that it was inefficient or that its performance would improve by a transfer to the private sector. There was no effort to assess the costs and benefits of its privatization nor to define a set of goals other than sale price maximization. What was striking was how little advance thought was given to the policy questions raised by privatization. Once attention was directed to these questions, even then the process was largely, though not exclusively, driven by a concern over who should be allowed to purchase Teleglobe rather than a concentration on policy principles and priorities.

Having described the origins, evolution and privatization of Teleglobe, two questions stand out. Why was Teleglobe created and permitted to operate in a public policy vacuum? More importantly, why did the privatization process take the form it did? We have already alluded to some of the answers to the first question. Teleglobe was not created because the government of Canada decided it needed a state-owned international telecommunications carrier; the decision was determined by international treaty obligations. Once established, Teleglobe was permitted, contrary to legislated public policy, to become an unregulated monopoly-provider of overseas telcommunications services without causing a ripple of concern. Clearly the absence of a policy rationale as a yardstick against which to judge its performance aided such a development. Furthermore, Teleglobe's economic performance reinforced its autonomy within an indifferent state apparatus. For almost all its years as a Crown corporation, Teleglobe lacked political salience but it is worth noting in this respect that the firm was not much different from the other Canadian telecommunications companies.[44]

The second question, why did the privatization process unfold as it did, is far more difficult to answer. Idiosyncratic factors such as Sinclair Stevens' ideological and personal preferences played an important role, but in themselves do not constitute a persuasive explanation. Nor do Teleglobe's uniqueness or variables such as symbolism and regional concerns identified as playing a major role in other privatizations explain the Teleglobe process.[45] In our view, the explanation for this process, and its larger significance for students of the Canadian political process, is to be found in the autonomy exercised by both elected and appointed state officials.

By autonomy we mean much more than what is usually associated with bureaucratic politics. We mean that state authorities developed and sought to impose their own policy preferences which were not, in Eric Nordlinger's words, "shaped [or] constrained by the expectations, demands, and pressures of . . . societal actors . . . ."[46] There is no evidence that state actors were representing societal interests or were influenced by such interests in the determination of their positions on the central issues. Nor did they feel compelled to employ recourse to such interests to buttress or advance their positions. The only apparent exception, and it is more apparent than real, was Marcel Masse's invocation of provincial support for Telecom Canada's right to acquire control of Teleglobe. We would argue that such support reflected the perception of the provincial politicians that such control served their best interests as representatives of provincial governments *per se* rather than as representatives of provincially-based social and economic interests. What is particularly impressive about the autonomy of state actors in this instance is the virtual exclusion of the telecommunications industry from the policy development and implementation process. This industry had dominated the telecommunications policy sector until very recently.

The autonomy of state officials in the Teleglobe process can be underlined by an understanding of the factors that shaped their positions on the central issues. For his part, Sinclair Stevens' opposition to Telecom Canada was influenced by his personal political and ideological position on carrier ownership and control. While it is true that he was seeking to advance his constituents' concerns in obtaining cheaper local telephone service, his opposition to Bell Canada did not reflect constituents' demands to meet such concerns.

Nor was his general antipathy to corporate concentration a reflection of any interest group demands; it reflected his personal experiences at the hands of what he perceived to be undue corporate power.

The preferred privatization outcome of the officials from the Bureau of Competition Policy in the Department of Consumer and Corporate Affairs reflected their organizational and personal preferences. The Bureau has a public mission to promote and enhance competition both in the development of federal public policies and in regulatory proceedings at both the federal and provincial levels. There was no need for private lobbying to persuade the Bureau and thus Bureau participants from the outset sought to block the domestic telephone companies from acquiring control of Teleglobe on the grounds that such control could only prove to be anti-competitive.[47] It was not insignificant, as well, that some of the Bureau officers responsible for representing the Bureau in the intragovernmental negotiations were former telephone company employees who understood but rejected the telephone companies' approach to telecommunications policy, especially the introduction of competition into telecommunications markets. One of the advantages possessed by Bureau participants was their statutory role which meant, as competition advocates, they could be neither excluded from the privatization process nor have their views treated perfunctorily. Other state authorities knew that, if either was attempted, the Director of Competition Policy had the independent authority to initiate a separate and public review of any purchase under the provisions of the Competition Act.

The Minister responsible for Privatization and her officials developed their positions on the Teleglobe issues unconstrained as well by external societal forces for a number of reasons. In the first place as a very new unit, it was not even a department *per se* but an office, external actors were thus inclined to underestimate its stategic importance especially as its minister was relatively junior. This ignored, however, the fact that the creation of the Office of Privatization established for the first time since the government had initiated privatizations the locus of responsibility for developing policies and making recommendations to cabinet on specific privatizations. The minister's position was further enhanced by the creation of a cabinet Committee on Privatization, Regulatory Affairs and Operations of which she was a member. The Office of Privatization was a natural ally for the Bureau of Competition Policy both for substantive and strategic reasons. On the substantive grounds, the Office, especially with respect to regulatory issues which constituted the other half of its mandate, was committed to lessening regulation which led its officers to prefer pro-competition policy alternatives. On strategic grounds, the Office faced the continuous threat that line departments would continue to seek to dominate the privatization and regulatory policy process. Consequently it would need to form alliances and coalitions with other bureaucratic participants who shared its preferred outcomes.

Even the position of the minister and officials in the Department of Communications on the key issue of carrier ownership or control represented less a positive response to external demands and more a championing of those demands for political and bureaucratic reasons. Departmental players feared the political fallout that would occur if an unsuccessful privatization threatened Teleglobe's viability. More importantly they wanted a sale which would pose a minimal threat to the Department's dominant role in the development of national telecommunications policy. For much of the past two decades, in the face of the threat of telecommunications competition, the Department of Communications has consistently sought to control the pace and direction of such competition. The sale of Teleglobe to the domestic carriers was preferred because it would result in a community of interest between purchaser and department and would prevent the introduction of a new, unknown and potentially volatile player in the policy network.

One of the interesting aspects of the Teleglobe privatization is the limited role played by the firm's managers. Although they had developed a preference for privatization several years earlier, they were denied any significant input into the process of determining their fate. Their greatest impact appears to have been during the CDIC process when they were able to impress upon CDIC officers the complexity of the policy issues. When Stevens assumed responsibility, Teleglobe management was effectively excluded from the process because of Stevens' dismissal of policy concerns. For his part, Marcel Masse was no more sympathetic to Teleglobe management playing a role because he was far more sympathetic than they were to Telecom Canada acquiring a dominant interest in Teleglobe. Teleglobe's managers were concerned that if this was permitted Teleglobe would probably disappear as a separate corporate entity. They had no role in influencing the positions of either the Privatization Minister or the Bureau of Competition Policy but when these two sets of participants advocated positions that were supportive of their preferred outcome they were relieved if somewhat annoyed over being denied an opportunity to influence the outcome.

In short, it is our contention that it was the nature of competing political and bureaucratic preferences which produced the lengthy, highly chaotic and very focussed Teleglobe privatization process. These preferences were autonomously developed in that they were not derived from, nor dependent upon, social and economic actors or influences. The autonomy of the process *vis-à-vis* society was reinforced by the confidential nature of the bidding process. Confidentiality was necessary for corporate and public reasons but it served to insulate effectively the process from external pressures. Neither the names of the bidders nor the content of their bids, except for the winner of course, were disclosed for either round of bidding.

The clash of bureaucratic preferences within a very insulated decision-making system may have implications for the long-term significance of the Teleglobe privatization. Perhaps more important than the sale itself was that it may have caused the premature closing of a window of opportunity to re-evaluate the structure of the telecommunications industry in Canada. As indicated earlier, the past decade has witnessed a debate over whether and how much competition should be allowed into the telecommunications industry. In other countries such as the United States, Japan and Great Britain the decision has been to favour the introduction of competition in varying degrees. In part because we chose not to have a public debate over the merits of privatizing Teleglobe, Canada opted to maintain the status quo. The nature of the process may also explain why, once the decision to sell was taken, state authorities fell into very traditional assumptions about the appropriate instruments of public control for the privatized Teleglobe.

Although the literature on privatization discusses the possible alternative accountability regimes that might accompany privatization, no such discussion occurred in the Teleglobe process.[48] This is not to say that such a debate was not attempted because in the first call for bids prospective purchasers were asked to suggest alternatives to traditional rate of return regulation. The fact that there was near unanimity among the bidders in favour of traditional regulation, combined with the fear that the privatized Teleglobe would not retain its monopoly status which lowered the original bids submitted to the government in 1985, may have caused the government participants to be less innovative than they might otherwise have been. In any event the result was the promise to continue the *de facto* monopoly for at least five years. Once the decision was taken on this issue, it was perhaps inevitable that regulation would be introduced in order to prevent monopolistic practices such as excess profit-taking or anti-competitive behaviour. It did not follow, however, that there should be no discussion of alternative forms of regulation. The decision was simply to subject, with minor modifications, a privatized Teleglobe to traditional CRTC regulation. This contrasts sharply with the rejection of such regulation in the United Kingdom for British Telecom and the creation of an innovative formula for price, rather than profit, regulation when British Telecom was privatized.[49] It is also in marked contrast to the coincidental debate in the United States about alternatives to rate of return regulation.[50]

The privatization of Teleglobe raised fundamental policy issues. These involved considerations about the preferred structure of the Canadian telecommunications sector as well as larger questions about the appropriate relationships between the state and the economy. Such questions required the government to direct its attention to issues about the concentration of private economic power and the availability and effectiveness of alternative public instruments to control such power. Unfortunately, because of the intragovernmental nature of the debate, the larger questions and issues were ignored. The pursuit of the largest possible sale price combined with the negative objective of preventing a purchase of Teleglobe by the telephone companies caused a major opportunity to be lost. The irony, of course, is the non-reviewable purchase by BCE of a one-third interest in Teleglobe's parent. Although the Teleglobe divestiture bill does not prohibit Teleglobe from entering new lines of business such as the Canadian-U.S. enhanced services sector, the BCE relationship may effectively inhibit such a development. Furthermore, if the emerging international competitive marketplace is stillborn or the government decides in 1992 to extend Teleglobe's *de facto* monopoly, then the privatization of Teleglobe may simply have been the substitution of private for public monopoly. Customers will benefit from the initial mandatory rate reductions, the managers of the firm are now subject to a greater degree of accountability than hitherto, albeit to the private owners, and the firm itself is regulated by the CRTC. But it remains to be seen if the results are worth the effort. The privatization of Teleglobe may turn out to be less a sale and more of a giveaway of the jewel in the crowns.

Notes

1. In writing this paper I draw on material and assumptions from an earlier paper on Teleglobe written before its privatization with Hudson Janisch entitled "Teleglobe Canada: Cash Cow or White Elephant?" in *Papers on Privatization* ed. by Thomas E. Kierans and W.T. Stanbury (Montreal: Institute for Research on Public Policy, 1985), pp. 185-242. In addition to this earlier debt, I want to acknowledge his assistance and advice, particularly his extensive press clipping file, for this paper. I also want to thank Robert Cairns for comments on an earlier draft and Allan Bartley for his research and editorial assistance. I am particularly indebted to Allan Tupper for his extensive editorial advice. Finally I would like to thank the numerous individuals in the government departments and agencies as well as in the telecommunications industry who were willing to be interviewed for this project. Although, as was agreed, I cannot identify them

by name, I want to express my gratitude for without their willingness to discuss the privatization process in great depth and in a few cases not without a little pain, I would not have been able to write this paper.

2. Charles M. Dalfen, "Deregulation and Privatization in the Canadian Telecommunications Sector: The Case of Teleglobe Canada." Paper presented to the International Colloquium on Privatization and Deregulation in Canada and the United Kingdom, Gleneagles, Scotland, 2-4 November 1987.

3. Although Teleglobe Canada only assumed its current name in 1975 after being known as the Canadian Overseas Telecommunications Corporation for the preceding 25 years, we shall use the name Teleglobe throughout this paper.

4. On the cultural predisposition see Herschel Hardin, *A Nation Unaware: The Canadian Economic Culture* (Vancouver: J.J. Douglas, 1974) but also see H.V.Nelles, *The Politics of Development: Forest, Mines & Hydro-electric Power in Ontario, 1849-1941* (Toronto: Macmillan, 1975). On the growth of public enterprise in World War II and immediately afterwards see S.F. Borins,"World War Two Crown Corporations: Their Wartime Role and Peacetime Privatization," *Canadian Public Administration,* 25 (Fall 1982), pp. 380-404.

5. Canada, Parliament, House of Commons, *Debates,* 30 September 1949, pp. 387-402; 21 October 1949, pp. 1033-36. (Hereafter referred to as *Debates*).

6. *Canadian Overseas Telecommunications Corporation Act,* R.S.C. 1970, c. C-11, s. 7.

7. *Ibid.,* s. 3(9).

8. *Ibid.,* s. 18 which makes the COTC subject to Part III of the *Telegraphs Act.*

9. Brownlee R. Thomas, "Teleglobe Canada: outside the (CRTC) regulatory camp," *Canadian Public Administration,* 29 (Fall 1986), pp. 425-444.

10. *Ibid.,* p. 432.

11. *Debates, ibid.,* p. 1033.

12. *Canadian Overseas Telecommunications Corporation Act, ibid.,* s.2.

13. For background on the creation of the TransCanada Telephone System and its original membership, see William Lederman, "Telecommunications and the Federal Constitution of Canada" in *Telecommunications for Canada: An Interface of Business and Government* ed. by H. Edward English, (Toronto: Methuen, 1973), pp. 67-68. Subsequently membership expanded to include Newfoundland Telephone Company, Telesat Canada and, as an associate member, Teleglobe. In 1984 the name was changed to Telecom Canada. For a listing of its current members, their ownership and regulators see Richard Schultz and Alan Alexandroff, *Economic Regulation and the Federal System* (Toronto: University of Toronto Press, 1985).

14. *Ibid.*, p. 85.

15. Philippe Faucher, "La stratégie de l'entreprise d'état," in *Hydro-Quebec*, ed. by Philippe Faucher and Johanne Bergeron (Montreal: Presses de l'Université de Montréal, 1986), pp. 19-34.

16. See Janisch and Schultz, *op. cit.*, p. 193, and the references cited therein.

17. Schultz and Alexandroff, *op. cit.*, p. 89.

18. This process reached its culmination in 1975 when Teleglobe assumed its present name. See *An Act to Amend the Canadian Overseas Telecommunications Corporation Act*, S.C. 1974-75-76, c. 77.

19. Canada, "An Act respecting Telecommunications" (Bill-43), First Reading 22 March 1977. See also Bill C-24, 30th Parliament, 3rd Session, 1978 and Bill C-16, 30th Parliament, 4th Session, 1978.

20. Teleglobe Canada, *Brief to the Minister of Communications Regarding the Bill Entitled An Act Respecting Telecommunications in Canada*, 31 Oct. 1977, pp.43-44.

21. Janisch and Schultz, *op. cit.*, pp. 227-231 and the sources cited therein. See also Jill Hills, *Deregulating Telecoms*, (Westport, Conn.: Quorum Books, 1986) especially ch. 6.

22. Roger Croft, "Five more Crown companies heading for the auction block," *Toronto Star*, (11 September 1979), p.A4.

23. Stephen Brooks, "The State as Entrepreneur: from CDC to CDIC," *Canadian Public Administration* 26 (Winter 1983), pp. 525-543; and Jeanne Kirk Laux and Maureen Appel Molot, *State Capitalism: Public Enterprise in Canada* (Ithaca: Cornell University Press, 1988), especially ch.6.

24. Giles Gherson, "Hard questions on privatizing," *Financial Post*, (10 November 1984), p.1.

25. Patrick K. Nagle, "Crown firms for sale as CDIC boss fired," *Vancouver Sun*, (31 October 1984), p. A10.

26. See, for example, Department of Regional Industrial Expansion, "News Release," 1 August 1985; Department of Communications, "Statement of Telecommunications Policy Respecting Teleglobe Canada," November 1986; and Lawrence Surtees, "Divestiture of Teleglobe draws criticism Ottawa is giving up lucrative dividends," *Globe and Mail*, (2 March 1987), p. B5. Charles Dalfen persuasively argues that the 1 May 1987 statement by the Minister of State for Privatization and Regulatory Affairs entitled "Excerpts from Statements by the Honourable Barbara McDougall on the Reasons for Privatization" do not hold up on close examination as applicable to Teleglobe. See Dalfen, *ibid.*, pp.15-17.

27. Technically the bid was made on behalf of all Canadian telecommunications carriers because provision was made for non-Telecom Canada participation. Some of the other carriers, most notably CNCP, had not agreed, however, to enter the proposed consortium.

28. The Department of Communications had announced by way of the *Canada Gazette* on 14 January 1984 a major review of telecommunications policy. No report has been issued by the department.

29. CRTC, *Report of the Canadian Radio-television and Telecommunications Commission on the Proposed Reorganization of Bell Canada* (Ottawa: CRTC, 18 April 1983). See also "An Act Respecting the Reorganization of Bell Canada," (C-19) assented to 25 June 1987.

30. Department of Regional Industrial Expansion, "News Release: Government Calls Bids for Teleglobe Canada," 1 August 1985.

31. See Janisch and Schultz, *op. cit.*

32. News release, Department of Regional Industrial Expansion, 1 August 1985, p. 2.

33. David Hatter, "Privatization gamble," *Financial Post*, (24 November 1986), pp. 1-2.

34. Minister of State, Privatisation, "Divestiture of Teleglobe Canada: Conditions and Process of Sale," November 1986. The Minister of Communications simultaneously released what was termed a "Statement of Telecommunications Policy Respecting Teleglobe Canada" which was largely a reiteration of that issued by the Minister of State, Privatization. Although Communications referred to "policy objectives" the closest thing to an objective in the document was the statement that "It is in Canada's national interest that telecommunications services between locations in Canada and from Canada to other locations shall, to the greatest extent feasible, be provided over Canadian-owned and controlled facilities."

35. Minister of State, Privatization, *ibid.*, p.5.

36. Hatter, *op. cit.*, p. 2.

37. Minister of State, Privatization, "News Release and Information Package," (11 February 1987); Karen Howlett, "Win puts underdog Memotec in the big league," *Globe and Mail*, (12 February 1987), p. B.1; Ann Gibbon, "Meet the minnow that swallowed Teleglobe," Montreal *Gazette*, (14 February 1987), p. H.1.; David Hatter, "Memotec-Teleglobe buy raises serious questions," *Financial Post*, (16 February 1987), p. 10. For examples of earlier speculation about the likely winner in the bidding process see David Hatter, "Teleglobe victor could find prize bittersweet," *Financial Post*, (2 February 1987), p. 1 and Hatter, "Power Corp likely Teleglobe winner," *Financial Post*, (9 February 1987), p. 3.

38. *Globe and Mail, Report on Business Magazine*, "Big Deal", (June 1987), pp.55-56.

39. Gibson, *op. cit.*; Christopher Waddell, "Ottawa joins TSE, ME probes into trading in Memotec stock," *Globe and Mail*, (13

February 1987), p. B.7; Harvey Enchin, "Blaikie denies insider charges," *Globe and Mail*, (30 September 1987), p. B.1.

40. Ken Romain, "BCE to buy one-third interest in Memotec," *Globe and Mail*, (8 May 1987), p. B.1; Lawrence Surtees, "BCE proposal opens door to major Teleglobe stake," *ibid.*, (9 May 1987), p. B8; Mathew Horsman, "BCE moved fast to beat Ottawa on Teleglobe," *Financial Post*, (18 May 1987), p. 19.

41. Harvey Enchin, "Memotec Data reduces proposed share offering following BCE purchase," *Globe and Mail*, (12 May 1987), p. B.5.

42. Some sources indicated in interviews that there was some consternation within Telecom Canada that BCE had unilaterally purchased the share of control available to telephone companies. One indication of that concern, and BCE's attempt to placate it, was the nomination by BCE of Frank Degenstein, President of Telecom Canada, as one of its members to the Board of Directors of Memotec.

43. Lawrence Surtees, "BCE proposal . . .", *op. cit.*

44. See Schultz and Alexandroff, *op. cit.*, pp. 76-86.

45. See, for example, G. Bruce Doern and John Atherton, "The Tories and the Crowns: Restraining and Privatizing in a Political Minefield," in *How Ottawa Spends 1987-88: Restraining the State*, ed. by Michael J. Prince, (Toronto: Methuen, 1987) pp. 129-175; and W.T. Stanbury "Privatization in Canada: Ideology, Symbolism or Substance?" paper prepared for the conference "Privatization In Britain and North America: Theory, Evidence and Implementation", sponsored by the Bradley Policy Research Center, William E. Simon Graduate School of Business Administration, University of Rochester, Washington, D.C., November 6-7, 1987.

46. Eric A. Nordlinger, "Taking the State Seriously" in *Understanding Political Development* ed. by M. Weiner and S. Huntington (Boston: Little Brown, 1987), p.353. See also Eric Nordlinger, *On the Autonomy of the Democratic State* (Cambridge, Mass.: Harvard University Press, 1981) and *Bringing the State Back In*, ed. by P. Evans, *et. al.* (Cambridge: Cambridge University Press, 1985) especially chs. 1 and 11.

47. For a particularly instructive example of both institutional mission and personal preferences shaping policy outcomes, also drawn from the telecommunications sector but in the United

States, see Peter Temin's analysis of the role of the Anti-Trust Division of the Department of Justice and its head, William Baxter, in the AT&T divestiture in Temin, *The Fall of the Bell System* (Cambridge: Cambridge University Press, 1987).

48. Michael Beesley and Stephen Littlechild, "Privatization: Principles, Problems and Priorities," *Lloyds Bank Review*, (July 1983), pp. 1-20, and Thomas E. Kierans, "Privatization if Necessary but not Necessarily Privatization," *Choices*, (November 1984).

49. See Beesley and Littlechild, *op. cit.*, Irwin M. Stelzer, "Regulating Telecommunications in Britain: A New Alternative to the U.S. Approach," *Telematics*, 3, (September 1986) and B. Carsberg, "Review of British Telcom's Tariff Changes, November 1986," Report issued by the Director General of Telecommunications, Office of Telecommunications, November 1986.

50. Mark Fowler, Albert Halprin and James D. Schlicting, "Back to the Future: a Model for Telecommunications," *Federal Communications Law Journal*, 38 (August 1986), pp. 145-200; Dennis R. Patrick, "Long Distance Carrier Service: Other Modes of Regulation," *Public Utilities Fortnightly*, 119 (5 March 1987), pp. 11-15 and United States Department of Commerce, National Telecommunications and Information Administration, *NTIA Regulatory Alternatives Report*, July 1987.

Chapter IX

The Farm Credit Corporation and the Federal Business Development Bank

G. Bruce Doern and John F. Devlin*

In the 1970s, the assets of the four largest federal financial crown corporations were the fastest growing of the federal crown-owned sector.[1] In the 1980s, asset growth rates have reduced in the wake of increased political scrutiny of the banking crowns. At no time, however, have these state-owned banks been anything other than a small part of the total banking and finance sector. In the late 1980s, financial crowns constituted just over 10 percent of the assets of the financial sector with federal crowns accounting for less than half of this figure. This modest role perhaps helps explain why the banking crowns have received little sustained scholarly analysis. They have nonetheless been politically controversial at key points in Canadian history.

This chapter fills part of the research gap by analyzing the origins, evolution and operations of two of the four federal banking crowns, the Farm Credit Corporation (FCC) and the Federal Business Development Bank (FBDB) and their predecessor bodies, the Canadian Farm Loans Board and the Industrial Development Bank. The operations of these two financial crown corporations engage

* We gratefully acknowledge the research assistance of James McEwan and John Heimbecker.

several policy fields. Although the size of their assets is not sufficient to assign to them any significant role in macroeconomic policy, they are instruments of both economic and social policy affecting the agricultural and small business sectors. In these roles, they serve primarily regional and rural concerns. At the same time, their lending activity places them squarely in the financial sector along with the banks, finance, mortgage, and venture capital firms. They are thus influenced by the evolution of the financial sector particularly as this evolution is shaped by government regulation.

As instruments of policy, the financial crowns do not stand alone — they operate alongside diverse policy instruments focussed upon similar and often overlapping policy objectives. The question of instrument choice is thus relevant. Why use a state bank rather than a loan guarantee, a direct subsidy program or a change in the structure of financial regulation? We shall explore the reasons and influences that gave rise to the selection of the state bank option. The reasons and influences do not come together in a complete and coherent way. This is because policies do not emerge as responses to single pressure situations but in complex multifaceted contexts where both objectives and instruments are the subject of often heated debate rooted in conflicting interpretations of the problems to be addressed. Where there is agreement over basic policy objectives there may still remain substantial room for disagreement over the "best" instrument. Where there is agreement over the choice of instrument there may remain disagreement over the objectives pursued.

The chapter comprises four sections. We begin with an overview of the period from creation of the FCC and the FBDB's predecessor bodies until the approximate end of the expansive phase of the post-war Canadian economy in the mid 1970s. The focus here is on the political interests pressing for and against change. This is followed by a more intensive analysis of the behaviour of the financial crowns under restraint in the 1975 to 1986 period. The penultimate section reviews the neo-conservative critique and the Mulroney agenda and their impact on the financial crowns. Finally we comment on the prospects for these two crown corporations and for state banking in general in the 1990s. Because we are examining and comparing two companies, space precludes discussion of their internal managerial dynamics and of all of their business activities. Reference is made to the changing accountability regimes in a broad sense but the chapter's primary concern is the political economy of the two companies.

Origins and Development to the Mid-1970s

The Canadian Farm Loans Board was created in 1929 and became the Farm Credit Corporation in 1959. The Industrial Development Bank was formed in 1944 and restructured in 1975 to form the Federal Business Development Bank. These moments of creation and metamorphosis were preceded and accompanied by important debates over the problems of agriculture and small business credit. The second generation corporations show important continuities with their precursors but also important differences reflecting evolution and change in the political economy of agricultural and small business credit.

The availability of financing is a vital concern to most small enterprises. Large firms can often finance their needs from retained earnings, or the sale of bonds, stocks or other securities. Whether starting up, seeking to expand or weathering a market downturn a small firm does not always have this range of options and is forced to rely primarily on equity or secured credit from banks and finance companies. Where the market satisfies demand at an acceptable cost, there is little likelihood that the issue of credit availability will move from the market to the political arena. But conversely, when the demand for credit is not met, the potential for the politicization of credit is large. For farmers historically, the relationship to the providers of private credit, especially the chartered banks, has been politically volatile. For small business, credit became politicized at the national level only in the early 1970s.

Creation of the Canadian Farm Loans Board

During the early 1920s, the price and demand for Canadian wheat was falling. As the provincially-run agricultural credit programs were becoming less active in the face of deficits and inadequate resources, farmers found themselves unable to obtain loans at 'reasonable' rates of interest from private lenders.[2] The belief that credit was not available at 'reasonable' rates was a crucial point of contention.

Behind the notion of the reasonable rate lies an elaborate infrastructure of ideas concerning the nature of the market. Most farmers believed the credit market was distorted by financial monopolies based in central Canada which were in a position to restrict credit and raise its price above competitive rates. A reasonable rate in the view of farmers would be a competitive rate established by a mechanism outside the control of the vested financial interests. In the Parliamentary debate over the creation of the Canadian Farm Loans Board, Robert Gardiner, Progressive member for Acadia, captured the underlying perception of many farmers:

> The only basis of real credit is the ability of the Canadian
> people to create and deliver goods and service(s) . . . . It is

because of the existence of such high (interest) rates and the fact that they are controlled by a financial group in this country that we farmers find ourselves in the position we are today . . . . We could not resist (them) because of the fact that parliament in the past gave over to financial interests in this country the total credit that the people of the Dominion produced.[3]

Farmers aggressively pressured the government to correct monopolistic practices through government intervention. The Fielding Committee[4], as part of its review of agricultural conditions, concluded in 1923 that Canadian farmers were paying more for long-term credit than either farmers in other countries or Canadians outside of agriculture. The Committee recommended that the federal government promote the extension of long and medium-term credit to farmers. A follow-up examination of rural credit was commissioned. Under the guidance of Henry Marshall Tory, two studies of agricultural credit were produced, the first in 1924 and the second in 1925.

In his first report, Tory observed a lack of competition in private sector lending in the West. The private sector explained the lack of competition as arising from government restrictions in the mortgage lending field. They argued that the elimination of such restrictions would result in a reduction in administrative costs equivalent to two percentage points on lending rates. However, Tory was not smitten with any fundamental faith in the capacity of the market to pass on savings from the deregulation of credit to farmers through reduced interest rates.

In his supplementary report which included an international survey of public agricultural boards, Tory concluded that farm lending required a specialized public institution. Private lending firms regarded agricultural credit as a secondary activity. He suggested the creation of a joint federal-provincial board whose exclusive concern would be the provision of long-term loans to farmers. Why a state agency rather than some other program? Tory was clearly influenced by the model of the U.S. Farm Loan Board and by the realization that many countries were introducing such agencies. He expressed the belief that Canada had to follow suit if it was to compete effectively in international markets. Tory saw the need for a state agency in what with hindsight appears to be a strikingly post-war developmental and technocratic vision:

(If) we desire to have Canadian agriculture maintain its place in world competition in the future, the time to begin to plan for the rational administration both of its finances and its scientific development is the present.[5]

The role of the Canadian Farm Loan Board would be to serve the ends of rational administration and scientific development in agriculture in order to protect and enhance Canada's international competitiveness.

This essentially economic rationale for the creation of the CFLB was lost on most of its critics who chose to see it as a program for redistribution to the western farmer. Although there was general consensus over the need for some sort of agricultural credit program, political criticism of the concept was made on the grounds that such a policy promoted sectoral and regional inequality. Thomas Church, a Conservative MP from Toronto, saw benefits for farmers but costs for "artisans and toilers."

> There are 2,900,000 people in Ontario who will have to contribute to this scheme although they will not share in its benefits .... This is class legislation of the worst kind which gives to the farmers of one province a benefit at the expense of the rest of the people. Those who will have to foot the bill are the artisans and toilers in the various centres of population. The farmers do not want any reduction in the income tax which these people [the artisans and toilers] have to pay, because they [the farmers] pay no income tax; but they want the rest of the country to provide taxes for legislation to meet their demands for agricultural credits.[6]

Another M.P., R.B. Hanson, raised the flag for Maritime fishermen:

> If there is to be any easy money for a particular class, then let us have no discrimination for the western farmer. I am not by any means opposed to rural credits, but if the government desires to put easy and cheap money in the way of the farmers of the west, I demand at least equal treatment on behalf of the fishermen of the Maritime provinces.[7]

The assumption that the program would provide "easy money" at taxpayers' expense fundamentally misunderstood the intent of the program as envisioned by Tory who wanted a program for the provision of well-secured credit to fill a gap in the credit market created by the generally weak financial infrastructure established on the prairies. The importance of filling this gap lay in the concern over the long-term competitiveness of the prairie agricultural economy in international markets. If Canadian agriculture could not obtain credit at prices at least equal to those of the American and European competition, how was it to succeed in maintaining its export markets?

Was the CFLB to be an instrument of economic policy or social policy? To a degree its complexion lay in the eye of the beholder. To eastern politicians, public credit was social redistribution. To the financial industry it was an extension of undesirable state intervention. To western farmers it was a correction to distorted financial markets. For H.M. Tory, who was strongly influenced by the existence of public agencies for the delivery of agricultural credit in other countries, it was a step towards a more economically rational agricultural sector.

The creation of an institution is in itself a policy output. It does not assure that the activities of the institution will meet all the demands that led to its creation. From the perspective of farmers, the creation of the CFLB should have been seen as of secondary importance to the future impact of its operations. It appears, however, that the agency and its program were not separated. The creation of the CFLB was a concession to the demands of the populist agricultural movement of the late nineteenth and early twentieth century rooted in the provincial and federal electoral successes of the Progressive Party in Ontario and on the Prairies. It was not, however, an immediate or automatic concession. Indeed, only a decade of pressure through the 1920s led to change. The political demands of agricultural populists also had their economic source in the market driven pressure for technological improvements and land consolidation, a pressure that would lead to secular decline of the subsistence farm and a proportional reduction in the number of farm families in Canada. The breakeven operations of the CFLB could do little to offset this structural feature of agricultural development. The strength of the Progressive Party waned following the 1926 federal election but the political punch of the agricultural producers continued. Energized by continual evidence of individual financial disasters, the farmers pressed for a more redistributive agricultural policy.

The Canadian Farm Loan Act was given Royal assent in April 1927 but the creation of the CFLB was delayed. It began operations in January 1929 just a few months before the stock market crash that would drag the Canadian agricultural economy from crisis into depression.[8]

Creation of the Industrial Development Bank

While the Canadian Farm Loan Board emerged in response to a severe economic crisis in agriculture and a political climate strongly influenced by agrarian pressures, the creation of the Industrial Development Bank was, in contrast, the product of government officials working in an environment devoid of direct public pressure and in the anticipation of a post-war economic crisis. The concept of a development bank was generated within government in response to problems anticipated by government. There were no public hearings or special public investigations. A vision of the "problem" and its "solution" emerged from the Department of Finance in Ottawa and the Bank of Canada in Montreal.

In the early 1940s, economic analysts in the Bank of Canada turned their attention to the prospects for the post-war economy and projected a rapid fifty percent increase in the labour force after the war. To absorb this increase would require significant related increases in capital investment and national consumption.[9] The study of potential post-war economic policy was assigned to the interdepartmental Economic Advisory Committee. The Bank of Canada was asked to study the capacity of the private markets to finance the conversion of small and medium-sized industries from war production. The Bank concluded that in the post-war period both new firms and firms seeking to convert their production would have difficulties in finding resources. They would have little collateral to secure needed medium and long-term loans and existing financial institutions were not well-situated to offer such loans even where adequate security did exist. Chartered banks restricted themselves to short-term lending. Insurance, trust and mortgage companies served the housing not the manufacturing sector. The Bank of Canada perceived a gap in the services of the financial industry, a gap that might restrict the conversion and growth of small industry. It was suggested that the gap should be filled through the creation of a special public credit agency.[10]

The government's intention to create a publicly-owned industrial credit institution was announced as part of the broad interventionist program of the Mackenzie King government in 1944. This package represented the first sweep into Canada of Keynesian concepts of social welfare and state-led economic expansionism. The creation of the Industrial Development Bank was thus one specific program among a bundle of programs all fitting into a broad framework of mutually reinforcing economic and social policy. The bundle included, in addition to the creation of the IDB, the creation of the Export Credit Insurance Corporation, the National Housing Act, support for agricultural and fish prices, guarantees for farm improvement loans, family allowance payments and the payment of war veterans gratuities and benefits.[11]

The need for an institution to fill the credit gap between short-term bank lending to business and the long-term, but large scale, activity of the bond and securities markets was broadly accepted by the financial industry. The suggestion that this gap was created by government regulation of the financial industry was not pushed. The new public institution was accepted as fulfilling an important function within the financial industry and one that held little attraction for the private sector.

The parliamentary debate over the creation of the new bank brought forward criticisms grounded upon the anticipation that the bank would be subject to political presure, could not function as an independent financial institution and would inevitably lose money.[12] Dr. W.C. Clark, Deputy Minister of Finance and Graham Towers, Governor of the Bank of Canada, stressed that the IDB would fulfil a market-correcting function, was not intended to do anything but finance economically viable, well-secured projects and was not intended to engage in social redistribution. Its political independence would be assured by its status as a subsidiary of the Bank of Canada operating under the direction of the Governor of the Bank of Canada and not directly under a Minister of the Crown.

Why create a public agency rather than attempt to influence a change in the behaviour of private financial institutions? A loan guarantee program was considered but rejected on the grounds that it might not be sufficiently responsive to the specific needs of diverse small manufacturing businesses. The private sector did not have experience in the type of lending anticipate, and given the variety of circumstances likely to arise under such a program, it would be difficult to assure accountability without detailed familiarity with the clients.[13]   Since the private sector did not have the experience and infrastructure to deliver such a credit program it appeared reasonable to create a new public institution.

It was continuously reiterated that the objective of the IDB was to provide loans to small industries where funds were not available on reasonable terms and conditions from the private sector. The credit gap concept suggested that economically viable firms with adequate security and with the capacity to meet the borrowing costs might still be unable to obtain credit due to inadequacies in the range of services provided by the private sector. The rationale was essentially economic but the notion of 'reasonable terms and conditions' was reminiscent of the farmer's critique of the financial system. For the defenders of the new bank, however, the desire to provide to borrowers credit on 'reasonable terms and conditions' carried no implications about fundamental inadequacies in the private financial industry.

The CFLB and the IDB in Operation

The CFLB operated for thirty years (1929-1959) before it gave way to the Farm Credit Corporation, the IDB for thirty-one years (1944-1975) before being transformed into the Federal Business Development Bank. Although both institutions were intended to function independently, it is not surprising that they were drawn into the ebb and flow of agricultural and industrial policy as it unfolded. Both agencies operated on a "break even" basis. This reflected the implicit willingness of the government to allow them to carry on as independent businesses. The greater their independence, the less they could be used as instruments of short-term policy. Alternate policy instruments were ultimately created to respond to redistributive concerns in both sectors.

CFLB Operations

The central critique levelled at the CFLB quickly became that it was too conservative in its lending practices. It was not an instrument for social redistribution. Loan applications were carefully reviewed, mortgages foreclosed and farms auctioned off when repayment was not made. Moreover, throughout the Depression, the CFLB showed a profit.[14] As the agricultural economy collapsed the CFLB prospered. The federal government responded to the Depression through a variety of other programs including: federally managed international wheat sales, the creation of the Canadian Wheat Board, and attempts to create national marketing programs. In the agricultural finance and credit field, several programs were introduced including guarantees for bank loans to the wheat pools, the Farmers' Creditors Arrangements Act (1934), the Prairie Farm Rehabilitation Act (1935) and the Prairie Farm Assistance Act (1939).[15] These acts created programs to encourage the restructuring of existing mortgages and provide loans for that purpose (FCAA, 1934), to rehabilitate land affected by drought and drifting soil (PFRA, 1935) and to provide indemnities to grain farmers (PFAA, 1939).[16] Only the Farmers' Creditors Arrangement Act was administered by the CFLB. This was a program which continued the pattern of secure lending that had been established by the Board.

From 1929-1959 the CFLB disbursed $191.4 million. Almost fifty percent of this amount was disbursed in its last eight years.[17] During the Depression, war and early post-war years, the CFLB played a small role in long-term agricultural credit. During this period, private institutional lenders left the long-term credit market en masse. In 1932, private institutional lenders held $167 million in outstanding loans but by 1952 this had been reduced to $27.5

million.[18]   The CFLB did not take up the slack. Its activity was surpassed by the individual private lenders who by 1951 were estimated to hold nearly fifty percent of long-term farm credit[19] and by other public programs such as the Veterans' Land Act.   Only in 1956-57 did CFLB disbursements exceed $10 million for the first time. A decade later under the Farm Credit Corporation disbursements would be over $200 million and climbing.[20]

In 1956 the CFLB's last commissioner suggested that the role of the CFLB had been to influence the interest rates charged in the private market:

> To provide moderate and stable mortgage interest rates for farmers across Canada, this Board has always been predicated upon a competitive and self-sustaining operation without the benefit of government subsidies, so that the mortgage interest rates charged to farmers by all mortgagees could properly and fairly be influenced by that charged by this Board.[21]

The suggestion that the CFLB could have influenced private sector mortgage rates, given the volume of loans it was willing to issue, seems quixotic.   The CFLB hardly made a dent in the long-term mortgage market prior to 1952.

Throughout the Depression and war period, the consolidation of farms into larger-sized operations and the introduction of increasingly expensive technology continued.   By the early 1950s, as the devastation of the pre-war period faded somewhat from view a stronger case could be made for interpreting agricultural credit as primarily an issue of agricultural efficiency. This had been the concept that originally justified H.M. Tory's argument for the CFLB's creation. Pressure for increased lending came from several quarters. In 1953 it was observed by G.C. Elliot, the manager of mortgage investments for Great West Life Assurance, a private institutional lender, that without expanded state intervention, mechanization and land consolidation would only proceed at a pace determined by the individual farmer's ability to save.[22]   In 1955 a Saskatchewan Royal Commission noted that the CFLB's lending activities were seriously flawed since they did not help younger farmers just entering agriculture. Its loan limit was too small, and the Board was too conservative in accepting risk.   The Royal Commission recommended that the federal government take another look at the mandate of the CFLB.[23] The Canadian Federation of Agriculture in 1956 observed that only the most successful commercial farmers were likely to receive loans from the Board.[24] In 1957, a supporting study for the Royal Commission on Canada's Economic Prospects repeated the criticism that the CFLB was too cautious and ineffective.[25] Publications aimed at the agricultural community began to carry articles on the problem of agricultural credit. Agricultural policy, including farm credit, emerged as a major election issue in the 1957 and 1958 campaigns. With the landslide victory of the Progressive Conservatives under John Diefenbaker in 1958, a major revamping of agricultural programs was expected.

A resolution to amend the Canadian Farm Loan Act was put to Parliament in the spring of 1959. A new agency would be created with an advisory committee composed largely of farmers; maximum loan limits and available capital would be increased; and higher risk producers would be eligible for loans. Criticism of the new act was limited, but one point of dispute was the rate of interest to be charged by the new agency. The government's original intention had been to leave the rate to be set by the agency, but during committee hearings the government agreed to fix the rate by statute at five percent. The intention had been to see the agency operate on a break-even basis. However, this last minute alteration guaranteed that the Farm Credit Corporation would never see a year pass without net losses. The stage had been set for the evolution of the agricultural credit agency into an agent of income redistribution. After thirty years dedicated to the principle of market correction this was a significant watershed. The politicization of agricultural credit had taken a decisive step.

The creation of the FCC was only one component of a package of expenditure programs directed toward regional development. The Diefenbaker government introduced vocational training, created the Atlantic Development Board, designed a program for the expansion of resource extraction (Roads to Resources) and encouraged rural development under the Agricultural Rural Development Act.[26] The mood was expansive and buoyant. The FCC disbursed more loans in its first four years than the CFLB had over the preceding thirty. Public credit was now flowing rapidly into agriculture and for the first time it was effectively flowing at below market rates.

Despite the increased flow of credit into agriculture, the continuing consolidation and mechanization of agricultural production intensified the concern that farming was dying as a way of life. The subsidization of credit by the FCC probably accelerated this process even though it was perceived as a means to ease the economic pressure on farmers. Subsidized credit did not relieve the income problems of the more marginal producers but did allow some of the more successful farmers to expand more easily. The marginal farmers contracted, found other work, farmed part-time and demanded more relief. The resentment associated with this process could be drawn upon to mobilize political pressure for additional policies to save farms. Nor did the expansion of credit prevent the decline of agriculture as a source of direct employment. Between 1961 and 1971, agricultural employment fell by 167,000.[27] The cheaper credit was a boon to those who could profit from expansion and technical improvements. It was primarily a subsidy to the business-oriented farmer not to the marginal producer. It was thus a perverse social program encouraging to a considerable extent what in fact it was advertised to prevent.

During the late 1960s and early 1970s, the lending activity of the FCC slowed although the absolute volume of lending continued to rise. The chartered banks were in a position to enter the long-term farm mortgage market following the 1967 amendments to the Bank Act which removed the statutory restriction on mortgage lending by chartered banks. This deregulation, combined with the good prices being enjoyed by farmers, made lending in the agricultural sector particularly attractive. The private institutional lenders looked with envy upon the volume of lending in the publicly serviced credit market. The undercurrents of economic crisis that were to open that market up to them were already being felt in the stagflation of the post-OPEC period. The imposition of wage and price controls in 1975 marked the onset of the politics of restraint and another watershed in the political economy of agricultural credit as private institutional credit re-entered the market it had abandoned in the pre-war period.

IDB Operations

Like the CFLB the IDB was repeatedly criticized for its lending practices. Throughout its thirty-one years it never registered a net loss and on its final balance sheet in 1975, it showed a cumulative reserve fund (into which all its profits and allowances for loan losses for each year had been placed) of $37.7 million. The principle of "break-even" banking had been scrupulously maintained. For those who chose to interpret the bank's mandate as involving the encouragement of small business, industrial or regional development, this was a limited virtue. The bank's firm and conservative security requirements were seen to have limited its effectiveness as a development agency.

Criticisms of the lending practices with respect to small business grew through the 1950s. The average size of loans was increasing rapidly, from $40,000 in 1945 to $79,000 in 1955, but the number of loans approved was still small (201 in 1955). The IDB Act enjoined the Bank to lend to 'industrial enterprises' and not exclusively to small businesses. As the average size of loan increased to $113,000 in 1956, the bank's activity was moving toward larger firms. The meaning of 'industrial enterprise' was broadened somewhat in amendments to the IDB Act in 1956 and went some way to increasing the numbers of applicants and reducing the average loan size.

During the election campaigns of 1957 and 1958, the concerns of small business were addressed. The Progressive Conservatives promised a special advisory committee composed of cabinet members and representatives of small business as well as a low interest loan fund for small business. The Liberals countered with promises of special assistance and an extension of the IDB Act to allow lending to retailers.

Prior to 1960, the only new small business lending program came with the establishment of a small business section within the Department of Trade and Commerce. However, following upon their electoral campaign promise, the Conservatives introduced the *Small Business Loans Act* which was given Royal assent. This act guaranteed loans to small business disbursed by chartered banks and would be instrumental in attracting the private financial institutions into longer-term business lending for small firms. In July 1961, amendments to the IDB Act broadened the definition of an industrial enterprise to include industrial, trade or other business "of any kind." Additional new applicants came to the bank and the average loan size fell back to the $45,000 range where it would remain for the rest of the bank's life.

The expansion of IDB lending to retail and other firms activated concerns from a new source. Chartered banks and particularly finance companies complained that the IDB was active in lending that they were willing to perform. They suggested that they were suffering from the unfair competition of a bank which paid no income taxes, had easy access to funds, maintained a lower rate of interest and did not have to show a commercial rate of return.

The problem centered around the IDB's mandate to lend when the private market could not provide reasonable terms and conditions. What after all were reasonable terms and conditions? The private institutional lenders were beginning to fear that reasonable was being defined in reference to IDB's costs. Since the IDB operated with subsidized capital it could always offer lower rates. These complaints marked the beginning of the effort by the financial sector to deny the continued existence of the credit gap that had been the original justification for the creation of the IDB.

Such concerns were presented by the Federated Council of Sales Finance Companies and by several large financial firms to the Porter Commission on Banking in 1961. Public expressions of concern over the threat to free enterprise were heard and the need for a state bank was brought into question. The Porter Commission accepted some of these arguments and suggested that the IDB should keep its interest rates more in line with those of private lenders and seek not to "inhibit" the private sector. As concerns over inflation and unemployment re-emerged in the late 1960s and as questions of industrial and regional development came to dominate the policy agenda, the IDB came under increased scrutiny. Credit gap filling, if it was even recognized as an important function, was still seen as a micro-issue in relation to the overall performance of the Canadian economy. There was no sustained public pressure to change the IDB but the concern over industrial policy and the role of small business was once again moving onto the policy agenda.

The eventual creation of the FBDB in 1974 can be attributed to a series of economic events and pressures only one product of which was the FBDB. As a result of the "Nixon shocks" of 1971 (a 10 per cent surcharge on manufactured goods entering the United States) the federal government was mobilized to examine widely what its "industrial strategy" ought to be. The 1972 industrial strategy statement asserted that the strategy must embrace all sectors of economic activity from resources to services. Thus the service sector, whose escalating contribution to job creation was only beginning to be internalized in the consciousness of industrial policy makers, came to be more officially recognized. The importance of technological change through research and development was also becoming clearer. A Ministry of State for Science and Technology (MOSST) was established in 1972.

It was in the midst of this larger search that several government departments initiated studies of the IDB's activities and in June 1972, the Department of Finance was asked to suggest changes in IDB operations. In December an interdepartmental committee encompassing nine departments and a representative of the IDB was established. In the Speech from the Throne in January 1973, plans for increased aid to small business and improvements to the IDB were announced. It was decided to absorb the IDB into a new crown corporation owned directly by the government and reporting to Parliament through the Minister of Industry, Trade and Commerce. The new crown corporation would take over existing business counselling, management training and consulting activities from other departments as well as continue the lending activities of the IDB.

The emergence of the FBDB, however, was also a product of pressure from a newly formed lobby, the Canadian Federation of Independent Business (CFIB). Composed of thousands of small primarily Canadian businesses, especially in the rapidly growing service sector, the CFIB was openly suspicious of big business (especially the banks) and big government. It was anxious to gain legitimacy and recognition as the main representative of small business. In the early 1970s, well before the effects of the 1967 bank deregulation had worked their way through the economy, the CFIB strongly believed that credit gaps existed for small business and that the big banks and the IDB were still insensitive to the needs of small business.

The bill to create the Federal Business Development Bank was introduced in April 1974 and given Royal assent in December 1974. The initiation of FDBD operations was delayed for almost a full year as the government wrestled with an increasingly unruly economy and suffered internal divisions. The IDB stopped operations and the FBDB began operating in October 1975. Within two weeks Prime Minister Trudeau announced the program of wage and price controls that served for most Canadians as the welcome mat to the new politics of restraint.

The Companies Since 1975: Mandate, Structure and Performance

By the mid-1970s, the two banking Crowns had mandates that exhibited some similarities as well as some unique features forged out of the separate political economies in which each functioned. The FCC's mandate, derived primarily from the *Farm Credit Act* but also from the *Farm Credit Syndicates Act*, is the provision of long term loans and management counselling to enable farmers to establish, develop, and maintain viable farms.[28] Funds are directed to farmers lacking either the equity or the track record normally required by private lenders. Farmers are charged interest rates determined by cost of funds plus a 1.25 percent margin. The FCC is required to maintain an undefined "reasonable" return on capital.

The FBDB's mandate is derived from the *Federal Business Development Act* and enables the company to provide loans or loan guarantees to Canadian business where credit is not otherwise available on reasonable terms.[29] The FBDB is also expected to give particular emphasis to the needs of small business. It must recover its costs in fulfilling its mandate. As a lender of last resort, its interest rates are typically 2 to 4 per cent above the prime rate. The FBDB has also been involved in equity investment and this aspect was given additional emphasis in 1983 when an Investment Banking Division was established. The Bank performs this risk capital catalyst role by full syndication, by underwriting, and by investing jointly with the private sector in small or medium-sized companies with high growth potential.

Organizationally, the two banks are similar in form in that they report to their respective line ministers, Agriculture, and Regional Industrial Expansion (in contrast to their predecessor bodies which reported to the Finance Department) and are governed by a board of directors whose purpose is to shield the bank from undue political interference as well as to guide the bank's overall development. The banks' corporate plans must be approved by three ministers, the line minister, the Minister of Finance, and the President of the Treasury Board. The two banks have advisory committees intended to provide greater regional input in their deliberations.

In other respects, the companies diverge organizationally. While both are small in comparison with most government entities, the FBDB is about four times larger in terms of employees (about 2000 versus 550 for the FCC) but with fewer branch offices (about 80 for the FBDB and 100 for the FCC). In the mid 1980s, the FBDB served about 17,500 customers compared to 78,000 for the FCC. Of special importance is the regional distribution of the offices and of the loans. The offices of the FCC are especially concentrated in Western Canada while the FBDB is focussed in Ontario and Quebec. This regional presence, as we will see later, is of significance in assessing the political support for the two Crowns when they are under attack. The regional distribution of loans will be examined later.

From the early 1970s to the early 1980s, the two firms operated in a fairly stable environment well away from the political limelight. It was basically business as usual with even modest growth. But gradually the debate about their performance took on increased currency and following the 1982 recession the pressures on the two firms became far less subtle and also less consistent. Before assessing this performance we must examine data for the overall pattern of loans, operating efficiency and sources of financing.

Tables 1 and 2 present basic financial statistics for the FBDB and FCC respectively. These data show that financial difficulties for the companies increased in the 1980s after, first, high inflation rates and interest charges and then the 1982 recession. The greater volatility of the agricultural sector is shown by the fact that the FCC also had a period of losses in the mid 1970s and that its escalation of losses in the 1984-87 period was much greater, in part because of falling grain prices.

When one looks at the number of branches and size of staff, as well as the nominal customer base of the two companies, the pattern of instability changes. The FCC has stayed fairly steady in overall size whereas the FBDB has experienced a sharp drop in these indicators, suffering a 30 percent cut in branch offices and a 25 percent reduction in employees.

In the 1980s the FBDB was losing business and/or its clientele in three senses. First, as Table 1 shows, more funding was being carried out under the *Small Business Loans Act*. These funds were allocated through the regular banking system and by 1985 these loans equalled

Table 1
Federal Business Development Bank Selected Financial Statistics 1975-1986

Year	SBLA Loans Out-standing	FBDB Loans[1] Out-standing	Net Income[2] (Loss) $1000	%Loss Rate[3] (Provision for Losses $1000)	No. of Customers[4]	No. of Branches[5] (No. of Staff)	Average Loan Size[6] [8]
1975	160,000	1,171,300	4,470	.007 N/A	27,508	79	N/A
76	211,000	1,275,257	3,700	.005 (5,799)	29,274	80 (1600)	45,343[8]
77	236,000	1,408,382	2,100	.014 (19,932)	31,925	89 (1855)	45,546
78	319,000	1,481,677	1,200	.013 (19,509)	33,224	92 (2062)	48,378
79	447,000	1,638,927	541	.011 (18,440)	35,376	99 (2160)	54,486
80	661,000	2,025,699	(29,310)	.022 (43,737)	39,947	103 (2464)	52,286
81	787,000	2,046,975	(44,809)	.030 (60,955)	38,270	103 (2299)	60,748
82	896,000	1,995,515	(75,622)	.043 (86,457)	35,209	104 (2053)	102,802
83	1,142,000	1,354,921	(81,021)	.049 (91,839)	31,263	104 (1940)	99,091
84	1,420,000	1,626,727	(64,278)	.045 (73,557)	24,741	90 (1685)	148,898
85	1,458,000	1,560,019	(4,695)[7]	.011 (17,052)	20,292	77 (1198)	183,029
86	1,291,000	1,646,695	4,829	.015 (24,041)	17,496	77 (1232)	175,324

Table 1 (cont'd)

Sources:

For SBLA Loans Outstanding
Bank of Canada Review, Statistical Table C8 Chartered Banks:
Quarterly Classification of Non-Mortgage Loans p. S47

For FBDB Loans Outstanding, Net Income, etc.
Annual Reports 1975-86
except - No. of Branches and Employees 1983 and after which were provided through FBDB staff interviews.

Notes:

1. FBDB Loans Oustanding
   From Loans (Receivable) in Assets shown on Balance Sheets. Does not include FBDB's venture capital investments.

2. Net Income (Loss)
   FBDB is exempt from income tax.

3. % Loss Rate equals 'Provision for losses on loans, guarantees *and* venture capital investments' from financial statements divided by FBDB Loans Outstanding in Column 2 of chart above (i.e. Note 1 figures).

4. Includes loan and investment customers although the breakdown in annual reports shows that the majority are loan customers.

5. No. of Branches (No. of Staff)
   No. of Branch and sub-branches and CASE officers – does not include regional offices.

6. Average Loan Size
   Equals amount of loans authorized in a particular year (does not include investments) divided by the number of loans authorized in that year.

7. The 1985 Net Income was actually a small net income of $932,000 but an extraordinary item of $5,027,000 reduced it to a net loss of $4,695,000. The extraordinary item was incurred as a result of organizational realignments and cost reduction measures i.e. staff reductions, write-off of fixed assets, moving costs, costs of carrying surplus space, etc.

8. The figure is for the 6 months ending at March 31, 1976 i.e. 1/2 of a fiscal year. The FBDB started operations on October 2, 1975 when the Act under which it was established was proclaimed in force.

Table 2
Farm Credit Corporation Selected Financial Statistics 1975-1986

Year	FCC Loans Outstanding[1] $1000	Net Income (Loss)[2] $1000	%Loss Rate[3] (Provision for Losses $1000) %	%Loss Rate[3] (Provision for Losses $1000) $1000	No. of Customers[4]	No. of Branches[5] (No. of Staff)		Average Loan Size[6] $
1975	1,695,897	(4,220)	N/A	N/A[9]	70,219	115	640	49,279
76	2,003,687	(3,458)	.005	109	72,088	112	658	64,449
77	2,287,946	(1,618)	.022	512	72,977	108	638	67,510
78	2,593,735	946	.029	740	73,625	108	624	78,995
79	2,867,736	2,616	.051	1,461	73,292	108	626	94,929
80	3,192,006	6,030	.063	2,018	72,563	103	615	110,298
81	3,842,006	7,688	.097	3,725	72,663	103	605	108,587
82	3,847,805	3,461	.226	8,711	74,637	103	585	101,007
83	4,291,462	(24,459)	.740	31,758	77,609	105	626	115,369
84	4,917,100	(53,395)[7]	1.34	65,708	80,112	104	614	135,763
85	4,992,728	(30,178)	.927	46,278	79,270	104	579	116,123
86[8]	5,018,898	(121,406)	2.669	133,972	78,183	105	571	108,413

Table 2 (cont'd)

Sources:

FCC Annual Reports 1974/75 to 1985/86

Notes:

1. FCC Loans Outstanding is 'Amount of Loans Receivable' i.e. principal outstanding on loans to farmers and farm syndicates, and on agreements for sale.

2. Net Income - *before* taxes.

3. % Loss Rate equals 'Provision for Doubtful Accounts' i.e. for Loan Losses divided by Loans Outstanding (Note 1 above figures).

4. No. of Customers. No. of Customers figures in annual reports. Estimate based on 'Total Loans Receivable'. However, this assumes one loan per customer which will be too high because some customers will hold more than one loan. Note also that 'Total Loans Receivable is for *all* FCC loans i.e. FCC Act, Farm Syndicates Act, etc.

5. No. of Branches uses number of district field offices – does not include regional offices.

6. Average Loan Size is average size of loans authorized during each year. Includes Farm Credit Act loans only, it does not include Farm Syndicate Credit Act loans.

7. 1983-84 Loss was $56,714,000 prior to write-off of deferred income taxes by $3,319,000 yielding a $53,395,000 loss. The write-off of deferred taxes was due to a management decision.

8. Figures may be affected by moratorium on FCC foreclosure actions announced on September 17, 1985.

9. 1975% Loss Rate

   Allowance for doubtful accounts (Provision for Losses) was not included in financial statements prior to 1976-77. The 1975-76 figure of 109 appeared in the 1976-77 Annual Report and was approved retroactively.

those of the FBDB. Second, in 1982 and thereafter there is a sharp increase in the average loan size for FBDB loans. This reflects a desire to be more risk averse in the wake of the recession but it simultaneously led to criticism from some pockets of the small business lobby that the FBDB was not serving the very small firms. Other studies show that the FBDB share of all business term loans under $5 million dropped from 11 percent in 1980 to 8 percent in the mid 1980s.[30]

The third aspect of the FBDB's declining clientele concerns activities not revealed in Table 1. These activities are in the spheres of training, information and counselling activities. Space does not allow us to focus on these areas but they collectively represent a dilemma for the company. About one quarter of FBDB staff are engaged in these service roles that often reach very small firms in smaller Canadian centres. This generates a dispersed but quite supportive clientele that filters to MPs in the usual imperceptible ways. At the same time, the value of the service is difficult to quantify. Moreover, among some small businesses engaged themselves in business consulting activity, this aspect of the FBDB's business is often viewed to be taking away business from them. This of course is simply another manifestation of the emergence of the small business service sector of the economy as a whole. The FCC has similar but more indirect service roles. In the agricultural sector, however, such activities are less of a threat to the private service sector, in part due to the lack of private consulting expertise in agricultural matters and in part because of the strong traditions of state-sponsored agricultural research.

Another performance indicator of the two companies is operational efficiency. Table 3 indicates one measure. It compares the ratio of operating expenses to total assets and indicates that the FBDB has a ratio that is three to four times that of the FCC. This spread in itself may simply reflect inherent differences in the nature of the lending and business activity in the two sectors. We must therefore ask, are comparisons with the private sector more meaningful? One study in 1984 compared the efficiency of the FBDB with Roynat and Credit Industriel Desjardin, two firms which were at least partly comparable in terms of their basic business, but still not lenders of last resort.[31] It found that the FBDB's operating costs were three times that of Roynat and also much higher than Credit Industriel Desjardin. The study suggested the need for strong caution on even these measures since the mandates of the firms were not fully comparable.

It is useful to pause at this point to consider some of the inevitable confusion over, or contradictions in, the various performance

Table 3
Operating Expenses for FBDB and FCC as a Proportion of Total Assets 1975-1986
(all figures in $000 or $)

Year	FBDB			FCC		
	Administrative Expense[1]	Total Portfolio Assets[2]	%	Administrative Expense	Total Portfolio Assets	%
1975[4]	N/A	1,170,746	N/A	11,906	1,702,283	0.70
76[5]	17,109	1,277,994	1.34	14,276	2,006,435	0.71
77	39,551	1,417,259	2.79	15,791	2,293,186	0.69
78	49,625	1,493,576	3.32	16,125	2,595,620	0.62
79	52,488	1,631,303	3.22	17,943	2,869,719	0.63
80	63,726	2,001,309	3.18	19,160	3,191,826	0.60
81	66,710	2,046,528	3.26	21,481	3,483,054	0.62
82	71,693	1,957,963	3.66	24,350	3,853,897	0.63
83	74,065	1,907,341	3.88	28,233	4,300,126	0.66
84	68,010	1,615,873	4.21	31,643	4,901,222	0.65
85	54,988[3]	1,566,085	3.51	32,086	4,940,229	0.65
86	50,621	1,594,987	3.17	34,961	5,015,036	0.70

Table 3 (cont'd)

Sources:
Annual Reports of FBDB and FCC (see Financial Statements)

Notes:

1. Is Net Non-Interest Expenses i.e., all expenses except Provision for Losses (Doubtful Accounts). Includes salaries and employee benefits, premises and equipment expenses, and other expenses e.g. travel. For FBDB, the figures are Financial Services - Management Services are not included.

2. Total Assets at year end i.e., March 31.

3. Personnel in the Loans Division was reduced by almost 25%, from 1,233 to 925 in 1985. Over the 5-year period between March 31, 1980 and March 31, 1985, the Bank reduced the staff in its Loans Division from 2159 to 925, a reduction of 57 per cent.

4. As of October 2, 1975.

5. For the six months from inception to March 31, 1976.

indicators discussed above. They can lead to highly selective evaluations by the firm, its critics, and its supporters. For example, whether the company is expected to earn a reasonable return, or is to recover costs, it is still not clear how annual data showing profit or loss should be interpreted. Presumably, given the riskier nature of the lending a longer period of time or a cycle of time should be considered to be fairer than annual periods of assessment. If bad debts increase in tough economic times for the sector this could be an indication of bad management by the company or, conversely, of an appropriate form of behaviour for this kind of bank of last resort. Similarly the operational efficiency comparisons with some private lenders may be ultimately totally misleading because the output or product of the firms are different. Finally, data showing a loss of market share by the firms may simultaneously be either evidence of the success of other policy instruments such as deregulation, or may simply be behaviour that one cannot attribute to the company's management, no matter what they might have done.

A further aspect of performance which is especially revealing of the privatization pressures and of the growing aggregate concerns of the Department of Finance is found in the data on the sources of funds for the two banking Crowns. Table 4 indicates the effects of federal policy to force the two companies to obtain increasingly their funds from private markets. For the FBDB this policy pressure began in 1980 and for the FCC in 1983. In both cases it sharply escalated under the Mulroney Conservatives who saw it as a way of managing the deficit, saving funds, and possibly preparing the companies for partial privatization.

Last but hardly least among the performance indicators for the two firms is the regional distribution of their loans. We have already seen that the distribution of employees is regionally concentrated. The lending activity reinforces these positions, though interestingly, the regional patterns are not aggressively paraded in annual reports. For the FCC in 1985-86, about 63 percent of the loans approved under the Farm Credit Act went to farmers in the three prairie provinces, with Saskatchewan alone accounting for 42 percent of the total loans approved.[32]

Data on the regional distribution of FBDB loans indicate that they were skewed towards Ontario, Quebec and British Columbia with about 30, 25 and 25 percent respectively in the early 1980s but with a small shift away from these percentages and towards poorer regions in the mid 1980s.[33] In broad terms, however, it is still the case that the FCC is a prairie Crown and the FBDB is a central Canadian Crown.

Table 4
Funding of FBDB and FCC by Government of Canada and Private Market 1975-1986
(all figures in thousands of $ and negative figures are in brackets)

Year	FBDB						FCC					
	Government of Canada			Private Market			Government of Canada			Private Market		
	Capital Contributed[1]	Equity Held[2]	Loans[3]	Loans[4] From Capital Markets	Short Term Notes	Total	Capital Contributed	Equity Held	Loans	Loans From Capital Markets	Short Term Notes	Total
1975[8]	79,000	116,740	Nil[9]	Nil	Nil	Nil	N/A	N/A	N/A	Nil	Nil	Nil
76	10,000[7]	130,358	108,000	Nil	Nil	Nil	11,400	74,209	358,000[5]	Nil	Nil	Nil
77	19,000	151,535	396,000	Nil	Nil	Nil	10,700	84,016	350,500[6]	Nil	Nil	Nil
78	14,000	166,656	623,000	Nil	Nil	Nil	11,500	96,507	294,254	Nil	Nil	Nil
79	14,000	181,198	876,000	Nil	30,000	30,000	10,300	109,095	261,279	Nil	Nil	Nil
80	48,000	199,888	1,073,000	230,000	115,000	345,000	11,800	124,151	295,446	Nil	Nil	Nil
81	38,000	193,079	934,000	631,870	63,211	700,081	10,400	138,703	265,436	Nil	Nil	Nil
82	46,000	163,457	763,000	879,280	60,447	939,727	13,148	153,720	335,023	Nil	Nil	Nil
83	125,000	207,436	592,000	909,280	94,443	1,003,723	23,185	163,697	371,263	50,000	5,000	55,000
84	56,600	199,758	420,000	820,968	99,926	920,894	23,900	130,883	354,334	255,599	(5,000)	250,599
85	7,000	202,063	263,000	703,708	318,889	1,022,597	28,400	129,105	(199,825)[10]	167,543	97,333	264,876
86	Nil	206,892	144,000	818,371	365,359	1,183,370	Nil	7,699	(214,368)	273,459	140,164	413,623

Table 4 (cont'd)

Source:

Annual Reports of FBDB and FCC 1975-86.

Notes:

1. Capital Contributed for FBDB or FCC taken from Statement of Changes in Financial Position for each year. For FCC, is pursuant to Section 12 of the Farm Credit Act i.e. is subject to statutory limits which were periodically raised until the early 1980's.

2. Equity Held by Canada for either FBDB or FCC equals Accumulated Capital Contribution *minus* (plus) annual deficit (profit).

3. Loans for FBDB or FCC equals Net Loans received each year i.e., gross amount of loans minus principal repaid and refinanced. Does not include annual repayment of loans from Canada on financial statements.

4. Loans from Capital Markets are long term.

5,6. Gross amount of loans only. Net amount could not be determined from annual reports. However, the annual reports do not indicate any refinancing or repayment.

7. For 6 months only to March 31, 1976. FBDB was formally begun October 2, 1975.

8. As of October 2, 1975.

9. Outstanding debentures issued to and held by the Bank of Canada which were assumed by October 2, 1975 amounted to $1,029,646,470. The debenture was gradually paid off.

10. During 1984-85 and 85-86, FCC was repaying loans in excess of loans received.

While a decade of data supplies a convenient performance package and useful way to see how the companies evolved, it is misleading in that it does not convey the subtleties of pressure on the two companies especially in the context of the conservative critique of government and of public sector management but also of developments that predate the direct emergence of the privatization ethos.

The Conservative Critique and the Privatization Pressures

The emergence of the overall critique is most usefully examined in the context of three sources of pressure: the emergence of professional quasi-bureaucratic criticism; the shifting positions of key interest groups familiar with the two companies; and the views and initiatives of the Mulroney Government.

In the late 1970s and early 1980s, criticism of the two firms began in professional evaluation circles and was first directed at the broad problem of the government's overall lending activities. The Auditor General drew increasing attention to the government's contingent liabilities especially in the light of the increasing use of loan guarantees.[34] The AG was also critical of the manner in which the overall assets and liabilities were accounted for in public financial data. In the 1970s as a whole, the banking Crown corporations enjoyed the fastest rate of asset growth among state-owned companies.

In 1982 the Economic Council of Canada published its study of government credit and credit guarantees to the private sector as a whole.[35] It focussed attention on the efficiency of government intervention as a supplier of credit. In terms of allocative efficiency the Council's argument was that government should only intervene when there are "genuine" gaps in the credit market. With respect to the FBDB and the FCC, the Council portrayed the state of credit markets in the small business and agricultural sectors as one in which few gaps now existed. Much of the reduction in the gap-filling role was attributed to the deregulation of banking following the 1967 Bank Act revisions and the enhanced competition it fostered. The extent of private sector provision of credit to farmers and small business had also expanded because of the relative prosperity of these sectors in the 1970s. For the farm sector, this was especially the case in the early 1970s when the banks moved extensively into short term farm credit.

The Council recognized the need for some social gap-filling role but here too the efficiency theme was paramount. These gaps might include regional pockets or groups such as young farmers but the instruments used should be transparent and tailored to avoid building in hidden subsidies.

This general line of argument found considerable support in the central budgetary agencies in Ottawa and in the Department of Regional Industrial Expansion but it is doubtful that professional-bureaucratic criticism alone would have generated change. The views of some of the main interest groups also changed in the late 1970s and early 1980s. Consider first the views of the small business lobby and of the banks regarding the role of the FBDB.

As pointed out earlier, the Canadian Federation of Independent Business was an active supporter of the FBDB. This was because of the CFIB's view that a credit gap did exist in the early 1970s but also because the CFIB was engaged in an even larger grass roots campaign to have the needs of the small business sector recognized and supported by the federal government. By the early 1980s, the CFIB had succeeded in gaining legitimacy for itself in the corridors of Ottawa. Provincial governments had also responded by establishing programs for small business. Accordingly, the CFIB was now focussing its attention on other aspects of government activity that it believed were harming its members, including the "burden" of government regulation, postal rates and strikes, and tax levels. Meanwhile, the FBDB's role was increasingly questioned by the small business lobby, especially its loan operations. This was because the banks, seeing the growth of the service sector, had begun to serve this sector quite extensively. This was a product of both the banks' business strategy as well as a further unfolding of the effects of deregulation. This did not mean that there were no remaining credit gaps. For example, surveys of small business operators indicated a need for start-up funds for *very* small firms and in *some* regions.

The banks meanwhile were quite happy to continue with the increased penetration of business financing they had secured in the 1970s and early 1980s. Though the Canadian Bankers Association saw the profitable small business sector as theirs to supply with credit, their overall view of both the farm sector and the small business sector was similar. For farmers, they believed that the FCC's activities did not represent unfair competition if it remained the lender of last resort to the more "pre-commercial" farmer.

As for the traditional supporters of the FCC, the "last resort" role of the FCC was seen as an abandonment of the true role of the company set up by the Diefenbaker government. Interest groups such as the Canadian Federation of Agriculture, echoing an earlier populist view, urged in 1985 that the FCC should be returned to its "central role in farm financing with a renewed mandate, government support, and the required resources so that it can serve the credit needs of all farmers who wish to use it".[36]

By the time the Mulroney government took office in 1984, and with the added impetus of a $30 billion deficit, the basic critique of the banking Crowns had congealed. If there were any doubts about how to treat these arms of government finance, they were put to rest by the work of the Nielson Task Force on program review. Two different task force teams reached similar conclusions and suggested policy changes that could pave the way for the full or partial privatization of the two companies.

The Nielson study team that examined the FBDB concluded that, given increased private sector involvement as well as other federal and provincial programs, there was no longer a general need for the federal government to provide loans through the FBDB.[37] It observed that there may be some needs in particular regions but that these could be met by other mechanisms. Its overall preference was to wind up the company and assign its other services to other agencies.

The FCC study team saw that firm somewhat differently. It concluded that some gap-filling role was still viable but that changes should be instituted in preparation for possible privatization.[38] First, it wanted to eliminate any borrowings by the FCC from the Consolidated Revenue Fund and to require that the FCC obtain its funds from private markets. Second, if there were subsidies built in to any programs they should be assigned to a "Canada Account" with full costs borne by the government. Third, the FCC should be required to achieve a reasonable return on funds to reduce losses and eventually to attract future equity capital from the private sector.

The Mulroney government's actions only selectively reflect the spirit and content of the Nielson study team views and of the overall conservative critique portrayed above. Table 3 shows that the most significant action taken was the requirement to obtain funds from the private sector. This policy was begun under the Liberals at the insistence of the Minister of Finance but the Conservatives have followed the policy with conviction rather than reluctance.

The Tories, however, have resisted to date the pressure to windup the FBDB primarily because of pressure from its caucus and especially from Quebec members, the province in which the FBDB is headquartered. It is possible that the FBDB could eventually be dismantled but probably only in the context of the announcement of substitute package of services for small business or incentives for venture and equity capital.

With respect to the FCC, the Mulroney government has not dared even to suggest its privatization. For most of the 1984 to 1988 period, the depressed state of farm prices and the subsidy wars between the United States and the European Common Market countries required more, not less, scarce federal dollars in agriculture, mainly through income stabilization payments. The FCC, moreover, reached a particularly perilous state in its finances when, at the end of its 1986-87 financial year, its liabilities exceeded its assets. During the year it set aside over $200 million to cover loans it feared would never be repaid. This situation meant that it would be difficult to raise funds in the private sector and, as a result, the Minister of Agriculture promised the agricultural community that the government would ensure that the farm community's credit needs would be met.

Conclusions

Three overall conclusions emerge from the six decades of history and corporate evolution covered above. The first conclusion is that over the period the direct public provision of credit has been marginal never amounting to more than a small percentage of the total assets of financial markets. Agricultural credit has, however, been regionally important and often politically controversial. One is tempted to regard both Crowns as social banks but if so this aspect can only be regarded as a mild tilt in their operations. However, the determination of what is a social role is itself not always clear. To the extent that the two banks provided credit to some farmers and small businesses that would not otherwise have obtained it, the banks have served a broad equity role, a form of distributive justice. "Break-even" policies assist this function, even if borrowers are individually charged interest rates above normal market rates. A social role can also be defined purely in regional terms. In this case the FCC was seen as an institution supportive of Western Canada farmers.

The second conclusion is that both companies are products of relatively short bursts of political creation followed by long periods of "business as usual" when they laboured in relative obscurity. In each set of political bursts, the engine of pressure came from a different interplay of private and state led interests. The IDB was more obviously a state-led initiative in the reconstruction era. However, the FBDB emerged partly from pressure exerted by a newly aggressive small business lobby anxious to establish its legitimacy and from an internal governmental effort to devise an industrial strategy which was itself a reaction to the actions of the American government. The CFLB was the product of populist pressure but mediated by professional interests. It took sustained pressure to achieve a policy innovation but only to yield a bank that thereafter became a tiny, very conservative institution. The FCC emerged from a second populist burst brought to fruition by a government headed by a prairie Prime Minister. The FCC became a more expansive entity for a longer period than its predecessor but is now setting into a more restrained existence.

The explanation for these long periods of quite conservative normalcy is also multi-faceted. In part they arise from a form of interest group cooptation. Agrarian interests and the small business lobby are quieted not necessarily just by the existence of the two banks but by the whole array of initiatives taken by the government. Once a new set of programs becomes operational, both the interests and the government turn to other priorities. For the government, this means a wide array of competing priority issues well outside the realm of small business, agricultural or even banking policy. The remaining pockets of the farm lobby or of small business variously defined (e.g., young farmers, or very small firms) for whom there is still a credit gap are either too small to be effective politically or they mobilize in other ways, perhaps at the provincial level.

These periods of burst and then stability cannot be directly attributed to the internal organizational dynamics of the two companies. We have not examined the roles of the companies' leaders nor their boards of directors and thus we must be cautious about this point. We have, however, observed the shift in reporting relationships that occurred when the FCC and FBDB were established. Both reported to a line minister and department which in principle would be more sympathetic to the basic mission of the banks than was the Finance Department to which the earlier corporate versions reported. Finance clearly ran the IDB and the CFLB on a tight leash. But these aspects of accountability were partially external to the companies themselves and thus could not be counted as a purely internally driven pressure. The professional and bureaucratic staff and leadership of the two companies undoubtedly contributed to some internal program development, expansion and refinement over the years. But as fairly marginalized banks and as small players even among the Crown corporation community in Ottawa, it is clearly the case that the key changes in the company at these major moments were externally driven either by the central agencies of the government, key interest groups, international developments, or a combination thereof.

The third conclusion deals with privatization. For the two banks these privatization pressures predate the Mulroney era. The first significant privatization pressure was the 1967 Bank Act revisions which allowed the banks freer rein to compete. In the overall context of the 1970s this reduced the size and nature of the credit gap that the two banks were designed to fill. The second privatization pressure came in the early 1980s when the Finance Department, worried about deficits, insisted that the companies obtain their financing from private markets. The third impetus came from the Mulroney government which practiced this policy to an even greater extent and which contemplated the winding-up of the FBDB.

It is at this point that one must be especially sensitive to the issue of instrument choice. Whether we are assessing the performance of the two companies as normal operating entities or as wholly or partially privatized entities, the interlaced choices of diverse policy instruments must be fully acknowledged even if they cannot be precisely evaluated. Changes on the program side of the policy environment may be made by other departments of the federal government and indeed by other governments. In addition to the two forms of instrument change noted above, bank deregulation and severe spending restraint, there have been others that have affected the banks' performances. These range from the choice of the separate small business loans legislation operated through the regular banks which itself adversely affected the FBDB's market shares in the 1980s, to the massive increases in the mid 1980s of agriculture support payments which in part were a *de facto* substitute for both increased loans or increased foreclosures on farmers threatened by declining grain prices in the world grain subsidy war between the United States and Western Europe.

As to the future political economy of the two banks, two scenarios seem plausible. If general liberalization-privatization continues either under free trade or under financial market deregulation, then a further reduction of credit gaps may occur leading to a smaller role for the FBDB or even to its demise. There may still be a needed role for some of the bank's service activities and for regional pockets of credit gap-filling, in which case a more decentralized provincially delivered scheme may emerge. While similar pressures may be present for the agricultural sector, the FCC is likely to have a continuing role. In part, this is because the farm sector is more volatile and in part it is due to the fact than the farm lobby is arguably stronger and more sympathetic to state support.

The above scenario is one premised on the continued functioning of normal competitive markets and indeed of their expansion. A second scenario is always possible. If through external crises, sharp price declines occur, or, in short, if markets are jarred, then it will not be surprising if a new coalition is formed demanding an expansion of state banking or some politically acceptable alternative to meet the needs of those most adversely affected by the continuing evolution of the Canadian economy.

Notes

1.   The four crowns are the Canada Mortgage and Housing Corporation, the Farm Credit Corporation, the Export Development Corporation and the Federal Business Development Bank. For general comparisons and data see: Economic Council of Canada, *Minding the Public's Business* (Ottawa: Minister of Supply and

Services, 1986), pp. 10-12 and Economic Council of Canada, *Intervention and Efficiency* (Ottawa: Minister of Supply and Services, 1982).

2. Farm Credit Corporation, *The Development of Farm Credit in Canada*, (Ottawa, 1980), p. 4.

3. Canada, Parliament, House of Commons, *Debates*, 1 June 1926, p. 3960 (hereafter cited as *Debates*, date, page).

4. A Parliamentary Committee, chaired by the Minister of Finance, W.S. Fielding. It was struck in 1922 and reported in January 1923.

5. Canada, Parliament, House of Commons, Select Committee on Banking and Commerce, *Minutes of Proceedings and Evidence*, 28 May 1924, p. 250.

6. *Debates*, 1 June 1926, p. 3958.

7. *Debates*, 1 June 1926, p. 3925.

8. Jean E. Brassard, *Financial Assistance for Farmers: A Lawyer's Guide to Federal Programs*, (Toronto: Carswell, 1987), p. 4.

9. R. Clarke, *The IDB: A History of Canada's Industrial Development Bank*, (Toronto: University of Toronto Press, 1985).

10. *Ibid.*, pp. 15-16.

11. *Ibid.*, p. 17.

12. Ibid., pp. 22-23.

13. W.E. Scott, unpublished monograph prepared for the Bank of Canada, cited in Clarke, *The IDB*, p. 16.

14. B. Wilson, *Beyond the Harvest: Canadian Grain at the Crossroads*, (Saskatoon: Western Producer Prairie Books, 1981).

15. E.L. Menzie, "Developments in Canadian Agricultural Policy, 1929-79," *Canadian Farm Economics*, 15 (April 1980), pp. 15-16.

16. Brassard, *Financial Assistance For Farmers*, pp. 45-47; Canada Task Force on Agriculture, *Canadian Agriculture in the Seventies*, (Ottawa: Information Canada, 1969), p. 390.

17. Farm Credit Corporation, *The Development of Farm Credit*, Table 2, p. 173.

18. *Ibid*, p. 77.

19. R.S. Rust, "How Much Farm Credit in Canada," *Economic Analyst*, 33 (February 1963), Table 1, p. 9.

20. Task Force on Agriculture, *Canadian Agriculture in the Seventies*, p. 376.

21. Canada, Parliament, House of Commons, Standing Committee on Banking and Commerce, *Minutes of Proceedings and Evidence*, 6 March 1956, p. 10.

22. Address to the conference "Problems in Farm Credit," Canadian Agricultural Society (1953).

23. Saskatchewan Royal Commission on Agriculture and Rural Life, *Report* (Regina: Queen's Printer, 1955).

24. Canada, Parliament, House of Commons, Standing Committee on Banking and Commerce, *Minutes of Proceedings and Evidence*, 12 April 1956, p. 116.

25. W.M. Drummond and W. MacKenzie, *Progress and Prospects of Canadian Agriculture*, (Ottawa: Queen's Printer, 1957), pp. 113-115.

26. H. Lithwick, "Federal Government Regional Economic Development Policies," in *Disparities and Interregional Adjustment*, ed. by K. Norrie (Toronto: University of Toronto Press, 1986), pp. 118-120.

27. Economic Council, *Intervention and Efficiency*, p. 91.

28. Canada, Farm Credit Corporation, *Annual Report*, 1986.

29. Canada, Federal Business Development Corporation, *Annual Report*, 1986.

30. Study Team Report to the Task Force on Program Review, *Economic Growth - Services and Subsidies to Business*, (Ottawa: March 1985), p. 168.

31. See Donald McFetridge, "The Federal Business Development Bank", (Ottawa: Carleton University Department of Economics, 1984), p. 6.

32. Farm Credit Corporation, *Data Tables*, Table 6 (supplied to authors).

33. Economic Council, *Intervention and Efficiency*, p.39.

34. Canada, Auditor General of Canada, *Report to the House of Commons* (Ottawa: Minister of Supply and Services, 1983), pp. 12-14.

35. Economic Council, *Intervention and Efficiency*.

36. Canadian Federation of Agriculture, "Statement on the Farm Credit Corporation and Farm Credit," Ottawa, October 1985, p. 1.

37. Study Team Report to the Task Force on Program Review, *Economic Growth - Services and Subsidies to Business*, (Ottawa: 1985), pp. 167-184.

38. Study Team Report to the Task Force on Program Review, *Economic Growth - Agriculture*, (Ottawa: 1985), pp. 196-205.

Chapter X

The Provinces and Privatization: Are the Provinces <u>Really</u> Getting Out of Business?

Maureen Appel Molot *

As the *Economist* noted, "*Privatization* — everybody's doing it, differently.[1]" Indeed, privatization is now a catchword of the 1980s, pursued by states around the world anxious for a variety of reasons to restructure their public enterprise sectors. In Britain we see the dramatic sell-off of state-owned assets; by the end of its second term the Thatcher government had dismantled much of the infrastructural and industrial state sector created since World War II and reduced the state share of GDP to about 6.5 per cent from the 10 per cent it held in 1979 when the Thatcher Conservatives were first elected.[2] In Europe, Japan, Africa, Latin America and parts of Asia we see the same phenomenon — not the sweeping sale of state-owned corporations that has occurred and continues in Britain but nonetheless some diminution of state ownership of both competitive industries and monopolies.[3] In Canada, the Mulroney government has implemented its election promise to take the state out of business by selling a number of Crown corporations, including Canadair, Canadian Arsenals, DeHavilland and Teleglobe, as well as some subsidiaries of CN and by dismantling a number of inactive and small companies.

* The research assistance of Mark Chapnick and the critical comments of Jeanne Kirk Laux, June Corman and Allan Tupper are gratefully acknowledged.

Several Canadian provinces have also begun to privatize their commercial holdings, for example, Raffinerie du Sucre de Québec, Pacific Western Airlines (owned by Alberta until 1984), and Ontario's Urban Transportation Development Corporation. In October 1987 the British Columbia government announced a broad privatization package that included both the sale of commercial holdings such as the gas, rail, and research and development divisions of B.C. Hydro and that of government services, for example, bridge and road maintenance and tree nurseries.[4] Saskatchewan, Ontario and Quebec have within the last few years reviewed their public enterprise sectors[5] with a view to reducing the size of the state sector. Given the long history of state intervention in Canada at both levels for public policy purposes and particularly, the extensive post-1960 creation of Crown corporations, what does this provincial reassessment mean? Are the provincial states *really* getting out of business – or are we seeing a rationalization of provincial holdings to facilitate adjustment to the changing fiscal and commercial realities of the late 1980s and beyond?

I will argue that privatization at the provincial level is similar to that federally (with the possible exception of British Columbia about whose program it is too early to make a judgment) and has as its purpose not the dismantling of the state sector but rather its streamlining to ensure the continued viability of commercial state enterprises. The vagaries of Canadian federalism, including provincial state autonomy and the character of regional capital may in fact make it more difficult for provincial governments than for Ottawa to divest. Governments are selling uncompetitive corporations and transforming others into mixed enterprises through the sale of shares. What we are seeing, in other words, is yet another reassessment of the character of the state sector and of the ways in which the state can participate most effectively to attain its ends.

Evolution of the Provincial State Sector

Provincial public enterprises date back to the establishment of Ontario Hydro in 1906. Ontario's example of state ownership of electricity was followed by a number of other provinces including Nova Scotia, New Brunswick, Manitoba and Saskatchewan, and ultimately Quebec. Pressure for better service led to the creation of state-owned telephone companies in the three prairie provinces. But with the exception of Saskatchewan, where the CCF government of Tommy Douglas employed state enterprises as a conscious tool of economic development in the 1940s – thereby anticipating to some degree what would unfold across many provinces some two decades later – provincial state sectors remained small until 1960. In the years following 1960, however, the number of provincial Crown corporations grew rapidly as provincial states turned to direct investment in corporations producing goods and services for the market for purposes of province-building. By the mid-1980s, according to an Economic Council of Canada study, there were some 200 provincially owned or controlled enterprises which in turn owned outright or effectively controlled some 187 subsidiaries.[6] Among these provincial holdings are sixteen which ranked in the Financial Post's 1985 list of Canada's top 500 industrial companies ranked by sales.[7]

Explanations for the Canada-wide phenomenon of province-building have frequently been found in the postwar tensions in Canadian federalism that have amongst their origins regional disparities. Uneven economic development and increasingly active provincial governments generated support among different classes, including provincially based capital in some provinces – Quebec and Alberta among others – and farmers, for direct state participation in the economy.[8] Provincial states, unable to employ macroeconomic policies to promote economic growth and diversification within their borders, utilized more specific interventionist policies, including the creation of public corporations, to accomplish these goals. Governments in Quebec after 1960, regardless of political philosophy, consciously used state authority to promote economic growth and increase Francophone control over the provincial economy. Following the 1963 nationalization of the remaining private power producers in the province, Quebec governments created public enterprises in a number of strategic sectors including finance, pulp and paper, mining, steel, asbestos and oil and gas. In Saskatchewan, the NDP government of Allan Blakeney first elected in 1971 established a number of state-owned companies to increase provincial control over the development of non-renewable resources and to ensure that these were developed for the benefit of Saskatchewan residents. Other provinces also set up public corporations to further broadly defined provincial development goals by underwriting the start-up costs of some industry, or to pursue more specific objectives in particular sectors such as energy – the Ontario Energy Corporation or Nova Scotia Resources Limited for example – or high technology industries (Ontario's IDEA Corporation).

As the economic environment changes, so do the expectations and orientations of the state for its public corporations. Many, if not the majority of provincial Crown corporations, were established in an era of relative economic expansion when governments still adhered in large measure to concepts of Keynesian political economy. Resource prices were generally buoyant and governments were unconcerned with deficits. With changes in global economy brought about by

Privatization, Public Policy and Public Corporations in Canada

ongoing industrial restructuring and the recession of the late 1970s and early 1980s on the one hand and an increasing preoccupation with provincial indebtedness and budget deficits on the other, governments altered their expectations for the state sector. Social purposes were de-emphasized while those of financial performance, ie., the bottom line, were stressed. Government enterprises were often directed to be cognizant of their market environments and to act in a commercial manner.[9] This "commercialization" of public enterprises[10] thus involved a new profit orientation and a keener appreciation of competition both domestically and abroad. Some Crown corporations – the utilities, for example, have successfully diversified their activities and compete in domestic and international markets.[11] Others have been less able to do so for reasons of changing market conditions – the case with many provincially-owned resource corporations which face international conditions of oversupply, decline in demand, and fluctuating prices.[12]

Concomitant with this emphasis on profitability, provincial governments have sought alternative forms of investment to enhance their flexibility in meeting broad development goals. Governments are downgrading the big Crown corporation as an investment vehicle in favour of investment through holding companies and mixed enterprises, whether created by buying into existing corporations or by partial sale of shares in an established state company. Change in the governing party in many provinces since 1982 has also contributed to this ongoing reassessment of the character of the state sector. Thus we are witnessing the evolution of the provincial state sector as provincial governments reconsider their modes of economic intervention. By looking at Quebec, Saskatchewan and Ontario, each of which has an important state sector, we can examine the process of streamlining and rationalizing that is underway to determine both the extent of divestment and its justification.

Quebec

Since 1960, governments in Quebec have used the state as an agent of *rattrapage* (catching up). During its tenure the Parti Québécois government continued to employ both state-owned enterprises and state investment agencies like the Société générale du financement (SGF) and the Caisse de dépôt et placement (Caisse) to promote Quebec-based economic development and enhanced opportunities for Quebecers in industry. Toward the end of its tenure, however, there were signs that the PQ government was beginning to re-examine the size of the state sector in light of the financial requirements that it imposed. In early 1985 Jacques Parizeau, who had then just resigned as Finance Minister from the Levesque cabinet and who had presided over Quebec's entry into the asbestos industry, posed a number of questions about the role of both wholly-owned public enterprises and state capital pools. He suggested that his goverment had made mistakes with respect to some of its unprofitable enterprises – Sidbec (a plant manufacturing pelletized iron) and la Société nationale de l'amiante (asbestos) and that these should be sold or disbanded. Others, which had at one time fulfilled public policy purposes in stimulating development (the Société québecoise d'exploration minière – Soquem) but which had outlived their usefulness should be transferred in whole or in part to the private sector. Parizeau also recognized the enormous impact of SGF and, more importantly, the Caisse within the Quebec economy and the need to consider the future operations of both investment vehicles.[13]

Some restructuring of the state sector occurred under the PQ before its defeat in December 1985.[14] SGF, for example, responded to government pressures to reduce its losses and to generate its own financing for new undertakings by divesting some of its assets, issuing shares in some subsidiaries to the public and negotiating joint ventures.[15] Beset with losses resulting from a declining market for asbestos, SNA, the state asbestos corporation, sought a partnership with one of the remaining private producers in the province with a view to rationalizing its mining and milling operations and removing itself one step from direct participation in the industry.[16] But more significant than the actual streamlining was the change in philosophy revealed by the PQ's spring 1985 budget speech. In the context of budget restraints, the Finance Minister argued that however crucial public enterprises had been for promoting Quebec-based economic development in the past, the size of the state sector and the assets it represented made it essential to reconsider its role. Moreover, although a lack of indigenous entrepreneurship had once made state participation essential, the Quebec economy had matured to the point where private capital could assume more of the initiative. The Minister enumerated four steps the government contemplated to reduce and restructure its holdings: (1) sale of assets provided fair market value was obtained; (2) joint ventures between state-owned and private sector firms; (3) new financing through stock issues in commercially successful state-owned companies; and (4) regrouping the operations of state enterprises undertaking similar activities.[17]

The Liberal party assumed office in December 1985 with a commitment to re-examine the role of the state in the economy. Premier Bourassa immediately appointed a Minister of Privatization, Pierre Fortier, with a mandate to review all provincial state enterprises and to sell the commercial ones unless the public interest could justify continued state ownership. In a statement issued shortly after he assumed his position, the Minister outlined the government's perspective: henceforth the state would act as a "catalyst" to economic growth rather than as an "entrepreneur" in competition with the private sector. Privatization was not "an end in itself but a means to help reduce the deficit and to give Crown corporations new life, through private capital and by forcing them to play by the rules of international competition."[18] To seek advice on this task and assistance in designating which commercial enterprises and their subsidiaries should be sold, the government established an Advisory Committee on privatization (comprising prominent Quebec businessmen) which reported in June 1986.

The recommendations of the Advisory Committee were clear — the ten strategic enterprises[19] established between 1962 and 1985 and their subsidiaries which pursue economic development activities and which operate in competition with private capital should be privatized. The rationale for this recommendation differed little from that advanced by the PQ in its last budget: although these strategic enterprises had been created by the state to compensate for weaknesses in the Quebec political economy, these weaknesses no longer existed; Francophone capital had developed to the point where it could take the lead in Quebec's economic development. Moreover, the Committee noted, many of these state enterprises functioned in industries which were not at the leading edge of economic change. The Committee also strongly suggested that the status of Quebec's public monopolies, including Hydro-Quebec, be re-examined, with a view to revising their statutes to allow for competition.[20]

The Bourassa government did not wait for the report of the Advisory Committee to implement its divestment agenda. In March 1986 it sold its money losing sugar refinery, Raffinerie de Sucre du Québec, to a competitor (for $48.5 million of which $10 million was cash) which then closed it. This was followed by the sale of Québecair for $21 million of which $10 million was to be profit, (but which, when the true state of the airline's finances were known, was only $5 million), and of Soquia's (Société Québécoise d'Initiatives Agro-Alimentaires — the state agro-food enterprise) six percent interest in Provigo.[21] Two small subsidiaries (each with less than 50 employees) of the state-owned asbestos company, SNA, were transferred to the private sector in July 1986 as part of SNA's ongoing rationalization.[22] Finally during 1986, the government regrouped the profitable operations of its mining company, Soquem, into a new company Cambior, which issued two-thirds of its shares to the public. This enabled Soquem, still state-owned, to pay off its debts and retain an interest in the very attractive Cambior holdings.[23]

In early 1987 SGF sold its stake in the forest products company, Donohue for some $320 million and Madelipêche Inc, a fish processing plant for approximately $2 milliion.[24] In August 1987 Quebec's oil and gas corporation, Soquip, agreed to sell its Alberta subsidiary (Soquip Alberta Inc.) to Sceptre Resources Inc. for $227 million; as a result of the transaction Soquip will hold 22 per cent of Sceptre's shares.[25] In April 1988, after three years of intermittent efforts to sell Seleine Mines Inc., the salt-mining subsidiary of Soquem, the Quebec government announced its sale to Canadian Salt Co. Ltd. for $35 million. Though this price is less than one-third of the slightly over $125 million the Quebec government invested in the mine between 1979 and 1983, the year it commenced production, the sale relieves the goverment of an unprofitable venture created by the PQ government to generate employment in Îles-des-Madeleines.[26]

In March 1987, some thirteen months after he assumed his portfolio, the Minister of Privatization was ecstatic over his accomplishments.[27] While undoubtedly there have been some sales, in fact, when compared to those remaining in state hands the size of state assets sold to the private sector is quite small. Not only does Quebec rank first amongst Canadian provinces with respect to state enterprise assets[28], as Table 1 illustrates, the state sector remains large despite the privatizations. Moreover, at the same time as Quebec sold all or part of its stake in some corporations, it was acquiring or enhancing its position in others.

Shortly after the sale of Donohue to a Quebec-based company, it was announced that Donohue and the Quebec government, through its state forestry agency, Rexfor, would join forces to construct a paper mill in a depressed part of the province.[29] Although actual construction of the joint venture may depend on federal financial assistance, the publication of the agreement between the parties illustrates the continued willingness of the state to invest in production. While SGF was negotiating its Donohue divestment, another SGF subsidiary, Marine Industries Inc. (in which SGF holds 65 percent) concluded a long discussed arrangement to take over Versatile Davie Ltd., thereby protecting Quebec jobs and creating Canada's largest shipbuilding conglomerate.[30] Quebec's agency which has financially assisted capital to develop technology, La Société de développement industriel, was converted from a grant-giving to a lending institution with the option of acquiring shares in recipient companies.[31] Quebec capital may have matured but a role for the state as a lender remains. Hydro-Québec, the largest Crown corporation in the province, continues to grow by expanding its international activities: Hydro has been an active participant in a Canadian consortium seeking contracts in China and early in 1987 it concluded a joint venture agreement with a Maine utility company to form a transmission company to facilitate power exports to the United States.[32] Soquip formed a consortium with Quebec and non Quebec-

Table 1
Assets of Quebec State Sector
(Commercial enterprises only)
as at March 31, 1986 (in thousands of dollars)

Enterprise	Assets
Hydro-Québec	29,183,000
Caisse de dépôt	22,543,379
Société générale de financement	1,399,022
Sidbec	524,789
Société québécoise de d'iniatives pétrolières*	419,739
Société québécoise d'exploration minière*	201,406
Société nationale de l'amiante*	160,256
Société de récupération, d'exploration et de développement forestier	158,282
Société québécoise de transports*	148,150
Raffinerie du sucre#*	81,473
Société québécoise d'iniatives agro-alimentaires	51,126
Madelipêche*	26,135
Sepaq	30,323

*   Sold in whole or in part
\#   Value in 1983

Source: Report of the Committee on the Privatization of Crown
           Corporations, *From the Quiet Revolution...*, p. 20;
           Economic Council of Canada, *Minding the Public's
           Business*, p. 160; and Jeanne Kirk Laux and Maureen
           Appel Molot, *Report on the Control and Accountability of
           Government-Owned Corporations in Selected Provinces in
           Canada* (Prepared for the President of the Treasury
           Board), February 1984, pp. 70-71.

based firms to distribute natural gas in Montreal[33], Cambior developed and pursued a strategy to improve its position in gold mining, milling and marketing[34], and the Caisse continues to diversify its portfolio.[35] In April 1988 the Quebec government announced that it would retain its shares (28 per cent) in the paper company Domtar held through SGF's subsidiary, Dofor Inc. Offered for sale at the same time as Donohue the possible sale of the government's interest in Domtar generated considerable speculation about possible purchasers, but after two years on the market it was clear no one was prepared to pay the asking price. The Quebec government thus decided to take the profitable company off the auction block.[36]

Thus the Quebec divestment record is mixed — some sales and a contribution to provincial deficit reduction, but at the same time an expansion of the activities of the remaining state companies. With the blush of first success now past, the high profile sale of state assets has assumed a lower priority for the government. According to the Minister of Privatization, "the money-losers have been sold" and there's no rush to sell more companies. "We're still committed to the program."[37] Improved provincial economic conditions in 1987 made the need for the proceeds from privatization to meet budgetary constraints less urgent.

The government has discovered, moreover, that privatization may be more difficult than expected, with unanticipated problems. The Bourassa government's decision to halt the sale of Société des Alcools du Québec (SAQ) stores brought lawsuits against the state from those who had submitted bids for the stores.[38] The sale of Québecair only generated half the anticipated profit and also has resulted in job losses heavier than predicted and in a deterioration in service. Worries persist that the transfer of Madelipêche Inc. will reduce jobs in the fishing industry with a negative impact on the economy of the Isles-de-la-Madeleine.[39] In its efforts to sell its holdings in Culinair (held through the Société québécoise d'initiatives agro-alimentaires) the Quebec government discovered the problems of being a minority shareholder; sale of state shares in this instance was dependent on the stance of the controlling shareholder, in this case one opposed to a takeover bid.[40]

Although the Privatization Minister suggested that close to 50 per cent of Quebecers "support the initiatives we have already taken"[41], there is considerable opposition to divestment from labour as well as from regional interests in the province. Job loss resulting from privatization is thus a politically sensitive question. Whether private capital in Quebec has the wherewithal or the interest to purchase what the government would like to sell is uncertain, particularly given the size of some of the assets, yet the sale of state assets to buyers outside the province might well be as unacceptable to the business elite as it would be to labour. In sum, although the Quebec state might suggest that it wants to "get out of business", for political and economic reasons it will find this difficult to accomplish. We will continue to see a rationalization of state holdings, some additional sales, and the ongoing search for flexible investment tools but privatization is already less central to the Bourassa government's priorities than it was immediately after its return to power.

Saskatchewan

Under CCF-NDP governments, the state sector in Saskatchewan was a conscious economic development tool. During its terms, the Blakeney government created a number of state-owned enterprises, particularly in the resource sector (Potash Corporation of Saskatchewan [PCS], Saskatchewan Mining Development Corporation [SMDC], Saskatchewan Oil and Gas Corporation [Saskoil]), to increase provincial control over resources and to reduce dependence on multinational corporations. To ensure that state corporations fulfilled public policy purposes, cabinet ministers sat as chairmen of Crown corporations' boards of directors. In relation to the size of the provincial economy, state-owned and controlled corporations were and are more significant economically in Saskatchewan than elsewhere in Canada.[42]

The 1982 election victory of the Progressive Conservatives (PC) under Grant Devine brought to power a government determined to reduce the size of, and to depoliticize, the state sector. Indeed, an attack on what was viewed as a large and publicly unresponsive state enterprise sector was a central theme in the Conservatives' campaign. At the same time, the new government recognized the limitations of an agriculture and resource-based provincial economy without large indigenous pools of capital and thus the need to retain some state participation to protect provincial interests. Moreover, in the eyes of Saskatchewan residents, Crown corporations, most notably the public utilities, fulfilled a need private capital was not prepared to play in providing essential services. Therefore, the sale of state assets would have to proceed cautiously. It would not include divestment to eastern capital; rather the government looked to "public participation" in the state sector, instead of privatization.[43]

To launch the examination of the state sector, the government established the Crown Investments Review Commission (known as the Wolff Commission) with a mandate to assess all government holdings and their manner of financing and control. This Commission concluded that the objectives of state-owned enterprises were inadequately defined, that political control rather than corporate autonomy was emphasized, and that these enterprises provided an insufficient return to the state on investment. Among its recommendations were the replacement of ministers as chairmen of enterprise boards of directors by private sector nominees and the restructuring of the state-enterprise holding company (renamed the Crown Management Board from the Crown Investment Corporation) to include amongst its directors persons other than ministers. The state-enterprise holding company was to take "as its central objective the maximization of dividend payments to the province." Moreover, each commercial Crown should "pay grants to the province equal to taxes on income paid by similar businesses in the private sector."[44]

Like Quebec the Saskatchewan government moved quickly to rein in the state sector. Two low profile state enterprises, the Saskatchewan Fur Marketing Service and Saskatchewan Media, were eliminated. The Potash Corporation was directed to disband an offshore marketing subsidiary and to rejoin the offshore marketing cooperative in which it had participated with the private sector; moreover, PCS's plans to build a new mine were terminated. Saskatchewan Telecommunications lost its monopoly on telephone equipment and was instructed to stop the sale of office equipment. Saskatchewan Mining Development Corporation lost the right to automatic participation in any new uranium development in the province and Saskatchewan Government Insurance was told it could not expand into life insurance and auto body shops.[45] The government also sold its share of a meat packing company to the private sector.[46] In short, in its first eighteen months in office, the Devine government privatized some holdings, admittedly small ones, and ordered others to shelve plans for either expansion or diversification. The state sector declined in terms of numbers of enterprises but not really in size since the value of their assets continued to appreciate.

In March 1986, the government sold its pulp company to the subsidiary of a US forest company; as part of the deal, the new owner of Prince Albert Pulp Co., Weyerhauser Canada Ltd., promised to construct a new integrated paper mill in Prince Albert. The financial arrangements of the deal were complex and did not include any direct payment—critical to a government with as severe a deficit as Saskatchewan.[47] The PCs also created two new Crown corporations in 1986, one to manage government lands and buildings, the other, the Agriculture and Commercial Equity Corporation (which was modeled on the Alberta Energy Company) to invest in agribusiness projects in the province.[48]

What was crucial for the Devine government was the need to ease its debt. Faced with the first budget deficit in twenty years, the government used the state sector to generate some much needed cash.

Although Saskatchewan's Crown corporations collectively lost $125 million in 1982, the state holding company paid the government a $42 million dividend.[49]   Declining prices for resources, which in turn produced large losses for a number of major state-owned ventures, meant that the Crown Management Board has incurred operating losses annually since 1982, with the exception of 1984.   It paid the government a dividend again only in 1985.[50]

By 1984 the Conservative government had formulated a new strategy for its state enterprises which reflected the realities of the Saskatchewan political economy — a recession which had its origins internationally but which translated into depressed prices for natural resources and wheat, high interest rates, and budgetary constraints on the one hand, and continuing popular support for Crown corporations on the other.   The strategy was to encourage public participation — to sell different types of securities in major state enterprises to the public thereby raising much needed monies for the government and enhancing political accountability and control. Through this approach, a combination of pragmatism and populism, the Tories hoped to create "an equity mentality" in a population not given to equity purchases by allowing people to invest their money in the province.[51]   As the Premier explained it, "We have the largest savings per capita in the world.   Why should I go to New York and borrow $200 million at U.S. rates and pay them interest when I can do it from my own folks?"[52]

Since mid-1984 the government has sold three Saskatchewan-only bond issues, two for Saskatchewan Power and one for Saskoil. Although the sales period for the first bond issues had to be extended to raise the required amount ($61 million), subsequent issues were oversubscribed; a target of $65 million for the second Sask Power bond realized $91 million.   In the words of Grant Devine, the people "just love it.   They are actually cashing Canada Savings Bonds to buy Saskatchewan."[53]   The Tories introduced a second mode of popular participation in state enterprises in late 1985 when shares of Saskoil went on the market.   The heavily publicized sale of linked common and convertible preferred shares brought in $110 million and altered the status of Saskoil from a wholly state-owned company to a mixed enterprise in which the state held 58 per cent of the voting shares.[54]   A second Saskoil common share offering of $50 million in 1987 reduced the government's stake in the oil company to 47 per cent of the voting shares.[55]

Thus we see in Saskatchewan that a government which entered office committed to reducing the state sector has done so to some degree.   Table 2 illustrates the size of the province's assets.

Table 2
Assets of Saskatchewan State Sector
(Commercial enterprises only)
at end of 1983 (in thousands of dollars)

Enterprise	Assets
Agdevco	2,158
Potash Corporation of Saskatchewan	1,161,550
Prince Albert Pulp#*	
Sask Computer Utility Corp.	7,267
Sask Forest Products Corp.	29,746
Sask Grain Car Corp.	54,916
Sask Govt. Insurance	366,611
Saskatchewan Minerals	19,809
Saskatchewan Mining Development Corporation**	812,985
Saskoil*	214,883
Sask Power	2,355,976
Sask Telecommunications	873,453
Sask Transporation Co.	12,624
Sask Water Supply Board	13,360
Saskatchewan Economic Development Corporation	162,354

\#   Wholly owned subsidiary of Crown Management Board with no financial statement available.

*   Sold in whole or in part

**   To be combined with Eldorado Nuclear to form a new company effective July 1, 1988.

Source: Adapted from Economic Council of Canada, *Minding The Public's Business*, p. 162 and Laux and Molot, *Report on the Control....*, pp. 67-68.

The Conservatives, now in their second term, remain intent on encouraging "private investment in Saskatchewan while simultaneously reducing government involvement in the business sector." No longer can the government afford to be the "exclusive owner" of cyclical commodity based resource industries but must seek alternative forms of risk sharing.[56] Contributing to the pressure to divest is the climbing budget deficit (at $3 billion in early 1988) which presents its own political strictures.

To implement this strategy the government created a new portfolio of Public Participation in early 1988. Nonetheless, there is recognition of the limitations of a regionally-based political economy without large pools of local capital in which there is continuing support for the provision of essential services by government owned corporations. Herein lies the justification for public participation, a theme emphasized by Premier Devine as he explained the establishment of the new department "that will be quite powerful". According to the Premier, the department "will be given the responsibility to allow us in Saskatchewan to participate in government and to facilitate the public being involved. That is, owning shares or being part of government operations financially."[57] The first move in this direction since the change in status of Saskoil came at the end of February 1988 when the Saskatchewan and federal governments announced the merger of the Saskatchewan Mining Development Corporation and Eldorado Nuclear. Saskatchewan will own 61.5 per cent and Ottawa 34.5 per cent of the new company, which will be one of the world's largest uranium producers. The company will gradually be privatized through a series of public share offerings, the first of which will be in two years when market conditions in the uranium industry are expected to improve.[58] Cited as other potential candidates for sale are the general insurance division of Saskatchewan Government Insurance, Saskatchewan Minerals, Saskatchewan Forests Products Corp. and Saskatchewan Government Printing. To privatize these enterprises the government is considering a number of options including public share offerings, sales of assets to employees and contracting out of services.[59]

What is most interesting about the Saskatchewan case is the modality of divestment through public participation. In other provinces the sale of state assets has been to the private sector. Prior to the October 1986 provincial election the Conservatives' privatization program had lost its momentum. As the PCs first Finance Minister and minister responsible for privatization, Bob Andrew, commented, "Privatization is yesterday's theory .... It doesn't make sense for one government to build these things and for the next one to come and sell it all off."[60] However, in the first eighteen months of its second term the Devine government, driven as much by the provincial debt as by philosophy, reinvigorated its commitment to reducing the size of the state-owned sector. At the same time, like its NDP predecessor, the PC government sees the advantage to the province of having large enterprises headquartered there. Reflecting this philosophy, Saskoil was encouraged to diversify its activities into Alberta[61] and the headquarters of the new venture created by the merger of the Saskatchewan Mining Development Corporation and Eldorado Nuclear will be in Saskatoon. Moreover, despite Premier Devine's stance on private investment, Saskatchewan favoured a slower approach on the divestment of the new uranium company than did the federal government.[62] Whatever additional restructuring and divestment occur in Saskatchewan two things are clear: the state sector will remain a significant component of the provincial economy and Saskatchewan residents will have additional opportunities to invest directly in it.

Ontario

The history of state intervention in Ontario is different from that of the other two provinces examined in this chapter. Although the creation of Ontario Hydro in 1906 stands as a landmark, the province has few high profile commercial Crown corporations. Moreover, state enterprises have never been viewed by Ontario governments as an important public policy tool. Nevertheless, the Conservative government, in power from 1943 to 1985, did establish a few state-owned enterprises to participate with private capital in the development of either energy or high technology sectors. These were the Urban Transportation Development Corporation (UTDC) set up in 1973 to develop and market new public transportation technology, the Ontario Energy Corporation (OEC) created in 1975 to promote secure sources of energy for Ontario industry and the Innovation Development for Employment Advancement (IDEA) Corporation, established in 1981 to encourage technological innovation. The current Liberal government, critical while in opposition of these enterprises and a government owned tourist facility (Minaki Lodge), moved to divest once it came to power.

Like the new governments in the other two provinces discussed in this chapter, the Peterson Liberals appointed a team to examine the province's public enterprises.[63] In contrast to Saskatchewan and Quebec, the Ontario review was conducted by a small group of bureaucrats who worked closely with senior officials of the province's Management Board. No public document was produced; rather, the group reported directly to the Premier. Following the attitude of Premier Peterson on privatization, the approach was pragmatic, balancing political versus philosophical needs. Privatization was not

to be undertaken only to increase revenue to the provincial treasury
but to ensure that activities better performed by the private sector
were returned there and to stop the hemorrhage of public monies to
some Crown corporations.[64]

The Special Advisory Group examined twelve Ontario public
enterprises and recommended the sale of several of them, including
the four mentioned above. Some, such as the Ontario Stockyards
Board and Ontario International Corporation, were brought under
closer government control. Others, such as the Ontario Northland
Telecommunications Corporation, in which there was some private
sector interest, were not sold because divestment would have entailed
costs to state enterprises – in this case Ontario Northland Transportation Commission which needed its subsidiary's revenue – that served
public policy purposes.[65]

Although the concept of providing venture capital to stimulate
the development of high technology in Ontario was, in the words of the
responsible minister, "valid, the IDEA Corporation has proved to be
an inappropriate vehicle"[66] and the Corporation ceased operations on
June 30, 1986. Ontario did not get out of assistance to industry
completely since IDEA's portfolio of investments was turned over to
another Crown corporation, the Ontario Development Corporation
and some of the preventure capital activities of IDEA were to be
continued through the Ministry of Industry, Trade and Technology.
The Ontario Energy Corporation, which had become a significant
player in both the search for new energy sources and energy-related
technology, began to wind down its activities in late 1985 at
government direction. Some of its investments in joint ventures were
sold to the private sector and no new investments were made.[67] Total
privatization of OEC was impossible, however, because of the
province's 25 per cent ownership of Suncor (purchased in 1981 to give
the province a window on the petroleum industry). Ironically, the
very individual who advised the Premier on privatization discussed a
possible Ontario purchase of majority control in Suncor.[68] This did
not materialize, nor did the sale of Ontario's investment in Suncor.
Given the uncertainties of the oil and gas industry, the government
decided to retain its Suncor shares until the market improves;
therefore Ontario's energy enterprise continues to function, primarily
through OEC's participation in two joint ventures. UTDC was sold to
Lavalin Inc. in 1986 in a controversial sale which the government
justified in terms of preventing further losses. Not only did Ontario
assist Lavalin to finance the purchase, but it also retained
responsibility for completing outstanding contracts which were
expected to result in losses. The province has not divested completely
but has kept a 15 per cent interest in the new UTDC and a 25 per cent
share in future pre-tax profits.[69] Because it was such a money loser,

Minaki Lodge was difficult to sell, but the province eventually struck a deal with the Four Seasons chain to take the lodge. The sale made no money but the government did relieve itself of an extremely costly venture.

In sum, Ontario has privatized some assets and, in so doing, has ended its obligation to pour money into unprofitable enterprises. Nonetheless, the size of the state sector has not been dramatically reduced because the enterprises sold were not large and because the largest Ontario public enterprise, Ontario Hydro, continues to grow.

In some instances the state did not divest completely because circumstances — the situation of the oil industry or the needs of a buyer — made total privatization unfeasible. Privatization in Ontario was far less visible as a political issue than in either Quebec or Saskatchewan — or than it will be in British Columbia — because the province's enterprises have generally been low profile and have not played a central role in the Ontario economy. With the divestment of some controversial state holdings the topic has disappeared from the government's agenda.

Conclusion

New governments in the three provinces examined came to office determined to reduce the size of their state sectors and all three did so to some degree by terminating unprofitable or inactive enterprises or by selling holdings. In Quebec and Saskatchewan the economic significance of the public sector was, and continues to be, far greater than in Ontario. Not surprisingly the debate in these two juris-dictions over privatization was more heated. In both provinces the government argued that direct state intervention both strained public finances and acted as a damper on private investment. In Saskatchewan in particular the sale of state assets was seen as a means to reduce a politically embarrassing provincial deficit. The debate over privatization in British Columbia is just beginning as that government gears up to reduce the size of the state sector. Given the philosophy of the Vander Zalm administration, we might well witness a Thatcher-style sell off of state assets.

The experience of three provinces in their efforts to "get the state out of business" suggests that the divestment process is more complicated than generally assumed or anticipated. After the initial sale of some assets to make good on electoral promises, the process slows down. Privatization, despite its rhetorical appeal, has limits. These include the economic realities of resource-based provincial economies, the relatively fewer number of economic levers available to provincial governments than to Ottawa which has resulted in their

Table 3
Assets of Ontario State Sector
(Commercial enterprises only)
at end of 1983 (in thousands of dollars)

Enterprise	Assets
Algonquin Forestry Authority	1,543
Eastern Ontario Development Corp.	78,120
IDEA Corporation*	40,884
Metro Toronto Convention Centre Corporation	10,362
Minaki Lodge Resort Limited*	------
Niagara Parks Commission	40,446
Northern Ontario Development Corp.	65,063
Ont. Centre for Advanced Management	8,070
Ont. Centre for Automotive Parts Technology	989
Ont. Centre for Farm Machinery and Food Processing Technology	1,302
Ont. Centre for Microelectronics	2,096
Ont. Centre for Resource Machinery Technology	2,153
Ontario Dvlpmt Corporation	196,855
Ontario Energy Corporation*	702,729
Ontario Food Terminal Board	8,289
Ontario Hydro	23,193,894
Ontario Northland Transportation Commission	190,197
Ontario Stockyards Board	1,332
Ontario Waste Management Corporation	1,564
Urban Transportation Development Corporation*	156,094

* Sold in whole or in part

Source: Adapted from Economic Council of Canada, *Minding The Public's Business*, p. 161 and Laux and Molot, *Report on the Control.....*, pp. 68-70.

greater reliance on more direct instruments of intervention[70], continuing public support for Crown corporations, the number of enterprises realistically available for privatization[71] — i.e., which are financially attractive and in sectors which are vibrant — and the problems of finding interested (and appropriate) buyers.

Economic, historical and practical political reasons intruded into the privatization calculus in all three provinces and resulted in decisions not to divest or to do so only partially. Some enterprises of which the state was once the sole owner became joint or mixed as shares were sold either to private capital or to the public. Rationalization of holdings and concerns about profitability became increasingly important. Privatization may have been seen as a means to defray growing provincial government deficits, but with a couple of exceptions (SGF's sale of Donohue and Saskoil's sale of shares), the returns to the provincial treasury were small; rather monies gained through divestments or the sale of corporate bonds went to pay off enteprise debts. Of the three provinces discussed in this chapter, only in Saskatchewan is privatization still high on the political agenda, a function of a renewed government mandate, political philosophy and fiscal necessity. Acknowledgement of the limits of privatization has promoted an interesting approach to divestment, that of public participation, which allows the state to relinquish its position as sole owner of some enterprises and thereby raise much needed revenue, yet retains the state as major shareholder.

Given the economic and political realities of the late 1980s, pressures for reducing the size of the state will continue in some provinces, most notably those in which parties adhere to diametrically opposed views of the appropriate role of the state in the economy and in which the government has made divestment an important part of its political rhetoric. Arguably there is no reason for the state to own commercial enterprises. Nonetheless, the very fact that at the same time as divestment was on the agenda, we saw the opposite process occurring — growth of the state sector through the continued expansion of the activities of existing enterprises or the creation of new ones — illustrates the difficulty provincial governments have in surrendering Crown corporations as a public policy tool.[72] The state enterprise is too important to all provincial governments for the provinces to get out of business entirely. What the provinces are trying to do in an era of fiscal restraint is to be more businesslike.

Notes

1.   *Economist* (21 December 1985), p. 71.

2.   *Ibid.*, p. 85.

3.   In France, the state has privatized a variety of its enterprises including banks and manufacturing companies, West Germany has reduced its ownership of the state holding company, VEBA, and the socialist government of Spain ordered its holding company INI to divest itself of industries which could not survive in international competition. Japan has sold part of its take in the telephone monopoloy NTT and governments in Malaysia and the Philippines are looking to reduce the size of the state sector. The same is true in Ghana, Nigeria, Senegal, Tanzania, Mexico and Brazil, among other countries.

4.   "B.C. to sell $3 billion in assets, Vander Zalm says," *Globe and Mail* (24 October 1987), p. A4. For a description of previous B.C. government privatizations (under former premier, William Bennett in the late 1970s), see J.W. Langford and N. Swainson, "Public and Quasi-Public Corporations in British Columbia" in *The Administrative State in Canada*, ed. by O.P. Dwivedi (Toronto: University of Toronto Press, 1982), pp.63-88.

5.   Crown Investments Review Commission, *Report to the Government of Saskatchewan*, December 1982; Quebec, Minister Responsible for Privatization, *Privatisation de Sociétés D'État: Orientations et Perspectives*, February 1986 and Report of the Committee on the Privatization of Crown Corporations, *From the Quiet Revolution . . . To the Twenty-First Century*, June 1986. The Ontario report was never made public.

6.   Economic Council of Canada, *Minding the Public's Business* (Ottawa: Minister of Supply and Services Canada, 1986), Table 2-1, p. 7.

7.   *Financial Post 500* (Summer 1985). The editors note that two other provincial state enterprises qualified to be on the list — Alberta Government Telephones Ltd. and Potash Corporation of Saskatchewan — but late submission of data prevented their inclusion.

8.   See Jorge Niosi, *Canadian Capitalism* (Toronto: James Lorimer and Co., 1981), pp. 94-96 and John Richards and Larry Pratt,

Prairie Capitalism: Power and Influence in the New West (Toronto: McClelland and Stewart, 1979).

9.   For example, the Ontario government's Memorandum of Understanding with its Urban Transportation Development Corporation stated that "the Corporation shall operate in a totally commercial manner...." Memorandum of Understanding Between the Minister of Transportation and Communications and the Urban Transportation Development Corporation, 12 June 1979, article III.1.

10. Jeanne Kirk Laux and Maureen Appel Molot, *State Capitalism: Public Enterprise in Canada* (Ithaca: Cornell University Press, 1987), passim but particularly chapter 3.

11. For example a number of provincial hydro companies compete with each other for sales in the US market; Hydro-Quebec and B.C. Hydro, to name but two, have moved into the international consultancy market as has Alberta Government Telephones.

12. Companies such as Potash Corporation of Saskatchewan, Quebec's Société nationale de l'aminante (asbestos) and some of the provincially-owned oil and gas companies have all been affected by fluctuating prices and demand and have been forced to adjust their operations by reducing staff, internal reorganizations and termination of some activities. In addition to the examples discussed below see the chapter in this volume on the Potash Corporation of Saskatchewan.

13. Jacques Parizeau, "Public Enterprises: The Quebec Experience" in *Papers on Privatization,* ed. by W.T.Stanbury and Thomas E. Kierans (Montreal: Institute for Research on Public Policy, 1985), pp.89-99.

14. Some of the material in this paragraph is drawn from Laux and Molot, p.196.

15. SGF sold its shares in Forano Inc., Volcano Inc. and Artopex, reduced its ownership of Dofor to 91 percent, and agreed to participate in the Bécancour aluminum refinery as a joint venture partner. Le Group SGF, *Annual Report 1984* p.4 and *ibid.,* 1985, p.2.

16. "Quebec begins cutting ties with asbestos industry," *Globe and Mail* (11 September 1985), p. B18. The joint venture came into effect in 1986.

17. Gouvernement du Québec, Budget 1985-86, *Discours sur le Budget*, pp. 26-28.

18. Gouvernement du Québec, *Privatisation de Sociétés d'État: Orientations et perspectives*, pp. 11-13, 31, 50.

19. These are SGF, Sidbec, Soquem, Rexfor, Soquip, Soquia. Madelipêche, Société nationale de l'aminante, SQT (and Québecair), and Sepaq.

20. Report of the Committee on the Privatization of Crown Corporations, *From the Quiet Revolution . . .* , pp.9-10, 29, 63-4.

21. "Quebec sale of sugar firm means closing," *Globe and Mail* (11 March 1986), p. B4 and "Sparking Donohue privatization may be hard to match," *Globe and Mail* (23 February 1987), p. B4. On the reduced profit from the sale of Québecair see "Quebec to get only half of profit expected from sale of airline to Nordair-Metro," *The Ottawa Citizen* (9 September 1987), p. C9.

22. "Quebec is privatizing asbestos subsidiaries," *Globe and Mail* (31 July 1986), p. B4.

23. "Quebec set to privatize Soquem with planned offering to public," *Globe and Mail* (30 April 1986), p. B6 and "Cambior strikes gold for Quebec," *Financial Post*, (9 March 1987), p. 25.

24. "Sparking Donohue privatization may be hard to match," *Globe and Mail* (23 February 1987), p. B4. SGF held its shares of Donohue (as well as Domtar the sale of which, according to Minister Fortier, has only been postponed) through Dofor Inc. Dofor sold about 10 percent of its stock to the public in 1985 with SGF holding the remaining 90 percent of Dofor's equity. The sale of Donohue attracted considerable media interest through late 1986 and into 1987 and was finally completed in July 1987. "Quebecor completes acquisition of Donohue from Quebec Government," *Globe and Mail* (9 July 1987), p. B6.

25. "Sceptre agrees to buy assets of Soquip Alberta," *Globe and Mail* (14 August 1987), p. B3 and "Sceptre to pay $195 million for Soquip unit," *Globe and Mail* (29 October 1987), p. B14. The Caisse de dépôt et placement holds 17 per cent of Sceptre Resources Inc. In October it was announced that Sceptre would pay $195 million for Soquip Alberta, the lower price the result of a re-evaluation of Soquip Alberta's hydrocarbon reserves.

26. "Quebec to sell ailing salt mine for \$35 million," *Globe and Mail* (4 April 1988), p. B3.

27. Pierre Fortier, "La Privatisation Des Sociétés D'État au Québec", Notes pour une allocution devant, L'Institut d'Administration Publique du Canada Groupe Regional de la Capitale Nationale, Ottawa, le 23 mars 1987.

28. Report of the Committee on the Privatization of Crown Corporations, *From the Quiet Revolution . . .* , p. 22.

29. "New mill for Gaspé area hinges on aid," Globe and Mail (30 March 1987), p. B10.

30. "Delay in sale threatens Davie shipyard," *Globe and Mail* (7 January 1987), p. B6 and "Marine Industries, Versatile close Quebec deal," *Globe and Mail* (3 February 1987), p. B7.

31. "Quebec agency overhauled to become provider of loans, not a giver of grants," *Globe and Mail* (18 February 1987), p. B4.

32. "Hydro-quebec has big hopes for China," *Globe and Mail* (6 March 1987), p. B17 and "Quebec, Maine utility sign hydro agreement," *Globe and Mail* (11 February 1987), p. B2.

33. Soquip, *Annual Report 1985-86,* p. 28.

34. "Cambior wants all of Sullivan," *Financial Post* (20 July 1987), p. 19.

35. "Caisse '86 return nosedives to 13.5% but official calls the rate 'satisfactory'," *Globe and Mail* (20 March 1987), p. B7 and "Caisse reveals increase to 19.3 per cent in stake in CDC Life Sciences Inc.," *Globe and Mail* (20 July 1987), p. B2.

36. With a profit of \$41.6 million in 1987 and \$38.2 million in 1986 Domtar is the most profitable of SGF's holdings. Quebec also owns another 16 per cent of Domtar through the Caisse de Dépôt et Placement. "Quebec takes Domtar stake off sale block," *Globe and Mail* (30 April 1988), p. B5.

37. Quoted in "Innovation marks province's privatization spree," *Financial Post* (22 June 1987), p. S4.

38. "Bourassa sires privatization paradox," *Globe and Mail* (17 July 1987), p. A17.

39. "Quebec's 'private' concern," *Globe and Mail* (29 November 1986), p. D2 and "Quebec to get only half of profit expected from sale of airline to Nordair-Metro," *Ottawa Citizen* (9 September 1987), p. C9.

40. Soquia owns 35.4 per cent of Culinar. "Shareholders' rejection of Culinar takeover bid thwarts Quebec," *Ottawa Citizen* (10 February 1988), p. C11.

41. Pierre Fortier, "La Privatisation Des Sociétés D'État au Québec", p. 14. For a discussion of the new Quebec business class which strongly supports privatization see Alain G. Gagnon and Khayyam Z. Paltiel, "Towards Maître chez nous: The Ascendancy of a Balzacian Bourgeoisie in Quebec", *Queen's Quarterly*, 93 (Winter 1986), pp. 731-749.

42. Economic Council of Canada, *Minding the Public's Business*, p. 9.

43. See the views of Robert Andrew, first Minister of Finance in the Devine government expressed in "Public Participation in Crown Corporations: A Saskatchewan Perspective" in *Papers on Privatization*, pp. 101-07.

44. Crown Investments Review Commission, *Report to the Government of Saskatchewan*, December 1982, passim and pp. 40-45.

45. "Bit of burnish again for Crowns in Regina," *Financial Post* (1 January 1983), p. 5 and "Corporations valuable jewels in Devine government crown," *ibid.* (15 October 1983), p. 28. For additional information on PCS see the chapter by Maureen Appel Molot and Jeanne Kirk Laux in this volume.

46. "Meat packing business cut," *Financial Post* (18 June 1983), p. 2.

47. "Saskatchewan called loser over Papco sale," *Globe and Mail* (11 February 1987), p. B7.

48. "Budget fires talk of Sask. election," *Financial Post* (5 April 1986), p. 10.

49. "Crowns dividend eases government deficit," *Financial Post* (21 May 1983), p.6.

50. Crown Management Board of Saskatchewan, *Annual Reports* 1983 to 1986.

51. Andrew, "Public Participation in Crown Corporations" in *Papers on Privatization,* pp. 105-06.

52. Quoted in the *Financial Post* (31 August 1985), p. 30.

53. *Ibid.*

54. Saskoil, *Annual Report 1985,* pp. 1-2. To facilitate this change in status of Saskoil, the Saskatchewan legislature enacted The Saskatchewan Oil and Gas Corporation Act, 1985, which continued Saskoil under the province's Business Corporation Act and ended its status as a Crown corporation. Crown Management Board of Saskatchewan, *Annual Report 1985,* pp. 4, 8.

55. Saskoil, *Prospectus,* 6 July 1987, p.4. The value of Saskoil's shares has fluctuated considerably since they went on the market in January 1986, falling to about half their issue price within two months of sale.

56. Crown Management Board of Saskatchewan *Annual Report 1986,* p. 4.

57. "Sask. may sell shares in Crown firms," *Ottawa Citizen* (16 January 1988), p. A4. The Minister of Public Participation is Graham Taylor, the former minister of Small Business and Tourism. The alternative modalities for privatization are spelled out in "Saskatchewan plans peaceful privatization drive," *Financial Post* (1 February 1988), p. 7.

58. Saskatchewan Mining Development Corporation, *Annual Report 1987,* p.1. and "Merger leaves Ottawa with Eldorado's debts," *Financial Post* (29 February 1988), p.7. Under terms of the agreement the Saskatchewan government, which has assumed SMDC's debts, will get enough out of the merger to cover these debts. The federal government, on the other hand, will be reimbursed $230 million by the new company and will have to wait for the sale of its shares in the new company to get the rest of its money — some $340 million — back. This is because of the size of Eldorado's debt.

59. "Four firms on Saskatchewan privatization list," *Globe and Mail* (19 March 1988), p.A3. At other times additional Saskatchewan-owned enterprises, such as the Potash Corporation and the provincial bus line, have been listed as under consideration for

sale. "Devine announces more sales of Saskatchewan Crown firms," *ibid.* (21 July 1987), p.A5.

60. "Crown corporations aren't for sale," Moose Jaw *Times-Herald* (29 January 1985), p.3.

61. Saskoil purchased the significant reserves of Alberta light oil and natural gas of Thomson-Jensen Energy Ltd. and Thomson-Jensen Petroleum Ltd. in April 1987 as a means to complement its almost total dependence on Saskatchewan production of heavy and medium crudes. About $30 million of the $50 million July 1987 share issue went to pay off this Alberta purchase. "Saskoil issue to pay off Alberta buy," *Financial Post* (15 June 1987), p. 4.

62. "Merger leaves Ottawa with Eldorado's debts," *Financial Post* (29 February 1988), p.7.

63. Prior to their defeat the Ontario Tories commissioned John Gracey to examine the role of Crown corporations in the province. By the time the report was completed the government had changed.

64. Paragraph based on talk given by John Kruger, Chairman, Pensions Commission of Ontario and former Special Advisor to the Premier of Ontario, Special Advisory Group on Crown Corporations to Institute of Public Administration of Canada, National Capital Regional Group, Privatization, Contracting Out, Make or Buy: Managing Governments Better, Ottawa, 23 March, 1987.

65. *Ibid.*

66. Ministry of Industry, Trade and Technology, Ontario, *News Release* (19 February 1986).

67. Ontario Energy Corporation, *Annual Report 1985*, p.2.

68. "Ontario urged to raise Suncor stake," *Globe and Mail* (17 May 1986), p. B3.

69. "Ontario sweetens pot to sell UTDC to Lavalin," *Globe and Mail* (15 July 1986), p.A4, "Lavalin plans changes at UTDC plants," *ibid.* (23 July 1986), p. B4 and "UTDC's rocky road curbed potential," *Financial Post* (2 August 1986), p. 3. For a detailed discussion of the privatization of UTDC see Christopher J. Maule, "Privatization—The Case of the Urban Transportation

Development Corporation Ltd.," *Business Quarterly* 52 (Fall 1987), pp. 26-32.

70. Michael Jenkin, *The Challenge of Diversity: Industrial Policy in the Canadian Federation* (Ottawa: Minister of Supply and Services Canada, 1983).

71. John. W. Langford makes this point in the context of a discussion of the assumptions surrounding the privatization issue. "Privatization: A Political Analysis," in *Papers on Privatization*, p. 60.

72. The Alberta government has recently reversed its policy of reducing its holdings in Alberta Energy Co. Ltd. by purchasing slightly over one-third of the company's new share offering. "Alberta Energy stake bought by province," *Globe and Mail* (30 March 1988), p.B4.

Members of the Institute

Board of Directors

The Honourable Robert L. Stanfield, P.C., Q.C. (Honorary Chairman)
Ottawa

Roger Charbonneau, O.C. (Chairman)
Président du conseil, NOVERCO, Montréal

Rosalie S. Abella
Chair, Ontario Labour Relations Board, Toronto

Robert Bandeen
President and Chief Executive Officer, Cluny Corporation, Toronto

Nan-Bowles de Gaspé Beaubien
Vice-présidente du conseil d'administration, La Corporation Télémédia, Montréal

Larry I. Bell
Chairman and Chief Executive Officer, B.C. Hydro & Power Authority, Vancouver

Catherine Callbeck
Callbeck Limited, Central Bedeque, PEI

Allan F. (Chip) Collins
Special Advisor, Provincial Treasurer of Alberta, Edmonton

Peter C. Dobell
Vice-President & Secretary Treasurer, Institute for Research on Public Policy, Ottawa

Rod Dobell
President, Institute for Research on Public Policy, Victoria

Dianne I. Hall
Vancouver

David Hennigar
Atlantic Regional Director, Burns Fry Limited, Halifax

427

Roger A. Blais, O.C.
École Polytechnique de Montréal

Jill Bodkin
Director of Financial Services, Clarkson Gordon, Vancouver

George Cooper, Q.C.
McInnes, Cooper and Robertson, Halifax

James S. Cowan, Q.C.
Partner, Stewart, MacKeen & Covert, Halifax

V. Edward Daughney
Rosegreen Investments Ltd., Vancouver

H.E. Duckworth, O.C.
Winnipeg

Marc Eliesen
Winnipeg

Emery Fanjoy
Secretary, Council of Maritime Premiers, Halifax

Maureen Farrow
President, C.D. Howe Institute, Toronto

James D. Fleck
Chairman and Chief Executive Officer, Fleck Manufacturing Inc., Don Mills

Francine Harel Giasson
Directrice des programmes et professeure agrégée
École des Hautes Études Commerciales, Montréal

Margaret C. Harris
Past President, The National Council of Women of Canada, Saskatoon

Michael Hicks
Centre for Executive Development, Ottawa

David Hopper
Washington, D.C.

Richard W. Johnston
President, Spencer Stuart, Toronto

Leon Katz, O.C.
Saskatoon

Geraldine Kenney-Wallace
Chairman, Science Council of Canada, Ottawa

Verna J. Kirkness
Director, First Nations House of Learning, University of British Columbia, Vancouver

Claude E. Lafrance
Directeur, Direction de l'information industrielle et technologique
Centre de Recherche Industrielle de Québec, Sainte-Foy

David Leighton
Director, National Centre for Management Research and Development
University of Western Ontario, London

Terrence Mactaggart
Toronto

Judith Maxwell
Chairman, Economic Council of Canada, Ottawa

Milan Nastich
Canadian General Investments Ltd., Toronto

Roderick C. Nolan, P.Eng.
President, Neill & Gunter Limited, Fredericton
Robert J. Olivero
United Nations Secretariat, New York
Gordon F. Osbaldeston, O.C.
Senior Fellow, School of Business Administration, University of Western Ontario, London
Garnet T. Page, O.C.
Calgary
Jean-Guy Paquet, O.C.
Québec
Leonard Russell
Summerside, Prince Edward Island
Eldon D. Thompson
President and Chief Executive Officer, Telesat Canada, Vanier
Israel Unger
Dean of Science, University of New Brunswick, Fredericton
Louise B. Vaillancourt
Outremont
Ida Wasacase, C.M.
Winnipeg
R. Sherman Weaver
Executive Director, Alberta Environmental Centre, Vegreville
Blossom Wigdor
Director, Program in Gerontology, University of Toronto

Government Representatives
Roger Burke, Prince Edward Island
David R. Cameron, Ontario
Joseph H. Clarke, Nova Scotia
Ron Hewitt, Saskatchewan
Lynn Langford, British Columbia
Donald Leitch, Manitoba
Francis McGuire, New Brunswick
Barry Mellon, Alberta
Geoffrey Norquay, Canada
Norman Riddell, Quebec
Leonard Russell, Prince Edward Island
H.H. Stanley, Newfoundland
Gérard Veilleux, Canada
Louise Vertes, Northwest Territories

Institute Management

Rod Dobell   President
Peter Dobell   Vice-President and Secretary-Treasurer

Yvon Gasse   Director, Small & Medium-Sized Business Program
Jim MacNeill   Director, Environment & Sustainable Development Program
Steven Rosell   Director, Governability Research Program
Shirley Seward   Director, Studies in Social Policy
Murray Smith   Director, International Economics Program

Jeffrey Holmes   Director, Communications
Parker Staples   Director, Financial Services

Walter Stewart   Editor, *Policy Options Politiques*

Fellows- and Scholars-in-Residence:

Tom Kent   Fellow-in-Residence
Eric Kierans   Fellow-in-Residence
Jean-Luc Pepin   Fellow-in-Residence
Gordon Robertson   Fellow-in-Residence
Gilles Paquet   Scholar-in-Residence
David Cameron   Scholar-in-Residence
Klaus Stegeman   Scholar-in-Residence
Eugene M. Nesmith   Executive-in-Residence